Singing the News

Singing the News is the first study to concentrate on sixteenth-century ballads, when there was no regular and reliable alternative means of finding out news and information. It is a highly readable and accessible account of the important role played by ballads in spreading news during a period when discussing politics was treason. The study provides a new analytical framework for understanding the ways in which balladeers spread their messages to the masses. Jenni Hyde focusses on the melody as much as the words, showing how music helped to shape the understanding of texts. Music provided an emotive soundtrack to words which helped to shape sixteenth-century understandings of gendered monarchy, heresy and the social cohesion of the commonwealth. By combining the study of ballads in manuscript and print with sources such as letters and state records, the study shows that when their topics edged too close to sedition, balladeers were more than capable of using sophisticated methods to disguise their true meaning in order to safeguard themselves and their audience, and above all to ensure that their news hit home.

Jenni Hyde is Associate Vice-President of the Historical Association. A former music teacher, folk singer and classically trained soprano, she holds a doctorate in history from the University of Manchester and a PGCE in music from Edge Hill University College. She is Honorary Researcher in History at Lancaster University and an Associate Lecturer at Liverpool Hope University. She has published articles for both journals and popular magazines.

Material Readings in Early Modern Culture

Series Editor: James Daybell, and Adam Smyth

University of Oxford, UK and Plymouth University,
UK and Balliol College

The series provides a forum for studies that consider the material forms of texts as part of an investigation into the culture of early modern England. The editors invite proposals of a multi- or interdisciplinary nature, and particularly welcome proposals that combine archival research with an attention to theoretical models that might illuminate the reading, writing and making of texts, as well as projects that take innovative approaches to the study of material texts, both in terms of the kinds of primary materials under investigation and in terms of methodologies. What are the questions that have yet to be asked about writing in its various possible embodied forms? Are there varieties of materiality that are critically neglected? How does form mediate and negotiate content? In what ways do the physical features of texts inform how they are read, interpreted and situated?

Recent in This Series

Singing the News
Ballads in Mid-Tudor England

Jenni Hyde

Routledge
Taylor & Francis Group

NEW YORK AND LONDON

First published 2018
by Routledge
711 Third Avenue, New York, NY 10017

and by Routledge
2 Park Square, Milton Park, Abingdon, Oxon OX14 4RN

*Routledge is an imprint of the Taylor & Francis Group, an
informa business*

Library of Congress Cataloging-in-Publication Data
CIP data has been applied for.

ISBN: 978-1-138-55347-7 (hbk)
ISBN: 978-1-315-14860-1 (ebk)

Typeset in Sabon
by codeMantra

MIX
Paper from
responsible sources
FSC® C013056

Printed and bound in Great Britain by
TJ International Ltd, Padstow, Cornwall

To my family and my fiend.

Contents

List of Figures

List of Tables

Acknowledgements

Dover Publications for permission to use J. A. Fuller-Maitland &
W. Barclay Squire's edition of *The Fitzwilliam Virginal Book*. The staff
of Cambridge University Library Manuscript Reading Room; the Parker
Library, Cambridge; the British Library, London; the Bodleian Library,
Oxford; and the Library of the Society for Antiquaries, London.

Beth Quitslund, Anindita Ghosh, Diarmaid MacCulloch, Eva-Maria
Broomer, Jenny Spinks, Julianne Simpson, John Milsom, Janet Ing
Freeman, Alex Wheeler, Christopher de Hamel, Richard Wistreich, Kate
van Orden, Natalie Zacek, Jennifer Richards, Steven Veerapen, Marci
Freedman, Bradley Irish, Elspeth Jadelska, Mark Hailwood, Kirsty
Rolfe, Mathew Lyons, Rebecca Rideal, Ian Gregory, Jonathan Gibson,
Steve Tilston, Jane Brace, Steve Knightley, Anne Curry, Stephen Kelly
and Richard Hoyle.

Rosamund Oates, Jeremy Gregory, Daniel Szechi, Sasha Handley,
Rebecca Herissone, Joad Raymond and Thomas Schmidt.

Chris Hyde

Glyn Redworth

Abbreviations

APC	*Acts of the Privy Council*, ed. J.R. Dasent *et al.* (32 vols. London: HMSO, 1890–1907).
BL	British Library, London.
Bod.	Bodleian Library, Oxford.
CSPDom	*Calendar of State Papers, Domestic Series, of the Reigns of Edward VI, Mary, Elizabeth, 1547–1580,* ed. R. Lemon and M. A. E. Green (12 vols. London: Longman, Brown, Green, Longmans, & Roberts, 1856–72).
CSPDom Mary	*Calendar of State Papers, Domestic Series, of the Reign of Mary I, 1553–1558, preserved in the Public Record Office,* ed. C.S. Knighton (London: Public Record Office, 1998, revised ed.).
CSPFor	*Calendar of State Papers Foreign, Mary, 1553–1558,* ed. W. B. Turnbull (London: Longman, 1861).
CSPSpan	*Calendar of State Papers, Spanish,* xiii, ed. R. Tyler (London: HMSO, 1914–54).
FSL	Folger Shakespeare Library, Washington DC.
L&P	*Letters and Papers, Foreign and Domestic, of the Reign of Henry VIII,* ed. J.S. Brewer *et al.* (21 vols. London: HMSO 1867–1910)
STC	Short Title Catalogue.
TAMO	John Foxe *The Unabridged Acts and Monuments Online* variorum edition (Sheffield: HRI Online Publications, 2011), www.johnfoxe.org [accessed 6 February 2012].
TCD	Trinity College, Dublin.
Tottel's *Miscellany*	Henry Howard, Earl of Surrey. *Songes and Sonettes, Written by the Right Honorable Lorde Henry Haward Late Earle of Surrey, and Other* ([London], 1557) STC (2nd ed.) / 13861.
TRCS	*A Transcript of the Registers of the Company of Stationers of London, 1554–1640 A.D.,* ed. Edward Arber (3 vols. London: Privately printed, 1875).

Editorial Note

In all quotations, original spelling has been maintained, with the thorn *y* silently expanded to *th* and *vv* modernised to *w*. Original punctuation and capitalisation has been maintained also, with the exception of the virgule, which has been modernised to a comma in order to avoid confusion with the use of the oblique slash to demarcate line breaks in verse quotations. In order to differentiate between titles of ballad lyrics and titles of ballad tunes, the former appear in italics (even where they form a single entry in a manuscript collection) and the latter are enclosed by inverted commas.

The aim has been to make the musical examples accessible to modern readers. As far as possible, musical examples have been taken from early versions of the tunes, often in the form of lute or keyboard arrangements, often accessed in digital facsimile. Bar lines have been added silently to most of the transcriptions and most clefs have been modernised silently to the treble and bass. Other editorial alterations have been acknowledged in the footnotes.

As the instrumental arrangements used to provide the ballad tunes did not include words, the melodies were extracted from the arrangements and the appropriate lyrics were underlaid editorially. In order to fit lyrics to the tunes, it was sometimes necessary to alter the rhythm of the music to accommodate the words. The melodies are most often adapted to suit the words by the inclusion of what might be termed *additional sung notes*: the replacement of a single note by several of shorter duration, usually (but not invariably) of the same pitch. Additional sung notes enable the performer to sing the extra syllables that are required by the lyrics. The replacement of several short notes with one long one also occurs, although less frequently. The resultant variations of the tunes will be called revised melodies. Additional sung notes, with their requisite slurs and ties, have been added silently, although attention is drawn in the main text or footnotes to places where substantial alterations had to be made. These were most significant in part-songs, where the underlaid text had to be rearranged in an attempt to create a modern score from individual sixteenth-century parts, where the words were given separately to the tune.

The names of musical periods (e.g. Medieval, Renaissance and Baroque) have been capitalised for the purposes of clarity.

Unless otherwise stated in the main text or footnotes, printed primary sources have been accessed via Early English Books Online (EEBO), http://eebo.chadwyck.com/home [accessed between 1 January 2014 and 30 September 2017]. These items can be located by their name, title and/or bibliographic name/number. Unless otherwise stated, all biographical details are taken from the *Oxford Dictionary of National Biography* online edition, ed. Lawrence Goldman (Oxford: Oxford University Press), www.oxforddnb.com [accessed 9 September 2014].

All references to the works of William Shakespeare are to Stanley Wells and Gary Taylor (eds), *The Oxford Shakespeare: The Complete Works* (Oxford: Oxford University Press, 1989).

All musical definitions are based on those given in *Grove Music Online*, www.oxfordmusiconline.com/subscriber/book/omo_gmo [accessed 9 September 2014].

For the sake of consistency and to avoid confusion, Edward Seymour, 1st Viscount Beauchamp of Hache (1536), 1st Earl of Hertford (1537) and 1st Duke of Somerset (1547) will be referred to throughout this study by the title of Somerset. Likewise, John Dudley, 1st Viscount Lisle (1542), 1st Earl of Warwick (1547) and 1st Duke of Northumberland (1551) will be referred to by the title Northumberland.

Introduction

Without our stories or our songs
How will we know where we come from?[1]

Ballads and history meet in the stories. As a child, it was folk music that sparked my interest in history. From traditional songs that were clearly grounded in history if only we knew how, to contemporary writing that described historical events, these songs have always fascinated me. They form a thread that runs through the centuries, linking us to people in the past. So it was perhaps natural that I was drawn to ballads as a historical resource. How better to see into the lives of our ancestors than through the popular songs that seem to be so ubiquitous in the background picture? And so I found myself writing about the ballads that attempted to explain the anomaly that saw a woman sitting on the English throne for the first time. The problem was that none of the 'songs' had tunes. I was convinced that they were songs, but it was difficult to explain why.

This book was conceived with two main, interconnecting aims: the first was to address the disconnect between ballads as texts and ballads as songs; the second, to show that in the sixteenth century, ballads could play a significant role in the transmission of news. These two aims come together because of the social context in which the songs were spread from one person to another. The primary means of learning a song was 'by ear', that is, using internal hearing to imitate the pitches and rhythms that we hear someone else produce. If this sounds complicated, it is because it attempts to describe something that many of us do quite naturally and without being conscious of the procedure. It is the way in which we learn our first songs as children.[2] It is the way we learn to sing along with the radio. Although the means of transmitting songs has changed in the intervening 450 years, the method has not. Where we can now learn from compact discs and MP3 files, and many people never hear their favourite musicians live, in the Tudor period most music was passed directly from person to person through performance. This, of course, is blindingly obvious. But it is also fundamentally important to understanding popular song in the sixteenth century. Music facilitates recall of a text.[3] This makes it particularly useful if you want to communicate with people who cannot read, as many people who enjoyed Tudor ballads could not.

Ballads as Songs

Halfway through my research, I presented a paper at a conference in Manchester which investigated the means by which music has contributed to the public sphere from the sixteenth to the twenty-first centuries. The reception was reassuringly good, given that it was my first paper at a specialist music conference. Afterwards, Richard Wistreich approached me and said, 'I think you're at the wrong conference'. Initially taken aback, I quickly realised that this was not a damning criticism of my musical research, but an invitation to join the Arts and Humanities Research Council-funded 'Voices and Books, 1500–1800' research network, who were, at that moment, meeting further down Oxford Road at the Royal Northern College of Music. From there on, I never looked back. Surrounded by supportive colleagues from across the disciplines of history, music, English and more, I became convinced that these texts were intended to be voiced and that this, moreover, contributed much to their importance in English society at the time.

Indeed, the twenty-first century has seen growing recognition that songs had been silenced by a disproportionate concentration on their texts. This has led to something of a rethink about the nature of the ballad as a source. Up to then, most studies of the ballad had concentrated on the printed broadside. This first overlooked the significant contribution made by manuscript circulation and second, often sidelined the importance of oral transmission. Bruce Smith's *Acoustic World of Early Modern England: Attending to the O-factor* was the first modern study to incorporate songs from manuscript and oral sources systematically alongside those which had been printed.[4] This is something that I have sought to emulate, through the use of manuscript miscellanies and supporting documents such as court records and letters, as a means to broaden the debate beyond print to manuscript collecting habits and the nature of oral transmission itself. Many sixteenth-century manuscripts contain a few ballads, but a few contain many; these have something important to tell us about the types of songs that people chose to collect. Despite the stereotype of the 'bawdy ballad', these collections are, in fact, dominated by devotional material.

As well as incorporating manuscript ballads, though, Smith took a particularly novel approach to his work. It was based on the theory that sound is a combination of physical act, sensory experience, act of communication and political performance. His concentration on the way sound was experienced in the early modern world, however, proved controversial with critics who challenged his methodology.[5] Nevertheless,

Smith's most important contribution was his emphasis on the auditory aspects of the early modern world: it provided a clear reminder that song is, essentially, intended to be sung and heard.

Christopher Marsh's *Music and Society in Early Modern England*, the most influential contribution to ballad scholarship so far, sought finally to redress the balance of a social and cultural history of early modern England which had been written 'with only fleeting attention to music'.[6] Marsh devoted two chapters to ballad production and performance, particularly regretting that many historians study these inherently musical sources as texts alone. Marsh's belief that the choice of melody could affect the way in which a ballad was received has become central to my study of ballads. It explains why a book which is ostensibly about the relationship between ballads and news actually contains several chapters about music. Tunes, especially those which became popular and were repeatedly reused, had several functions. They were a mnemonic device, they were entertaining and they created mood. When tunes were recycled, they provided the comfort of familiarity. A balladeer might hope for instant success with new words, but the use of a popular tune could even help the audience to make associations between the new song that they heard and the ballads that they already knew. Because each person drew on their own experience when listening to ballads, Marsh argued that songs did not have one meaning but, rather, a central theme around which audiences embroidered their own connotations.[7] The magical combination of music, words and pictures on a broadside ballad contributed to their appeal.

One of the primary aims of this study, therefore, is to treat ballads as songs which were intended to be performed. Music is essential to understanding ballads. Even when no tunes can be identified for a particular set of lyrics, it is important to remember that those lyrics were the words of a song. While it was (and is) possible to read the words aloud as poetry, music was the unique selling point of the ballad: it helped the audience to remember and could also make its own contribution to the meaning of the words. The centrality of oral transmission meant that lyrics did not have priority over melody; words and music had something of a symbiotic existence. Wherever possible, therefore, I include musical examples of the ballads as an intrinsic part of the text. On occasion, I am able to use the skills of a folk singer to recreate ballads from music when, in the past, the compatibility of music and lyrics has not been immediately apparent. A website that accompanies this book features recordings of the ballads.[8]

Ballads as News

The early modern period certainly had its fair share of political upheavals. Among the many ballads on religious and moral issues (indeed, among the many, many ballads that mention death), I found clusters of topical ballads in circulation around times of crisis. These occasions included two rebellions in the north (the Pilgrimage of Grace and the Northern Rebellion); the downfall of Thomas Cromwell, Henry VIII's chief minister; and the reign of Mary I, England's first queen regnant. Later, there were various Catholic plots surrounding Mary, Queen of Scots. The seventeenth century saw, for example, Prince Charles's ill-fated visit to Spain to woo the Infanta and, of course, the descent into civil war. That balladeers were concerned by these events is probably predictable, given that broadside ballads were printed as a commercial enterprise, while few people write songs intending no one to hear them, even if they perform them for nothing. It suggests that there was an interested audience for topical songs.

But what marks out the sixteenth-century from later periods (which themselves have given rise to much more research) is the lack of a regular, periodical press. As a result, it is anachronistic to compare ballad news directly to newspapers during the mid-Tudor years, nor were they in a teleological relationship with the periodicals of the seventeenth century. Nevertheless, a substantial subset of the topical songs presented themselves as 'news', using the word in their titles and throughout their lyrics. Perhaps, then, rather than trying to trace a line back from newspapers to ballads, we should see them as two threads in a tangled web of information. The self-styled news ballad is best understood in its own terms: as a song, its primary function was entertainment, but as part of the oral news culture of the time, it was capable of spreading information and inciting debate.

The trouble was that in the sixteenth century, treason laws prevented free speech. In theory, this meant that no one was allowed to spread the sort of information that was carried by many of the topical ballads included in this study. In practice, the mid-Tudor regime only seems to have made a concerted effort to curb this sort of discussion when it criticised the monarch or their ministers.[9] When the content of songs verged on the seditious or libellous, balladeers often used an implicit subtext to hide the meaning of the words. In this way, they could, to some extent, control their audience. Those who were in the know would understand, but those who were not might only have a general idea of the meaning. Although, as a song, the ballad still had its intrinsic entertainment value, implicitness obscured the details. It might even have contributed to the enjoyment of people who understood. It was certainly a device which helped to protect the balladeer, as any seditious content was ultimately deniable. Furthermore, the process of oral transmission supported the ballad's role in spreading the news even when the subject matter was masked in allegory, metaphor or irony. Those who were not in the know could ask for an explanation.

Sources and Structure

This study is intended to be interdisciplinary, incorporating both musical and historical analysis of a period when important political and religious changes coincided with the first time we have access to a significant number of ballads. More than 430 ballads make up the main body of evidence. These include the extant broadside ballads printed between 1530 and 1570, as well as several manuscript collections of ballads whose contents can be dated to the mid-sixteenth century. The database was supplemented by contemporary ballads taken from a variety of other sources, including John Foxe's *Actes and Monuments* and conciliar records. These texts were analysed for their content, construction and, in particular, for the light that they shed on Tudor politics, religion and society.

Another invaluable source in the mid-Tudor period is the Register of the Company of Stationers. The company was granted a royal charter in 1557, although the back-payment of sixteen years' worth of quarterage by Anthony Clerke in 1561 shows that some form of association had existed prior to its incorporation.[10] Members of the company registered their right to print a particular item, in what amounted to an early form of copyright which protected the printer rather than the author. The company register usually recorded the printer's name and the title or first line of the work to which they wished to assert their right. Records exist covering the period 1554 to mid-1571, although the records from later years are more detailed and comprehensive than the earlier ones.[11] Although they certainly do not record every item printed during the period, they give us an insight into the sort of material which was being produced during these changing times.

Mid-Tudor ballads offer us an opportunity to examine popular perceptions of religion, monarchy, gender, the commonwealth and social authority: many of the issues, in fact, which in the sixteenth century contributed to an individual's understanding of news and current affairs. To appreciate this, however, it is necessary to understand the ways in which ballads were produced, sold, passed on and performed. Chapter 1 places the sixteenth-century ballad within its social context, giving an overview of what the ballad is and why it matters as a historical source. It presents the theoretical framework of implicitness and suggests that this technique allowed balladeers to take part in a temporary and informal public sphere. The following few chapters then seek to locate the news ballad in the context of the ballad genre as a whole. Chapter 2 investigates the world of the sixteenth-century ballad. It examines many features of the typical broadside ballad, including tune direction, black-letter font and woodcut illustrations, but it also shows that the word 'ballad' did not necessarily mean a printed broadside. It compares the broadside ballad to printed ballad collections and investigates the author-ship of these popular songs as well as looking at their links to the oral tradition.

As melody is a vital part of any ballad, Chapters 3 and 4 analyse many of the most popular sixteenth-century ballad tunes. The first of these heavily musical chapters looks at the sources for and composition of bal-lad tunes, to explain what features made them easy to pass from one person to another. Chapter 4 investigates how these melodies could con-tribute to meaning by examining the reuse of tunes in moralised ballads. These two chapters provide the essential musical background to the songs studied throughout the book. Although they do not focus on news ballads specifically, they demonstrate the ways in which music contributed to the ballad as a multimedia experience – something which was particularly important for those songs which sought to inform or persuade as well as entertain. They contribute to our understanding of the news ballad niche within the wider genre. Furthermore, this musical analysis serves to re-mind us that even when we do not know the tune to which a ballad was set, it must be understood (as far as possible) as a song for performance. These chapters inform all the case studies that follow: once we have seen how melodies added mnemonic features, entertainment value and some-times even an extra layer of meaning to songs, we can be confident that ballad news and current affairs were put across in an engaging and enter-taining fashion which promoted discussion and debate.

The central chapter of the study foregrounds the ballad's role in spread-ing news. Chapter 5 shows that popular song songs formed the per-fect medium for transmitting messages far and wide through the use of catchy tunes in face-to-face contexts. The remainder of the book is then made up of case studies. Each chapter in turn examines how a significant issue of the day was presented in mid-Tudor popular song. Chapter 6 deals with that most newsworthy event of Henry VIII's later years: the fall from grace of Thomas Cromwell. It investigates how Henry's re-ligious changes were interpreted and understood by balladeers. Some were loyal supporters of Cromwell, whereas others were opposed to ev-erything that he represented. Chapter 7 addresses the question of loyalty to England's first queen regnant, Mary I, examining the ways in which balladeers tackled head on the challenges raised by a woman on the throne. Finally, Chapter 8 concentrates on manuscript ballad collections to show that these were perhaps the best way of gathering socially criti-cal ballads which had a radical edge.

By using songs that circulated in manuscript and in print, and even oral transmission, the book demonstrates that ballads formed a hith-erto neglected part of sixteenth-century public debate about matters of state. The ballad, however, was a report that came with added enter-tainment value that allowed it to spread rapidly and widely, so before turning to *what* the ballads said about the issues of the day, we should investigate *how* they said it.

Notes

1 Show of Hands, 'Roots', *Witness* (HMCD23: Hands On Music, 2006). Used by permission of the author.
2 Robert H. Woody, 'Playing by Ear: Foundation or Frill?', *Music Educators Journal*, 99:2 (2012), pp. 82–3.
3 Wanda T. Wallace, 'Memory for Music: Effect of Melody on Recall of Text', *Journal of Experimental Psychology: Learning, Memory & Cognition*, 20:6 (1994), p. 1475.
4 Bruce R. Smith, *The Acoustic World of Early Modern England: Attending to the O-Factor* (Chicago: University of Chicago Press, 1999). For earlier studies which include manuscript ballads see C. H. Firth, 'The Ballad History of the Reigns of Henry VII and Henry VIII', *Transactions of the Royal Historical Society*, 2 (1908), pp. 21–50; C. H. Firth, 'The Ballad History of the Reigns of the Later Tudors', *Transactions of the Royal Historical Society*, 3 (1909), pp. 51–124; C. H. Firth, 'The Ballad History of the Reign of James I', *Transactions of the Royal Historical Society*, 5 (1911), pp. 21–61.
5 Smith, *Acoustic World*, p. 3; Audrey Ekdahl Davidson, 'Review: The Acoustic World of Early Modern England: Attending to the O-Factor by Bruce R. Smith', *Sixteenth Century Journal*, 30:4 (1999), p. 1160; Peter Holman, 'Review: The Acoustic World of Early Modern England: Attending to the O-Factor by Bruce R. Smith', *Journal of the Royal Musical Association*, 125:1 (2000), pp. 118 and 116.
6 Christopher Marsh, *Music and Society in Early Modern England* (Cambridge: Cambridge University Press, 2010), p. 25.
7 Marsh, *Music and Society*, p. 300.
8 Recordings are available at https://earlymodernballads.wordpress.com/singing-the-news-ballads-in-mid-tudor-england/.
9 See Debora Shuger, *Censorship and Cultural Sensibility: The Regulation of Language in Tudor/Stuart England* (Philadelphia: University of Pennsylvania Press, 2006).
10 *TRCS*, i, p. xix.
11 Unfortunately, there is a hiatus from 1571–76 in the detailed cash accounts which list the titles of registered copies; only the cash abstracts remain for these years.

1 'Now lesten a whyle & let hus singe'
The World of the Sixteenth-Century Ballad

The case of my writing vnto you att this time is to lett you vnderstand that I have reseved your token giveing you harti thankes for itt. willing you to send me vj of those pickturs, and one hundred of ballits, as monny of shaking of the shits [sheets] as you cane get and as many of manni[n]gton you shall have munny of the bearer.[1]

So wrote John Herrick of Leicester to his brother, William. The Herricks were a prosperous and upwardly mobile Tudor family. John's father was an ironmonger in Leicester and his elder brother, Robert, would go on to take over the family business in the 1580s. William Herrick was apprenticed to another brother, Nicholas, who was a goldsmith in Cheapside. William later became MP for Leicester and was a jeweller to James I. The two ballads that John Herrick requested that William send from London were *A dolfull daunce & song of death Entituled: the shakeing of the sheetes* and *A sorrowfull Sonet, made by M. George Mannington, at Cambridge Castle*.[2]

A sorrowfull Sonet was sung to the tune of 'Labandala Shot' (Figure 1.1).[3] Mannington was executed for armed robbery in 1576. His ballad advised specific sections of the audience such as prisoners and students not to follow in his fickle footsteps. Rather than containing explicit details of his offences, Mannington merely alluded to them with the words 'With wrong attempts, increase no wealth'. The audience were presumably expected to know about Mannington's crimes or to ask about them. Composed and published immediately prior to his execution, his 'goodnight' ballad was written first and foremost as a topical song. The level of moralising and lack of detail, however, suggest a simultaneous wish for longevity in the marketplace. John Herrick clearly anticipated that both this song and *A dolfull daunce & song of death* would have a substantial market in Leicester. Asking for 'as many copies as you can get' suggests not only that Herrick would be selling broadside copies of the song but also that he had reason to believe that the ballad would be a hit in the East Midlands. It implies demand: he would have no trouble hawking his wares.

Figure 1.1 Setting of *A sorrowfull Sonet, made by M. George Mannington, at Cambridge Castle* from Clement Robinson, *A Handefull of Pleasant Delites*, p. 65, to the tune of 'Labandala Shot', transcribed from Dublin, Trinity College, MS 410 (Dallis Lute Book), p. 14.

Although John appears to have been selling ballads in Leicester in the 1570s, the Herricks have no known direct link to the London ballad trade. They do not seem to have been balladeers themselves, nor (as far as we know) were they involved in printing or bookselling. Several of the brothers, however, seem to have been in the habit of sending each other songs that they thought might pique someone's interest. In January 1578, Thomas Herrick wrote to William, 'consarnyng the ballett that you write vnto me for I can not fynde hitt, neither can I in wordes rehearse hit'.[4] The Herricks' letters, therefore, reflect many aspects of sixteenth-century balladry. They remind us that ballads were printed, copied out and learned by ear, but also that they were interesting and important enough to be sent from one person to another. Furthermore, they could be a lucrative investment, and there was a significant market for these cheap, vernacular songs outside the capital.

This chapter makes a case for the centrality of ballads in sixteenth-century popular culture and provides the methodological framework on which the rest of the book is based. It attempts to define the ballad genre, not so much by virtue of the physical properties of the broadside ballad but by the stylistic features of the songs themselves. It begins to explore the relationship between ballads and news, which was predicated on the oral culture of the sixteenth century. By setting out a theory of 'implicitness', by which balladeers could hide the precise meanings of their songs when they approached sensitive political subjects, the chapter suggests that these ballads can be seen as part of a nascent public sphere.

The Ballad Genre

By the time the Herricks were writing in the 1570s, the broadside ballad was a fixture in the pack of the peripatetic hawker and chapman, and a staple of the London bookstalls. Production increased dramatically between 1550 and 1650.[5] Tessa Watt estimated that a minimum of 600,000 broadside ballads were in circulation during the second half of the sixteenth century, while the true figure might be closer to three or four million. They were cheap to produce, at four pence to register each 'copy' with the Stationers' Company, and cheap to buy, at a halfpenny a sheet.[6] Printed ballads were ephemera. They did not need to last long, but they were relatively easy to transport over long distances. Furthermore, although only a minority of the population was literate, people could learn by ear, so the spread of the ballad was not confined to the educated. These simple songs were a particularly useful way to spread messages because they combined print, oral and visual cultures.

The boundaries between ballads and other forms of song seem to have been fluid in the sixteenth century, with no contemporary consensus of what marked out a ballad from other songs. The genre was one which assimilated many forms of music and literature. Unlike many art songs

of the time (which were composed with an intended aesthetic outcome
in mind), comparatively few mid-sixteenth-century ballads specify their
tune by name, let alone appear with music, which can make it difficult
to separate ballads from other forms of music and verse. Even in the
twenty-first century, considered definitions of what constitutes a ballad
are few and far between, despite the increasing number of scholars who
have dealt extensively with the genre. Natascha Würzbach was concerned with the ballad as a literary form; therefore, she confined herself
to stating that it 'is immediately noticeable that the texts have a metric
and verse pattern, with rhyming couplets or alternate rhyme scheme',
while Claude Simpson identified the convention that a ballad was a form
of narrative poetry. Tessa Watt's description of the ballad was more
wide-ranging and formed the starting point for my own view. She noted
that 'the early modern notion of a "ballad" concealed a wide variety of
song-types, from courtly wooing song to Scottish battle legend'. The
distinctions between these categories broke down as 'a natural result of
the process of oral dissemination'. Another significant feature was that
ballads were performed in a wide variety of social situations: by minstrels, at dances, on stage as part of theatrical entertainments and in the
more intricate setting of the three-man-song.[7]

A ballad, then, is a popular song that contains an element of narrative
and often includes a recurrent refrain or burden. There is some degree of
overlap with 'folk' or traditional ballads of the sort collected by Francis
Child during the nineteenth century, which often have a very strong
storyline. Multiple variants of the texts and tunes for these traditional
songs exist. The melodies were, of necessity, easily passed on from one
person to another. Links between the Child ballads and the broadside
trade suggest that some printed material was originally drawn from oral
sources, and there is evidence of the *ad hoc* adaptation of popular broadsides to fit particular local situations. Further similarities can be seen
in the fact that many sixteenth-century ballads emerge from a culture
of anonymity, implicitly claiming the authorship 'of the people' by not
naming their composer. It is easy to imagine them being assimilated by
their audiences and adapted to suit new circumstances.

The ballad as a song certainly seems to have been a very adaptable
genre. The term 'ballad' was used alongside 'ditty', 'carol', 'rhyme',
'sonet' and 'song', amongst others, to indicate verses which could have
been sung. It spawned its own poetic metre – ballad metre – with four
lines which alternated between iambic tetrametre and iambic trime-
tre (a syllabic count of 8686) and a rhyme scheme of ABCB. By no
means all ballads, however, used this metre, and many other poetic
metres counted as 'ballads'. Sometimes, tunes were indicated; sometimes, they were not. As a result, I tend to define 'ballad' in a very
broad sense that encompasses a wide variety of vernacular song. For
the purposes of this study, 'ballad' will be used to describe narrative

verse in a popular style, with music in strophic or binary form. In strophic songs, all the verses are sung to the same melody which repeats throughout. Songs in binary form alternate different music for the verse and chorus. A ballad can be distinguished from a poem on account of its often commercial or populist nature. This in turn derives from content that makes reference to current events, imbues timeless themes with a contemporary relevance or tells an interesting story, be it gossip, news or an invented tale designed to entertain. Another feature that tends to set the ballad apart from the art songs that were composed and performed by trained musicians is that they could be sung without extensively challenging either performers or listeners. Unlike much art music, ballad singing did not require any formal musical training. Stylistic features of the ballad, therefore, include simple language and straightforward metrical patterns. Because balladmongers often performed songs in addition to peddling printed copies, many ballads opened with phatic phrases such as 'come all ye', 'give ear' or 'gather round', which were intended to attract the audience's attention rather than convey information. Another characteristic that appeared frequently in ballads was the refrain, which encouraged the audience to participate in the performance.

Ballads, of course, were only one part of the musical scene, but they were the most widely accessible and widely experienced form of Tudor song. Ballads took their tunes from the court, the church, the theatre and the street. Placing popular, vernacular song within its broader context contributes to the cultural, social, political and intellectual history of a period during which English society underwent significant change. Music itself was affected by these adjustments, as this was also a period of rapid liturgical change. The lines between sacred and secular music in the period were indistinct.[8] Protestants, for example, expressed their identity through the use of many types of music, including psalms, hymns, anthems and godly ballads, all of which were influenced by the political and religious environment in which they were produced.[9] This can clearly be seen in the different versions of the popular, vernacular psalter by Sternhold and Hopkins. Each edition was a product of its cultural context. For example, under the Protestant King Edward VI, the psalter concentrated on psalms of commonwealth and counsel. By the time, it was revised for the beleaguered Protestant community under Mary I, it foregrounded a tone of comfort during oppression and the means by which God's punishment would be meted out to tyrants.[10] In the early days of the Reformation, Protestants were happy to utilise secular tunes for sacred ends. Nevertheless, although psalms and popular songs might sometimes have shared tunes, the connection was not always a comfortable one: Miles Coverdale published his *Goostly psalms and spirituall songes* specifically to provide an antidote to what he saw as 'filthy' ballads.

Such condemnations of balladry also highlight the importance of the musical dimension of these songs – it was their tunes that made them particularly entertaining and memorable.

The Importance of Ballads

Ballads dealt with every aspect of life from the failure of a love affair, through recipes for good living, to rebellion and treason; and they did it in a manner that appealed to the public: by putting it to music. These apparently simple songs provide an insight into the attitudes that balladeers thought would be popular with their audience – an audience that had the potential to include a cross section of individuals from all social levels. These songs dealt with commonly held values and news items of a general nature that balladeers thought would strike a chord with their audience. Not only did they reflect the views and beliefs of the population, they sometimes sought to shape those attitudes.

Scholarly interest in this sort of cheap print was stimulated by Margaret Spufford's classic text, *Small Books and Pleasant Histories* and Bernard Capp's *Astrology and the Popular Press*, but the first major study of the broadside ballad was Tessa Watt's *Cheap Print and Popular Piety*.[11] Watt emphasised that the broadside ballad combined text, image and music in order to reach an audience far wider than just its literate readers.[12] Her monograph is an essential starting point for understanding sixteenth-century ballads. Watt concentrated on printed ballads to study the development of what she termed 'popular piety', so she studied only those ballads which played a part in spreading Protestant messages. Although Watt provided a few musical examples, her use of music's technical terminology is sometimes inaccurate. For example, she described 'The Black Almain' as having a 'syncopated rhythm [that] does not easily accommodate words'.[13] Syncopation emphasises unusual places in each measure or bar of music. The result is that those beats which we would normally expect to be strong (for example, the first and third beats of a measure in common time) are not emphasised. Heavier emphasis is placed off the beat. The rhythm of 'The Black Almain' that Tessa Watt described, however, is not syncopated; it is merely in compound time, where the beats in each measure are divided into three rather than two.

Nevertheless, the book remains a hugely important contribution to our knowledge of early modern ballads, not least because it spawned a new generation of interest in the subject. It helped scholars to see that ballads allow us to access and understand several complex relationships.[14] Like other forms of cheap print, they had several overlapping purposes. The first and foremost of these, obviously, was to entertain, whilst another was to make money for the balladeer. But they had a further purpose: to provide guidance and inspiration to the reader or listener.[15] Susan Dwyer Amussen noted that popular culture is created 'at the crossroads between theory and life' where theories about politics, society and religion from literate culture were 'shaped to fit local conditions'. Ballads epitomise the interaction between popular and elite culture, combining scenes from everyday life and experiences with Biblical and classical references.[16] Their invocation of social mores helped to promote stability during a period of uncertainty.

Sixteenth-Century Ballads and News

The relationship between ballads and news, however, is complex, not least because as songs that employed 'sensationalist language and affecting music', they had the power to move people in a way that other news reports could not.[17] This, in turn, made them a particularly effective means of spreading topical messages or even seditious material, because these features also contributed to easy memorisation. Although interest in ballads (and indeed, the relationship between ballads and news) has been widespread in recent years, the sixteenth century remains a relatively neglected area. The early days of the broadside ballad bear witness to a period that saw radical changes in the nature of monarchy and disputes within the church, as well as significant economic difficulties.[18] As such, ballads allow us to investigate high politics from a low perspective through the voice of popular song. The final years of Henry VIII's reign were characterised by court factionalism and widespread uncertainty as to what constituted royal policy. Henry was succeeded by a child-king, whose councils pursued increasingly radical agendas. Next came two queens regnant, each of whom found their own solution to the thorny problem of marriage, although neither entirely to the satisfaction of their subjects. Meanwhile, harvests failed, inflation grew and taxes rose. Protestantism succeeded Catholicism, then became heresy until finally, under Elizabeth, to be Catholic was equated with treason. Of course, in sixteenth-century England, even matters of religion and the economy were, in essence, political matters. At least in theory, the monarch made all the decisions and the regime could punish those who disobeyed. This in turn made the upheavals of the mid-Tudor period important to everyone. They were, in modern parlance, newsworthy.

The coincident upheavals of the mid-sixteenth century, however, allow us to probe the peculiarities of the relationship between ballads and news in a way that has two significant differences to later periods. First, during the sixteenth century there was no regular or reliable source of news available to most of the people whose lives would be affected by major political changes. It pre-dated the explosion of print in the seventeenth century and was a time when orality was still entirely central to the transmission of news and information. The wandering balladeer, arriving in the local market place, might be asked 'What news?'. He might bear the latest tidings from London in his pack and sing them abroad. Second, news was the subject of treason laws, which forbade the discussion of political matters. Topical ballads were open to the charge of sedition, especially when they dealt with contentious matters.

Ballads and Orality

Historians have sometimes been reluctant to engage with 'orality', or culture in which communication took place primarily through the spoken rather than the written word.[19] Despite an increase in literacy and the rise of printing, it was still verbal communication that was key to the transmission of knowledge.[20] Broadside ballads were a multimedia resource, designed to appeal by sight and sound so that they had the broadest possible audience. They were disseminated by oral means, but often they were written out too. This not only helped to maximise circulation, it also gave the ballad a visual dimension which could even be used to decorate homes or public places.[21] Adam Fox's innovative research into the effect of manuscript and print on oral cultures challenged historians' belief in the hegemony of print. By investigating a variety of resources including print, manuscript and court records, he showed that there was a 'promiscuous exchange between the oral, scribal and printed realms' that 'thoroughly undermines the extent to which a story can be assigned to any one medium'. By extension, we can see that ballads, in print and manuscript, voiced or on paper, should be placed firmly in their oral context, as one thread in the tangled web of information culture. Fox concluded that the entertainment value of English songs, with their attractive mnemonic features, made them 'one of the best means of communicating messages among the people'.[22] Furthermore, those who were unable to read were still able to access the text through the performance of others.[23]

It seems likely, however, that only a small minority of sixteenth-century ballads survive. Those that were transmitted only by oral means are the most likely to have disappeared. Tantalising glimpses of lost ballads appear in court records and contemporary chronicles, providing some evidence of the songs' place in oral culture. Court records in particular help us to investigate the performance and reception of popular song. In the seventeenth century, they sometimes describe the practice of 'ballading', where an unfortunate individual was singled out by his neighbours to have his misdemeanours ridiculed in libellous song. Court records for the mid-Tudor period tend to provide more evidence of seditious song than libel, but one principle remains true: the broadside or manuscript ballad tells us little or nothing of the ways in which ballads were performed, whereas court records provide access to the ways in which ballads were sung in markets and streets, alehouses and homes, while also documenting the way the songs spread from person to person. Although the evidence for the reception of Tudor balladry is thin, it is nonetheless possible with material from State Papers to investigate how songs could be heard and understood by contemporaries. These performative attributes are difficult to reconstruct in any other way, since where descriptions of ballad singers do appear, they tend to be either from later sources or disparaging authors, or both.

Ballads and Implicitness

As they were designed to sell (either as a material broadside ballad or as an entertaining song), topical ballads had to relate to the changes of the mid-sixteenth century. They could not stand apart from the upheavals of the period in the way that songs of romance and relationships could. The external demands of the cultural field dictated that some songs had to address what was happening in and to England at the time.[24] Vernacular songs were one way of processing and coming to terms with the changes in sixteenth-century society and culture. Furthermore, their meanings were not fixed, but multivalent. The relationship between the producer and the auditor, however, was not simply bidirectional. A third area allowed them to understand each other. Pre-existing knowledge informed the understanding of any new text. A passage that meant one thing to a particular individual might mean something entirely different to someone else.[25] Sixteenth-century balladeers left little or no definitive record of what they actually meant by their lyrics, which could sometimes be obscure. In order to understand the author's intentions, we must focus on what they said and how it related to the world around them. This makes it necessary to investigate their political world, one where 'an understanding of conventions, however implicit, must remain a necessary condition for an understanding of all types of speech-act'.[26]

Implicitness is therefore the means by which I investigate the ways in which balladeers protected themselves and their audience from the charge of treason when, in some cases, they hid the meaning of their songs in order to explore the controversial issues of the day. It also explains, in part, why some topical ballads contain only a small amount of detailed information. I examine how some ballads, through music and/or words, predispose their audience to a particular reception by 'textual strategies, overt and covert signals, familiar characteristics or implicit allusions'.[27] I demonstrate that the opportunity to assign meanings to the ballads is not only created but also constricted by the context of the words. Ballads sometimes contained an oblique meaning through the use, for example, of *double entendre*, irony or even melody itself, but the context in which they were heard helped to shape the audience's response and privileged certain paradigms whilst also implying that other people might interpret the words in a different way. Implicitness also depends upon a secrecy or exclusivity that is missing from standard reader-reception theory, where the understanding of a text is open to anyone with *or without* prior knowledge of the context. This was particularly important in the Tudor period, when there was no 'free speech' as we recognise it today. Writers used their own corpus of knowledge to compose the ballads, while the audience used their experiences to interpret and engage with the songs that they heard.

Various performative means and linguistic techniques were used to activate these hidden meanings, and irony was perhaps the master trope of implicitness during the Tudor period. An ironic reading of a song, then as now, rests on our pre-existing interpretations or assumptions about elements which were 'possible, necessary, telling, essential, and so on'. These assumptions, however, are so ingrained we simply do not realise that we are making them.[28] Furthermore, it is easy to imagine a balladeer using, for example, gesture or tone of voice to subvert the meaning of his words in much the same way as a stage performer would.

Implicitness as a theoretical framework for investigating sixteenth-century news ballads is heavily indebted to Peter Bailey's theory of 'knowingness'. This was a concept originally developed to elucidate his findings on the Victorian music hall, another potentially subversive mode of performance. Fundamental to knowingness are Bailey's 'conspiracies of meaning'. A conspiracy, of course, must have a common aim or aims. Knowingness was an act of performative collusion. Bailey described how, through knowingness, the audience was able to identify with the performer and recognise itself within the performance. In doing so, however, it assimilated the song – its understanding helped to shape the meaning.[29] The audience was expected to understand subtly allusive frames of reference because they shared common knowledge with the performer. This allusive meaning of the song was necessarily selective, implicating only the closed group who shared common points of reference with the performer.

There are, of course, potential pitfalls in taking a theory about nineteenth-century performance and overlaying it on (or even adapting it for) the sixteenth. The cultural situation had changed significantly in the intervening years, which perhaps explains why the knowingness of Victorian music hall was often related to sexual innuendo rather than seditious material. Yet both balladry and music hall were deceptively complex forms of popular culture. They required a robust voice and physical mode of performance, and their apparently simple songs dealt with the knowledge that enabled the individual to navigate his way through a changing environment.[30] Of course, ballads of this sort were a minority among the whole which were dominated by religious and moralistic material, but among topical ballads and those which dealt with current affairs, implicitness was an important trope.

Bailey's 'conspiracy of meaning' is based on the belief that the performer and his knowing audience had a common purpose in mind. As we shall see, however, common understanding in the Tudor period did not necessarily imply a common aim. Implicitness therefore acknowledges problems of cultural change by recognising that the cultural field of the sixteenth century was more restricted than that of the nineteenth. Certainly, a knowing sixteenth-century audience appropriated a ballad if it spoke to them, but there were also those who implicitly found themselves and their beliefs called into question. While knowingness described a performance which required other knowledge in order to understand it, implicitness describes a knowing performance which implied one meaning while also indicating that other less respectable or intelligent people would have a different view. On occasion, ballads that relied on a knowing audience could rouse an equally knowing yet contradictory response in the form of a retaliatory ballad. In an implicit reading of a text, it is therefore not necessary to share the opinions and beliefs of the author (as Bailey suggested was true in music hall) in order to engage with them. Implicitness does not require the same degree of partiality as knowingness and, as such, it creates subsets among the knowing. It was possible to 'know' the allusions created by the balladeers without agreeing with them. Although the balladeers' language assumed all *right-thinking* people would share their beliefs, there was an implicit acknowledgement that others would disagree. As such, some ballads divided their audience twice over. The audience was first divided between those who shared the common points of reference that allowed them to 'know' from those who did not. Implicitness then further separated the knowing into two groups: one that shared the beliefs of the balladeer and another group who disagreed with his values.

Throughout this study, there are references to both knowingness and implicitness, and the distinction between the two is, I acknowledge, sometimes fuzzy. I use knowingness as a more wide-ranging term when describing a covert meaning that requires some explanation, be it *double entendre* or irony, for example, or news of a general nature. In these cases, it is assumed that all listeners agree with the subtext when they understand it. Implicitness, however, is more specific. It is not just about understanding hidden meanings, it is about understanding hidden meanings and using them to engage in debate or even to take sides. Implicitness brings singing the news much closer to singing sedition. The personal nature of Tudor monarchy meant that the monarch's word was final – the people had no business discussing 'current affairs'. Through implicitness came a freedom to listen to people who were audaciously debating matters that should never have been open to discussion in the first place. In the sixteenth century, when free speech was barely imaginable, the crucial point is not so much *what* the audience was talking about, but that implicitness allowed some form of discussion to take place at all.

Ballads and the Public Sphere

So if implicitness in sixteenth-century ballads opened a space for debate among the commons, it naturally leads on to questions about the public sphere. Given the lack of a coherent state or organised bourgeoisie in the mid-sixteenth century, it would be anachronistic to suggest that the ballads represent a Habermasian 'bourgeois public sphere'.[31] Nonetheless, the songs perhaps represent an attempt to respond to religious or political uncertainty at moments when the unity of the regime was, for a time, fractured, or when people were unsure about how government policy might affect them.[32] The discussion of current affairs and news in mid-Tudor ballads provides evidence of an emerging sense of engaged opposition to the policies pursued by those in government, a conceptual space in which politics of all types and at all levels could be assimilated and discussed. In this respect, it is perhaps best seen as an evanescent or even a proto-public sphere.[33] Sixteenth-century implicitness exploited a conflict of authority, an antinomy between the official line presented by proclamation and policy and the view presented by the balladeer. It was both a product of, and a contributor to, the political, religious and social upheaval of the mid-Tudor period.

This, in turn, provides some explanation for repeated attempts to control and even censor ballads over the course of the sixteenth century. The dialectic function of the ballads presented the possibility of a significant challenge to social order. Although when taken at face value, sixteenth-century ballads often appeared trivial, an implicit performance could imbue them with much deeper significance. Ultimately, however, the existence of another layer of meaning was deniable, so implicitness helped to protect the author, the singer and their audience. Implicitness was therefore permissive, allowing the audience to address social change and set their experience against the dictates of those in power. Consequently, ballads allow us to investigate both the relationship between court and street, and the nature of the divisions between the two.

As such, ballads can be seen to play a part in what we might term 'popular politics', a concept which emphasises such diverse forms as social authority, riot, rebellion and parish government as important in defining the social relations between the 'ruler' and the 'ruled' during the early modern period.[34] Men, women and children at all social levels experienced ballads as part of their everyday life, ballads that reflected their interest in the world around them and the politics that 'reasserted, extended or challenged' the distribution of power in society.[35] Ballads both observed political developments and, on occasion, contributed to an informal, *ad hoc*, public sphere.[36] During a period of remarkable social and political change, vernacular song created a space where public debate could take place. It allowed the lower and middling sorts to come together to discuss the news and relate it to their experiences. The next few chapters will set out the means by which ballads spread their messages, before exploring the relationship between ballads and news in more depth.

Notes

1 Oxford, Bodleian Library, MS Eng. hist. c. 474, f. 159^r.
2 Possibly *The daunce and song of death* (London, 1569), STC (2nd ed.) / 6222 or an earlier version of *The dolefull dance and song of death; intituled; Dance after my pipe To a pleasant new tune* ([London], 1664), Wing (2nd ed.) / H2013B; *A sorrowfull Sonet, made by M. George Mannington, at Cambridge Castle* was registered in 1576 (*TRCS*, ii, p. 304) but was reprinted in Clement Robinson, *A Handefull of Pleasant Delites Containing Sudrie New Sonets and Delectable Histories, in Diuers Kindes of Meeter. Newly Deuised to the Newest Tunes That Are Now in Vse, to Be Sung: Euerie Sonet Orderly Pointed to His Proper Tune. With New Additions of Certain Songs, to Verie Late Deuised Notes, Not Commonly Knowen, nor Vsed Heretofore, by Clement Robinson, and Diuers Others* (London, 1584). The version of *A Handefull of Pleasant Delites* consulted for this study is that edited by Hyder E. Rollins (New York: Dover Publications, 1965).
3 Dublin, Trinity College, MS 410 (Dallis Lute Book), p. 14. Bar 4 is taken from marginalia at the beginning of the first line, as the first phrase of music is the only one which does not have four bars. The last four phrases are subject to an editorial repeat – in doing so, the music then fits the words perfectly. The final note, G, is also editorial. The top line of the lute part, often quoted as the tune, does not resolve successfully. The ear, however, would pick out the G in the accompaniment. Similarly, at the end of other phrases, the rhythmic decoration of the lute tune (which matches the rhythm of a galliard) is replaced by an editorial held note.
4 Bod. MS Eng. hist. c. 474, f. 152^r.
5 Marsh, *Music and Society*, p. 226. Many early modern English broadside ballads have been made freely available online, for example, on the websites *English Broadside Ballad Archive* (EBBA), http://ebba.english.ucsb.edu/ [accessed 20 July 2017] and *Broadside Ballads Online from the Bodleian Library*, http://ballads.bodleian.ox.ac.uk/ [accessed 20 July 2017]. As a result, I have chosen to focus on providing musical examples rather than images of broadside ballads to illustrate the text.
6 *TRCS*, i, p. 74; Tessa Watt, *Cheap Print and Popular Piety* (Cambridge: Cambridge University Press, 1991), pp. 11–12.
7 Natascha Würzbach, *The Rise of the English Street Ballad, 1550–1650*, trans. Gayna Wells (Cambridge: Cambridge University Press, 1990), p. 1; Claude Simpson, *The British Broadside Ballad and its Music* (New Brunswick, Rutgers University Press, 1966), p. 1; Watt, *Cheap Print*, p. 13.
8 Peter Le Huray, *Music and the Reformation in England, 1549–1660* (Cambridge: Cambridge University Press, 1978); Nicholas Temperley, *The Music of the English Parish Church* (2 vols. Cambridge: Cambridge University Press, 1979).
9 See Jonathan P. Willis, *Church Music and Protestantism in Post-Reformation England: Discourses, Sites and Identities* (Farnham: Ashgate, 2010).
10 Beth Quitslund, *The Reformation in Rhyme: Sternhold, Hopkins and the English Metrical Psalter, 1547–1603* (Aldershot: Ashgate, 2008), pp. 17–18.
11 Bernard Capp, *Astrology and the Popular Press: English Almanacs 1500–1800* (London: Faber, 1979); Margaret Spufford, *Small Books and Pleasant Histories: Popular Fiction and Its Readership in Seventeenth-Century England* (London: Methuen, 1981); Watt, *Cheap Print*.
12 Watt, *Cheap Print*, pp. 6–7.

13 Watt, *Cheap Print*, Introduction and pp. 8 and 63.

14 Patricia Fumerton and Anita Guerrini, 'Introduction: Straws in the Wind', in Patricia Fumerton, Anita Guerrini, and Kris McAbee (eds.), *Ballads and Broadsides in Britain, 1500–1800* (Farnham: Ashgate, 2010), p. 8.

15 Watt, *Cheap Print*, p. 8.

16 Susan Dwyer Amussen, 'The Gendering of Popular Culture' in Tim Harris (ed.), *Popular Culture in England c.1500–1850* (Basingstoke: Macmillan Press Ltd, 1995), p. 49.

17 Una McIlvenna, 'When the News was Sung', *Media History*, 22:3–4 (2016), p. 318.

18 R. W. Hoyle, 'Taxation and the Mid-Tudor Crisis', *Economic History Review*, 51:4 (1998), p. 649.

19 D. R. Woolf, *The Social Circulation of the Past: English Historical Culture 1500–1730* (Oxford: Oxford University Press, 2003), p. 273. The seminal work on the interplay of oral and literate cultures remains Walter Ong's *Orality and Literacy: The Technologizing of the Word* (London: Methuen & Co Ltd, 1982).

20 Adam Fox, 'Remembering the Past in Early Modern England: Oral and Written Tradition', *Transactions of the Royal Historical Society*, 6th Series, 9 (1999), p. 256.

21 Adam Fox, 'Ballads, Libels and Popular Ridicule in Jacobean England', *Past & Present*, 145 (1994), p. 51.

22 Adam Fox, *Oral and Literate Culture in England, 1500–1700* (Oxford: Clarendon Press, 2000), pp. 40 and 382.

23 Robert W. Scribner, *Popular Culture and Popular Movements in Reformation Germany* (London: Hambledon, 1987).

24 See Pierre Bourdieu, 'The Social Space and the Genesis of Groups', *Theory and Society*, 14:6 (1985), pp. 723–44; Pierre Bourdieu, 'Social Space and Symbolic Power', *Sociological Theory*, 7:1 (1989), pp. 14–25; David Gartman, 'Bourdieu's Theory of Cultural Change: Explication, Application, Critique', *Sociological Theory*, 20:2 (2002), pp. 255–77.

25 Hans Robert Jauss and Elizabeth Benzinger, 'Literary History as a Challenge to Literary Theory', *New Literary History*, 2:1 (1970), p. 10.

26 Quentin Skinner, 'Motives, Intentions and the Interpretation of Texts', *New Literary History*, 3:2 (1972), p. 404.

27 Hans Robert Jauss, 'Tradition, Innovation, and Aesthetic Experience', *Journal of Aesthetics and Art Criticism*, 46:3 (1988), p. 12.

28 Stanley Fish, 'Short People Got No Reason to Live: Reading Irony', *Daedalus*, 112:1 (1983), p. 190.

29 Peter Bailey, 'Conspiracies of Meaning: Music-Hall and the Knowingness of Popular Culture', *Past & Present*, 144 (1994), p. 146.

30 Bailey himself notes that music hall drew on the techniques of the street ballad singer (Bailey, 'Conspiracies of Meaning', p.143). What is more, a form of implicitness seems to appear in societies worldwide over the course of many years, when free speech was perceived to be threatened in some way. See, for example, Rachel Platonov's description of what she terms 'covert marginality' in subversive guitar songs in Soviet Russia during the 1960s and 70s in *Singing the Self: Guitar Poetry, Community, and Identity in the Post-Stalin Period* (Evanston, IL: Northwestern University Press, 2012). For an example of how knowingness could be used to protect the composer, see the case of Mukunda and the 'White Rat' in Robert Darnton, 'Literary Surveillance in the British Raj: The Contradictions of Liberal Imperialism', *Book History*, 4 (2001), pp. 133–76. The technique can also be seen in practice in Jacobite ballads such as *Killiecrankie* and *The Blackbird*, sometimes

known as 'disguised songs'. William Donaldson comments on the highly allusive nature of these pieces in *The Jacobite Song: Political Myth and National Identity* (Aberdeen: Aberdeen University Press, 1988), p. 28.

31 Jürgen Habermas, *The Structural Transformation of the Public Sphere: An Inquiry into a Category of Bourgeois Society*, trans. Thomas Burger with the assistance of Frederick Lawrence (Cambridge: Polity, 1989).

32 Peter Lake and Michael Questier, 'Puritans, Papists, and the "Public Sphere" in Early Modern England: The Edmund Campion Affair in Context', *Journal of Modern History*, 72:3 (2000), p. 591.

33 Massimo Rospocher and Rosa Salzburg, 'An Evanescent Public Sphere: Voices, Spaces, and Publics in Venice During the Italian Wars', in Massimo Rospocher (ed.), *Beyond the Public Sphere: Opinions, Publics, Spaces in Early Modern Europe* (Bologna: Il Mulino, 2012), pp. 93–114.

34 See, for example, Steve Hindle, *The State and Social Change in Early Modern England* (Basingstoke: Palgrave, 2000); John Walter, *Crowds and Popular Politics in Early Modern England* (Manchester: Manchester University Press, 2006); Andy Wood, *Riot, Rebellion and Popular Politics in Early Modern England* (Basingstoke: Palgrave, 2002).

35 Wood, *Riot, Rebellion and Popular Politics*, p. 16.

36 Thomas Cogswell, 'Underground Verse and the Transformation of Early Stuart Political Culture', in Susan Dwyer Amussen, Mark A. Kishlansky, and David Underdown (eds.), *Political Culture and Cultural Politics in Early Modern England: Essays Presented to David Underdown* (Manchester: Manchester University Press, 1995), p. 295.

2 'Lend listning eares a while to me'

The Production and Consumption of Sixteenth-Century Ballads

Amonge manye newes reported of late,
As touchinge the Rebelles their wicked estate,
Yet Syr Thomas Plomtrie, their preacher they saie,
Hath made the North countrie, to crie well a daye.[1]

In 1570, a ballad was written to celebrate news of the execution of a Catholic priest, Thomas Plumtree. The song related how Plumtree, like other Catholic churchmen that had 'chaunted the morowe masse bell', had been hanged as a traitor in Durham for his part in the Northern Rebellion that took place during the winter of 1569–70. The song emphasised that the poor rebels had been forsaken by their leaders. While Northumberland and Westmorland had fled to 'good saftie wher freedome is nieste', fathers and mothers were 'put to their trialles with terrible feare'. They had been abandoned, 'weeping & waylinge to sing well a daye'. Without the ballad, Plumtree would be all but lost to history. What little we know comes from passing references in other works: he had apparently been a priest since Queen Mary's reign; he consecrated the holy water for the rebels and preached in Durham Cathedral on 4 December 1569. A month later, Plumtree was dead, and the subject of a triumphant ballad.[2]

'W.E.' indicated that the song was written by the most prolific mid-Tudor balladeer, William Elderton. His song, *A ballad intituled, A newe well a daye / as playne maister papist as Donstable way*, was set to 'Welladay', which would go on to become one of the top 50 ballad tunes of the early modern period (Figures 2.1 and 2.2).[3] There is little to mark out Elderton's ballad from its contemporaries, but for this very reason, it is a useful starting point for a study of how mid-Tudor balladeers used their skills to spread the news. Through this song, we can see how ballads were produced: who wrote them, who printed them and how they fitted into the market for cheap print in the mid-sixteenth century.

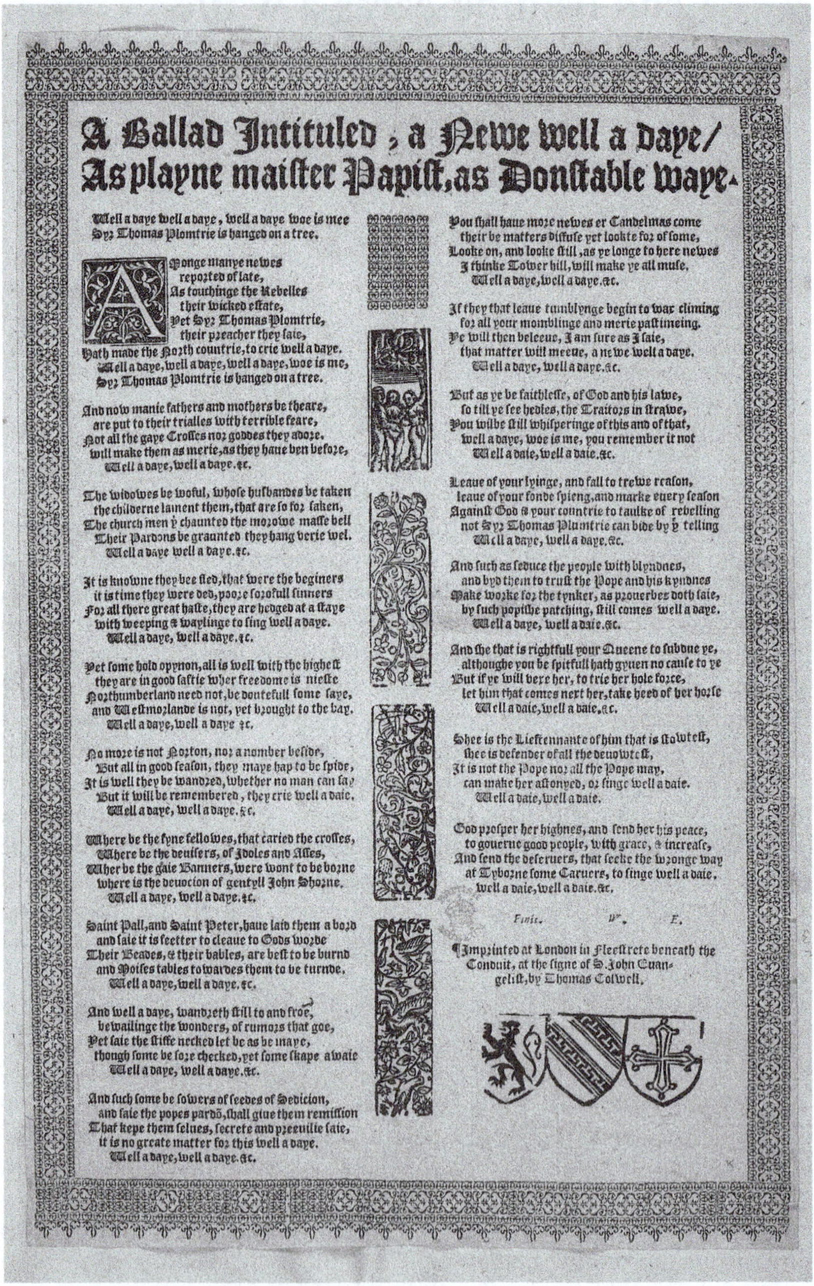

Figure 2.1 William Elderton, *A ballad intituled, A newe well a daye / as playne maister papist, as Donstable waye. Well a daye well a daye, well a daye woe is mee Syr Thomas Plomtrie is hanged on a tree* (London: 1570), STC (2nd ed.) / 7553. © The British Library Board (General Reference Collection Huth 50 (4)).

Figure 2.2 Setting of William Elderton's *A ballad intituled, A newe well a daye / as playne maister papist, as Donstable waye. Well a daye well a daye, well a daye woe is mee Syr Thomas Plomtrie is hanged on a tree*, to the tune of 'Welladay' transcribed from Paris, Bibliothèque nationale de France, MS Rés. 1186, ff. 25ʳ⁻ᵛ.

Figure 2.2 (Continued).

Ballads and Print

The typical sixteenth-century broadside ballad was printed, just like *A newe well a daye,* on only one side of a folio of rough paper. The text appeared in two columns of black-letter font, often surrounded by a decorative border. As the century unfolded, more and more broadside ballads included illustrative woodcuts. These copies became the stock-in-trade of the wandering pedlars and chapmen who were so memorably described as 'the ragged and colourful tassels on the outer fringe of the Elizabethan underworld'.[4] These songs were accessible to everyone, literate or illiterate, rich or poor, and they covered a wide range of themes through an equally diverse selection of melodies. In 1520, the price of a ballad was ½d. By the seventeenth century, it seems to have risen to 1d, but they were still affordable to a large proportion of the population at least occasionally. They were sold both by specialist ballad-mongers, who roamed the country singing and hawking their wares, and by chapmen and women who selected the songs that they thought would be profitable and carried them to the provinces among the other small items that they had for sale.[5] Despite the cacophony of voices complaining about the poor quality of ballad singers, much of the evidence against professional balladeers was culturally biased. Christopher Marsh painted a portrait of a tuneful ballad singer, working the crowd to draw them in to his performance, in the hope of persuading them to buy a copy to take home.[6] Ballads were perhaps the ultimate in sixteenth-century multimedia entertainment, with words, melody and pictures combining to create a multisensory experience designed to appeal not just to the literate, but to those who could only listen, look and join in with the singing.

It is easy to imagine William Elderton's *A newe well a daye* in the pack of a travelling balladeer. Printed in London, it nevertheless spread news from the 'north countrie', contrasting the papists of 'Donstable way' with the queen's loyal subjects in the south. The ballad trade was a lucrative part of the book trade, which was centred in England on London and, in particular, the area around St Paul's Cathedral. Printers, bookbinders and booksellers had been drawn to the area in the fifteenth century by the proximity of literate customers such as lawyers and schoolteachers.[7] Nevertheless, the earliest records of English ballad sales come not from London, but from Oxford, and the day book of John Dorne. Over the space of almost a year, he sold in the region of 180 ballads alongside his staple stock of university texts, as well as several copies of Christmas carols.[8] Although there was a boom in provincial printing during Edward VI's reign, it faced decline again when the Stationers' Company received its charter in 1557, putting an end to printing outside London.[9] From then on, with the exception of the university towns of Oxford and Cambridge, printing was supposed to take place only in London. Only one extant broadside ballad of the mid-sixteenth century claims to have been printed outside London: *Certayne versis writtene by Thomas Brooke Ge[n]tleman in the tyme of his impriso[n]ment the daye before his deathe who sufferyd at Norwich the 30 of August 1570* by Thomas Brooke. Despite the restrictions, the broadside states that it was printed in 'Norwich in the parish of St Andrews' by Anthony De Solempne.[10]

It is perhaps because of the emphasis placed on these printed broadsides by previous scholarship that the ballad has sometimes been seen as a particularly urban medium, in opposition to traditional ballads which that are associated with rural scenes. Elizabethan broadside ballads might often have been addressed to a London audience, but the literature itself often depicted rural settings.[11] Presumably, this helped ballads to appeal to the widest possible audience. An analysis of places in the British Isles that were mentioned in the lyrics of mid-Tudor ballads shows that the songs encompassed a whole range of places, both urban and rural, across the length and breadth of England. These are shown by triangles on the map in Figure 2.3. Of course, many more ballads referred to places outside the British Isles, especially Rome, while one even mentioned Florida. Moreover, if we look at the places where ballads are referenced in other sources, such as court and privy council records, it becomes clear that ballads were obviously attractive to and consumed by people across the country.[12] In Figure 2.3, these locations are represented with circles. These are places where we know ballads were in circulation, because there are records which show them being sung, distributed or discussed.

Although most printing took place in London, ballad singers wandered the country as pedlars and hawkers, singing their songs and selling their wares to any and all who would hear. Based on the portrayals of ballad-mongers in Shakespeare, Jonson and Cavendish, Christopher Marsh described the itinerant ballad-monger as 'a happy rogue, commercially motivated, criminally inclined and thoroughly manipulative'. They had, nevertheless, to be capable musicians in order to sell their songs and their wares. They were as much salesmen as performers, ready both to sing their songs and to engage in banter with their audiences,

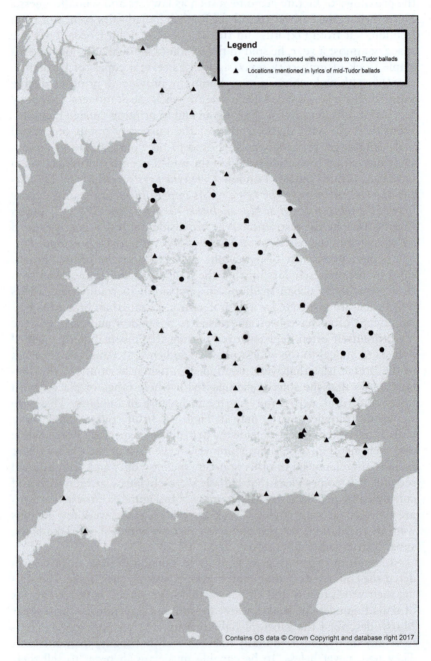

Figure 2.3 Map of locations mentioned in and with reference to mid-Tudor ballads.

with their wares (in the form of printed broadsides) on display while they sang.[13] This helped the audience to learn the songs and the messages they contained.

Specialist Printers

It remains true, though, that much of the evidence for Tudor ballads comes from the print trade. The detailed records of the Stationers' Company for the period 1557–71 provide us with an insight into the types of copy that were being produced and the number which were being registered, although they are certainly not comprehensive. Rather than being entered on a specific date, copies were normally entered during a year that ran from mid-July, usually (but by no means always) with a statement of the type of work, for example, a 'ballet' or 'boke'. It cost 4d to register each ballad copy. Ballads form the largest single category in the registers of this period. Of the 1636 items appearing in the Stationers' Company registers between 1557 and July 1571, 684 (41.8%) are known to have been ballads. Slightly fewer items (476) were categorised as books, although 283 entries in the register do not state the item's format. Some of the 283 items were certainly books, but it is likely that others will have been ballads, not least because their printers seem to have had a special interest in producing these simple songs. Thomas Colwell, William Griffith, John Alde, Alexander Lacy and William Pickering registered the highest number of ballads during the period.

The Stationers' Registers show that some printers specialised in ballads while others had a much wider output. Alexander Lacy registered 71 ballads, but only 7 books, while a further 7 copies are of unspecified format. John Alde, on the other hand, registered 72 ballads, 5 almanacs, 17 books, 2 epitaphs, and a play, as well as 7 unspecified copies. Although ballads dominate Alde's registered output at a minimum of 68%, he diversified far more than Lacy. Of course, all such figures are thrown into doubt by the high number of items that were never registered. Furthermore, printers sometimes undertook work on behalf of other members of the company. For example, although Lacy registered 71 ballads, the colophons of extant broadside ballads show that he also printed at least ten on behalf of other men. Lacy also printed at least five further ballads without registering them with the company.

Comparing the titles of items entered in the Stationers' Registers to those items which survive also gives us some idea of what proportion of ballads were registered. Of the 684 ballads entered in the Stationers' Registers, either for licensing or where a fine was given for printing without license, 670 are named in some way and therefore have the potential to be identified with extant ballads. Hyder E. Rollins undertook much of this work in his comprehensive 'Analytical Index to the Ballad-Entries in the Registers of the Company of Stationers of London'. Whilst it is an extremely useful starting point, Rollins's identifications are not always secure, nor does the ballad always exist in its entirety.[14] For example, there is no doubt that 'the lamentation from Rome', entered in the registers by William Griffith between July 1569 and June 1570, was the satirical ballad on the Northern Rebellion, *A lamentation from Rome, how the Pope doth bewayle, that the rebelles in England can not preuayle to the tune of Rowe well ye mariners*. Likewise, 'All Mars his men Drawe nere', entered by Richard Jones in 1568–9, is the first line of the broadside *Sapartons alarum, to all such as do beare the name of true souldiers, in England, or els wheare*, also allowing for a positive identification of the ballad.[15] Other claims made by Rollins, however, are rather less secure. In 1568–9, John Alde registered a ballad named *awake out of your slumbre*. Rollins suggested that it might be *the Bellmans good morrow*, in BL Add. MS 15225 (beginning 'From sluggishe sleepe and slumber, good Christians, all aryse'), or a ballad in Bodleian Library MS Ashmole 48 which begins, 'After mydnyght, when dremes dothe fawll, / Sume what before the mornynge gray, / Me thowght a voyce thus dyd me cawll, / lustye youthe, aryes, I say'. These ballads both begin with the subject of waking from sleep, but there is little more than that to connect them to *awake out of your slumbre*. Indeed, the dream vision is a relatively common theme in sixteenth-century ballads, whilst waking is also used as a metaphor for turning away from sin. So 'awake out of your slumbre' could just as easily be 'Aryse, Aryse, Aryse, I say / Aryse for shame, yt ys fayre day' in BL Add MS 15233, or 'Awak, all fethfull harttes, awake, / And with meeke myndes your selvis prepare' in Bod. MS Ashmole 48. Alde, however, appears to have registered his copies by their title, so it seems much more likely that *awake out of your slumbre* has not survived. If we make the generous assumption that most of Rollins's identifications were accurate, 162 (24%) of the ballads registered with the Stationers' Company have survived in some form. Only 56, a staggeringly low 8% of the total, are extant as contemporary broadsides. This shows that the survival rate for broadside ballads is extremely low. They were ephemeral in the true sense of the word. This, in turn, makes the ballads that people chose to collect far more significant. If the titles of ballads in the Stationers' Registers are indicative of their content, many more news ballads and songs of love were printed than have survived. Furthermore, by no means every broadside ballad that survives was registered with the company.

Ballad Garlands

Love songs, however, do survive in larger numbers in garlands and anthologies of short literary pieces, such as Tottel's *Songes and sonettes* (better known as Tottel's *Miscellany*) or Clement Robinson's *Handefull of Pleasant Delites*. Rollins suggested that several of the items entered in the Stationers' Registers could also be single-sheet editions of items in Tottel's *Miscellany*. Several items in the *Miscellany* do indeed survive in ballad forms. For example, the *Description of an ungodly world* from the *Miscellany* was definitely printed as a broadside which is no longer extant. Otherwise known by its first line, 'Who lovithe to lyve in peas', it was also included in several manuscript collections of ballads over the next 50 years. This moralistic but popular ballad provided a long list of the world's ills which required redress.

Tottel's *Miscellany* was full of such moralistic and decorous material. He was aware of the hostility towards 'bawdy ballads' felt by authors such as John Hall and the Calvinist, Thomas Becon. Tottel thus felt the need to assure his readers that his *Miscellany* was not, as he put it, 'euill doon'. Tottel's prefatory remarks created a virtual space between the 'lecherous ballades' in the miscellanies attacked by Hall, and the poetry in his collection which was intended to appeal to an educated audience which aspired to literati status.[16] That there was some overlap between the contents of his book and the single-sheet broadsides is perhaps remarkable given the difference in the affluence of the intended market. It speaks to both the broad appeal of ballads and the way in which the genre defies easy categorisation. We know nothing, for example, of the J. Canand who contributed two poems to the *Miscellany*, except that he also wrote a poem which was included on a broadside containing three poems, printed by Alexander Lacy in 1566. Lord Vaux's *The Aged Louer renounceth Loue* was included in the *Miscellany*, licensed as a broadside and gave its name to the tune used for the poem when it was sung as a ballad. His *Thassault of Cupide upon the Fort where the Lovers Hart Lay Wounded and how he was Taken* appears not only in the *Miscellany* but also was printed by John Awdelay in 1560 and licensed as a ballad in 1565–6.[17] So even if Tottel expected his audience to have the spending power to buy his book, some of the material it contained was later used in cheap print for the masses.

If Tottel's *Miscellany* was aimed at the aspiring mid-Tudor literati, then Clement Robinson's *A Handefull of Pleasant Delites* developed the printed 'collection' genre for another market: the wealthier ballad-buying public. Rather than containing a wide variety of poetic forms, the *Handefull* is made up of 33 ballads. It nevertheless modelled itself on its august predecessor, perhaps hoping to adapt the format for those with less money and more demotic tastes. The preface, after all, pointed out that although the book might appeal to music lovers and ladies who liked 'pretie thinges', it was still affordable because 'the price [was] not so high'. The wide range of poetic metres included in Tottel's *Miscellany* seems to have been one of its selling points, so the *Handefull* also highlighted the 'new sonets' in 'diuers kindes of Meeter', which could be found beneath its cover. Even so, the songs in the *Handefull* had even closer links to the broadside ballad trade than those in Tottel's *Miscellany* had done.

There is some uncertainty over the date of the ballads in the *Handefull* because although the book was first registered in 1566, the only extant copy is dated 1584. Edward Arber argued that six of the ballads in the 1584 volume were not included in the first edition because the individual ballads were themselves registered as broadsides with the Stationers' Company during the period 1566–82, after the first publication of the *Handefull*.[18] His assumption was that a ballad in the *Handefull* must necessarily have been published as an individual broadside before it was included in the collection. One ballad in the volume can be conclusively shown not to have been included in the first edition of the *Handefull*: *A sorrowfull Sonet, made at Cambridge Castle* by George Mannington. This was a 'goodnight' ballad, apparently written the night before Mannington's execution in 1576. *A sorrowfull Sonet* was one of three ballads in the *Handefull* that Hyder E. Rollins agreed dated after 1566.[19] Rollins's other decisions were based on the titles of tunes that were registered as songs between 1566 and 1584. Even this does not provide conclusive proof that the ballads could not have been in the first edition. Ballad tunes sometimes took on the names of a 'hit' song long after they began to be used, while others went by several names. These ballads could, however, have been registered individually after the collection was published, rather than before. Indeed, the market for a single broadside ballad and a book of songs was presumably somewhat different, as more people could afford to purchase a single sheet than a larger volume like the *Handefull*.

Clearly, the men and women we associate most closely with ballads, the labouring poor who most often found themselves represented in the songs, would have been unlikely to be able to afford a collection of ballads such as the *Handefull of Pleasant Delites*. Yet the ongoing popularity of volumes such as Tottel's *Miscellany*, the *Handefull of Pleasant Delites*, *The Paradyse of daynty deuises* and *A gorgious Gallery, of gallant Inuentions* points once again to an elision of art forms that we now consider to be distinct. Hall and Becon's failure to distinguish between courtly poetry and the doggerel verse of broadside ballads in their criticism only serves to reiterate this point.

Balladeers and Their Social Status

So who were the mid-Tudor balladeers? The fact that the vast majority of mid-sixteenth-century ballads were anonymous makes this a difficult question to answer. Anonymity has usually been taken to indicate that individual authors did not matter and ascription would add nothing to the song. Sometimes, however, an individual balladeer might be named because he had a reputation as an entertainer. William Elderton was the exception rather than the rule, as it seems that many of his ballads carried his name because it indicated a certain caché. Conversely, most balladeers were seen even at the time as 'hack versifiers'.[20]

Anonymity has also given rise to the belief that balladeers must have been of middling or low social status, otherwise they would have wanted to claim authorship of their work. Given the low cultural status of the ballad as an art form, however, we might question the truth of this assumption. Critics complained that ballads were detrimental to people's moral and spiritual health. As early as 1535, the preface to Miles Coverdale's *Goostly psalmes and spirituall songes drawen out of the holy Scripture, for the co[m]forte and consolacyon of soch as loue to reioyse in God and his Worde* expressed his specific intention to provide metrical psalms that could be sung by people at home, in order 'That they may thrust under the borde / All other balettes of fylthynes'.[21] Similarly, in 1547, the Bishop of Winchester, Stephen Gardiner, bewailed that Lent had been 'buried' in 'fonde... and foolyshe' rhymes. He complained that 'the people paye mony for them. And they can serve for nothyng but to learne the people to rayle'.[22] Forty years later, this association between ballads and vice was ingrained. The poet Robert Fletcher urged the Elizabethan regime to

> suppresse that huge heape, & superfluous rable of balde Ballads, Rimes & Ridles, Songs & Sonnets, yea, and whole volumes of vanity, which tend to the nourishing of vice, and corrupting of Youth, which be not written for our learning, but for the confusion of those that delight therin, to teach vnlawfull lust, and outragious ribauldry, and to trayne vp in the toyes of vanitie, the vaine, fickle, and fantasticall youth, yea, and some aged, whose modestie ought to be ashamed of such immoderate follie.[23]

Ballads contributed to society's moral and spiritual decay, and needed to be controlled or, better still, replaced with more edifying forms of music. If ballads were as poorly thought of as men such as Fletcher claimed, then it is possible that authors, particularly those of the middling sort, might wish to avoid people knowing that they had added a host of popular songs to their printed output, even if it generated welcome extra income. No amount of urging from the godly, however, was able to turn the tide of popular song.

Despite their association with the poorer sections of society, ballads and ballad authorship were by no means the exclusive preserve of the lower orders. Some balladeers derived status from their education or social standing. Several 'goodnight' ballads like that of George Mannington appear to have been written by noble prisoners who were about to be executed, although it must be admitted that the gentle authorship of some of these ballads is questionable. It is quite possible that these ballads were written to cash in on topical stories by just the sort of 'tabloid' balladeer of stereotype. But it is clear nonetheless that ballads were popular at Henry VIII's court, and some were composed to be sung at

Queen Anne's coronation in 1533.[24] Furthermore, Lord Vaux's *The Aged Louer renounceth Loue* became one of the most ubiquitous mid-Tudor ballads. Vaux's background is certainly not typical of mid-sixteenth-century balladeers, but it seems that when a name was attached to a work, it was attached because someone thought it would help the ballad to sell. It is possible, though, that anonymity might simply reflect a cultural norm – if ballads were supposed to appeal to the people, might it be better that they appeared to have sprung from the people? It was, in effect, a throwback to the *vox populi* tradition of the oral ballad.

In fact, we know something of the lives of some 46 balladeers who were active during the mid-Tudor period. Of these, at least 13 had a university education. Others moved in court circles or had connexions with a group of musicians, poets and playwrights associated with St Paul's Cathedral in London. The most prolific of these balladeers was the author of *A newe well a daye*, William Elderton. As well as writing ballads, it seems that Elderton had close links to Protestant courtiers. He appeared as the fourth son of the Lord of Misrule in a Twelfth Day entertainment at Edward VI's court in 1553, wearing a taffeta and silk fool's coat in crimson and white. The role of the Lord of Misrule was reprised by George Ferrers, who was a courtier, MP and former servant of the Duke of Somerset. Ferrers had been instructed to take on the role in 1552 by the Duke of Northumberland, as part of the lavish pageantry intended to divert attention from Somerset's execution. The 1553 celebrations, therefore, place Elderton at court at a time of evangelical Protestant ascendancy. Some years later, in 1569, he published a ballad praising his former patroness, the marchioness of Northampton, for her Protestant piety. His later ballads, especially those published during the progress of the Northern Rebellion, take a polemical Protestant and aggressively anti-Catholic stance. By 1573, Elderton was in charge of the boy actors of Eton College and the following year he took part in a play performed before Queen Elizabeth. One of his songs, *The Gods of Loue*, was used by Shakespeare in *Much Ado About Nothing*. Despite this, his first ballad, *The panges of Loue and louers fttes* [sic], is perhaps one of the lewdest survivals from the mid-Tudor period.[25]

As well as his involvement with the Protestant circle at court, Elderton had links with the legal profession. Hyder E. Rollins speculated that Elderton was an attorney in the sheriff's court between 1562 and 1568, although this connection is unclear.[26] Certainly Elderton's Lord of Misrule, George Ferrers, was trained as a lawyer at Lincoln's Inn. The social network surrounding the Inns of Court included Protestants such as Thomas Norton and William Baldwin; Jasper Heywood, poet and son of the propagandist and balladeer John Heywood (who was himself related to the famous Rastell printing family); George Puttenham, author of *the Arte of Poesie*; and the printer, Richard Tottel, who is best known to history as the printer of the poetic miscellany, *Songes and sonnettes*.

Lawyers in this circle were trained to be eloquent. They were encouraged to write poetry as practise for their careers. Each of the Inns of Court had a Master of the Revels who was responsible for providing entertainment and they may well have written some of the plays, poems and songs used at the revels themselves.[27] This makes it all the more possible that Elderton the balladeer had a parallel career in law.

Likewise, another Tudor balladeer led something of a dual life. Richard Sheale was an itinerant ballad-seller who was also one of the Earl of Derby's retainers. He has become particularly associated with a manuscript in the Bodleian Library which contains five ballads that bear his name. One of these ballads was an autobiographical account of his life on the road, which gives us one of few real insights into itinerant musicians' way of life. It described in detail Sheale's journey from Tamworth in Staffordshire to London. Sheale's wife was a silk-woman who made shirts and smocks to sell at fairs and markets along with items of haberdashery. Having sold much of her merchandise, Sheale converted the money to gold and, with his harp, rode towards London to pay off his debts. He had only reached Dunsmore Heath, near Rugby, when he was robbed by four thieves. He returned home, destitute, to Tamworth, where his friends rallied round to support him. Sheale's 'good lord and mastar' sent for him 'aftar a lovyng facion' and Lord Strange took compassion on the unfortunate minstrel. Like much of Sheale's verse, this song reflected a familiarity with the aristocratic Stanley family, for whom he seems to have acted in the capacity of minstrel. Likewise, William Elderton's *A proper new balad in praise of my Ladie Marques* referred to Elizabeth Parr as the woman for whom he 'spends the time to speak and write', implying that the marchioness was in some way his patron. These links between balladeers and the nobility rather undermine the claim that balladeers were independent of the system of patronage.[28]

Elderton and Sheale were not the only Tudor balladeers who seem to have had significant links to the great and the good of mid-Tudor society. John Philips was educated at Queen's College, Cambridge, but apparently took no degree. His father was a clothworker named Robart Philip, who was a member of a London livery company which had links to the duchess of Suffolk, Katherine, Lady Bertie. Philips' multifaceted output of ballads, news sheets, a historical novel and several moralistic and anti-papal tracts probably mirrored that of many Tudor balladeers. As well as producing *A balad intituled, A cold pye for the papistes wherin is contayned: the trust of true subiectes for suppressyng of sedicious papistrie and rebellion: to the maintenance of the Gospell, and the publique peace of Englande. Made to be songe to Lassiamiza noate*, he also wrote several broadside epitaphs about London luminaries and aristocrats, such as the wife of the lord mayor, Alexander Avenon, and Margaret, Countess of Lennox. Written in ballad metre, any of these could easily have been sung. In addition to these single sheets, he wrote several longer verse epitaphs including those of Sir Christopher Hatton, and another lord mayor's wife, Helen Branch.

Nevertheless, although women were the subject of many of these ballads, they appear notable by their absence from ballad authorship during the mid-Tudor years. All of the known Tudor balladeers were male, but this need not preclude the involvement of women in balladry. Pamela Allen Brown fashioned a convincing case for women as producers and consumers of ballads at a local level, pointing out that even though there is little evidence of women as ballad authors and printers, 'this consideration recedes in importance next to questions of transmission and reception'. She argued that women were 'undeniably present' in the print trade in jests, ballads and other ephemera, not only among the audience but also as sellers and performers, and possibly as authors too.[29]

Illustrating Ballads

The ballads written by these men (and perhaps women) were printed as illustrated broadsides. The woodcuts used to enliven broadside ballads such as those written by William Elderton were usually taken from a stock of existing images, rather than being specifically cut to the needs of the ballad in question. This should not, however, imply that images were chosen at random. Hyder E. Rollins promulgated the belief that printers illustrated their ballads with whatever image came to hand, regardless of its appropriateness. This became the accepted view of twentieth-century scholars. By contrast, recent work by Christopher Marsh has shown that although woodcuts were frequently reused to illustrate many different situations, they were usually relevant in some way to the text at hand. By reading the texts and using our imagination, it is possible to see that the illustrations were chosen with care in order to relate to the narrative.[30] This suggests that printers did, in fact, pick woodcuts with care even if they only had a limited stock from which to choose. For example, *A godly ditty or prayer to be song vnto God for the preseruation of his Church, our Queene and realme, against all traytours, rebels, and papisticall enemies,* by John Awdelay, was illustrated by a large cut of royal arms placed centrally under the title. Awdelay's *An Epitaph of Maister Fraunces Benison Citizene and Marchant of London and of the Haberdashers Company* contains a simple but beautiful image of Death, carrying his sting and a coffin, passing a standing cross in the corner of a wall, with houses in the background.[31]

Ballad illustrations were certainly reused extensively. Thomas Colwell had a stock of images which he used in many of his publications, not just ballads. These included a matching set of at least 12 small woodcuts which he used individually and combined in different groups. As well as images of well-dressed male and female figures, they included one of St John and several of St Luke with his symbolic bull, which suggests that the set was perhaps first used to illustrate a New Testament. The most frequently used image from the collection is that of a man with his left hand raised aloft to illustrate speech. Its first appearance in an extant publication seems to be on the title page of the 1562 *Erra Pater* almanac.[32] Colwell used it again in 1565 on the title page of John Larke's translation of the *Boke of Wisdome*, where it was accompanied by the image of a woman carrying a rose.[33] Seven of the set of images appear down the right-hand margin of Robert Burdet's devoutly Protestant ballad, *The Refuge of a Sinner*.[34] Like the author, the figures in each illustration are male. Written in the first person, this song repented man's tendency to sin and repudiated Catholic teaching on atonement. According to Burdet, nothing but God's grace, freely given, could save sinners. He chastised those who relied on pilgrimage, saintly intercession or the outward trappings of faith to save their souls, condemning the Catholic sale of redemption: 'Thy bloud hath bought my soule, and booteth all my bale. / And not mans workes nor chaunted charmes devised in Ma[m]mons dale'. Mammon as a personification of greed was associated with St Luke because the story of the unjust steward (or *the Parable of Wicked Mammon* as William Tyndale presented it) appears only in Luke's gospel. Tyndale's text, published in May 1528, examined the parable in its wider theological context. He used the parable to argue that good works were a result of faith in Christ rather than a means to gain salvation. Only God could grant pardon for sins and this assertion of solifidianism was emphatically Protestant. Three of the woodcuts on the ballad *The Refuge of a Sinner* are images of St Luke, which perhaps reinforced the association between the lyrics of the ballad and St Luke's parable.[35]

Colwell reused several of his set of images on William Elderton's ballads in 1569, although it seems that space did not permit him to use them on *A newe well a daye*. Five female figures were placed at the head of Elderton's *A proper newe ballad sheweing that Philosophers Learnynges, are full of good warnynges*.[36] Like Burdet's *Refuge of a Sinner*, Elderton's ballad bemoaned the folly of men. The images of women presumably illustrated the 'lyberties that lust desireth'. They represented the desires of the flesh that Elderton suggested were at the root of men's sinful behaviour. Meanwhile, four male figures and one female from the set adorned the top of *A proper new balad in praise of my Ladie Marques, Whose death is bewailed, To the tune of new lusty gallant*.[37] Interestingly, three of the males were images of St Luke. Elderton's ballad epitaph subtly emphasised the Protestant faith of Elizabeth Parr, who spent her time 'Homblie kneeling one her knee, / As her desire was still to praie'. Perhaps, then, the images of St Luke again reinforced the idea that faith alone guaranteed salvation. Furthermore, the images of St Luke were dressed more simply than the other, more elegantly dressed men we find in Colwell's collection.

As the ballad lamented Elderton's loss of income since the death of his patroness, the pictures were more appropriate than those of men in much richer costumes. By the time Colwell used these same images of St Luke on *The Plagues of Northomberland* in 1570, the bull, who originally identified the saint, was probably an implicit reference to the 'Westmere Bull'. Christopher Neville, Earl of Westmorland, had a coat of arms supported by a bull. The fact that the rebel Westmorland still sported St Luke's halo was probably unfortunate but unavoidable when the presence of the bull was so appropriate. Perhaps it was even a joke: it was ironic, given the way in which the rebels presented themselves as doing God's work in attempting to bring about a counter-Reformation. The figure of the speaking man stood between the rebels and a female figure which presumably represented Queen Elizabeth.[38]

On the other hand, not all of the ballads that Colwell printed during this period were illustrated quite so appropriately. The extant copy of *A Proper New balad of the Bryber Gehesie* might only be a printer's proof, given that the decoration down the centre of the page consists of several words in Latin, *ti et per* and *a muliere initum factum*.[39] This message, perhaps translated as 'by woman was the first sin committed', bears no relevance to the text of the ballad, which instead told the biblical story of Elisha's servant Gehazi, who was cursed with leprosy as a result of his avarice. When appropriate woodcuts were unavailable, broadside ballads were frequently decorated with simple, attractive borders. As *A newe well a daye* shows, the initial letter of the first word of the lyrics was often printed in an ornamental form rather than black letter, suggesting a stylistic link to illuminated manuscripts. Nevertheless, although ballads were often attractively illustrated, such illustration was subordinate to the text: there would, after all, be no ballad without the words. This was at least in part down to the how much text there was to fit on the page, so when space was at a premium, decoration was dropped. If the ballad was relatively short, it left plenty of space on the page for decorative borders, fleurons and illustrations. *Churchyardes Lamentacion of Freyndshyp* (1566), by contrast, was almost entirely undecorated, save for a single leaf motif and small illuminated letter. Sometimes the space available on the page dictated the ways in which ornaments were used, and printers were not above turning images on their side in order to fit them on the page.

Furthermore, it is likely that buyers used visual cues such as familiar woodcuts to identify songs by their favourite printers and balladeers. Only those ballads which depicted monstrous births seem to have guaranteed a specially cut illustration, as these unique wonders required striking, individual images which fitted the description of the fish, pig or child. Presumably, these news ballads could be expected to sell in significant numbers, making it worthwhile to go to the expense of producing a specific illustration which would add a significant visual dimension to the songs' 'wow' factor. Even popular balladeers such as Elderton did not warrant such an investment.

Printing Music

It is noticeable, however, that while ballads were often ornamented with borders and illuminated letters, musical notation rarely appeared on Tudor broadsides. Oral transmission meant that tunes were instead passed from one person to another. Mentioning the name of a tune or humming a phrase of music would almost certainly have been enough to prompt recall. Providing the name of a tune as part of the ballad's title was enough to remind people how it went, but even tune names appear on only a minority of mid-Tudor ballads, which suggests that the primary means of transmitting a ballad was not in fact by written or printed means, but from mouth to ear. The easiest way for most of us to learn a tune, even now, is by listening to someone else singing it. When we are confident that we have picked it up, we join in with the singing. Likewise, for the ballad-buying public, a new tune would have been learned in the first instance by ear from the ballad-seller on the street. From there, it would have been passed on by ear from one person to another. These tunes might undergo slight alteration as they were passed along, but their tunes retained their central characteristics. Like the melodies for the Child ballads, they kept their basic outlines over a long period.[40]

This lack of musical instruction was by no means exclusive to ballads, though. All sorts of lyrics could be notated without their music. A clear example of this is the early Tudor song *As power and wytt*. As well as being a song in several parts, its words can also be found in a variety of non-musical sources.[41] Just because there is no music on the broadside or notated in manuscript, therefore, we should not assume that the verses could not be sung. On balance, it seems reasonable to suppose that broadsides which look like ballads, printed in two columns in black-letter type; or manuscripts containing lyrics in a simple metre and using demotic language; or even the simple, strophic songs printed in pamphlet form, might well all have been sung as ballads even though we cannot be certain of the tunes.

Moreover, in the mid-sixteenth century, English music printing was in its infancy and the process of printing music was not straightforward.[42] One method involved two printing impressions: the first for the stave and a second for the note-heads. More common, however, was single-impression printing, where individual punches contained a single note, rest or other symbol on a small section of stave. Music printed in this way is easy to spot because it produces small gaps in the stave between each note, where the individual sections of the type face were lined up. This sort of single-impression printing was useful because the notes were dual purpose: they could be inverted to produce the opposite position on the staff. For example, a note on the top line of the stave could be inverted to produce a note on the bottom line of the stave if necessary. Whichever method a printer chose to use, however, music printing was an expensive and time-consuming undertaking with a limited market of musically literate buyers. As only a small percentage of the ballad-buying public would have been able to read the music, the rest would have learned by ear, making the expensive process of typesetting or producing a woodcut of music redundant.

The earliest broadside ballads to contain music use different single-impression music type faces. This tells us that more than one set of musical type was available to London printers at the time. Furthermore, William Griffith used a different musical type face for Richard Beeard's *A Godly Psalme, of Marye Queene* in 1553 to the one that he used in 1568 for Osborne's *A Newe Ballade of a Louer, Extollinge his Ladye*. Donald Krummel speculated that this first type face was one of those owned by John Day (who seems to have held the patent for printing psalm books), who then loaned it to other printers, including Griffith and William Seres, during 1553. Because the type face needed for psalms such as Beeard's was different to that used for Catholic plainchant notation, it became obsolete in England shortly after Mary I's accession in 1553. Day then moved to Emden, in Protestant Saxony, where he used the same typeface to print Dutch psalms.[43] The type face used by Griffith for *A Newe ballade* might also have been owned by John Day, while Abel Jeffes used a musical type face belonging to one of Day's successors, John Wolfe, for *A godlie Dittie to be song for the preseruation of the Queenes most excellent Maiesties raigne*.[44]

Although the first extant broadside ballad with music was printed in 1568, it was not until a century later that melody lines began appearing more regularly on broadside ballads.[45] It is, however, possible that there was a significant rise in amateur music-making during the sixteenth century.[46] There were enough musically literate people in sixteenth-century England to justify the mass-production of some printed music, even though they remained only a small minority of the population at this stage. Furthermore, the use of technical musical language, such as references to hexachordal solmization, was widespread, especially on the Tudor stage. This suggests that the terms were familiar to many of the audience: there would have been no point using them if no one in the audience was in the know and understood what they meant. Nonetheless, the practical difficulties involved in routinely printing music on broadside ballads during this period would have outweighed the benefits.[47] Reliance on oral transmission was clearly the cheaper and more effective option. Printed music was aimed at a more affluent market than the bulk of the ballad-buying public who might only be able to afford an occasional single-sheet copy, purchased from a London bookstall or a wandering ballad singer.

Ballads and Orality

Even so, it seems likely that many more people would have encountered a ballad by hearing it sung than by reading it in print or manuscript. The balladeer who sold broadsides may be a product of the world of print but nevertheless, ballads thrived in Tudor society where many people could not read. Despite the increasing availability of cheap print in the sixteenth century, news and information was most often passed on by word of mouth.[48] For those who wished to communicate with a wide cross section of society, ballads were a particularly enticing form of expression because their content was framed by mnemonic devices. These included patterns of syntax, semantics and metre, but perhaps the most obvious were the rhymes that organised and unified words.[49] Rhyme works quickly to cue recall by limiting the choice of concluding words in a line. By the same token, it helps to stabilise oral traditions.[50] It is only relatively recently that historians have begun to engage with orality, a term used for cultures in which communication took primarily through the spoken rather than the written word. For historians, orality poses a particular problem which is perhaps less exposed in other disciplines: our inability to place oral evidence at precise times and locations. In order for us to know about oral culture, it has to have been recorded in some way, sometimes much later.[51]

Ballads were most often disseminated by oral means through face-to-face contact. Songs were taught by one person to another. The combination of oral and visual forms in broadside ballads helped to reinforce people's memory of a song. Research on the transmission of knowledge in several European cultures has shown that oral, literate and visual cultures overlapped in creating human memory.[52] All three methods of transmitting a message were considered equally legitimate. The choice of one form of expression rather than another depended on what information could be portrayed, how long it was required to last and how widely it needed to be disseminated.

The overlap between printed and oral material is illustrated by the so-called Child ballads. Francis Child was Harvard University's first professor of English and an expert on early English literature. The extensive collection of 305 English and Scottish ballads which he gathered from the oral tradition during the mid-nineteenth century aimed to preserve every variation of each song. He described his collection as 'true popular ballads', that is, songs which had been transmitted exclusively through the oral tradition. Believing that the significant Pepys and Roxburghe collections of broadside ballads were 'veritable dunghills', he was nevertheless forced to include more than 250 texts taken from broadsides and garlands – there were simply too many places where traditional and commercial songs overlapped.[53]

Yet Child still believed that his popular ballads were quite different from commercially printed ballads. The basis for this distinction seems to have been that the popular ballad was the spontaneous creation of the illiterate rural population, rather than the artificial production of the professional ballad-writer. His evidence, however, was somewhat limited and rarely stated. If the English ballad can be described as a narrative song 'of largely (or effectively) anonymous origin', then, as we shall see, the majority of broadside ballads clearly also fit the bill and the barrier between the traditional and printed ballad is further demolished.[54] We cannot know who originally wrote the ballads collected from the oral tradition, and we do not know who wrote many of the sixteenth-century broadside ballads, so the main distinction between the two (historically speaking at least) is that in the case of broadsides we can more often tell *when* they were written. Nevertheless, there do appear to be some textual differences between the broadside and the traditional ballad. They arise from the singer's need to organise the narrative. Child ballads, for example, contain more refrains than the printed broadsides, although we should not underestimate the possibility that the balladeer might adapt a printed song by repeating lines in performance to achieve the same effect. Scribes who wrote ballads into manuscript might have had even more incentive to leave out repeated lines, in order to save both time and paper.

It was this breadth of appeal and their ease of transmission which placed ballads at the centre of sixteenth-century culture. These songs emphasised their orality, urging the audience to 'draw near' and 'listen awhile'. Repeated lines and refrains encouraged communal singing. People chose to write down the ballads that they enjoyed in manuscripts, sometimes collecting many ballad texts together. Even though printing was in its infancy, printers made the decision to make their ballads look as appealing as they sounded. It seems safe to assume that these were the songs that formed the background to much mid-Tudor life.

Notes

1 William Elderton, *A ballad intituled, A newe well a daye / as playne maister papist, as Donstable waye. Well a daye well a daye, well a daye woe is mee Syr Thomas Plomtrie is hanged on a tree* (London, 1570), STC (2nd ed.) / 7553. The chapter title is taken from *A merry new song how a bruer meant to make a cooper cuckold and how deere the bruer paid for the bargaine. To the tune of, In somertime* (London, 1590), STC (2nd ed.) / 22919.

2 Francis Fullwood, *The church-history of Britain from the birth of Jesus Christ until the year M.DC.XLVIII endeavoured by Thomas Fuller* (London, 1655), Wing / F2416, p. 83; Cuthbert Sharp, *Memorials of the Rebellion of 1569* (London: John Bowyer and Son, and William Pickering, 1840), pp. 123, 133 and 188; G. W., *The faithful analist:, or, The epitome of the English history: giving a true accompt of the affairs of this nation, from the building of the tower in London, in the days of William the Conquerour, to the throwing down the gates of the said city, by the command of the Parliament, which state before the secluded members were*

admitted, in the yeer 1660. In which all things remarkable both by sea and land from the yeer 1069. To this present yeer of 1660 are truly and exactly represented* (London, 1660), Wing (2nd ed.) / G69, p. 109.

3 Marsh, *Music and Society*, p. 236. The text has been underlaid using examples from two later sets of words given to the tune, with particular reference to how the 'welladay' refrain fits in these examples. The tune was transcribed from Paris, Bibliothèque nationale de France, MS Rés 1186, ff. 25^{r-v}. The pitch has been dropped by a tone to make it more suitable for voices and a key signature added for convenience.

4 Gamini Salgado, *The Elizabethan Underworld* (Stroud: Sutton, 2005), p. 139. A twenty-first century attempt to create a broadside ballad using early modern techniques is documented on the website, *The Making of a Broadside Ballad*, http://press.emcimprint.english.ucsb.edu/the-making-of-a-broadside-ballad/index [accessed 20 July 2017].

5 Marsh, *Music and Society*, p. 232.

6 Marsh, *Music and Society*, pp. 238–39.

7 C. Paul Christianson, 'The Rise of London's Book-Trade', in Lotte Hellinga and J. B. Trapp (eds.), *The Cambridge History of the Book in Britain* (6 vols. Cambridge: Cambridge University Press, 1999), iii, p. 129.

8 John Dorne, 'The Daily Ledger of John Dorne, 1520', in F. Madan (ed.), *Collectanea*, First Series (Oxford: Oxford Historical Society at the Clarendon Press, 1885), p. 137.

9 John N. King, 'The Book-Trade under Edward VI and Mary I', in Lotte Hellinga and J. B. Trapp (eds.), *The Cambridge History of the Book in Britain* (6 vols. Cambridge: Cambridge University Press, 1999), iii, p. 169.

10 Thomas Brooke, *Certayne versis writtene by Thomas Brooke Ge[n]tleman in the tyme of his impriso[n]ment the daye before his deathe who sufferyd at Norwich the 30 of August 1570* (Norwich, 1570), STC (2nd ed.) / 3835.

11 Watt, *Cheap Print*, p. 6.

12 Locations were taken from various volumes of the *Records of Early English Drama* (detailed in the bibliography) and from *State Papers Online*, http://gale.cengage.co.uk/state-papers-online-15091714.aspx [accessed 12 May 2015].

13 Marsh, *Music and Society*, pp. 240–42.

14 Hyder E. Rollins, 'An Analytical Index to the Ballad-Entries (1557–1709) in the Registers of the Company of Stationers of London', *Studies in Philology*, 21:1 (1924), pp. 1–324.

15 Thomas Preston, *A Lamentation from Rome, how the Pope doth bewayle, / That the Rebelles in England can not preuayle to the tune of Rowe well ye mariners* (London, 1570), STC (2nd ed.) / 20289; John Saparton, *Sapartons alarum, to all such as do beare the name of true souldiers, in england, or els wheare* (London, 1569), STC (2nd ed.) / 21745.

16 Christopher Warner, *The Making and Marketing of Tottel's Miscellany, 1557: Songs and Sonnets in the Summer of the Martyrs' Fires* (Farnham: Ashgate, 2013), p. 7; John Hall, *Certayn chapters take[n] out of the Prouerbes of Salomo[n], wyth other chapters of the holy scripture, [and] certayne Psalmes of Dauid, translated into English meter, by Iohn Hall. Whych prouerbes of late were set forth, imprinted and vntruely entituled, to be thee doynges of Mayster Thomas Sternhold, late grome of the kynges Maiesties robes, as by thys copye it maye be perceaued* (London, 1550), STC (2nd ed.) / 2760, sig. B1^{r}.

17 John Awdelay, *The cruel assault of Gods fort* (London, 1560), STC (2nd ed.) / 989.

18 Robinson, *Handefull of Pleasant Delites*, pp. ix–x.

19 Hyder E. Rollins, 'The Date, Authors, and Contents of "a Handfull of Pleasant Delights"', *Journal of English and Germanic Philology*, 18:1 (1919), pp. 57 and 47.

20 Hyder E. Rollins, 'The Black-Letter Broadside Ballad', *Publications of the Modern Language Association of America*, 34:2 (1919), p. ix.

21 Miles Coverdale, *Goostly psalmes and spirituall songes drawen out of the holy Scripture, for the co[m]forte and consolacyon of soch as loue to reioyse in God and his Worde* (London, 1535), STC (2nd ed.) / 879:22, p. i.

22 Stephen Gardiner, *The Letters of Stephen Gardiner* (Cambridge: Cambridge University Press, 1933), pp. 283 and 280.

23 Marie Ange Simard, *An introduction to the looue of God. Accompted among the workes of S. Augustine, and translated into English, by the right reuerend father in God, Edmund, Bishop of Norwitch, that nowe is, and by him dedicated to the Queenes most excellent Maiestie, to the glorie of God, and comfort of his chosen. And newlie turned into Englishe meter by Robert Fletcher* (London, 1581), STC (2nd ed.) / 936, sig. Bi^{r-v}.

24 *The noble tryumphaunt coronacyon of quene Anne wyfe vnto the moost noble kynge Henry the .viij.* (London, 1533), STC (2nd ed.) / 656, sig. Aiv^r & Av^r.

25 Alfred John Kempe, *The Loseley Manuscripts: Manuscripts and Other Rare Documents ... Preserved in the Muniment Room of James More Molyneux, Esq. At Loseley House, in Surrey* (London: Murray, 1836), pp. 47–48; Hyder E. Rollins, 'William Elderton: Elizabethan Actor and Ballad-Writer', *Studies in Philology*, 17:2 (1920), p. 201; Jenni Hyde, 'William Elderton's Ladie Marques Identified', *Notes and Queries*, 260:4 (2015), pp. 541–42; James M. Osborn, 'Benedick's Song in "Much Ado"', *The Times*, 17 November 1958, p. 11; William Elderton, *The panges of Loue and louers ftts* [sic] (London, 1559), STC (2nd ed.) / 7561.

26 Rollins, 'William Elderton', p. 201.

27 Warner, *Making and Marketing of Tottel's Miscellany*, pp. 20–23 and 5.

28 Würzbach, *Rise of the English Street Ballad*, p. 21.

29 Pamela Allen Brown, *Better a Shrew Than a Sheep: Women, Drama, and the Culture of Jest in Early Modern England* (London: Cornell University Press, 2002), p. 74. There is evidence of one female printer during this period – 'Mistress Toye' took over her husband's print shop on his death.

30 See Christopher Marsh, '"The Blazing Torch": New Light on English Balladry as a Multi-Media Matrix', *Seventeenth Century*, 30:1 (2015), pp. 95–116; Christopher Marsh, 'A Woodcut and Its Wanderings in Seventeenth-Century England', *Huntington Library Quarterly*, 79:2 (2016), pp. 245–62.

31 John Awdelay, *A godly ditty or prayer to be song vnto God for the preseruation of his Church, our Queene and realme, against all traytours, rebels, and papisticall enemies* (London, 1569), STC (2nd ed.) / 995; John Awdelay, *An Epitaph, of Maister Fraunces Benison, Citizene and Marchant of London, and of the Haberdashers Company* (London, 1570); Rollins, 'The Black-Letter Broadside Ballad', p. 263.

32 Erra Pater, *The pronostycacion for euer of Erra Pater: a Iewe borne in Iewery, a doctour in astronomy, [and] physycke Profytable to kepe the body in helth. And also Ptholomeus sayth the same* (London, 1562), STC (2nd ed.) / 439.15.

33 John Larke, *The boke of wisdome otherwise called the flower of vertue. Folowing the auctorities of auncient doctours [and] philosophers, deuiding and speaking of vices [and] vertues, wyth many goodly examples wherby a man may be praysed or dyspraysed, wyth the maner to speake well and*

wyselie to al folkes, of what estate so euer they bee. Translated first out of Italion into French, [and] out of french into English, by Iohn Larke (London, 1565), STC (2nd ed.) / 3358.

34 Robert Burdet, *The refuge of a sinner wherein are briefely declared the chiefest poinctes of true saluation* (London, 1565), STC (2nd ed.) / 4104.

35 William Tyndale, *That fayth the mother of all good workes iustifieth us before we ca[n] bringe forth anye good worke...* ([Antwerp], 1528), STC (2nd ed.) / 24454.

36 William Elderton, *A proper newe ballad sheweing that philosophers learnynges, are full of good warnynges. And songe to the tune of My Lorde Marques Galyarde: or The firste traces of que passa* (London, 1569), STC (2nd ed.) / 7563.

37 William Elderton, *A proper new balad in praise of my Ladie Marques, whose death is bewailed, to the tune of New lusty gallant* (London, 1569), STC (2nd ed.) / 7562.

38 John Barker, *The plagues of Northomberland. To the tune of Appelles* (London, 1570), STC (2nd ed.) / 1421.

39 Thomas Churchyard, *Churchyardes lamentacion of freyndshyp* (London, 1566), STC (2nd ed.) / 5223; Carole Rose Livingston, *British Broadside Ballads of the Sixteenth Century: A Catalogue of the Extant Sheets and an Essay* (New York: General Music Publishing Co., 1991), p. 300; George Mell, *A proper new balad of the Bryber Gehesie Taken out of the fourth booke of Kinges the .v. chapter. To the tune of Kynge Salomon* (London, 1566), STC (2nd ed.) / 17802.

40 Bertrand H. Bronson, *The Singing Tradition of Child's 'Popular Ballads'* (Princeton: Princeton University Press, 1976), p. xxx.

41 John Milsom, 'Songs and Society in Early Tudor London', *Early Music History*, 16 (1997), p. 245.

42 See A. Hyatt King, 'The Significance of John Rastell in Early Music Printing', *Library*, 26:3 (1971, 5th Ser.), p. 203; Donald William Krummel, *English Music Printing, 1553–1700* (London: Bibliographical Society, 1975).

43 Krummel, *English Music Printing*, pp. 42–45 and 161–62.

44 Bryan P. Davis, 'John Day', in James K. Bracken and Joel Silver (eds.), *The British Literary Book Trade, 1700–1820* (London: Gale Research, 1995), p. 85; R. Thacker, *A godlie Dittie to be song for the preseruation of the Queenes most excellent Maiesties raigne* (London, 1586), London, Society of Antiquaries, Book of Broadsides, STC (2nd ed.) / 23926.

45 Krummel, *English Music Printing*, p. 162.

46 John Milsom, 'Music, Politics and Society', in Robert Tittler and Norman L. Jones (eds.), *A Companion to Tudor Britain* (Oxford: Blackwell, 2004), p. 499.

47 Milsom, 'Songs and Society', pp. 278–82 and 276; Milsom, 'Music, Politics and Society', p. 503.

48 Fox, 'Remembering the Past', p. 256.

49 Reuven Tsur, 'Rhyme and Cognitive Poetics', *Poetics Today*, 17:1 (1996), p. 85.

50 David C. Rubin, *Memory in Oral Traditions: The Cognitive Psychology of Epic, Ballads, and Counting-out Rhymes* (New York; Oxford: Oxford University Press, 1995), pp. 75–85.

51 For a comprehensive digital archive of ballads collected by the twelve main Victorian folksong collectors, see The English Folk Dance and Song Society's *The Full English* project, www.vwml.org/search/search-full-english [accessed 31 August 2014].

52 See, for example, Fernando J. Bouza Alvarez, *Communication, Knowledge, and Memory in Early Modern Spain*, trans. Sonia López and Michael Agnew (Philadelphia: University of Pennsylvania Press, 2004); Fox, 'Remembering the Past'.

53 Letter from Francis Child to Svend Grundtvig, 25 August 1872, quoted in E. David Gregory, *Victorian Songhunters: The Recovery and Editing of English Vernacular Ballads and Folk Lyrics, 1820–1883* (Oxford: Scarecrow, 2006), pp. 294 and 318.

54 Francis Child (ed.), *The English and Scottish Popular Ballads* (5 vols. London: H. Stevens, Son & Stiles, 1882), i, pp. vii–viii; David Atkinson, *The Anglo-Scottish Ballad and Its Imaginary Contexts* (Cambridge: Open Book Publishers, 2014), p. 1.

3 'I praye thee Mynstrell make no stoppe'
The Music of the Mid-Tudor Ballads

In Ioye yt makes our mirthe abounde
in woo yt cheres our hevy sprites
be strawghted heads relyeff haith sounde
by musickes pleasaunts swete delightes
our sences all what shall I saye moore
are subiecte vnto musicks lore.[1]

A songe to the lute of musicke embraced music as a salve for the troubled mind and a fillip to the enraptured soul. It was, in short, the 'heavenly gyft that rules the mynd'.[2] This ability to move the human spirit was thought by many to be a result of the different modes, or scales, used for the music (see Appendix 1).[3] Archbishop Matthew Parker's description of the eight Gregorian church modes outlined a theory of how different modes affected the spirit in different ways:

The first is méeke: deuout to sée, [Dorian]
The second sad: in maiesty. [Hypodorian]
The third doth rage: and roughly brayth. [Phrygian]
The fourth doth fawne: and flattry playth, [Hypophrygian]
The fyfth delight: and laugheth the more, [Lydian]
The sixt bewayleth: it wéepeth full sore, [Hypolydian]
The seuenth tredeth stoute: in froward race, [Mixolydian]
The eyghte goeth milde: in modest pace. [Hypomixolydian][4]

The most common modes for mid-Tudor ballad tunes were the Ionian and Dorian, although a few were in the Aeolian and the Mixolydian. Occasionally, a tune could include more than one of these four modes. The modes have very different moods: the Ionian was the basis of the modern major scale that we tend to associate with happiness and positivity; the modern melodic minor scale (often associated with simplicity and sadness) developed from the Aeolian and Dorian modes; the Mixolydian is most familiar in the twenty-first century as the major scale with a flattened seventh, a common musical device in jazz and popular music.

Lyrics were undeniably important to ballads, but without music, those lyrics did not make a song. Rather than concentrating on words, this chapter will highlight the ways in which ballads used music to sell the songs and therefore spread the news. Tunes were important to help people remember song lyrics and their messages, so ballads naturally favoured melodies in the scales that were easier to sing. First, the chapter shows how ballad tunes were adapted to different modes of performance and to accommodate different words. Next, it investigates the most popular tunes for mid-Tudor ballads, to see what made them suitable melodies for oral transmission. It then shows that ballads as a whole drew their melodies from a wide variety of sources, including dance music, the stage and sacred music. It shows that the relationship between all these types of music was reciprocal and that the Reformation had an impact on ballads. Furthermore, because it shows that music was an important element of popular songs, the chapter provides the foundation for a musical form of implicitness.

Ballad Flexibility

The ballad was indeed 'a remarkably flexible art-form'.[5] It was appreciated by both the musically illiterate and trained composers. John Milsom, however, argued that many sixteenth-century 'ballads' were not intended to be the solo songs that we associate with balladry today. Milsom concluded that although *A godlie Dittie to be song for the preseruation of the Queenes most exclent Maiesties raigne* looked like broadside ballad because it was printed with a single line of vocal melody, it was in fact only one part of a song intended for several voices. The broadside is the single survivor of a multi-sheet part-song, because it contains three breve rests at the beginning of the first line. Similar polyphonic songs were printed on single sheets by John and William Rastell in the 1520s and 1530s. They were aimed at the ballad-buying public rather than the elite.[6] It is also possible, however, that other parts did exist, but that the song could be performed with or without them. All the indications suggest that ballads were many things to many people and that a single line from a part-song might have been sung alone in a simple, ballad-like style. It is quite possible that the parts were all tuneful in their own right because they were melodically rather than harmonically driven.

This tractability is illustrated by surviving manuscripts. In some cases, one or two known ballads are included among other verses that might be considered more sophisticated poetry or art song. This suggests that the compilers had eclectic tastes. Instead of making a distinction between ballads and other material, they wrote down anything that particularly interested them, regardless of the source. For example, a collection of 14 songs in a manuscript belonging to the Shann family of Methley in Yorkshire contains not only several verses without music, but also pieces with music and, in some cases, music for several voices. All of them were described as ballads by Hyder E. Rollins.[7] Although the manuscript probably dates from the early seventeenth century, the Shann family document usefully indicates the way in which people collected their musical material. The first of the 14 musical items is the hymn-like ballad *Jerusalem, my happie home*, which was set to a known ballad melody, 'Rogero'. The manuscript also contains at least one carol written by Richard Shann himself, with music for a single voice in the bass clef. As well as the religious material, there are several love songs. One of these, *A Pretie Songe in Com[m]endation of the Springe, called the Queene of Love*, can be identified with a broadside ballad registered in 1605, but the music in the miscellany appears to be the bass line of a polyphonic song.[8] *Venus (that faire lovelie queene)*, however, has music in four parts (Figure 3.1). In the manuscript, two musical parts are written on each of two facing folios, but the words are not underlaid. Instead, they appear as a poem with four verses on the first folio and five on the next. In order to render this music for a modern audience, it has been transcribed into a four-part score, with the words underlaid. There are two places where notes have been divided into additional sung notes in order to accommodate extra syllables. Furthermore, words are not always repeated the same number of times by each voice, while some lines need to be repeated in their entirety in order to fit the music. For example, in bars 17 and 18 of the second voice, 'by A tree' is repeated in order to make use of three notes which would otherwise be redundant. Thus, it is clear that the words and music in the manuscript needed to be adapted by the singers in order to create the song. The written notation of either words or music was not an accurate record of the song as it was voiced; it merely represented an outline which needed to be adapted for performance.

Rollins suggested that *Venus (that faire lovelie queene)* might be the *Venus and Adonis* which was entered in the Stationers' Registers in 1656.[9] If this is the case, then it shows that the ballad was a malleable genre: something that could be sung by one voice or many, in unison or in parts. Richard Shann himself described the inherent adaptability of four-part-song, commenting that 'Ye maye, if ye please, let the triplex [soprano or treble] singe the dittie by him selfe, and let the three other partes allwaies take hould at "hey downe," and likewise when the last voice beginneth, and so to the ende'.[10] This, perhaps, explains how some sixteenth-century 'ballads' were in fact part-songs: spontaneous or precomposed harmonisations were both possible, in addition to solo performance.[11] A melody could be taken from a part-song and sung independently, while a song for solo voice could easily be harmonised by a group of singers in a manner not unfamiliar to the audience of many modern folk clubs. No formal training is required, simply a keen ear and confident voice.

Figure 3.1 Transcription of *Venus (that faire lovelie quene)* from London, British Library, Add. MS 38599 (Shann family commonplace book), ff. 137ᵛ–138ʳ, underlaid by the author.

Figure 3.1 (Continued).

The Shann family manuscript contained a variety of music in different styles and with different combinations of voices. Similar wide-ranging tastes can also be seen in the Stanhope Manuscript (BL Add. MS 82370). This long-neglected, late sixteenth-century document demonstrates the interplay between so-called traditional folksong and broadside ballads.[12] It contains the lyrics to two previously lost broadside ballads on the Spanish Armada, as well as a long historical ballad on the fourteenth-century feud between the Eland and Beaumont families.[13] This latter item, although unknown to Francis Child, is stylistically similar to the epic narrative ballads collected in his *English and Scottish Popular Ballads*. Furthermore, the Stanhope Manuscript also contains Lord Vaux's *The aged louer renounceth loue*, a poem which had a life in print, in manuscript and on the stage. It appears in Tottel's *Miscellany* of 1557 and in the Bodleian Library's MS Ashmole 48, as well as being registered as a broadside in 1563–4, and being sung by the first clown in Shakespeare's *Hamlet*.[14] So popular was the poem as a song that its first line gave the name to its tune: 'I loathe that I did loue'.

Popular Songs

Nevertheless, the challenge facing ballad scholars is to understand the texts as songs that were intended for performance. Many ballad tunes have simply not survived. Although William Chappell and Claude Simpson provided excellent resources for those who wish to identify ballad tunes, they often took their melodies from later printed copies, or edited melodies without explanation.[15] Going back to the original manuscript sources, however, is not without its own problems. Contemporary or near contemporary sources, such as the Ballet Lute Book in Trinity College, Dublin, and the Folger Shakespeare Library (FSL) book of lute music, V.a.159, contain instrumental rather than vocal arrangements of tunes. They give us an indication of melodies but often include ornamentation that would not have been sung.[16] On the other hand, we cannot discount the possibility that ballads were sung to instrumental accompaniment, and, indeed, it is relatively easy to fit lyrics to many of these tunes.

Although the number of surviving ballad tunes from the mid-sixteenth century is limited, it is not insignificant. Of the 433 ballads included in this study, 75 (17%) state the tune to which they were to be sung. These include 34 individual extant tunes, which between them account for 56 (13%) of the ballads. As a result of the culture of oral transmission, in which music was mainly learned by ear, these ballad tunes were, of necessity, catchy and memorable. The lack of printed music is not, therefore, as much of a handicap as it might, at first, appear. Several musical features contribute to how easily a person can pick up and remember a tune, which is of course especially important in oral transmission and when one wishes to remember both melody *and* words. These features include the use of repetition, both of whole phrases and of short musical figures, such as that in bars 7 and 8 of 'The Downright Squire' (Figure 3.3). The use of sequence, where a short musical figure is repeated in an ascending or descending pattern, was also common in orally transmitted tunes. An example of a descending sequence can be found in bars 10–12 of 'The Queen's Almain' (Figure 3.8). A third feature was the use of strong rhythmic patterns, such as those that can be seen in 'The Lusty Gallant' (Figure 3.2).[17]

Where a ballad named a tune, it must suggest that the melody was widely known by its title. It was commonly assumed that singers would already know or could learn these tunes from another person even if they had to read the lyrics. The first printed collection of ballads, *A Handefull of Pleasant Delites*, contained 33 songs, of which 28 were set to tunes that must have pre-existed because they already had a name. The remaining five songs were presumably intended to be set to their own, new tunes. For example, *The scoffe of a Ladie, as pretie as may be, to a yong man that went a wooing: He went stil about her, and yet he went without her, because he was so long a doing*, from the *Handefull of Pleasant Delites*, did not indicate the name of its tune, presumably because it was a new one without pre-existing associations. Its first line was 'Attend thee, go play thee'. 'Attend the goe play the' was then named as the tune for a ballad in the *Gorgeous Gallery* of *Gallant Inventions* in 1578. So *The scoffe of a Ladie* was almost certainly set to a new tune which took on the name of the first line of the song. It was then used, under that name, as the melody for other ballads.[18]

Like 'Attend the, go play thee', many Tudor ballad tunes have been lost over the intervening centuries. Fortunately, some tunes became so widely known that they were assimilated by instrumentalists who notated their arrangements in manuscript. These lute and keyboard versions give us an insight not only into the melodic content that made the tunes easy to learn, but also the way in which they could be accompanied. The mid-sixteenth century's top four ballad melodies have several things in common: they all stay close to a home note; they have rhythms that are simple and repetitive; and they are easy to sing because of their range and melodic contour. The most strikingly simple and memorable is 'The Lusty Gallant' (Figure 3.2). As well as the extant ballads that specify 'The Lusty Gallant', several items registered with the Stationers' Company also used this tune. In long metre (8.8.8.8), it easily fits a large number of lyrics, including *A proper Song, Intituled: Fain Would I have Some Pretty Thing to Give Unto My Ladie*.[19] The tune also seems to have been commonly known by this name. Its simplicity makes it easy to see why it was so popular. The melodic contours of the first and third phrases rise and are answered by the second and fourth phrases which fall. The majority of 'The Lusty Gallant' is in the Dorian mode based on C; however, the second of the four phrases is in the Ionian mode based on C because the third note of the scale is raised from E flat to E natural.

Figure 3.2 Setting of *A proper Song, Intituled: Fain Would I have Some Pretty Thing to Give Unto My Ladie*, to 'The Lusty Gallant', transcribed from Dublin, Trinity College, MS 408 (William Ballet Lute Book), p. 85.

Simple tunes, however, did not necessarily imply straightforward harmonisations. Lute arrangements follow the principles of modal harmony and sound, to us, more like folk song than pop song. Whereas modern major/minor harmony is based around chords built on the first, fourth and fifth notes of the scale (known as chords I, IV and V in Baroque harmony, or, for example, the chords C, F and G in C major), modal harmonisation creates chordal relationships which now sound unusual to our ears. The chords are made up not just of the notes in the mode but also include accidental notes from outside the mode. This sometimes gives the impression that the melody note was harmonised using any chord in which that note appears.

For example, the majority of the tune in the earliest lute arrangement of 'The Downright Squire' is in the Ionian mode (Figure 3.3).[20] It opens with two three-bar phrases and a hook, reminiscent of a horn call, forms the centrepiece of the verse. Bar 9 contains a hemiola, a rhythmic feature common in Medieval and Renaissance music in which the articulation of two units of triple metre is notated as if they were three units of duple metre. In the first three-bar phrase, the harmonic progression creates an unusual series of triads on C, F and D. This produces movement from F sharp to F natural, followed by C sharp and back to F sharp in a piece whose modal centre is C natural. In tonal music (based on a key rather than a mode), it would be natural to harmonise the A of the tune in bar 3 with a chord of F major or D minor; instead it is harmonised with a chord of D major. Of course, the triads would not have gone by those names in the mid-sixteenth century, but the effect is the same. A similar thing happens in bars 10 and 11, where the harmony is a chord of B flat. To our ears, this sounds unusual because it is so remote from the chords around it. The final three-bar phrase uses chords on F, G and C.

By contrast, the mood of 'King Solomon' (Figure 3.4) is much more sombre.[21] The tune is based in the Dorian mode (similar to the modern minor scale) with some of the sevenths raised and some not. In the first phrase, however, a C sharp appears. This is the raised fourth of the scale and suggests the Hypodorian mode. The version taken from the Mulliner Book, a mid-sixteenth-century music manuscript, is harmonised in a similar fashion to the 'Downright Squire', with the musician creating harmony by forming triads based on the notes of the tune.[22] Again, because modal music is melodically rather than harmonically driven, this creates anomalies within the chordal harmony, such as the F sharp to F natural in bar two and the B flat to B natural in bar three.[23] Despite these accidentals, the tune never moves far from G as its home note.

Figure 3.3 Setting of *A New Sonet of Pyramus and Thisbie* from Clement Robinson, *A Handefull of Pleasant Delites*, p. 35, to 'The Downright Squire' transcribed from Washington, DC, Folger Shakespeare Library, V.a.159, ff. 18ᵛ–19ʳ.

Figure 3.4 Setting of *The Ballad of constant Susanna* (London, 1624), to 'King Solomon', transcribed from London, British Library, Add. MS 30513 (Mulliner Book), ff. 123^r–v.

The serious nature of many the ballads set to 'King Solomon' is reinforced by the solemn feeling of the Dorian mode. William Elderton wrote what appear to be the original lyrics: a love song that used several classical examples to display the balladeer's devotion to his 'deare lady'. Despite the apparently erudite framing of the text, in fact the piece was much earthier. The words left little to the imagination, with the lover trying to persuade the woman to fulfil his sexual desires. The sombre tune therefore gave the piece the ironic overtone of a mock-courtly love song. The second extant song to 'King Solomon' was a loyal ballad in praise of Queen Elizabeth. The third was based on the story of 'the Bryber Gehesie Taken out of the fourth booke of Kinges', in which Gehazi was cursed with leprosy for fraudulently obtaining clothes and two talents of silver by claiming that they were for his master, Elisha.[24] This biblical tale was imbued with wider significance both by the moralising gloss that cautioned Christians 'to deale with trueth at all assaies' and by warning the Queen and her council to expel bribers from the country. A further song to the same tune, *The Ballad of constant Susanna*, was registered in 1562–3.

'Row Well Ye Mariners' was easily the biggest hit among mid-Tudor ballad tunes. It took its name from a ballad registered in 1565–6, for which the words are now lost.[25] The melody is well within the vocal range of most people, having a range of a ninth. Bouncy and appealing, it is in compound time and opens with an anacrusis or upbeat – a note or set of notes that occur before the first bar line. Despite carrying a name that invokes nautical associations, the tune is not in the style of a hornpipe. The melody is easy to remember because several phrases are repeated. Indeed, the final two phrases have the feel of a chorus, not only because the music repeats but also because the rhythm becomes much simpler and stronger. Figure 3.5 demonstrates that, even though the melody has been transcribed from lute tablature, the tune easily fits the words of *A proper sonet, wherin the Louer dolefully sheweth his grief to his L[ady] and requireth pity*. Only slight adaptations to the rhythm of the tune, the removal of some repeats and the removal of a bar of lute accompaniment at the end of the first line are required to accommodate the lyrics.

The earliest known version of the music is an elaborate and often contrapuntal arrangement for lute, found in Thomas Robinson's *The Schoole of Musicke*, published in 1603.[26] It is in the Ionian mode based on G, which is similar to the modern G major scale. Much of the contrapuntal movement, where independent melodies combine to create a more complicated harmonic texture, is in thirds and sixths. The more chordal sections primarily use the triads based on the first, fourth and fifth notes of the scale. Intriguingly, these are the chords most commonly used as the basis of western harmony for the last 500 years, especially in blues-based popular music. As a result, this accompaniment seems familiar to our ears, modern even, in a way that modal music tends not to.

Figure 3.5 Setting of *A proper sonet, wherin the Louer dolefully sheweth his grief to his L[ady] and requireth pity* from Clement Robinson, *A Handefull of Pleasant Delites,* p. 22, to 'Row Well Ye Mariners' transcribed from Thomas Robinson, *The schoole of musicke,* sig. Dii[r].

Musical Transition

The sixteenth and seventeenth centuries formed a period of musical transition. It moved slowly and erratically away from the modal and hexachordal towards the triumph of major and minor harmonies in the Baroque. It is possible that the balladeers were contributors to this process through their oral conveyance of music to the unskilled masses. For example, 'Chi Passa' is known to have been used as the tune for two different ballads.[27] The melody is a Neapolitan villanella, a form of popular song. A heavily decorated version of the tune can be found in the Ballet Lute Book, but here it is taken from the Mulliner Book (Figure 3.6).[28] It opens with a four-bar phrase, which is heavily rhythmical, swapping from compound to simple time and back again. The second phrase is a decorated repeat of the first. The six-bar phrase that follows is also repeated and decorated. There is a hemiola in the penultimate bar of each phrase, while the harmony is based on a pedal (a held note on the fifth of the scale). As the whole tune has a range of only five notes, it is easy to imagine 'Chi Passa' being played for a country dance by a simple bagpipe with a drone. In order to set the words of *A Proper Newe Ballad Sheweing That Philosophers Learnynges, Are Full of Good Warnynges* to the tune, I have, as instructed by William Elderton, used only 'the Firste Traces of Que Passa', a melody which had ten phrases in total. A master balladeer was at work: although two alternatives are given (the other is My Lord Marques Galliard which is now lost), *Philosophers Learnynges* fits perfectly to the first four phrases of 'Chi Passa'.

The harmonic settings of melodies like 'Chi Passa' point to the diachronic nature of music in this period of transition between modality and tonality. Even trained musicians learned music predominantly by ear, harmonising melodies by what sounded pleasant and effective. 'Chi Passa' can, of course, be described modally, even though the melody's limited range makes it impossible to identify a precise mode for each section. There are only three notes in the melody's first two phrases (E, F sharp and G) and the harmony used in the Mulliner Book is that of chords on the first, fourth and fifth notes of the G major scale. In bars 9–11, where the tune predominantly uses the notes A and B flat, the melody is harmonised as if the music were centred on F, using chords on the first and fourth notes of the F major scale. It then returns to music centred on G in bars 12–14. This process is repeated through bars 15–20. Taken together, the five notes of the tune are the essential notes of the G minor scale. The G minor scale was not classified until much later, and therefore the lutenist was not thinking in that way when he harmonised the tune. Instead, his harmony is that of the major triads only because they include the notes of the tune. The resulting harmonic progression at the end of each of the four phrases foreshadows the standard chord progression of a perfect cadence (I, IV, V, I) in Baroque harmony.[29]

Figure 3.6 Setting of William Elderton's *A Proper Newe Ballad Sheweing That Philosophers Learnynges, Are Full of Good Warnynges* (London, 1569), to 'Chi Passa' transcribed from BL Add. MS 30513 (Mulliner Book), ff. 122ᵛ–123ʳ.

Figure 3.6 (Continued).

Dance Music

If it is easy to imagine 'Chi Passa' in a rural setting, providing the music for a dance, maybe this is in part because the word ballad itself derives from a song used to accompany a dance. The tune 'Greensleeves', famous as a ballad melody, was, over many years, appropriated by dancers in several tunes, including the 'Bacca Pipes' and 'Green-Sleeves and Pudding Pies'.[30] It is no surprise, then, that ballads drew on dance tunes too. Both dances and songs would have repeated the same tune over and over again, making it easier for the audience to remember the melody and, therefore, the message contained in the song. Furthermore, dances depend on music with a strong rhythmic character, so lend themselves to carrying words. It is easy to set poetic texts to repetitive rhythmic patterns and phrases of a regular length, so much so that the common 8.6.8.6. stanza pattern became known as ballad metre.

The simplest of the extant dance tunes used for mid-Tudor ballads was the volta, 'Light o'Love'.[31] The volta was a dance from Provence which became particularly popular at the French court in the late sixteenth and early seventeenth century. In England, it was considered to be risqué because, uniquely for dances of the period, the couple danced in a close embrace. It is perhaps curious, then, to see this tune used as the setting for the moralising ballad, *A very proper dittie: to the tune of lightie loue Leaue lightie loue ladies, for feare of yll name: and true loue embrace ye, to purchace your fame* (Figure 3.7).[32] Leonard Gibson's song chastised women for using alluring enticements to deceive men. Women treated love as a sport, fishing for men and then abandoning them when they had taken the bait. Unlike a stream of classical paragons, women of the 1560s and 1570s apparently left their men dangling rather than remaining constant in their love. Men could not resist their beauty, 'Suche wiles, and suche guiles', but women did not follow through on their promises. Gibson hoped that women would amend their wicked ways.

It is interesting to speculate whether another, less moral, ballad had previously been set to the same tune.[33] It could, of course, simply have been a joke, with the audience intended to recognise the volta's patterns in the music and to contrast the dance with the words of the song. In a lilting, compound time, 'Light o'Love' opens with two similar two-bar phrases formed as question and answer. The melody is easily memorable because the phrases are well balanced, so that they rise and then fall. The harmony in the Ballet Lute Book suggests a major key, through its use of chords on the first, fourth, and fifth degrees of the scale. Furthermore, the first phrase ends on the second note of the scale and is harmonised by a chord on the fifth, while the second phrase resolves on the key note and chord. This is very reminiscent of tonal harmony where the intermediate phrase often ends on the half close or dominant chord (technically known as an imperfect cadence) and the final phrase brings the music to a close with the chord on the home note (usually a perfect cadence).

Figure 3.7 Setting of Leonard Gibson's *A very proper dittie: to the tune of lightie loue Leaue lightie loue ladies, for feare of yll name and true loue embrace ye to purchase your fame* (London, 1570), to 'Light o' Love' transcribed from TCD MS408 (William Ballet Lute Book), p. 103.

Several mid-Tudor ballads were set to allemandes, an instrumental dance form which became particularly popular in the Baroque period. The earliest known version of the popular 'Queen's Almain' is William Byrd's highly embellished keyboard arrangement in the Fitzwilliam Virginal Book, which dates from the mid-to-late sixteenth century.[34] A setting of John Barker's 1569 ballad *Of the horyble and woful destruccion of Ierusalem And of the sygnes and tokens that were seene before it was destroied: which distruction was after Christes assension.xlii. yeares* (Figure 3.8) shows that words easily fit the dance rhythms as long as some minims are divided into crotchets and an anacrusis is added.[35] Once again, a raised leading note (the seventh of the scale) is included in a tune that otherwise appears to be in the Dorian mode on G. This is suggestive of major/minor tonality. The first four bars are repeated, as are the final eight bars, giving the melody a binary structure. The second section is far more elaborate than the first and includes a descending

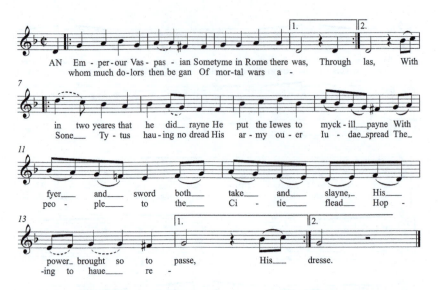

Figure 3.8 Setting of John Barker's *Of the horyble and woful destruccion of Ierusalem and of the sygnes and tokens that were seene before it was destroied: which distruction was after Christes ascension xlii yeares. To the tune of the Quenes Almayne* (London, 1569). The tune was adapted from *The Fitzwilliam Virginal Book, Edited from the Original Manuscript with an Introduction and Notes by J. A. Fuller Maitland and W. Barclay Squire; Corrected and Edited by Blanche Winogron; (translated into German by John Bernhoff),* ed. J. A. Fuller-Maitland & W. Barclay Squire (2 vols. New York, 1963), i, pp. 217–19. © Dover Publications.

sequence. Links might easily be drawn here with the melodic minor scale, as the change from F sharp in the ascending phrase in bar 9 to F natural in the phrase that descends in bar 10 is a feature of the key of G minor.

Similar suggestions of tonality may also be seen in the 'The Black Almain' (Figure 3.9). A lute arrangement of the tune can be found in FSL V.a.159.[36] 'The Black Almain' is a lively melody, as we might expect from this type of dance tune. The piece of music as a whole is suggestive of the much later melodic C minor scale with a modulation (key change) in the middle section into G minor. The first and final phrases include the sharpened leading note of C minor (B natural) and the middle section contains the sharpened leading note of G minor (F sharp). The presence of the natural and sharpened leading notes within the piece make it sound like many later pieces that modulate from one minor key to its most closely related minor key, the dominant minor.

We cannot, therefore, rule out the possibility that, rather than chanting out tuneless performances of songs, balladeers were capable singers. This song required a more able singer than any of the ballad tunes examined

Figure 3.9 Setting of *A proper Sonet, Intituled, Maid wil you marrie* from Clement Robinson, *A Handefull of Pleasant Delites*, pp. 39–40, to 'The Black Almain' transcribed from FSL v.a.159, f. 20ʳ.

so far. Nevertheless, despite its range of a tenth and the change of key, it was used as the melody for at least four ballads between 1530 and 1572.[37] The men and women who hoped to make money from singing ballads had to be able to perform songs like this to a successful level if they were to interest an audience and persuade them to buy a broadside. They were, then, capable performers who used their practical musicianship to sell their songs. In laymen's terms, practical musicianship is the ability to think in sound. It is the skill of producing out loud the music that you can hear inside your head. A musician produces music which is based on his or her conceptual knowledge of how it should sound. This is born from previous experience and intuitive perception. Sometimes that might mean reading notation; at other times, it might mean playing by ear or even improvising; but it always relates to the ability to create music which responds to the situation rather than only as the product of many rehearsals.[38]

The implications of this practical musicianship are important: we have only limited evidence for the performance practice of sixteenth-century ballad repertory but scholars, basing their judgements on disparaging remarks made by contemporary commentators, have tended to cast doubt on the quality of balladeers' singing. Adam Fox commented that it is difficult to tell if verse libels were 'intended to be chanted or sung', while Tessa Watt referred to ballads being 'chanted out by petty chapmen'.[39] Bruce Smith, referring to ballads on the fall of Thomas Cromwell that make up my case study in Chapter 6, pointed out that we cannot tell if they were meant to be sung, chanted or whether these two styles of performance were combined in some way.[40] Chant is, of course, a word with several meanings. Whilst it can be used to describe a declamatory, speech-like style of performance, it could also be used for the singing of chant in a religious setting. The educated minority, from whom the commentators were drawn, tended to denigrate the quality of ballads performed on the streets, but they might have been comparing balladeers to trained singers and to a type of singing that many people would never have experienced. Such a comparison, analogous to comparing a cathedral chorister to a member of a boy band, is as unhelpful when looking at the sixteenth century as it is today. The evidence of tunes such as 'The Black Almain' suggests that ballad singers were competent performers despite the allegation that popular, vernacular songs were 'bawled... from the street corners of London'.[41]

Sometimes, however, it was the rhythmic patterns of the music that presented a challenge to the ballad singer rather than a wide vocal range. 'The Quatre Branles' can be found in lute tablature in several mid-sixteenth-century manuscripts, but is here taken from FSL V.a.159.[42] It was named as the tune of *The Historie of Diana and Acteon* in the *Hande-full of Pleasant Delites* (Figure 3.10). The branle was a sixteenth-century

Figure 3.10 Setting of *The Historie of Diana and Acteon* from Clement Robinson, *A Handefull of Pleasant Delites*, p. 25, to 'The Quatre Branles' transcribed from FSL V.a.159, ff. 15ᵛ–16ᵛ.

Figure 3.10 (Continued).

French circle dance, similar in form to the pavane. In England, the form was often known as the 'brawl' but, although there were English branles, it never became common. A ballad published in 1569 described the novelty of branles in English dance culture:

> GOod fellowes must go learne to daunce,
> the brydeall is full nere a:
> There is a brall come out of Fraunce,
> the tryxt ye harde this yeare a.
> For I must leape and thou must hoppe,
> and we must turne all three a:
> The fourth must bounce it lyke a toppe,
> and so we shall a gree a.
> I praye thee Mynstrell make no stoppe,
> for we wyll merye be a.[43]

According to the French dance manual *Orchésographie*, every French dance began with the same set of four branles – the Double, Simple, Gay and Burgundian – and the complicated phrase structure of 'The Quatre Branles' is reminiscent of structures used by those four dances. It opens with a repeated four-bar phrase where the Double Branle had two of two-bars. This is followed by a repeated three-bar phrase typical of the Simple Branle. The second half of the melody has three two-bar phrases like the Gay Branle and, finally, a repeated two-bar phrase that is suggestive of the Burgundian Branle. Rhythmically reliant on crotchet movement with running quavers for interest, the tune contains many repetitive patterns. Its range is limited to seven notes in the Ionian mode, making it easy to sing, but the metrical patterns created by the references to the different branles are much more complicated than the allemandes and the volta.

Theatre Music

As part of entertainment culture, ballads featured regularly on the stage as well as at dances. Shakespeare, of course, included many references to ballads in his plays: 'Greensleeves', for example, is mentioned in *The Merry Wives of Windsor*; 'Chi Passa' in *The Two Noble Kinsmen* and 'Light o'Love' in no less than three plays. The lyrics to *Come Away Death* from *Twelfth Night* match the unusual metre of 'King Solomon', while in *Othello*, Iago sings a verse of the Scottish ballad *The Auld Cloak*.[44] But Shakespeare was not alone in alluding to ballads on stage, and ballads likewise sometimes took their tunes from plays. The melody 'Damon and Pythias' was used for *A Newe Ballade of a Louer, Extollinge his Ladye*, published in 1568.[45] It was the first (and for several years the only) extant broadside ballad to include a notated tune (Figure 3.11). The melody was taken from Richard Edwards' play 'Damon and Pythias' and therefore could be considered art music rather than folksong. Nevertheless, the fact that this tune was appropriated by at least two ballads shows that the boundaries between different forms of music were not fixed.

Furthermore, 'Damon and Pythias' appears similar to the tunes in the Sternhold and Hopkins *whole boke of psalmes*. Manuscript sources for the music show substantial differences to the broadside in their treatment of the melody. The manuscripts suggest a tune in the Dorian mode, while the rests and harmony produce triple, not duple, time.[46] Certainly, the music as it appears on the broadside is very difficult to sing, as the interval of the augmented fourth (or tritone) appears several times. The tritone is known to this day as the *diabolus in musica*, and it was rejected by hexachordal theorists as an unstable interval. The eccentricities of the broadside suggest that the music was put together by a printer who was not particularly familiar with musical notation, but who nevertheless attempted to give an indication of the melody to the ballad's purchasers. When the C clef is replaced by a treble clef and the position of the notes on the stave is maintained, however, the melody no longer contains the tritone and it sits comfortably in the Aeolian mode (Figure 3.12). Here, a few minor editorial alterations have been made to the music in order to bar it in triple time. The metre of the words 'burne within my brest' are indicative of triple time rather than the hemiola given on the broadside.

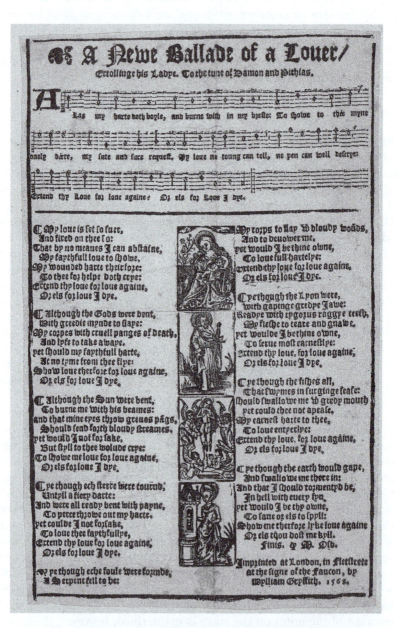

Figure 3.11 M. Osborne, *A Newe Ballade of a Louer, Extollinge his Ladye. To the tune of Damon and Pithias* (London, 1568), Early English Tract Supplement / A3:4[26]. © The British Library Board (General Reference Collection Huth 50 (27)).

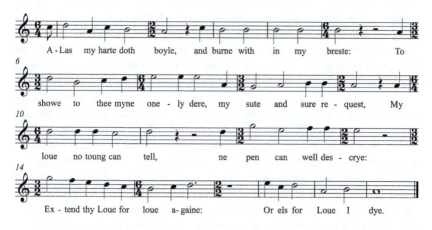

A-Las my harte doth boyle, and burne with in my breste: To showe to thee myne one-ly dere, my sute and sure re-quest, My loue no toung can tell, ne pen can well des-crye: Ex-tend thy Loue for loue a-gaine: Or els for Loue I dye.

Figure 3.12 Setting of Osborne's *A Newe Ballade of a Louer, Extollinge his Ladye* to music adapted from the broadside.

Ballad Music and the Reformation

All of these tunes, whether from art music, dance or the stage, have features that make them easy to pick up, recall and reproduce. It was precisely these memorable features of the ballad that the Protestant church drew on in its attempts to create congregational music. Just as ballad music appropriated melodies from many sources, the early Reformation church recognised the value of a good tune, especially when it was familiar to the audience. The Protestant church was prepared to assimilate many forms of pre-Reformation musical culture.[47] Protestant church music across Europe was influenced not only by art music written by trained composers, but also by traditional songs. In England, three polyphonic mass settings based on the traditional tune 'Western Wynde' were written, probably in the 1540s, by influential composers: John Taverner, Christopher Tye and John Shepherd. This sort of cultural appropriation should not surprise us because during the early days of congregational singing, folksongs were the only type of music that the majority of the population knew how to sing. The fact that folksongs were the only form of communal singing that most people had experienced made them especially significant in the development of church music.[48] Miles Coverdale's *Goostly psalmes and spirituall songes*, for example, used mainly German folk tunes with simple lyrics in order to cultivate broad appeal.[49]

This simplicity had an important antecedent, however: it was already a feature of vernacular song in the form of medieval carols. At the time, of course, the word 'carol' did not necessarily imply a religious subject, but even where the subject was devotional, they were not intended for use in church. Early English carols such as *The Corpus Christi Carol, The Coventry Carol*, and *Ther Is No Rose of Swych Vertù* are examples of religious folk songs that used simple but attractive melodies for mass appeal and had a refrain that encouraged participation. This sort of communal in-volvement in singing is an accepted feature of balladry. Conversely, plain-song melodies also influenced the development of English vernacular song. These simple tunes in duple metre were adapted into carol melodies by ex-tending their notes into a bouncier triple time.[50] This rhythmic alteration made them more accessible, sounding as it does like a childhood rhyme.

By the mid-sixteenth century, the issue of what made a tune suitable for use in church had become a question of confessionalism. The main musical differences between Roman Catholicism and still-emerging Protestantism lay in their attitude to polyphony (music with several voices or parts that moved independently) and to the use of secular tunes. These attitudes re-flected 'competing visions of reform, not simply reformed and unreformed practices'.[51] The Protestant church's emphasis on *sola scriptura* meant that their leaders were concerned with people's understanding of biblical text.[52] As such, they preferred mensural music in a homophonic style (such as metrical psalms) where one note was given for each syllable and all the voices moved together. In England, early reforms under Henry VIII moved towards the vernacular and discouraged polyphonic singing in church. In his oft-quoted letter to the king, Archbishop Thomas Cranmer stated his personal view that singing in church should 'not be full of notes, but as nere as may be for every sillable a note so that it may be songe distinctly and devoutly'.[53] Four years later, in 1548, Cranmer asked commissioners to report if there were those that 'saie it [the litany] or sorte as the people connot vnderstande the same'.[54] Polyphony, where several different me-lodic lines interwove, allegedly subjugated the text to the music, making it difficult to hear and understand the words. Nevertheless, polyphony was probably not widespread in England even before the Reformation, as most parish churches did not have the highly trained choirs needed to per-form music in this way. Instead, where a parish church had a choir with some trained singers, they would probably have sung plainsong, perhaps adorned by faburden (a method of improvising harmony above and below the line of the chant according to a simple series of rules).[55]

Although the Catholic church was also concerned about how polyphony might interfere with the congregation's understanding of scripture, it worried far more about whether the use of secular tunes within church services might constitute profanity. There were few restrictions on the use of music in the mass, but while the Council of Trent permitted polyph-ony and made no mention of the intelligibility of the words, it explicitly prohibited the use of 'lascivious' or secular music.[56] Such assimilation of secular music was not only tolerated by the early Protestant church, it was actively encouraged by men like Martin Luther who recognised several advantages to the use of secular melodies. In the German Protes-tant church, it was common to compose religious poems to pre-existing secular melodies in a process known as contrafacta.[57] The Protestant church's emphasis on lay involvement in worship meant that it privileged the vernacular and the simple tune. What else could you do if you wanted the congregation to join in? In practical terms, Latin polyphony (and probably faburden) was impossible for the majority of people. In order to involve the congregation in singing, the church had to use familiar forms. Hence, English church music drew on carols and ballads, in which the importance of a strong narrative and a memorable melody had already combined to create a popular medium of entertainment and, sometimes, a moving means of expression. During the Edwardian period, the Church of England had to produce music for an entirely new liturgy that replaced the Latin texts, often adapting what had gone before because it was quicker than composing entirely new works.[58] But it had the added benefit of drawing on music which was already familiar and, in addition, the tunes were easy to pick up. Although congregational singing did not become common in England until after the accession of Elizabeth I in 1558, these moves towards reform 'enfranchised the lay voice'.[59]

Ballads, Psalms and Implicitness

Although the Protestant church across Europe exploited tunes from the traditional repertoire, there was cross-fertilisation between sacred and secular music. There were even similarities in the material nature of printed ballads and early Lutheran metrical psalms, which were both printed on broadsides.[60] Protestant music drew on the vernacular song tradition and, in turn, supplied both stories and melodies to balladry. The tunes for congregational psalm-singing were familiar melodies in the mid-to-late sixteenth century and, indeed, the majority of the tunes in Sternhold and Hopkins's *whole boke of psalmes* were written in ballad metre (8.6.8.6). This made it possible for the many ballads in the same metre to be sung to them. Psalm tunes were officially sanctioned as the melodies for metrical anthems of thanksgiving for the church and the queen in 1578 which were published as ballads on broadsides.[61] This had happened as early as 1569, when John Awdelay published perhaps the most knowingly godly example of the extant mid-Tudor ballads: *A godly ditty or Prayer to be song vnto God for the preseruation of his Church, our Queene and Realme, against all Traytours, Rebels, and Papisticall Enemies* (Figure 3.13).[62] This topical ballad passed on news of the Northern Rebellion. In November 1569, the Earls of Westmorland and Northumberland rose in opposition to Queen Elizabeth. The rebels occupied Durham, where they restored the Catholic mass in the cathedral. But people actively sought out ways to associate new works of music and literature like Awdelay's *godly ditty* with those they already knew. It is likely that reusing tunes in this way leant them an extra layer of meaning. This might usefully be described as a musically contrived form of knowingness, where previous lyrics to a tune accentuate the meaning of new ones.

On the face of it, *A godly ditty*, like most topical ballads, dressed the news as the just desserts of the people whose 'syns haue moued thee / Iust plagues on vs to poure'. It hoped that God would take whatever steps necessary, however painful, to correct people's behaviour so that

Figure 3.13 Setting of John Awdelay's *A godly ditty or prayer to be song vnto God for the preseruation of his Church, our Queene and realme, against all traytours, rebels, and papisticall enemies* (London 1569), to the tune of 'Psalm 137' from Thomas Sternhold, *The whole boke of psalmes,* pp. 350–51.

they would not fall into the hands of those 'That do thee and thy truth withstand / Like diulysh deadly foes'. Only through God's help could Elizabeth's loyal, Protestant subjects avoid being driven into hell by the Catholic rebels. The ballad played on people's fears, pointing out that, because of the insurrection, widows would weep while their children were left fatherless and crying. The final two verses made it plain that to be loyal to the queen was to be a Protestant, whereas to be a Roman Catholic was in itself sufficient to be considered traitorous:

> Defend O God our gracious Queene,
> From Pope Rebel, and all:
> And as by her thy woorkes be seene,
> So let thy wrath now fall

Vpon all those that vexe thy truth,
Our Queene, our Realme and state:
And let their vicious prankes of ruth
Light vpon their own pate.

So shall thy name be magnified,
So shall thy power be knowne:
So shall our Christ be sanctified,
By them that be his owne.
Wherefore O Lord graunt our requestes
Which here to thee we make:
And make vs loue and lyue thy hestes,
For thy Christ Iesus sake.

But Awdelay's ballad was more sophisticated than it at first appears. It was to be sung to the tune of Psalm 137, whose words are familiar even today:

WHen as we sat in Babylon, [the] riuers rounde about:
and in reme[m]braunce of Sion the teares for grief burst out.
We ha[n]gd our harps & instruments, the willow trees vpon,
for in that place men for their vse, had planted many one.

The psalm tells the story of the exiled Jewish community, their wish to return to Jerusalem and their desire for revenge on the Babylonian conquerors who had taken their city. The parallels between the two situations are abundantly clear. It is highly likely that the people who sang *A godly ditty* were expected to link the Babylonian oppressors of Psalm 137 with the 'raging enemies' of Elizabeth and Christ, who were, of course, the Catholic rebels. The music, and the music alone, surely made the association between two occupied cities, Jerusalem and Durham. The Catholic rebels represented the Babylonian oppressors and Protestants embodied the faithful Jews, crying to God for help and retribution:

OVr liuyng God to thee we cry,
Now tend vnto our playnt:
Behold thy Church and family,
Which enmies seeke to faynt.

Clearly, it would be fallacious to suggest that every ballad's meaning was enhanced by its melody in this way, but it is equally important to note that when we study ballad lyrics without reference to their tunes, we might at the very least be missing a shade of meaning. The melody could, in fact, carry subtle but significant extra nuances that can only help us to interpret how ballads were heard and understood by their audience. On occasion, a tune could carry a layer of meaning of its own that had important implications for spreading the news.

Notes

1 London, British Library, MS Cotton Vespasian A-XXV, *A songe to the lute of musicke*, f. 137^r. The chapter title is taken from *A newe ballade intytuled, Good fellowes must go learne to daunce* (London, 1569), STC (2nd ed.) / 12019.
2 BL MS Cotton Vespasian A-XXV, *A songe to the lute of musicke*, f. 137^r.
3 Appendix 1 also explains the rationale behind the musical analysis in this study.
4 Matthew Parker, *The whole Psalter translated into English Metre, which contayneth an hundreth and fifty Psalmes. The first Quinquagene* (London, 1567), STC (2nd ed.) / 2729, sig. VViv^r.
5 Marsh, *Music and Society*, p. 276.
6 Milsom, 'Music, Politics and Society', p. 47; Thacker, *godlie Dittie to be song*.
7 London, British Library, Add. MS 38599 (Commonplace Book of the Shann Family of Methley, co. York); Hyder E. Rollins, 'Ballads from Additional Ms. 38,599', *Publications of the Modern Language Association of America*, 38:1 (1923), pp. 133–52. A similar variety of songs can be found in London, British Library, Stowe MS 958 and London, British Library, Add. MS 82370 (Stanhope Manuscript). BL Add. MS 38599 was incorrectly catalogued as a commonplace book by British Museum staff. It is more correctly described as a manuscript miscellany but the title of commonplace book is nevertheless the name under which it can still be found on the British Library catalogue and therefore this is the title I use in footnotes and captions.
8 Rollins, 'Ballads from Additional MS. 38,599', p. 147.
9 Rollins, 'Ballads from Additional MS. 38,599', p. 144.
10 BL Add. MS 38599, f. 138^r.
11 Milsom, 'Music, Politics and Society', p. 497.
12 Steven W. May, 'Matching Hands: The Search for the Scribe of the "Stanhope" Manuscript', *Huntington Library Quarterly*, 76:3 (2013), p. 347.
13 For a description of the manuscript and its contents, see Arthur F. Marotti and Steven W. May, 'Two Lost Ballads of the Armada Thanksgiving Celebration [with Texts and Illustration]', *English Literary Renaissance*, 41:1 (2011), pp. 31–63.
14 BL Add. MS 82370 (Stanhope Manuscript), f. 50^v; Tottel's *Miscellany*, f. 73^{r-v}; Oxford, Bodleian Library, MS Ashmole 48, ff. 23^v–24^v; Shakespeare, *Hamlet*, V.i.61–64, 71–74, 91–94 and 117–18.
15 For example, Simpson changed all the B naturals in 'Damon and Pythias' to B flats, presumably to avoid the interval of the augmented fourth (Simpson, *British Broadside Ballad and its Music*, pp. 157–59), see below.
16 Dublin, Trinity College, MS 408 (William Ballet Lute Book); Washington, DC, Folger Shakespeare Library, V.a.159.
17 Temperley, *Music of the English Parish Church*, i, pp. 33–34.
18 John Ward, 'Music for "a Handefull of Pleasant Delites"', *Journal of the American Musicological Society*, 10:3 (1957), pp. 154, 152 and 156.
19 Robinson, *Handefull of Pleasant Delites*, pp. 57–59. An editorial E flat has been added to the voice line at the end of bar 4 to begin the third phrase in the same manner as the first; another in bar 5 of the voice line accommodates the words through the use of a sequence, equivalent to the sequential pattern in the first phrase.
20 The title given for the tune in FSL V.a.159 is 'The upright esquier', but it is clearly the same tune as 'The Downright Squire'. In the tablature, the first half of bars 2 and 3 appear to contain a duplet (two crotchets in the time of three). These have been edited to a minim-crotchet rhythm in order to conform to the rhythm of the rest of the music. In bars 11 and 12, further editorial alterations have been made to standardise the rhythmic patterns.

In bar 7, it is more likely that the bottom note of the first triad (C) is the note of the melody than the top note, G. For this reason, C has been used in the melody line with the lyrics. An editorial repeat has been placed at the end of the second phrase and a repeated note has been added at the end of the melody line in bar 14 in order to accommodate the words.

21 London, British Library, Add. MS 30513 (Mulliner Book), ff. 123^{r-v}.

22 John Caldwell (ed.), *The Mulliner Book* (London: Stainer and Bell, 2011), pp. xxvi–xxvii. According to Caldwell, the book's compiler, Thomas Mulliner, was probably known to (and possibly a pupil of) the playwright and balladeer, John Heywood (on Heywood, see Chapters 5 and 7 below).

23 F sharp (the raised seventh) is used as part of the chord on the fifth of the scale. F natural is used as part of the chord based on the seventh of the scale. In major/minor harmony, this progression would be seen as false relationships.

24 Elderton, *panges of Loue*; Mell, *A proper new balad of the Bryber Gehesie*; R.M., *A Newe Ballade* (London, 1560), STC (2nd ed.) / 17147.

25 *TRCS*, i, p. 305.

26 Thomas Robinson, *The schoole of musicke wherein is taught, the perfect method, of true fingering of the lute, pandora, orpharion, and viol de gamba; with most infallible generall rules, both easie and delightfull. Also, a method, how you may be your owne instructer for prick-song, by the help of your lute, without any other teacher: with lessons of all sorts, for your further and better instruction. Newly composed by Thomas Robinson, lutenist* (London, 1603), STC (2nd ed.) / 21128, sig. Dii^r. In Thomas Robinson's version, each phrase repeats. In order to fit the words to the melody, though, all these repeats have been removed apart from the repeat of bars 18–20.

27 Elderton, *A proper newe ballad sheweing that philosophers learnynges*; *A Sonet of two faithfull Louers, exhorting one another to be constant* in Robinson, *Handefull of Pleasant Delites*, pp. 53–54.

28 BL Add. MS 30513 (Mulliner Book), ff. 122^v–123^r.

29 A cadence is the melodic and harmonic progression at the end of a musical phrase. These progressions became standardised during the Baroque period.

30 John Ward, 'And Who but Ladie Greensleeues?', in John Caldwell, Edward Olleson, and Susan Wollenberg (eds.), *The Well Enchanting Skill: Music, Poetry, and Drama in the Culture of the Renaissance: Essays in Honour of F. W. Sternfeld* (Oxford: Clarendon, 1990), pp. 181–211.

31 TCD MS 408 (William Ballet Lute Book), p. 103, also reproduced in Simpson, *British Broadside Ballad and its Music*, p. 447.

32 Editorial Cs have been taken from the lute harmony to provide the melody at the beginning of each of the first, second and final phrases. This is likely to be how the ear would have heard the tune in this lute arrangement.

33 Leonard Gibson, *A very proper dittie: to the tune of lightie loue Leaue lightie loue ladies, for feare of yll name: and true loue embrace ye, to purchace your fame* (London, 1571), STC (2nd ed.) / 11836.

34 J. A Fuller-Maitland & W. Barclay Squire (ed.), *The Fitzwilliam Virginal Book, Edited from the Original Manuscript with an Introduction and Notes by J. A. Fuller Maitland and W. Barclay Squire; Corrected and Edited by Blanche Winogron* (2 vols. New York: Dover Publications, 1963), i, pp. 217–19; Simpson, *British Broadside Ballad and its Music*, p. 590.

35 *TRCS*, i, p. 380; John Barker, *Of the horyble and woful destruccion of Ierusalem and of the sygnes and tokens that were seene before it was destroied: which distruction was after Christes assension .xlii. yeares* (London, 1569), STC (2nd ed.) / 1420.

36 FSL V.a 159, f. 20^r. An editorial repeat of the final phrase has been added to accommodate the lyrics.

37 Simpson, *British Broadside Ballad and its Music*, pp. 42–43.

38 Associated Board of the Royal Schools of Music, 'Practical Musicianship Examination Syllabus', http://us.abrsm.org/en/our-exams/other-assessments/practical-musicianship/ [accessed 1 September 2014].
39 Fox, 'Ballads, Libels and Popular Ridicule', p. 58; Watt, *Cheap Print*, p. 37.
40 Smith, *Acoustic World*, pp. 180–81.
41 Ward, 'Music for "A Handefull of Pleasant Delites"', p. 168.
42 See Simpson, *British Broadside Ballad and its Music*, p. 586; 'Ward, 'Music for "A Handefull of Pleasant Delites"', pp. 159–60.
43 *Good fellowes must go learne to daunce.*
44 Ross W. Duffin, *Shakespeare's Songbook* (London: W. W. Norton, 2004), pp. 177–79, 95, 253, 98 and 248–50.
45 M. Osborne, *A Newe Ballade of a Louer, Extollinge his Ladye. To the tune of Damon and Pithias* (London, 1568), Early English Tract Supplement / A3:4[26].
46 Temperley, *Music of the English Parish Church*, i, pp. 34–35; Thomas Sternhold, *The whole boke of psalmes, collected into English metre by Thomas Sternhold, Iohn Hopkins, and others: conferred with the Ebrue, with apt notes to syng them wyth all. ; Newlye set foorth and allowed to bee soong of the people together, in churches, before and after moring and euening prayer: as also before and after the sermon, and moreouer in priuate houses, for their godlye solace and comfort, laying apart all vngodly songes and balades, which tend onely to the nourishing of vice, and corrupting of youth* (London, 1566), STC (2nd ed.) / 2437.
47 Friedrich Blume, 'The Period of the Reformation', in Friedrich Blume (ed.), *Protestant Church Music: A History* (London: Gollancz, 1975), p. 3.
48 Temperley, *Music of the English Parish Church*, i, pp. 12 and 19.
49 Timothy Duguid, 'Sing a New Song: English and Scottish Metrical Psalmody from 1549–1640', PhD Thesis, University of Edinburgh, 2011, p. 13.
50 Robin A. Leaver, *'Goostly Psalmes and Spirituall Songes': English and Dutch Metrical Psalms from Coverdale to Utenhove (1535–1566)* (Oxford: Clarendon, 1991), p. 56.
51 Willis, *Church Music and Protestantism*, p. 45.
52 Robert W. Scribner, *The German Reformation* (London: Macmillan, 1986), p. 14.
53 *L&P* xx, SP 1/208, f. 166, p. 251, no. 539, 'Cranmer to Henry VIII, 7 October 1545'.
54 Thomas Cranmer, *Articles to be enquired of, in visitacions to bee had, within the Diocese of Cantorbury: in the seconde yere of the reigne of our moste drad souereigne Lorde Edward The .VI. by the grace of God, Kyng of Englande, Fraunce, and Irelande, defender of the faithe and in yearth of the Churche of Englande and also of Irelande, the Supreme Hedde* (London, 1548), STC (2nd ed.) / 10148, sig. Bi[r].
55 Temperley, *Music of the English Parish Church*, i, pp. 8–11.
56 Craig A. Monson, 'The Council of Trent Revisited', *Journal of the American Musicological Society*, 55:1 (2002), pp. 11–12. Monson goes on to point out that the only significant addition to the decree in later sessions was to delegate decisions on what constituted appropriate music to local bishops (pp. 17–18).
57 Blume, 'Period of the Reformation', p. 29.
58 Temperley, *Music of the English Parish Church*, i, pp. 14–15.
59 Matthew Milner, *The Senses and the English Reformation* (Farnham: Ashgate, 2011), p. 296.
60 Leaver, *'Goostly Psalmes and Spirituall Songes'*, p. 3.
61 Willis, *Church Music and Protestantism*, p. 187.
62 Awdelay, *A godly ditty or prayer to be song vnto God*. Although bar lines have beeen added silently to many of the settings in this study, it would be inappropriate to add them to a psalm tune such as this.

4 'Sung to filthy tunes'
The Meaning of Music

> And therefore the Apostle Iames biddeth vs, if we be merry, to sing
> Psalmes, & if we be sadde or sorrowfull to pray: by whiche rule of the
> Apostle is forbid and condemned all filthye talke or communication
> contrary to the word of God, all vncleane woordes, wanton songues,
> lasciuious sonettes, bawdye ballades, and all other prophane talke
> whatsoeuer.[1]

Writing in 1585, the Puritan pamphleteer Philip Stubbes articulated the
familiar division between spiritual psalms and bawdy ballads. Psalms
were good for the soul, but ballads were obscene. Stubbes, however,
was merely putting into words (albeit with characteristic forcefulness)
an opinion that had been widespread among the cognoscenti for many
years. One of Erasmus's most influential works had described how the
Christian knight should keep

> farre of from the eares of lytle bodyes wanton songes of loue, whiche
> christen men synge at whom & where soeuer they ryde or go, moche
> more fylthy than euer the comen people of the hethen men wolde
> suffre to be had in vse.[2]

The reuse of the catchy tunes that made these ballads so memorable and
popular also helped to impart meaning to the words.

This chapter will investigate the possible reasons why ballad melodies
were recycled in this way. It takes as its starting point an appreciation
of the familiar that was the basis of creativity during the Renaissance. It
develops the idea of balladeers as practical musicians who were not only
able to sing attractive tunes, but were skilled in adapting their source
melodies to fit new words. First, it describes the process of contrafacta,
whereby new words were fitted to existing tunes, looking both at the ways
in which oral traditions organised their material in order to help singers
remember and the ways in which singers and musicians adapted this material to keep it fresh. The chapter then looks at the ways in which music
might have an implicit meaning which amplified or subverted the text.

It investigates the bawdy ballads which were so heavily criticised by contemporaries. I show that by moralising these songs, some balladeers created a space for the self-fashioning of a godly persona that directly related to the bawdy version of the song as well as the moralised one. In doing so, I highlight the importance of melody as a vehicle for lyrics in the sixteenth century, demonstrating once again that ballads should be seen as songs rather than texts whenever possible.

The main focus of the chapter is the group of moralised ballads which took advantage of successful tunes in order to subvert the meaning of the song, attempting to replace secular and sordid songs with godly or edifying content. Despite the emphasis placed on them by scholars, it is possible to overstate the importance of moralised ballads. A survey of the Stationers' Registers from the beginning of the records to 1570 reveals that, in fact, only nine ballads appear with the word 'moralised' in their title. None of these ballads survive, so it is impossible to compare them with the original ballad. A further 14 songs entitled 'proper' ballads can be found in the database of 438 extant ballads. The use of 'proper' in the titles of these ballads points to a contrast with an 'improper' version, especially as, for all but two of them, the names of popular tunes are indicated. Nine of these ballads are from one volume: Clement Robinson's *A Handefull of Pleasant Delites*. There are no ribald ballads in *A Handefull of Pleasant Delites*. Quite the contrary, it is made up of moralised contrafacta, many of which are entitled 'proper sonet' or 'excellent song'. Moralised ballads played only a small role in the mid-Tudor ballad genre as a whole. Instead, their significance lies in their important role in contrafacta. They serve to show how the mid-Tudor mind connected new songs with old, and understood what they heard now in the context of what they already knew. Without contrafacta, moralised ballads lose their force.

To propose that every ballad relied on a perfectly fitting tune to add an extra layer of meaning to the words is clearly fallacious, since so few mid-Tudor ballad tunes are even named in the sources. Nevertheless, when John Ward commented that the tune 'Raging Loue', shared by two poems, was 'a purely neutral element, providing a means of performance without contributing any special character of its own to the resulting song', he underestimated how sophisticated the relationship between words and music could be. Describing the collection of songs in *A Handefull of Pleasant Delites*, Ward commented that 'the marriage of texts and music is strictly one of convenience'.[3] As a generalisation, he was undoubtedly correct in pointing out that many ballad tunes were in fact *arie per cantar*, that is, utilitarian tunes that could be fitted to any words in the given metre and stanzaic form. Nevertheless, it is also a mistake to suggest that this was always the case. The ability of the early modern audience to make links between new works and those with which they were already familiar has been recognised widely.

Ballad Contrafacta

The process of setting new words to an existing tune is known as contrafactum. It is a technique that has been in use since at least the twelfth century. The term is particularly useful for balladry because it emphasises the relationship between the music and the words rather than reinforcing the dominance of the text over the melody. Although during the Renaissance and Baroque periods the term contrafactum took on the specific meaning of replacing a secular text with a sacred one, this has not been maintained in modern usage. In this study, contrafactum will therefore be taken in its wider sense, that is, to describe a new set of ballad lyrics written to a pre-existing tune, irrespective of whether this was a sacred or secular melody.

The early modern mind was predisposed to hear the connections created by the process of contrafacting. People actively sought out links between the new pieces of music that they heard and those with which they were already familiar and there is little evidence to suggest that originality was prized or sought in the way that it is now. Renaissance humanism emphasised the teaching of rhetoric through techniques such as *imitatio* (where new pieces of literature were modelled on existing texts by another author). Later, a similar method was used by Restoration musicians to learn composition, which often involved the adaptation of existing material as the basis of a new work. The aim was not so much to be original or novel as to build on existing knowledge.[4] It is hardly surprising, then, that balladeers reused tunes too. It offered them the opportunity to build on the distinctive associations that ballad tunes took on in a musical form of knowingness, as well as the chance to cash in on the latest hit.[5] It does not seem to have been necessary, however, to remember the exact words of the original song; the effect was produced by recalling the mood and theme.[6]

At a conservative estimate, at least 16 popular tunes from the period were used for over 55 contrafacta that can be shown to exist between 1530 and 1570. Forty-eight of these are extant broadsides, so we can be confident that their lyrics fit the given tune because they have suitable metrical and stanzaic patterns. Other ballads were registered with the Stationers' Company which contained the name of the tune in the title, so even though the lyrics and tune have been lost, we can call them contrafacta too. In addition, we can surmise that other ballads listed in the Stationers' Registers are also contrafacta because their titles are similar, even though their texts no longer exist. For example, it is likely that *The Squyre of Low Degre* entered by John Kynge in 1559–60 was a version of 'The Downright Squire' and that the *Tow Lamentable Songs Pithias and Damon* entered by Alexander Lacy in 1565–6 were set to the 'Damon and Pithias' tune, especially as the melody seems to have been particularly current around this time.[7] Ten ballads can be considered 'known unknowns': that they once existed is proved by the survival (either physically or as a title in the Stationers' Registers) of a moralised or answer song. For example, even when no tune is given, it is highly likely that the words of *The paynter in his prynteshod* and *The paynter in his prentes hood moralized* would have been sung to the same tune, otherwise there would be little point in presenting the second ballad as a moralised version of the first.[8]

Constraints and Adaptations in Oral Traditions

Because ballads appealed both to those who could read a broadside and those who learned by ear, they were of necessity, memorable. They achieved this retention through the use of organisational techniques. In his work on epic poetry, counting-out rhymes and ballads, David Rubin developed a theory of 'constraints', or forms of organisation in oral traditions. Constraints limited the choices available to the performer, thereby making it easier to remember long texts. These factors were precisely what made ballads memorable. One of the most obvious constraints on a ballad is rhyme, as all ballads have some form of rhyme scheme. Rhyme limits the words that a singer can use to complete a rhyming phrase, so by restricting the possible word combinations it increases a person's ability to remember lyrics. For example, to take a ballad from Bod. MS Ashmole 48 in ballad metre with a rhyme scheme of ABCB:

> Aryse and wak, for Cristis sake,
> Aryse, I say agayn;
> Awake, all ye that synfull be,
> Awak, for fear of payn.[9]

The final word of line 4 could not be 'death', for example, because although it makes sense and has the correct number of syllables to fit the metre, it would not complete the rhyming couplet. Other constraints that Rubin identified include imagery, theme, metre and melody, all of which contribute to the overall stability of an oral tradition. Variation occurs frequently between performances of the same song, but only within these constraints.[10] At the simplest level, melody is a constraint on the words and therefore tunes cannot be randomly assigned to the lyrics. The metre of both the words and the tune must be at least compatible.

Nevertheless, in order to make contrafacta possible, singers used a flexible approach to melody. If the desired tune did not quite fit the lyrics, a singer could alter the rhythm of the melody to accommodate the words. Singers in the oral tradition are still known for decorating and subtly or even substantially altering a melody in order to make it better fit the words.[11] Claude Simpson failed to grasp that musical rhythm and verbal metre can be altered to enable words to fit a tune, so he sometimes denied that lyrics could fit the melody that was specified for them, as we shall see. By way of contrast, Bertrand H. Bronson was more sympathetic to the malleability of melody within the oral tradition. In his survey of the Child ballad tunes, Bronson pointed out that 'the fluid stuff of folk melody lends itself with extraordinary flexibility and sympathy to any given material'. He reminded us that folk singers utilise 'rhythmical irregularities' during the performance of songs.[12] In order to make new words fit an old tune, the balladeer had to demonstrate an element of practical musicianship in adapting the melody and rhythm. That we know this occurred is clear from the way different verses of the same song might require different rhythmic variants. Furthermore, the scribe of the Shann family manuscript advised singers that, 'Yf the verses will not agree with the tune, ye may breake A sembreefe into two minnems, or otherwise, as ye thinke good'.[13]

Even where music was notated, tunes might be adapted in performance. It was not particularly expected that a singer or instrumentalist would perform a piece exactly as it was written, nor that each performance would be the same. Instead, performers reworked and revised their material through repeated performances.[14] Trained musicians often used written music as a basis from which to create a performance complete with such embellishments as passing notes, ornaments and cadenzas. Even such celebrated composers as John Dowland and Thomas Campion would have continued to develop their lute songs in performance after the music was printed.[15] This undermines the modern assumption that the final version of any piece is the most authentic, or, contrariwise, the supposition of folk musicians that the original version of a tune is its purest form. Later in the Renaissance, a trained musician or singer was expected to be able to decorate a tune without any written instruction to do so: it was the convention of the time. How much more might a ballad tune, passed orally from one person to another, go through a process of performative change? Nonetheless, it was the 'gist' of the tune that was important and, indeed, Rebecca Herissone argued against drawing a 'conceptual line' between the transmission of popular music and that of theatre or dance music. Both amateur and professional musicians remembered the core characteristics of a piece and although these were maintained, other features could be adapted at will.[16] As a result, a single tune could develop in many different ways over time.

Ballad contrafacta also show that the balladeer was adept at altering an existing melody in order to fit new words. This was necessary because the ballad's prosody was primarily based on the number of stressed beats per line. The singer could therefore alter the rhythm of the unaccented syllables however he pleased, without affecting the line's overall shape. It allowed singers to ornament and develop their tunes, and consequently affected the sorts of tunes to which ballads, particularly in the oral tradition, were sung. With its regular and simple stress count, ballad metre leant itself to this sort of extemporisation.[17] Sometimes it was necessary to add an anacrusis at the beginning of a line. Sometimes different verses of the same ballad had different scansions to each other. It was therefore imperative that the rhythm (and perhaps with it, the pitch) was altered to accommodate the words. For example, the second lines of the first and second verses of *the Ballad of constant Susanna* have only eight syllables, whereas the second line of the third verse has nine. Although the scansion of the lines is different, in fact, there are still only four stressed beats in each, meaning that the rhythm of the melody can be altered without substantial change to the overall melodic line.[18]

If the tunes cited on the ballads were to be used, then adaptation was often imperative. For example, 'The Cramp' was given as the tune for *A new ballad entytuled, Lenton stuff, for a lyttell munny ye maye have inouwghe*. The melody can be found in the medius voice of *A Round of Three Country Dances in One* in Thomas Ravenscroft's 1609 book of vocal rounds and catches, *Pammelia*.[19] Claude Simpson claimed that Ravenscroft's melody 'does not fit the latter part of [William] Elderton's complex seven-line stanza':[20]

> Lenton stuff ys cum to the towne,
> The clensynge weeke cums quiklye,
> You knowe well inowghe you must kneele downe;
> Cum on, take asshes trykly,
> That nether are good fleshe nor fyshe,
> But dyp with Judas in the dyshe,
> And keepe a rowte not woorthe a ryshe.[21]

He maintained that a second song, *A ballad from the countrie sent to show how we should fast this lent*, 'agrees metrically with Elderton's, offering another bit of evidence that the surviving tune has little relation to the ballads here cited':[22]

> Prepare yourselves to fast this lent,
> as princesse law hath willed;
> to obay the same be you content,
> and let it be fulfilled.
> Submit yourselves, most humbly,
> to the hyare powers hartely;
> for cons[c]ience sake, doe not denie.[23]

Simpson concluded that these ballads were set to a different tune named 'The Cramp' which is now lost.[24]

The revised melodies in Figures 4.1 and 4.2 show that it is, in fact, relatively easy to make the words of *Lenton stuff* and *A ballad from the countrie sent* fit the tune of 'The Cramp', simply by creating additional sung notes. In Figure 4.1, for example, minims have been altered to two crotchets on the second line, while dotted minims have been amended to a minim-crotchet rhythm on the third and fourth lines of music. In Figure 4.2, these changes have been augmented by the alteration of some anacrusic crotchets to quavers in order to accommodate the words. An editorial rest has been added at the beginning of Figure 4.2, where the anacrusis appears in Ravenscroft's version. The only difficulty in fitting Elderton's words to the melody of Ravenscroft's *The Cramp* lies in the last two bars, which fit the refrain of the original song identified by Simpson ('the Crampe a') but for which there are no lyrics given in *Lenton Stuff*. This need hardly preclude the tune of 'The Cramp' being that of the ballad, as many words could have been used for a refrain here. The most obvious of these is the repetition of the final words of the preceding line ('worth a ryshe' and 'not denie'), as shown in Figures 4.1 and 4.2, but *The Cramp*'s refrain itself is another possibility.

As a large proportion of the Lent ballads' audience would probably not have been able to read the words, they would have used mnemonic devices to memorise the ballad. Accordingly, the necessity to write down every detail would be reduced. There is no particular reason why repetitions would need to be included in the broadside, as within the oral tradition of ballad-singing it remains common to vary a basic tune or set of lyrics during performance. Likewise, singers could interpret the music in their own way. The absence of a written record of these changes does not mean that they did not happen. By their very nature, 'oral traditions need not leave any written trace'.[25]

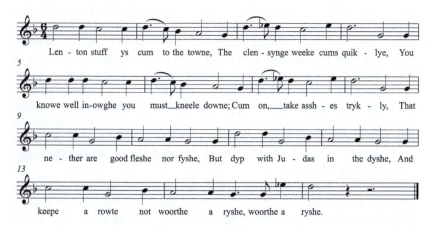

Figure 4.1 Setting of *A new ballad entytuled, Lenton stuff, for a lyttell munny ye maye have inouwghe; To the tune of the Crampe* from Oxford, Bodleian Library, MS Ashmole 48, ff. 115ᵛ–117ʳ, to 'The Cramp' from Thomas Ravenscroft, *Pammelia* (London, 1609), sig. F1ᵛ–F2ʳ.

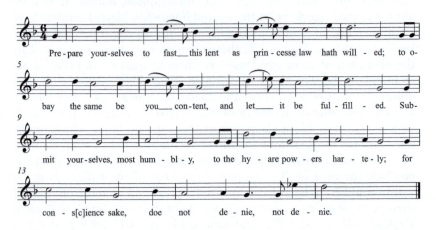

Pre-pare your-selves to fast__this lent as prin-cesse law hath will-ed; to o-

bay the same be you__ con-tent, and let__ it be ful-fill-ed. Sub-

mit your-selves, most hum-bl-y, to the hy-are pow-ers har-te-ly; for

con-s[c]ience sake, doe not de-nie, not de-nie.

Figure 4.2 Setting of *A ballad from the countrie sent* from *The Shirburn Ballads, 1585–1616*, ed. Andrew Clark (Oxford, 1907), p. 347, to 'The Cramp' from Thomas Ravenscroft, *Pammelia* (London, 1609), sig. F1ᵛ–F2ʳ.

Contrafacting in Practice

Despite minor variations that required the adaptation of melody, the metrical structure of the music can occasionally give a clear indication of which ballad texts might have fitted them. William Elderton's first known ballad was *The panges of Loue and louers ftts* [sic], published in 1559 (Figure 4.3).[26] The first line, 'Was not good Kyng Salamon', gave the tune its title.[27] A ballad called *kynge SALOMAN* was registered on 4 March 1560 and the tune was then used for at least five further ballads in the succeeding ten years.[28] The characteristic refrain 'Lady lady... my deare lady' makes contrafacta to the tune of 'King Solomon' relatively easy to identify, as it creates an unusual metrical pattern of 8.8.8.8.8.4.8.4. Any verse in ballad metre (8.6.8.6.), for instance, would be difficult, if not impossible, to fit to the tune. As the melody appears to be mainly based in the 'meeke and devout' Dorian mode (although the lack of the sixth of the scale makes the Aeolian a possibility for the first half of the tune), this may have made it especially suitable for some of these ballads: several are biblical stories and one counselled the queen on matters of religion.[29]

The audience for *The panges of Loue* was expected to have a wide knowledge of both Biblical and classical learning, but also to enjoy a ballad that chose to use this knowledge for earthier ends. The ballad was couched in the trope of a courtly love song addressing the lover's 'deare lady'. It used examples from classical mythology and even the Bible to encourage the lady to give in to the charms of the lover. Some of the examples display the ideals of pure courtly love: Pyramus 'For

Figure 4.3 Setting of William Elderton's *The panges of Loue and louers ftts* [sic] (London, 1559), to 'King Solomon'.

Tysbies sake hymselfe he slewe / ... / To proue that he was a louer trewe'; Paris endured 'sturdy stormes' to win the heart of Helena; Iphis committed suicide when he could not win the love of the hard-hearted beauty Anaxaretis. From the very first verse, however, Elderton's song shows that, even in the sixteenth century, sex sold: the aim of the ballad's lover was to get his lady into bed, just as his Biblical and classical predecessors had managed to woo their beloveds. The Biblical King Solomon, known not only for his wisdom but for his hundreds of wives and concubines, was 'ravished in sondry wyse / With euery liuelie Paragon'. Leander 'swomme the waters perilous / of Abidon those surginge sease / To come to her [Hero] where as she lay' in order to engage in sexual intercourse. Finally, Jupiter 'changed his shape as fame hath spred / ... / To come to Alcumenaes bed' when her husband was away. As a result, she gave birth to Hercules.

'King Solomon' was, then, an interesting choice of tune for a ballad addressed to Queen Elizabeth. Perhaps the sombre mood of the melody rendered it suitable, despite its associations with Elderton's ballad, or perhaps the pro-Elizabethan ballad was a conscious attempt to replace the salacious with something more edifying (indeed, all the known contrafacta on 'King Solomon' take a much more sober line than Elderton's lyrics). Undoubtedly, though, one of the primary reasons for recycling an old tune such as 'King Solomon' was to benefit from its popularity. *A Newe Ballade,* beginning 'O Dere Lady Elysabeth', has the correct stanza pattern to fit the 'King Solomon' tune.[30] It is clear that the words of *A Newe Ballade* used the 'King Solomon' tune because of its unusual metre and the similarity of the refrain's lyrics, but in order to make the rest of the lyrics fit the melody, it is necessary to change some minims to two crotchets and tie some crotchets together. The identity of the author, R.M., is unknown, but he was responsible for at least one other extant ballad, *An epytaphe vpon the death of M. Rycharde Goodricke Esquier*, printed in 1562.[31] Simpson conjectured that R.M.'s *A Newe Ballade* was *a new ballett after the tune of 'kynge SALOMON'* entered in the Stationers' Registers in 1561–2 by John Tysdale.[32] But the internal evidence of the ballad suggests that this might be incorrect. In *A Newe Ballade*, R.M.'s intent is to 'counsayle' the queen to 'beware of the spiritualtie', that is, the priests and ecclesiastical officials of the church. The only time anyone had reason to doubt the Protestant spirituality of Elizabeth's church was in the early months of her reign, prior to the meeting between representatives of Parliament and Convocation at Easter 1559, while several of Mary I's Catholic bishops were still in office. This suggests that *A Newe Ballade* was written very soon after *The panges of Loue*, somewhat earlier than the date *a new ballett after the tune of 'kynge SALOMON'* was registered.

In order to counsel the queen, R.M. relied on the weight of history to give authority to his words. He evoked images of her predecessors, William II, John, Richard II, Henry VI and, latterly, Elizabeth's father, brother and sister. According to the balladeer, some of these monarchs fell victim to priestly plots against their persons, while Elizabeth's father and siblings were unduly influenced by wicked ecclesiastical counsellors who held back the necessary reform of the church. In doing so, R.M. attempted to privilege English supremacy over the papacy. This was a common enough trope in Protestant Tudor England, when historical figures were given a role in current affairs by relating them directly to newsworthy events.[33] King John presented an interesting paradox to a Protestant Tudor author like R.M.: he could be praised for challenging the authority of the Pope over the appointment of a new Archbishop of Canterbury on the death of Hubert Walter in July 1205, but, in order to make this possible, King John's poor reputation had undergone a transformation during the early Tudor period.[34] Likewise, the figure of Richard II was used to exemplify the wages of sin. It was possible to see the consequences of one's actions through the example of people who had gone before.

Another contrafactum on 'King Solomon' which appealed to the authority of history was George Mell's ballad, *A Proper New balad of the Bryber Gehesie*, published in 1566–7 by Thomas Colwell.[35] It told the Biblical story of the briber Gehazi, who was punished by God with leprosy for his sinful behaviour. The ballad stressed the continuity of Elizabethan Protestant church with the early church, saying 'The Lord he is that same God still / That he was than vndoubtedlie'. The trappings of the church may have changed, but the God being worshipped

Figure 4.4 Setting of *Wysdom woold I wyshe to have,* from Oxford, Bodleian Library, MS Ashmole 48, ff. 122ʳ–123ʳ, to 'King Solomon'.

in Elizabethan England was the same one worshipped by the early Christians. Even while it looked backwards and appropriated history, it did so for topical reasons: it was intended to stress the superiority of Elizabethan Protestantism which had its roots in scripture over the corrupted papal church.

The metrical pattern of 'King Solomon' makes it almost certain that another religious ballad, *the Ballad of constant Susanna,* and an incomplete, untitled ballad from *A Handefull of Pleasant Delites* were also sung to this tune.[36] Two other ballads on the subject of Solomon can be found in Bod. MS Ashmole 48.[37] Neither specifies a tune, but the second, beginning 'Wysdom woold I wyshe to have', could easily fit 'King Solomon' with the repetition of the last few words of each line of the refrain, or using the 'lady, lady' refrain as in Figure 4.4.

Contrafacta and Implicitness

Likewise, all of the extant mid-Tudor ballad texts known to 'The Downright Squire' reflect men's attitudes to women, suggesting that the tune perhaps accumulated a set of implicit associations with this subject that balladeers drew on in the hope of selling a new 'hit'. In 1566, 'The Downright Squire' was used as the tune for two ballads in *A Handefull of Pleasant Delites.* As the preface to the *Handefull* stressed that it was a collection of songs which were suitable for ladies, these were songs which idealised women. The first was *L. Gibson's Tantara, wherin Danea welcommeth home her Lord Diophon fro[m] the war.* We know nothing of Leonard Gibson apart from his two ballads (the other being *Leaue lightie loue ladies, for feare of yll name*, published as a broadside in 1571). His *Tantara* was a mock-classical love song, in which the hero, Lord Diophon, returned to Syria from the war to find his wife, the queen Danea, waiting for him. Danea described his return 'from battered field / That valiantly thy foes did foile, / with speare and shield', showing that he was worthy of 'sounding praise' for his exploits during the war. Diophon described his wife as his 'ioy and life'. She had 'the trustiest hart, / that man can find'. The 'tantara' of the title was the onomatopoeic sound of the trumpet, which reappeared as a refrain throughout the song. Diophon, however, is not a familiar character from Greek history or myth, so it seems likely that Gibson was creating his story along courtly lines rather than turning to classical literature for direct inspiration.

The other ballad set to 'The Downright Squire' in the *Handefull* was *A new Sonet of Pyramus and Thisbie* (Figure 3.3). It was addressed to a female audience with the words 'You Dames (I say) that climbe the mount of Helicon, / Come on with me, and giue account'. Mount Helicon was home to the muses who inspired learning, poetry and music. It was itself seen as a source of poetic inspiration. The ballad told the Ovidian tale of the doomed lovers Pyramus and Thisbe, urging 'You Ladies all, peruse and see, the faithfulnesse, / How these two Louers did agree, to die in distresse'. It celebrated the constancy of 'These louers twaine, who with such paine, / did die so well content'.

These two songs showcased paragons of the female sex as constant and faithful lovers, but some of the women in the 'Downright Squire' ballads were less admirable. Later in the sixteenth century, the melody was used again for Thomas Rider's *A merie newe ballad intituled The pinnying of the basket* (Figure 4.5).[38] To 'pin the basket' is an obsolete phrase meaning to conclude matters. In this song, the matter concluded was the domination of men over women. The ballad told the 'pretie jeste' of two scolding wives who were beaten by their husbands. When the joiner arrived at the chandler's shop to spend his money, the chandler, Rafe, was not there to serve him. A drunken gambler, Rafe was instead at the alehouse playing at 'dice and drinke'. His wife, understandably upset that her husband was wasting money when he should have been making it, went forth 'in a rage' to find him. The clear implication of the ballad is that the man went to the alehouse to escape his railing wife. She was a 'bedlam beaste' who engaged in 'rough talke', while he was a good and quiet man who waited patiently while she scolded him in public, then took her back to their shop. Only once he had reached the privacy of his own home and served his customer, did the chandler try to teach his wife a lesson. He ordered her to pin the basket for the joiner's page and when she refused, he beat her into submission.

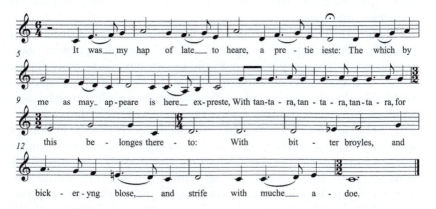

Figure 4.5 Setting of Thomas Rider's *A merie newe ballad intituled The pinnyng of the basket: and is to bee songe to the tune of The doune right squire* (London, 1590).

The brawl, however, was witnessed by the joiner's page. He was forced to watch the spectacle while waiting for his master's goods. Returning to his master and mistress, who were angry about his lateness, he reported what he had seen as an excuse for his apparently tardy behaviour. The page reported that it was the scold's refusal to do as she was bidden by her drunken husband that had led to the brawl. The joiner was pleased that the woman had been forced to submit to her husband's will, but the disorderly conduct of one woman set a subversive example for another and the joiner's wife began to sympathise with the victim of the beating. She took the beaten woman's part and claimed that she too would refuse to pin the basket for her husband. The joiner then took his wife to bed and raped her in an attempt to settle the matter. The page, on the other hand, went straight to the maid and repeated his story. She became the third woman in the ballad to attempt to defy her gender and have her own way. Calling the page 'knave' and 'sot', she hit him over the head and reprimanded him 'for makyng strife, ... / betwixt the maister and his wife, where love should be'. Angered by the maid's actions, the page violently assaulted her and 'made her grone', possibly emulating his master's deeds. By this he regained the upper hand: she was forced not only to make his supper, but to sit and eat with her attacker. The joiner was delighted by his page's mastery over the maid, but his wife was less than impressed. When she still refused to pin the basket for her husband, he began 'with a bedstaffe he[r] to baste' in a neat piece of balladic *double entendre*. Afterwards, the joiner's wife ran to the Justice of the Peace for protection. When the justice's wife heard the tale, she agreed to intercede for her friend, asking for the joiner to be bound over to keep the peace. The justice, however, was far from sympathetic to the woman's plight.

Instead, he laughed heartily at the 'jeste' and was tempted to teach his wife the same lesson.

As such, the ballad might have simultaneously appealed to different groups in the audience and implicitly divided them along gender lines. One group might sympathise with the beaten wives who were forced to rely on their neighbours for support, while the other supported the scolded husbands who were forced to assert their authority over their spouses. Nevertheless, mastery over the women of the ballad came at a price because none of the women acquiesced meekly to their husband's authority.[39] None of the women in the song got their own will in the end, and indeed the message of the song was twofold: that disorderly conduct spread like a disease among women and that they should submit quietly to their husbands in order to avoid conflict or even violence. The disorderly women in the song contrasted sharply with the ladies who epitomised feminine virtues in the *Handefull of Pleasant Delites*.

Dealing with Bawdy Ballads

The most widely recognised examples of ballad contrafacta, however, are the 'moralised' ballads, which cashed in on a popular and usually bawdy song by providing a 'godly' or 'improving' alternative. Use of the same tune was imperative if the ballad was to be subverted in this way, as to change the tune would destroy the relationship between the old and new versions of the song. It is reasonable to assume that in order for a moralised ballad to be written, the original song was considered in some way dissolute. There would be little point moralising an already 'proper' song. Few of the surviving printed mid-Tudor ballads were as full of sexual connotations as William Elderton's *The panges of Loue*. More vulgar ballads appear in manuscript than print, although not as many as might be imagined, given the attitudes of men like Philip Stubbes and Robert Fletcher. One of these was a ballad in Bod. MS Ashmole 48, which described an illicit erotic encounter, or perhaps just an erotic dream. In ballad metre, the tune for this song, which began 'fa re my la' (that is, F, D, E, A in the key of C), has not yet been successfully identified.[40] Although it was relatively unusual in traditional songs for the night visitor to be a woman going to a man's chamber, she is entirely familiar to the early modern audience in her insatiability:

> On tyme I layde me downe to rest,
> On slumbrynge sleepe I felle,
> Me thawght I saw her cum to me
> Whom I had loved well.
>
> And as I musynge thus do lye,
> That sleepe inclosde myne eye,

Then strayte way to the dore she came,
And shut yt by and by.

Then bold was she to stand by me
With myrthe and merry chere,
She vewde the chaumber rownd abowte,
She saw the cost was cleare.

Me thawght I sawe her blushe was red,
As red as any rose;
And when she sawe howe nakte I laye,
She covered me with clothes.

Save won part that she dyd leve bare,
Her cherry lypps to staye;
The nyght I past so plesawntly,
I forced not for daye.

The lips were a familiar euphemism for the labia, so 'cherry lypps' has a double meaning that could refer either to kissing or sexual intercourse. Double entendre like this was indispensable to the bawdy ballad. It was perhaps the most widely understood form of implicitness and yet it was equally deniable. It is easy to imagine the balladeer performing these songs with movement, gestures, facial expressions and pauses all contributing to the overall effect. It is also easy to imagine a critical voice being wrong-footed by such sexual innuendo: by complaining about the material, you had to admit having understood it, but you also ran the risk of making a connexion that had never been intended. Furthermore, you could be accused of exposing your own sexual proclivities through your own interpretation of the words. Even if the implicit meaning had been intended, if you complained you might find yourself being accused of being a wanton degenerate.

This did not, however, stop the godly trying to provide more decorous forms of entertainment to replace bawdy ballads like *Adew, My Pretty Pussy*:

Adew, my pretty pussy,
Yow pynche me very nere;
Yowre sudden parture thus
Hath chawnged much my chere.
But turn agayne, and bas me,
For yf that yow pas me,
A better grownd shall gras me,
Untyll another yere.
Thowghe yow make yt daynty,
Wemen wyll be plenty,
When won man shall have twenty,
There wyll be bownsynge chere.

Prynce Arthur cums agayne, sir,
So tellethe me myne host;
Dick Swashe keepes Salesbury plane, syr,
And schowrethe styll the cost.
But Jayne wyll jest no more, syr;
Tyb was borde before;
Kate she keepes the schore, syr,
And schores yt on the post.
Talk of other knaks, syr,
Fyll no empty saks, syr,
Put no fyre to flax, syr,
Lest all youre gaynes be lost.

The market wyll be mard, syr,
Yf corn and cattell faule;
The syt but at reward, syr,
That sarve in slovens haull.
But pres amunghst the best, syr;
Smell owt every fest, syr;
Shrynke not for a jest, syr;
Stand up and take no fawle.
For he that fumes and frets, syr,
Syldom payse hys dets, syr;
Smaull gaynes myne ostys gets, syr,
When cards are cownted all.

My pretty wenche dothe smyle, syr,
To here me tell thys tale;
I wowld ryde many a myle, syr,
To carry suche a male.
For she can syt asyde, syr,
Lyke a vyckars bryde, syr,
With all her poynts untyde, syr,
When she hathe in her ale.
But when she cums in place, syr,
Then she hydes her face, syr;
Thys ys all her grace, syr,
When her ale she sets to sell.

The peopell talk and prate, syr,
Of pus and her short lyff;
And of her mariage late, syr,
Men say there ys grete stryff.
But the gyrld ys gon, syr,
With a chokynge bon, syr;
For she hathe got her John, syr,
And ys ower vyckars wyff.

This ys no less in deede, syr,
Then holy churche dothe breede;
Suche serves at neede, syr,
To whet a blunted knyff.

Syns pus wyll part from me, syr,
And do me thus muche wronge;
Chyll have as good as she, syr,
Before that yt be longe.
Pus ys not contented,
Full oft she hathe repented
That ever she consented,
And thynks she hathe gret wronge.
But cowrtyers can not carve,
Except the tyme dothe serve, syr;
Thowghe thys be overthwart, syr,
Remember me amunge.

The alehouse invoked by this bawdy ballad was a social centre where gossip, news and entertainment could be shared among women and men. Alehouses figured frequently in many later ballads, although they are less present in the mid-Tudor ballads than one might expect. Women took a lead role in the brewing and sale of ale, but alehouses were also associated with the prostitution which is central to *Adew, my pretty pussy*.[41] 'With all her poynts untyde' implied that Pus was given to a state of undress when in her cups, which was hardly surprising given that she was a whore or bawd, like the other 'cattle' in the song. 'A better grownd shall gras me' implies that the women in the ballad provided sexual pasture for men and that if one were unavailable, another could easily be found. 'Bownsing chere' and 'ryde' referred, of course, to the motion of sexual intercourse, while 'jest' 'serve', 'press' and 'bore' leave little to the imagination. Kate kept score on the bedpost, a phrase still in common usage even today, but 'post' was also a euphemism for the penis, as were 'dick', 'bone' and the 'knife' which would be whetted in intercourse. 'Knaks' and 'sak' applied to the sexual organs of either sex.

Of course, enjoying sexual relations with a whore like Pus also meant risking infection with venereal disease. While 'fire' often referred to burning passion, 'Put no fyre to flax, syr, / Lest all youre gaynes be lost' suggested that the fire in this case was a symptom of gonorrhoea. Likewise, the market of verse three was probably the vulva, which could be marred by syphilis, although the marketplace was also a euphemism for the location where a prostitute would pick up her clients. 'Corn' implies semen, in this case probably female. We may as a rule be overzealous in pursuit of 'come' as a euphemism for orgasm in early modern texts, but considering the rest of the sexual innuendo in the ballad, there is little doubt about its meaning here.[42]

Even in a ballad as ribald as *Adew, my pretty pussy*, however, the balladeer could not resist investing his words with wider implications; the song displays an unmistakable anti-Protestant tone. Pus the whore was to marry a vicar, which in itself meant that the vicar must be Protestant. The implication was that vicars' wives were prostitutes, who provided sexual services for the clergy. The name of the vicar, John, was presumably selected for its association with the penis. The singer pointed out that the 'holy church doth breede', something which was (at least in official terms) a novelty in mid-Tudor England. It is difficult to tell whether the 'grete stryff' which apparently accompanied the wedding was intended to relate to disagreement between the couple themselves or to a wider disapproval of clerical marriage. Pus apparently regretted the wedding, thinking that instead she should have aimed for a man of the court. The balladeer perhaps counselled that these Protestant preachers could not 'carve' as well as the socially ambitious Pus would like.

Ballads like *Adew, my pretty pussy* and *On tyme I layde me downe to rest* were entirely typical in their emphasis on women's need for sexual fulfilment. They reflected the way in which the body was believed to be controlled by the humours, with women being particularly cold and moist. This meant that they were voracious, with a much stronger need for sexual fulfilment than men. Once aroused, female desire could not be quenched and women's enjoyment of sex was taken for granted by men, not least because it was believed that the woman's orgasm was a prerequisite for conception.[43] In *Adew, my pretty pussy*, the balladeer exhorted his listeners not to succumb to impotence but to 'Stand up and take no fawle'. 'To fall' often referred to assuming a sexual position, but in this case, it was probably a contrast between the erect penis and the limp one. The debt was a sexual one to the 'hostess', which could not be fulfilled if impotence prevented intercourse. Early modern women were believed to be susceptible to chlorosis, or greensickness, if marriage and its concomitant sexual fulfilment were postponed for too long.[44] Courting often went on for many years, as early modern women tended to marry late. One maiden bewailed her virginity with the refrain, 'For I have bene a meaden so longe, / That my tyme wyll be paste or I shall begynne'. Her lover, 'Good Robyne' had embraced her, but she 'dar not fullfyll thy desyare'. She complained that 'my body wastithe, my hart is clonge, / My face ys wrynckylde, and pale is my skin': all this because she had to forego intercourse with her lover.[45] This fear was likewise displayed in *A New Merry Ballad of a Maid that would Marry with a Serving Man*, which suggested that serving men made particularly good husbands because they were 'lustie and ful of yonge bloude, / Stronge and nymble, and very quicke of eye, / Clene, brave in apparel, and made properlye'. Nevertheless, the heroine of the ballad complained that 'My fleshe wyll pine awaye even to the bone' for the love of her serving man, if her parents forced her instead to make a socially expedient match. The singer of *Adew, my pretty pussy*, however, noted that people talked about 'pus and her short lyff'. Although women's desires were agreed to be insatiable and sexual abstinence was often considered dangerous to women, by contrast, frequent ejaculation (which was thought to occur in both men and women) was believed to exhaust the body and thereby shorten an individual's lifespan.[46]

Moralised Contrafacta

The trend to moralise ribald ballads was started by zealous reformers as part of an attempt to 'appropriate pre-Reformation cultural forms in the service of Protestantism'.[47] We have already seen this trend in the secular tunes for the liturgy. Godly men now began to use contrafacta in an attempt to stamp out salacious songs. They replaced the bawdy lyrics of popular tunes with biblical content or homiletic discourses to instruct the degenerate. Moralisers feared that popular songs displaced more fitting pastimes. It is not difficult to see why someone chose to publish *Mawken was a Counttry mayde moralysed* in 1563–4. Sadly, the moralised version no longer exists, but a fragment of the original Mawken ballad can be found in Thomas Ravenscroft's *Pammelia*:

> Malkin was a country maid,
> a country maid tricke and trim,
> tricke and trim as might be,
> she would needes to the Court shee said
> to sell milke and firmenty, hey hoe,
> haue with you now to Westminster,
> b[u]t before you come there,
> because the way is farre
> some pretty talk lets heare.
> Adew you dainty dames,
> goe whether you will for me,
> you are the very same
> I tooke you for to be.[48]

Malkin was used as a name for a woman of the lower orders, especially one who was lewd or considered a slut. Seeking social advancement, in this ballad she headed for the court at Westminster, a place associated with bawds and their clients. 'Tricke and trim' referred not just to the neatness of Malkin's dress, but also to the act of sexual intercourse. Given that 'milk' could refer to semen and was closely related to sexual activity, it is quite possible that there was a knowingly sexual connotation to furmety (a sweet and spicy dish made from wheat and milk) too.

Likewise, the lyrics of the original ballad *Roowe well ye marynors &c* are now lost, but the existence of so many moralised versions suggests that the original was in some way bawdy. The word 'roowe' could easily have been a pun on 'roe', the sperm of a fish, and it is possible that the ballad was rich in sexual innuendo because 'shot his roe' was a euphemism for ejaculation. The fact that the melody took on the name of the ballad indicates that *Roowe well ye marynors &c* quickly became very popular. At least 11 ballads were set to the tune 'Row Well Ye Mariners' between 1530 and 1570. One of these was Steven Peele's *A letter to Rome, to declare to the Pope, Iohn Felton his freend is hangd in a rope and farther, a right his grace to enforme, he dyed a papist, and seemd not to turne* (Figure 4.6), a satirical ballad on the 1569–70 Northern Rebellion.

The number of contrafacta on *Roowe well* suggests that the tune's popularity was maintained over several years. Due to its frequent reuse, it would have remained particularly familiar in people's minds. It was, after all, used for at least four ballads between July 1565 and July 1567; another 4 in the 12 months from July 1567; and a further four the following year. Moreover, even though the lyrics for most of these ballads are equally as obscure as the original song, it is clear from their titles that the vast majority of these songs were godly or moralised. One third included the word 'moralised' or 'proper', another two might

Figure 4.6 Setting of Steven Peele's *A letter to Rome, to declare to the Pope, Iohn Felton his freend is hangd in a rope and farther, a right his grace to enforme, he dyed a papist, and seemd not to turne.* To the tune of *Row well ye mariners* (London, 1570).

be considered 'godly' and at least three were topical, anti-Catholic ballads. Not only did Protestants presumably wish to use 'Row Well Ye Mariners' to make a godly point in contrast to a bawdy set of original lyrics, but also the tune's popularity may have helped to sell the moralised songs. In this case, the use of a popular melody enabled balladeers to make a moral or religious point. It contrasted the new lyrics with the old. Of course, we must also assume that the printer and balladeer hoped to make money from a new success with an established tune.

The Reformation of Manners

This trend to moralise licentious songs might be seen as a forerunner to the late sixteenth-century Puritan Reformation of Manners. This movement eventually gave rise to a belief in divisions between the godly, who were chosen by God for heavenly reward, and the reprobate, who were predestined for damnation. During the early years of Elizabeth's reign, however, it reflected a more general concern with immoral behaviour that could, in turn, lead to irreligion. Early Elizabethan policy was concerned with maintaining social order through control of both church and traditional customs.[49] Although in the localities there was a drive to increase rates of literacy and religious tuition, this was twinned with the suppression of traditional pastimes such as dancing, which were associated with dissolute behaviour. There has been some debate over how far Puritanism was at the root of this concern for the moral health of the community, but it is impossible to deny that many Puritans believed their neighbours' lifestyles to be immoral and dissolute. If these activities were left unchecked, they threatened to undermine the whole community and even the salvation of the godly themselves. The example provided by the reprobate might tempt others into sin. As such, the godly believed that they needed to take action against immoral behaviour.[50]

Moralised ballads, at first, provided one weapon in their armoury. The heyday of the godly ballad was the 1550s and 1560s, but this was not necessarily because there a large number of zealous reformers writing to improve the pastimes of ordinary folk. The idea, however, was then taken up by other writers and publishers who were rather less concerned about the spiritual welfare of their audience. Instead, writers and publishers took advantage of ballad moralisation as an opportunity to make money rather than as a means to enlighten the population.[51] But one effect of the trend for moralised ballads was that it allowed people to appear godly in front of others. They were able to fashion a self-image of politesse and refinement.[52] Listening to or performing a moralised contrafactum contributed a godly persona because you had chosen a decent ballad rather than a libidinous one. People who knew both ballads would be able to draw knowing, multivalent readings from the text of the moralised version. At a simple level, the two ballads set to one tune both work as pieces of entertainment, but a knowing audience would be able to make the comparison between the moralised ballad and its lewd antecedent and conclude that the performer was someone who valued manners, decency and the social order. The decline of the godly ballad in the late sixteenth century seems to have resulted from a belief that ballad-singing and psalm-singing 'were now mutually exclusive, and (at least for the reformers) there could be no such thing as a "godly" ballad'.[53] Over time, moralised and godly ballads came to be seen as 'a device for "singing psalms to horn-pipes"'. They pandered to people's baser instincts because they relied on secular rather than religious forms.[54]

Furthermore, ballads could be moralised in line with the social mores of the time without actually being 'godly': that is, a moralised ballad did not necessarily directly refer to God or have a Christian dimension. *A proper sonnet, wherin the Louer dolefully sheweth his grief to his L.& requireth pity* (Figure 3.5) from *A Handefull of Pleasant Delites* was set to the tune of 'Row Well Ye Mariners'. As *Roowe well ye marynors &c* appears in the Stationers' Registers before the publication of the *Handefull* in 1566, there is little doubt that *A proper sonnet* formed part of the *Handefull*'s first edition as well as the second, especially considering the popularity of the tune 'Row Well Ye Mariners' during the late 1560s. Considering the close registration dates of the first three contrafacta set to 'Row Well Ye Mariners' in 1566–7, it is even possible to speculate that *A proper sonnet* might be the lost *Roo well ye marynors moralyzed*. The passing reference to 'God' in the song is neither particularly Protestant nor Catholic in nature, nor is it central to the message of the song. Nevertheless, *A proper sonnet* is a moralised contrafactum of 'Row Well Ye Mariners' because it demonstrates the ideals of courtly love. The ballad captures the essence of the courtly lover, who praises the virtue and beauty of his lady 'deckt, / with worthie gifts aboue the rest'. His heart is held in his 'captiue breast' and he laments that 'Without redresse I die for loue'. This lack of religious ardour is entirely normal for a courtly love song, but contrasts with the three 'Row Well Ye Mariners' ballads which promote their religious character in their title: *Row well ye marynors moralyzed with the story of Jonas, Rowe well GODes marynours* and *Rowe well ye CHRISTes marynours*.

Another moralised contrafactum that was not reliant on religious morality was based on the tune 'All in a Garden Green'. Even though the second set of lyrics does not have the word 'moralised' in its title, the two lyrics contrast the actions of their protagonists through their single tune. The original text, *A merrye new ballad of a country wench and a clown* (Figure 4.7), was registered in 1565–6.[55] It is a salacious song set

Figure 4.7 Setting of the second verse of *A merrye new ballad of a countrye wench and a clown* from *The Shirburn Ballads, 1585–1616*, ed. Andrew Clark (Oxford, 1907), pp. 220–221, to 'All in a Garden Green' transcribed from TCD MS 408 (William Ballet Lute Book), p. 56 (first verse is incomplete).

in a rural location, where the rustic lover has his wicked way with a lass behind a tree, despite her protestations that it would be improper even for him to lay his hand on her knee. The clown, with his rustic ways and rude manners, attempts to seduce the wench, 'courting her with all his skyll, / working her vnto his will', but when his attentions fail to produce the desired effect, he becomes more aggressive. This prompts her to complain

> Lord, how yow hurt my hand;
> for god's sake let me goe:
> By my fayth and my troth,
> I did little thinke, forsooth!
> yow would haue servd me so.

There is some doubt over whether the sexual intercourse that is implied was consensual or not. The clown leaves the girl crying 'Since now yow haue me won / To yeeld and let you haue your will, / if yow would not love me styll, / I were quite vndone'. But happy endings were important and the pair do seem to part fondly.

The coarse *A merrye new ballad of a countrye wench and a clown* contrasts starkly with *An excellent song of an outcast lover*, which appeared in *A Handefull of Pleasant Delites* later the same year, specifying the tune 'All in a Garden Green' (Figure 4.8). In *An excellent song of an outcast lover*, the lover is a courtly servant of his lady, for whom 'No toile, nor labour great, / could wearie me herein'. The outcast lover's courtship is much more sophisticated than that of the clown, being based on the exchange of kind words, sighs and tokens rather than lust and physical desire:

> And friendly did we treat of loue,
> as place and time we got.
>
> Now would we send our sighes,
> as far as they might go,
> Now would we worke with open signes,
> to blaze our inward wo.
>
> Now rings and tokens too,
> renude our friendship stil,
> And ech deuice that could be wrought,
> exprest our plaine goodwill.

The outcome for this lover was not so satisfactory. Despite all the effort he put into courtship, the object of his affections cast him aside in favour of another man. What is important here, though, is that the scorned lover remained constant to his lady.

Although *An excellent song of an outcast lover* retained the theme of courtship from *A merrye new ballad*, the disparity between the behaviour of the country clown and the courtly lover could not be clearer. All suggestion of extra-marital sexual intercourse was removed. The

Figure 4.8 Setting of *An excellent Song of an outcast Lover* from Clement Robinson, *A Handefull of Pleasant Delites*, pp. 46–47, to 'All in a Garden Green'.

outcast lover behaved properly throughout, maintaining his affection for the lady with faithfulness, constancy and self-control, in stark contrast to the clown of *A merrye new ballad*, whose actions were controlled by lust. In short, the outcast lover shows the clown how he ought to behave. Furthermore, even without explicit reference to a Protestant, let alone Calvinist, God, the second ballad can be interpreted as a piece of subtle, moralistic propaganda. *An excellent song of an outcast lover* informed its audience about appropriate behaviour, both as a lover and a citizen. It stressed constancy in these 'inconstant daies'. Although a personal experience of a failed love affair might make an individual pick up the ballad, the inconstancy of women could also be seen as a symptom of wider problems in society. In a period of upheavals in monarchy, politics, religion and the economy, the effects of inconstancy were potentially much more serious than an individual broken heart. Constancy was a measure of a person's faith in the monarch. Inconstancy might lead to the failure of the commonwealth, or even to rebellion and treason. These stories formed part of the news of the day. Given their novelty, one might expect news ballads to be sung to new melodies. Even here, however, contrafacta could help to add extra meaning to the words.

Notes

1 Philip Stubbes, *The theater of the Popes monarchie wherein is described as well the vncleane liues of that wicked generation, as also their Antichristian gouernment, and vsurped kingdome: togeather with their horrible superstition, and blasphemous religion, as it is now vsed at this present, where Antichrist the Pope & his members do beare rule, by Phillip Stubbes* (London, 1585), STC (2nd ed.) / 23399.2, sig. A2ᵛ. The chapter title is taken from Shakespeare, *I Henry IV*, II.ii.55.

2 Desiderius Erasmus, *A booke called in latyn Enchiridion militis christiani, and in englysshe the manuell of the christen knyght replenysshed with moste holsome preceptes, made by the famous clerke Erasmus of Roterdame, to the whiche is added a newe and meruaylous profytable preface* [trans. William Tyndale?] (London, 1533), STC (2nd ed.) / 10479, sig. L6ʳ.

3 Ward, 'Music for "A Handefull of Pleasant Delites"', p. 154.

4 See Howard Mayer Brown, 'Emulation, Competition, and Homage: Imitation and Theories of Imitation in the Renaissance', *Journal of the American Musicological Society*, 35:1 (1982), pp. 1–48; Rebecca Herissone, *Musical Creativity in Restoration England* (Cambridge: Cambridge University Press, 2013), p. 41.

5 Marsh, *Music and Society*, p. 319; Christopher Marsh, 'The Sound of Print in Early Modern England: The Broadside Ballad as Song', in *The Uses of Script and Print, 1300–1700*, ed. Julia C. Crick and Alexandra Walsham (Cambridge: Cambridge University Press, 2010), p. 176; Una McIlvenna, 'The Power of Music: The Significance of Contrafactum in Execution Ballads', *Past & Present*, 229:1 (2015), pp. 47–89.

6 Christopher Marsh, '"Fortune My Foe": The Circulation of an English Super-Tune', in *Identity, Intertextuality, and Performance in Early Modern Song Culture*, ed. Dieuwke van der Poel, Louis Peter Grijp and Wim van Anrooij (Leiden: Brill, 2016), p. 324.

7 *TRCS*, i, pp. 128 and 304.

8 *TRCS*, i, pp. 297 and 331.

9 Bod. MS Ashmole 48, f. 101^v.

10 See Rubin, *Memory in Oral Traditions*, Chapter 11.

11 Tristram P. Coffin, 'Remarks Preliminary to a Study of ballad metre and Ballad Singing', *Journal of American Folklore*, 78:308 (1965), p. 150.

12 Bertrand H. Bronson, 'On the Union of Words and Music in the "Child" Ballads', *Western Folklore*, 11:4 (1952), p. 242 and 245.

13 BL Add. MS 38599, f. 140^v.

14 Herissone, *Musical Creativity in Restoration England*, p. 210.

15 Milsom, 'Music, Politics and Society', p. 502.

16 Herissone, *Musical Creativity in Restoration England*, p. 367.

17 Coffin, 'Remarks Preliminary to a Study of ballad metre', p. 150.

18 See Derek Attridge, *The Rhythms of English Poetry* (London: Longman, 1982), Chapter 4.

19 Thomas Ravenscroft, *Pammelia Musicks miscellanie. Or, Mixed varietie of pleasant roundelayes, and delightfull catches, of 3. 4. 5. 6. 7. 8. 9. 10. parts in one. None so ordinarie as musicall, none so musical, as not to all, very pleasing and acceptable* (London, 1609), STC (2nd ed.) / 20759, sig. F1^v–F2^r.

20 Simpson, *British Broadside Ballad and its Music*, p. 139.

21 Thomas Wright (ed.), *Songs and Ballads, with Other Short Poems, Chiefly of the Reign of Philip and Mary* (London: J.B. Nichols and Sons, 1860, repr. Forgotten Books, 2012), p. 188.

22 Simpson, *British Broadside Ballad and its Music*, p. 139.

23 Andrew Clark (ed.), *The Shirburn Ballads, 1585–1616* (Oxford: Clarendon Press, 1907), p. 347.

24 Simpson, *British Broadside Ballad and its Music*, p. 139.

25 Rubin, *Memory in Oral Traditions*, p. 262.

26 Elderton, *panges of Loue*.

27 Simpson, *British Broadside Ballad and its Music*, pp. 410–12.

28 *TRCS*, i, p. 127.

29 Parker, *whole Psalter*, sig. VV4^r.

30 R.M., *A Newe Ballade* (London, 1560), STC (2nd ed.) / 17147.

31 R.M., *An epytaphe vpon the death of M. Rycharde Goodricke Esquier* (London, 1562), STC (2nd ed.) / 17145.3.

32 *TRCS*, i, p. 181.

33 Thomas Betteridge, *Tudor Histories of the English Reformations, 1530–83* (Aldershot: Ashgate, 1999), p. 68.

34 See Carole Levin, 'A Good Prince: King John and Early Tudor Propaganda', *Sixteenth Century Journal*, 11:4 (1980), pp. 23–32.

35 *TRCS*, i, p. 331.

36 *The Ballad of constant Susanna* (London, 1624); Robinson, *Handefull of Pleasant Delites*, pp. 29–31; Simpson, *British Broadside Ballad and its Music*, pp. 410–11.

37 Bod. MS Ashmole 48, *The reare and grettyst gyfte of all*, ff. 29^v–30^v; Bod. MS Ashmole 48, *Wysdom woold I wyshe to have*, ff. 122^r–123^r.

38 Thomas Rider, *A merie newe ballad intituled The pinnyng of the basket: and is to bee songe to the tune of The doune right squire* (London, 1590), STC (2nd ed.) / 21037.

39 Brown, *Better a Shrew Than a Sheep*, pp. 138–39.

40 Bod. MS Ashmole 48, *On tyme I layde me downe to rest*, ff. 24^r–124^v.

41 Bod. MS Ashmole 48, *Adew, my pretty pussy*, ff. 137^r–138^r.

42 All definitions of sexual language in this section are taken from Gordon Williams, *A Dictionary of Sexual Language in Shakespearean and Early Stuart Drama* (4 vols. London: Athlone Press, 1994).

43 Anthony Fletcher, *Gender, Sex, and Subordination in England, 1500–1800* (London: Yale University Press, 1995), p. 51.

44 Laura Gowing, *Gender Relations in Early Modern England* (Harlow: Pearson Education, 2012), p. 17.

45 Bod. MS Ashmole 48, *In a sartayn place apoyntyd for pleasur*, ff. 81ʳ–83ʳ.

46 Fletcher, *Gender, Sex, and Subordination*, p. 46.

47 Watt, *Cheap Print*, p. 41.

48 *TRCS*, i, p. 102; Ravenscroft, *Pammelia*, sig. F2ᵛ–F3ʳ.

49 Edwin Davenport, 'Elizabethan England's Other Reformation of Manners', *English Literary History*, 63:2 (1996), p. 257.

50 Christopher Durston and Jacqueline Eales, 'Introduction: The Puritan Ethos, 1560–1700', in Jacqueline Eales and Christopher Durston (eds.), *The Culture of English Puritanism, 1560–1700* (Basingstoke: Palgrave/Macmillan, 1996), p. 26.

51 Watt, *Cheap Print*, p. 40 and 41.

52 See Stephen Greenblatt, *Renaissance Self-Fashioning: From More to Shakespeare* (London: University of Chicago Press, 1980).

53 Watt, *Cheap Print*, pp. 68–69.

54 Evelyn K. Wells, 'Playford Tunes and Broadside Ballads' *Journal of the English Folk Dance and Song Society*, 3:2 (1937), p. 87.

55 *TRCS*, i, p. 296; Clark (ed.), *Shirburn Ballads*, p. 220.

5 'Ye never herd so many newes'
The Social Circulation of Information in Ballads

Some of his neighbors doth inquire
What newes abrode there is:
If that he any thinge doth here,
Of those that dyd amisse.
Some longeth here to tell,
Of those that did Rebell,
And whether they be fled or take,
Thus still inquirie they do make.[1]

So sang Thomas Bette in the summer of 1570. *A newe ballade intituled, Agaynst rebellious and false rumours* was set to the attractive and rousing tune of 'The Black Almain' (Figure 5.1).[2] A version of the melody was popular for moralising ballads such as Steven Peele's *A proper new balade expressyng the fames, concerning a warning to al London dames to the tune of the blacke Almaine*, which reminded listeners that worldly wealth and beauty were no substitute for living a faithful Christian life: 'When Christ shall come to judge our deeds / No fairenes nor clerenes can helpe you than, / The corne to seperate from the weeds'.[3] Bette's song was likewise conventional in that it invoked religious authority, reminding the audience that 'surely Plagues we do desarue, / Most horrable and great: / Because from God we still do swarue., / and dayly doth him frette'. Yet although *Agaynst rebellious and false rumours* contained its fair share of religious moralising, it was different to the other mid-Tudor ballads set to 'The Black Almain'. It was a topical song, printed in the wake of the rebellion by the Earls of Northumberland and Westmorland against Queen Elizabeth I. Bette placed the revolt in the context of other religious conflicts, reporting that in France 'many a Noble hath bene slayne / A Duke and eake a Prince certayne', while the Dutch saw 'there Countrye cleane dispoyld' by Spanish troops led by the Duke of Alva. What is more, Bette's ballad reflected his understanding that 'euery one doth talke' about the news of the day.

This central chapter highlights the ways in which the music and lyrics of sixteenth-century ballads were mobilised to circulate the news, a term understood to include many aspects of current affairs. It shows that

Figure 5.1 Setting of Thomas Bette's *A newe ballade intituled, Agaynst rebellious and false rumours To the newe tune of the Blacke Almaine, vpon Scissillia* (London, 1570).

ballads presented themselves as part of information culture through the language they used. Even when the information that they contained was limited, their editorial stance was important. Furthermore, the chapter aims to set the songs firmly in their oral context, to show that the social framework surrounding the songs supported their newsworthiness through discussion and explanation. It demonstrates that the Tudor regime repeatedly attempted to control ballads precisely because they were an effective means of disseminating news and rumour and, finally, that implicitness created a space for the discussion of sensitive and seditious news and information.

The Meaning of 'News'

Although the early modern news trade has been much studied, the word 'news' remains surprisingly ill-defined.[4] Of course, one impediment is the fact that at least two very distinct forms of 'news' exist. The first is the abstract form of news: the retelling of an idea, story or message. The second form is concrete: the material means of presenting a message to other people, when this is necessary, perhaps by manuscript letter, proclamation, pamphlet, periodical or song. This distinction is reflected in recent scholarship about news. At an ideational level news is itself a construct, being simply what someone chooses to tell another person.[5] But ballads were part of a culture in which material forms of news such as pamphlets and, later, the first news periodicals formed a 'basis for verbal (and partly visual) exchange'.[6] They provided a starting point for people to talk about current affairs. News was as much about social networks in the early modern period as it was about intelligence. It was a matter of what information you chose to pass on and to whom.[7] Like ballads, news was mainly passed on by word of mouth. Although printed material was increasingly available and accessible during the early modern period, it was still a primarily oral society in which 'the whole process of social organisation and decision making was organised round an inherited tradition of communal activity, verbal expression and face to face contact'. News was understood to be about major events such as 'developments at court, wars, battles, pestilence or the fall of the great'. No matter how ephemeral the news print, though, the information it carried was always placed in a moral context to give it purpose.[8]

Sixteenth-century news might then be defined as the broadcast or reporting of interesting events and information considered to be novel, relevant to contemporary society and/or worthy of discussion, in whatever way it was transmitted. Consumers may have believed information to be noteworthy because it could affect them in some way, or simply because they had an interest in gossip and rumour. Perhaps it just became newsworthy by the act of being passed from one person to another. Producers wrote or printed news in various forms because they were told to by the ruling elite, as part of a commercial venture in which they could make money, or because they believed in the importance of the message itself.

Nevertheless, news in the sixteenth century would not necessarily appear important to the modern mind, nor even be a recent occurrence. Instead, it might be an apparently minor event or one that happened some time before, which had been imbued with a wider significance that rendered it topical and newsworthy.[9] As such, news was rarely objective. The addition of editorial opinion was as common in the sixteenth century as it is today, perhaps much more so. Early modern printed news, in the form of ballads, pamphlets and newspapers, attempted to influence the audience's response to the information received. Often the authorial voice assumed that all right-thinking people would agree with its opinion, or caricatured those who disagreed as malcontents or simply as the 'other'. Editorialising challenged the audience to think about the news. It encouraged the audience to share the opinion of the newsgiver, challenged them to disagree or even provoked them into finding out more. News was presumably more likely to cause discussion if it came loaded with opinion. By generating excitement and debate, it was more likely to sell to a wide audience. Ballads in particular heightened this excitement by presenting their message in an entertaining and memorable format which was especially appropriate for people who could not access printed material directly because they were unable to read.

Ballads and News

The idea that ballads were a forerunner of newspapers is a longstanding one. At the beginning of the twentieth century, Hyder E. Rollins was unequivocal in his belief that many ballads were journalistic and that 'the best way in which to judge the broadside ballad as a whole *is* frankly to compare it with the modern newspaper'.[10] Others were more circumspect, however. They pointed out that it might be misleading to present the ballad as an early form of newspaper and yet acknowledged that there were songs which might have been used as news reports in their day.[11] Natascha Würzbach, for example, argued persuasively that prior to the development of newspapers, ballads were a form of journalism. She posited that as well as expressing the political and religious views of pressure groups, they provided recreation which had a didactic function. This homiletic purpose was common to all early modern literature, but it was the unique entertainment value of the ballad that eased the reception of these messages.[12] It made them an invaluable persuasive tool. The broadside was certainly a medium of mass communication and many twenty-first century scholars agree that ballads were an early form of news media, even if they were not in a teleological relationship with newspapers.[13]

A pattern of news reports in the form of ballads and pamphlets was replicated across early modern Europe. During the war of the League of Cambrai in the early sixteenth century, Italian ballads had 'a significant informative function' and that, owing to their 'habitual mobility and adaptability, the singers were well placed to gather and disseminate news to large audiences'. Venetian street singers emphasised the *novità* (novelty), *verità* (truth) and sometimes the speed at which their accounts had been brought to the press.[14] Similarly, following the Saint Bartholomew's Day Massacre in 1572, French singers composed songs about the news which were then printed.[15] Even earlier, in fourteenth-century Spain, the ballad 'originated as a means to spread news and propaganda'. These songs arose directly from historical events. It was only after short news ballads became popular and had created a market for vernacular song that epic stories from literary sources, chronicles and folk tales entered the ballad genre.[16]

By the seventeenth century, fascinating differences between the form and content of English black-letter and white-letter ballads had developed. White-letter ballads were aimed at a more politically aware audience – a knowing audience – and relied on wider background knowledge; black-letter ballads, on the other hand, were more demotic and required less context.[17] Nevertheless, Angela McShane argued that the lack of detail in ballads indicated that their audience must already know the news. Ballads, according to this reading, were intended to argue rather than inform. She suggested that the purpose of ballads was 'not to narrate news', but that instead they were intended 'to expound upon the moral, political or comic potential of any story'.[18] McShane alleged that 'There was no such thing as a "news-ballad". Contemporaries did not use this term'.[19] The anachronistic term 'news-ballad' was coined by scholars who wanted to see the ballad as a poor relation of the newspaper.

Nevertheless, a subgenre of ballads that presented themselves as news certainly existed in the sixteenth century and was recognised as such by contemporaries. One balladeer, known only as R.B., unwittingly presented incontrovertible evidence that the news ballad existed in sixteenth-century England. His own ballad, *To such as write in metres* described three distinct types of ballad: alongside 'balades of loue not worth a beane' and 'open sclander', other ballads were sold 'vnder pretence / Of newes'.[20] He suggested that, instead of printing 'what commeth to hand', the printer should 'Pourge chaff from corne'. This would ensure that once the balladeers 'haue written their learned tale', only 'that which is meete to bring in pence' would reach the presses. R.B. set out to condemn the inaccuracy of some ballads that purported to sell news, but in doing so, he provided evidence that the 'news ballad' was recognised as a popular and lucrative genre in the sixteenth century.

The Lexicon of News

What matters here is not the amount of hard information that the ballads contain but the fact that they claim to contain any information at all. Most mid-Tudor ballads were not obviously topical, but of those that were, many used language that endorsed their newsworthiness. No fewer than 19 extant mid-Tudor ballads use terms that Joad Raymond describes as 'the lexicon of news' in their titles.[21] These were words which highlighted a text's relationship with news culture. The most obvious of these terms was, of course, the word 'news' itself, but they also included words like 'description', 'declaration', 'discourse' and 'report'. The number of self-proclaimed news ballads increases when titles from the Stationers' Registers are included. Many more ballads use news lexicon in their lyrics. Some ballads, such as *A Balade specifienge partly the maner, partly the matter, in the most excellent meetyng and lyke Mariage betwene our Soueraigne Lord and our Soueraigne Lady, the Kynges and Queenes Highnes* and *A discription of Nortons falcehod of Yorke shyre, and of his fatall farewel The fatal fine of traitours loe: by iustice due, deseruyng soe* emphasise their factual nature.[22] Other titles (for example, *The true fourme and shape of a monstrous childe*) highlight the accuracy of their story.[23] No matter how much or how little hard information these ballads contained, the fact remains that they used words such as 'discourse', 'declaration' and 'report' to create an association with information culture. In short, they presented themselves as news ballads.

Topical Ballads

Of the 205 extant printed ballads included in this study, 54 were classified as topical, so the survival rate for this type of ballad appears to be relatively low. Nevertheless, Alexandra Walsham suggested that topical ballads and pamphlets probably had a higher mortality rate than other similar texts. She pointed out that 'stale and obsolete news seems less likely to have been treasured than romantic tales of courtship and un-requited love, legends of Robin Hood, or favourite stories from Scripture'.[24] The evidence of the four mid-Tudor manuscript miscellanies examined in Chapter 8 confirms that topical ballads were less likely to be collected than those with more timeless themes.

Furthermore, it is likely that some topical ballads were so seditious that they were never transmitted by material means at all. After all, the ballad was not confined to the page. Conversation, letters and printed documents all provided additional contextual knowledge to the information provided in songs. Fundamental to our understanding of ballads, especially news ballads, should be their social context. Ballads were sung at community events such as fairs, markets and weddings. These social settings created a space for the public discussion of topical or political songs. This occasionally allowed them to leave a mark in court records rather than on a broadside. One such case occurred in February 1538, when William Smyth confronted the minstrel William Hunte in a vict-ualling house at Braintree in Essex. Smyth alleged that Hunte had sung a 'song that did it rayle agaynst saynt[es]' at a wedding.[25] Hunte defended himself, arguing that the saints were set up by the Pope, but 'now the Kyng ys Supreme hed of the churche in this realme And the bysshop of Rome hath no thyng to do here'. Smyth enquired, 'were ther not in tymes past as wise kyng[es] Rayneng over es as this kyng ys now and yet all they obeyed the popes power. And I pray the who gave thise kyng leve to put hym downe'. Smyth was duly reported to the sheriff of Essex, Sir Giles Capell, who in turn sent Smyth for trial by Thomas Cromwell and the other Privy Councillors in London. Smyth and Hunt's discussion of the topic took place as a result of a ballad that they had shared. The papal supremacy was a hot political topic in 1538 with the potential to result in a treason conviction.

Selling Ballads as News

Ballad news was therefore most often delivered orally by an intermediary such as a minstrel or balladmonger like William Hunte. Shakespeare alluded to this in Act 5 of *The Winter's Tale* when several gentlemen discuss the news. The first gentleman addresses the second with the words 'The news, Ruggiero!' The second gentleman replies that there is so much wonder abroad that 'Ballad-makers cannot begin to express it'.

'Ruggiero' (or 'Rogero') was the name of a popular ballad tune based on the Italian ground bass pattern of the same name. It was used for extemporising sung epic poetry, giving the second gentleman's name an impressive play on words.[26] We can be sure that the wonder ballads would have been sold as news, perhaps by the very character who discussed the news with the two gentlemen: Autolycus, the most famous and most quoted of all early modern ballad sellers. Useful precisely because he is a stereotype, Autolycus is intended to exhibit traits which would have been recognisable to an early modern audience familiar with petty chapmen and hawkers. What is more, Shakespeare presents his ballad seller unmistakably as a facilitator in the business of news. Autolycus takes advantage of his audience's credulity by selling songs as true reports:

> Here's another ballad, of a fish that appeared
> upon the coast on Wednesday the four-score of April,
> forty thousand fathom above water, and sung this
> ballad against the hard hearts of maids. It was thought
> she was a woman, and was turned into a cold fish for
> she would not exchange flesh with one that loved her.
> The ballad is very pitiful, and as true.[27]

Questioned by Dorcas about the veracity of the report, Autolycus replied that it had 'Five justices' hands at it, and witnesses more than my pack will hold'.[28] He stressed the accuracy and authority of his songs, wanting Dorcas to believe that they were not written by hack balladeers but that they came from a trusted source in the shape of men with significant social standing.

The exchange between Mopsa, Dorcas and Autolycus reveals that, even if the ballads were in fact tall tales, the balladmonger had no qualms about selling them as recently published, genuine reports of real incidents. Whatever they actually were, the fact is that Autolycus sold them as news:

> Autolycus: Here's one to a very doleful tune, how a
> usurer's wife was brought to bed of twenty money
> bags at a burden and how she longed to eat adders'
> heads and toads carbonadoed.
> Mopsa: Is it true, think you?
> Autolycus: Very true, and but a month old.[29]

The trade routes used by petty hawkers such as Autolycus and his real-life counterpart, the minstrel Richard Sheale, were not dissimilar to those that later would be used by the early postal system to deliver the first newspapers from London to the provinces.[30] Although wealthier individuals may have relied on messengers and letters to receive their information, for other people, the latest news may have been gleaned from urban gossip or from travellers to rural areas. Hawkers and chapmen travelled the country in this way, making it at least possible that ballads and balladeers could sometimes be the first to bring news from urban centres to rural areas.[31] It was via this network of travelling salespeople that the men and women of the provinces became well informed about current affairs.[32] The arrival of a travelling ballad salesman with a topical song gave listeners a chance to talk over the news, questioning the bearer of tidings from London. Rather than being dependent on an audience that already knew the news from alternative channels, ballads could in fact play a part in that oral dissemination of news by stimulating inquiry, causing people to ask questions about what they heard.

Information in Ballads

Although it is true that many ballads focused on the moralistic and religious ramifications of events, there were also songs that comprised detailed, narrative reportage.[33] For example, Thomas Watertoune's ballad *A ninuectiue against treason* describes Mary I's triumphal entry into London following her victory over the Duke of Northumberland's puppet queen, Jane.[34] As well as relating the progress of the attempted coup by the Duke of Northumberland, Watertoune gives a lovingly detailed description of how Mary was proclaimed in London, so much so that it reminds one of a special supplement provided by a modern-day newspaper to celebrate a great royal event:

> ...cappes and syluer plenteously, about the stretes dyd flye
> The greatest ioy and most gladnes, that in this realme myght be
> The trumpetres blewe vp all on hye, our Maries royall fame
> Let vs therfore styll gloryfy, and prayse his holy name.

> The nobles all consented than, together with one accorde
> To go to Paules churche euery man, to gyue thankes vnto the lorde
> Wheras they harde a songe of praise, as custome it hath bene
> To rendre thankes to god alwayes, for the victorie of our queene.

> Suche chere was made in euery strete, as no man can expresse
> In settyng forth wyne and plentie of meate: and fyers of much
>   gladnes.

The attention to detail creates the effect of reportage. Many of these particulars are also to be found in Henry Machyn's diary. Both the ballad and the diary mention heralds, the nobles, the singing of the Te Deum at St Paul's, banquets, bonfires and the distribution of largesse. Machyn's more detailed account recorded that trumpeters heralded the proclamation in the presence of

the erle of Arundell, the erle of Shrossbery, th'erle Penbroke, my lord
Tressorer, my lord of Preveselle, my lord Cobham, my lord Warden,
master Masun, and my lord Mare, and dyvers odur nobull men;
and thys was done at the crosse in Chepe, and from that plasse thay
went unto Powlls and ther was *Te Deum Laudamus*, with song, and
the organes playing, and all the belles ryngyng thrugh London, and
bone-fyres, and tabuls in evere strett, and wyne and bere and alle,
and evere strett full of bonfyres, and ther was money cast a-way.[35]

Watertoune and Machyn were probably both eyewitnesses to the celebrations. It is possible, however, that the two descriptions were each
taken from a common source which is now lost. This level of detail,
familiar perhaps to news chronicles, is not usually associated with balladry. It argues strongly for the relevance of ballads to news culture not
least because no other contemporary printed account of Mary's entry
into London survives.

Ballads and Editorial Comment

The early modern audience did not, however, expect information about
recent, important or downright titilating events to arrive without a thick
coating of gloss, be it religious, moralistic or mixed with the constant
appeal for loyalty to the crown. Ballads were no exception. Conversely,
those early seventeenth-century newspapers which tried to present only
the facts struggled to survive because the 'desiccated sequence of bare,
undecorated facts made them difficult to follow – sometimes, plainly
baffling'.[36] News that was sung therefore came with a heavy dose of
editorial content that contextualised the information. Such moralisation
was common in ballads, whether or not they were topical, but the use
of a moralistic or religious trope in a song did not preclude the presence
of news and information. Rather, the theme of proselytising provided
a form of editorial commentary in addition to the reporting of events,
presenting the information in a more interesting and enticing manner.

The timeless themes invoked by the ballads presented a form of moral
authority supplementary to the formal authority of the crown, the church
and the courts. These complementary forms of authority in early modern
England all had a 'power or right to define and regulate the legitimate
behaviour of others'.[37] Likewise, the social norm exerted a pressure of
its own that was widely accorded respect. Moral authority of this sort
relied on the common acceptance of an unwritten code of responsible
and appropriate behaviour. It was based on personal restraint and treat-
ing others with respect, but it was also underpinned by religious belief
and loyalty to the monarch.[38] This was reflected, for example, in ballads
which promoted the religious aspects of the news, or closed with a loyal
prayer to the king or queen.

Ballads certainly promoted a hegemonic viewpoint and they were not objective, but the modern belief that news reporting should be objective is anachronistic to the sixteenth century. Since objectivity in general was a concept barely understood, if at all, in the Tudor period, it is not surprising that balladeers took the opportunity to editorialise while they entertained and – at times – informed their audience. As a consequence, many ballads that reported news also emphasised the 'timeless and providential patterns that lay behind particular events'.[39] Even the most sober of early news pamphlets usually contained preambles that emphasised the enduring themes and moral implications of the reports, while later news books, printed between 1641 and 1660, were unmistakably partisan in addressing the fast-moving events of the Civil Wars.[40] By the time of the Cavaliers and Roundheads, of course, the political scene had undergone significant change from that experienced a century earlier by the Tudor monarchs and their ruling elite. Under the Tudors, there was virtually no formalised opposition to the crown, at least in the sense that would become obvious in the next century. The subject 'had no recognized right to political information, which was doled out selectively on a need-to-inform basis by the Crown or Parliament through authorized printers'.[41] Ballads, therefore, played a less punctilious part in the social exchange of information, as and when the need arose. Judging by the clusters of ballads around events such as the Pilgrimage of Grace and Thomas Cromwell's spectacular fall from power in 1540, that need was often created by an interest in politics as it affected the security and lifestyle of the middling sorts.

Ballads as Propaganda

One event that occasioned significant popular interest was the Northern Rebellion in 1569–70. In the years following Elizabeth's accession, several northern aristocrats had been removed from their offices because their conservative religious beliefs made them untrustworthy in the eyes of the queen's advisers. These conservative nobles included Charles Neville, Earl of Westmorland, and Thomas Percy, Earl of Northumberland. Their rebellion centred on a botched plot to settle the succession. They aimed to marry the most plausible Catholic heir to the English throne, Mary, Queen of Scots, to England's premier noble, the Duke of Norfolk. In the wake of the plot's failure, Northumberland and Westmorland rose in revolt against Elizabeth. They entered Durham, where they ejected the Protestant clergy and restored mass in the cathedral on 14 November 1569. Although the earls had contacted the Duke of Alva in the Low Countries to request Spanish assistance, none was forthcoming. The Earl of Sussex was dispatched to put down the rebellion. Furthermore, the majority of the English nobility rallied to Elizabeth's defence. On 15 December, the rebel earls disbanded their followers and made for Scotland. As a result of the rebellion, more than 700 men were hanged on Queen Elizabeth's orders.[42]

The broadside ballads published during the course of the rebellion were designed to entertain as well as inform. They were another, more demotic, means of spreading the news that the Tudor regime sought to promote more formally through pamphlet or proclamation. Although there is no evidence that the songs were directly commissioned by Elizabeth's chief advisor, William Cecil, these pro-government ballads contained significant linguistic similarities to the pamphlets written by men such as Thomas Norton and William Seres. Norton had a history of close collaboration with Cecil and it appears that he and his counterparts were passed information by the government about the course of the rebellion, such as copies of the northern earls' proclamation, in order to produce propaganda for the crown. These pamphlets were then used as the basis for the pro-government ballads, implying a 'unity of purpose' with the regime's aims even if they do not prove a direct link.[43]

Propaganda is, by its very nature, related to current affairs. It is a reflection upon what is happening at the time even when it talks about the past. The printed ballads include three self-confessed news ballads: *A ballat intituled Northomberland newes Wherin you maye see what Rebelles do vse*, *Newes from Northumberland* and *Ioyfull Newes for true Subiectes*. These songs related the fast-changing situation in the north-east. An additional three ballads used the word 'news' in their first few lines.[44] Two more remarked on 'what word I bring ye' and 'Who list to know', both phatic phrases that emphasised the way in which news was spread from person to person. Furthermore, *Newes from Northumberland* and *Ioyfull newes for true subiectes* are linguistically similar. They both use the same rhyme scheme, metre and similar texts. This suggests that although the tunes are unspecified, they were probably contrafacta with a melody that the knowing audience would have recognised and associated with the Northern Rebellion. Another pair of ballads on the Northern Rebellion, *A Lamentation from Rome, how the Pope doth bewayle, / That the Rebelles in England can not preuayle* and *A letter to Rome, to declare to the Pope, Iohn Felton his freend is hangd in a rope* both use the tune 'Row Well Ye Mariners', suggesting that the reuse of the tune helped to make an implicit association between two ballads on the same subject as well as cashing in on a previous success.[45]

These ballads are important not just because they use news lexicon. They also combine information with religious and political propaganda whilst emphasising their contemporaneity. Although the Northern Rebellion ballads do not provide a detailed narrative account of the uprising, there is sufficient information within their anti-papal propaganda to date many of the songs.[46] One song described how the rebels claimed 'Our banners and staues shall bringe vs Renowne', because, in an appeal to history, the rebels bore banners of the five wounds of Christ, which had also been carried during the Pilgrimage of Grace and the Prayer Book Rebellion.[47] Both of these earlier uprisings had been in favour of the maintenance of the Catholic faith. The ballads, in common with other polemical literature of the period, present the Northern Rebellion as an uprising that aimed at restoring papal authority in England. This was a move calculated to appeal to Elizabeth's faithful Protestant subjects. Once the involvement of the earls themselves had given the rebellion a traditional, feudal legitimacy, the northern commons were encouraged to support the uprising by the promise that Catholicism would be restored.[48] Indeed, the Council of the North reported that the rebels had been 'some w[i]th ther force in armo[u]r to p[er]suade the people to take ther partes, and some of ther comepany have throwen downe the com[m]union table and torne the holy bible in pieces' in a show of anti-Protestant aggression.[49] According to one ballad, this model was repeated across the north-east, 'In coming through ech Towne: / The Bibles they did rent and teare, / Like Traytors to the Crowne'.[50] It is clear that for the balladeers, Catholics were not just disloyal to Elizabeth, they denied the authority of God's word as set out in scripture.

By 1570, the news for the queen's loyal subjects was good. *Ioyfull Newes for true Subiectes* recounted how God had been pleased 'to vanquish the Rebels that troubled the Crowne'.[51] Later, as the earls abandoned their supporters, more news appeared. Following the flight of Northumberland and Westmorland, *Newes from Northumberland* reported that 'to Sainte Androwe, be they gone, / with very harde shyfte to make theare moane, / And som of theare Ladies lefte behind, / with very small wages vnder the wynde'.[52] 'To wag' also meant to be hanged from the gallows, so this is probably a reference to the punishment of the rebels by the provost general, Sir George Bowes. Although Anne Percy, countess of Northumberland, was the only woman to be attainted in her own right for her part in the rebellion, many women suffered after the rising for their husbands' actions.[53] Even Thomas Preston's satirical ballad, *A Lamentation from Rome, how the Pope doth bewayle, / That the Rebelles in England can not preuayle* reinforced the relationship between ballads and news. It began with a 'come all ye' which underlined the ballad's topicality, though it provided a fly's eyewitness account of the Pope's reaction to news of the rebellion's failure which was designed to entertain the audience: 'ALl you that newes would here, / Geue eare to me poore Fabyn Flye'.[54] The use of the fly was a many-layered insult: flies were insignificant and associated with spying, since they were small and could fit into tiny and private spaces; however, the fly was also believed to be a familiar or demon. Finally, William Elderton's ballad reporting the execution of Thomas Plumtree, the celebrant of the Durham mass, promised 'You shall haue more newes er Candlemas come'.[55]

The Effectiveness of Ballads as News

If these ballads were semi-official propaganda for the Elizabethan regime, gauging their effectiveness is nonetheless challenging. Nevertheless, various forms of Tudor propaganda were disseminated widely and with varying degrees of success, so indirect evidence such as sermons and court records can be vitally important to understanding how such texts were received.[56] A range of sources can be used to investigate the impact of balladry. At the simplest level, ballads could provoke a response in kind, perhaps a moralised version of the song or a contrafactum reply. Personal letters sometimes include references to popular songs, while later published sources complained about the bawdiness and ungodliness of ballads. As the seventeenth century opened, Sir William Cornwallis's *Essayes* famously made reference to his use of 'News, and two penny Poets' as scrap paper in his privy.[57] At the opposite end of the spectrum, royal proclamations bear testament to the perception that the ballad could be a conduit of seditious words. Despite the fact that much of the material that poured from the London presses was highly moralistic and fiercely loyal to the monarch, ballads were seen as a possible threat to the Tudor regime, which made repeated efforts to control their production and dissemination. A 1538 proclamation ordered that no book in English was to be printed without a license in order to prevent the production of heretical or seditious works. Bible or ballad, everything printed was supposed to be licensed by royal officials and, later, registered with the Stationers' Company. Censorship was, however, 'essentially *ad hoc*, inconsistent, opportunistic and usually ineffective'.[58] Whatever the theory, in practice, the licensing rules seem to have been routinely ignored.

Furthermore, because their melodic and mnemonic nature made them suitable for oral transmission, many contentious ballads were probably never written down. Evidence that these seditious songs existed can be found in the State Papers and court records, which provide much of our evidence for the reception of vernacular song. They show that ballads travelled the country, entertaining diverse audiences, informing their listeners and inciting debate. Among the State Papers is a letter from a Knutsford schoolmaster, Richard Oldfelden, to his son, Philip, at Oriel College, Oxford, written in 1536. He enclosed 100 verses 'concernyng thys insurrection or Rumpll i[n] the northe' and 'oth[er] englyshe Rymes and news'.[59] The insurgence to which he referred was the Pilgrimage of Grace. Not only did Oldfelden want to pass on the information to his son, he also instructed him to 'let your ma[ster] se them'. Nevertheless, as he finished his letter Oldfelden decided that the news was too sensitive to send with the messenger in case he was searched, so he altered the text to promise to send the verses under separate cover. Oldfelden was right to worry: his messenger, William Rede, was examined by the constable of

Wotton and Oldfelden's letter was passed on to the Privy Council. Songs and rhymes like these formed part of a wider oral and literary culture that helped to disseminate messages to the people. That message was news.

Controlling Ballads

The fact that something as apparently simple as a ballad could arouse the interest of the Privy Council shows what an impact the wandering balladeer could have when he turned his talents to singing the news. Indeed, the State Papers provide one particularly fascinating account of the way in which news ballads were performed and received in Tudor England. In February 1537, the wandering balladeer John Hogon performed a topical version of the popular ballad *The Hunt is Up* with his 'crowd', or fiddle, in several houses in the small Norfolk town of Diss. Several versions of *The Hunt is Up* are known.[60] George Puttenham's *Arte of English Poesie* attributed the song to 'one Gray', describing 'what good estimation did he grow vnto with the same king *Henry,* & afterward with the Duke of Sommerset Protectour, for making certaine merry Ballades, whereof one chiefly was, *The hunte it vp, the hunte is vp*' [sic].[61]

Like other popular songs, *The Hunt is Up* is found in manuscript, print and oral traditions. It underwent many changes over time. The melody is found in a lute arrangement in FSL V.a.159.[62] It is in the Ionian mode with a compound rhythm. The musical phrasing closely follows the textual phrasing by including a half close at the mid-point. It is a simple, easily remembered tune with some interesting rhythmical features. The earliest extant version of the lyrics is attributed to John Thorne and can be found in BL Add. MS 15233, alongside songs by John Redford and John Heywood (see Figure 5.2; also Chapter 7 for Heywood's celebratory ballads on the accession of Mary I).[63] In the late 1540s, Redford was an organist, playwright, poet and master of the choristers of St Paul's Cathedral, while Heywood was the vicar-choral of St Paul's. During this period, John Thorne was probably the singing man of St-Mary-at-Hill in London, although he would be appointed organist at York Minster in July 1542. Louise Rayment suggested that BL Add. MS 15233 was compiled during the period 1550–1560, but it remains likely that the men knew each others' work from their contemporaneous time in London.[64] Redford and Heywood were known to have court connections and, alongside Puttenham's comment about the song being popular with Henry VIII, they give *The Hunt is Up* a fascinating provenance at the centre of court life. Not only does it help to place ballad music squarely in court circles in the mid-sixteenth century, it could add an extra dimension to our understanding of Hogon's song. Is it possible that a knowing audience would have recognised the melody as being popular at court and made a comparison between Henry VIII's court and the implicit, seditious critique of Henry's religious policy contained in Hogon's lyrics?

Figure 5.2 Setting of John Thorne's version of *The Hunt ys Up*, from London, British Library, Add. MS 15233, ff. 33ʳ–34ᵛ, to the tune transcribed from FSL V.a.159, f. 12ʳ.

The version of *The Hunt is Up* that Hogon sang in early 1537 was anything but John Thorne's moralistic version. Unlike a printed broadside ballad, the one thing that an orally transmitted ballad such as *The Hunt is Up* most emphatically was not, is static. On paper, a ballad was constrained by the written word. In oral transmission, ballads could be continuously updated; in performance, a ballad text could be subverted by gesture or tone of voice. Hogon's version of the song related the events of the Pilgrimage of Grace, complaining that 'the masters of arte and doctors of dyvynyte / have brought the realme owght of good unite'.[65] Hogon apparently claimed to have twice previously sung the song in the home of the Earl of Surrey, Henry Howard. Surrey was the courtesy title given to the eldest son of the Duke of Norfolk. Although Thomas Howard, 3rd Duke of Norfolk was sent to quash the rebellion, his son's loyalty was suspect. Shortly after Hogon was investigated by the authorities, Surrey fell victim to incriminations by Thomas, Lord Darcy, that he was sympathetic to the rebels' cause. Furthermore, Surrey was himself a poet who had close links to Sir Thomas Wyatt, the great court poet. *The Hunt is Up* was sung at court and in the provinces, by the acolytes of the monarch as well as by wandering minstrels and balladeers, reinforcing the point that we should not associate balladry solely with the poor and less educated members of society. Instead, these songs had wide appeal and assimilated music from a variety of sources.

The report in State Papers describes how Hogon decided to sing his news in the homes of Robert Frauncez, John Ketylbergh and John Harlewyne. Crucially, on this occasion, he misjudged his audience: his auditors were loyal subjects of the king. When their friends and neighbours heard 'this report', John Jamys and Thomas Bek gathered at the house of the local butcher, Edmund Browne, where they asked Hogon to sing again. Hogon's version of the ballad named Norfolk, Surrey, Shrewsbury and Suffolk as men who 'myght a made Ingland mery', but the men in his rural audience claimed to be unable to understand some of the implicit references in the song. It is impossible to tell from the report whether they were genuinely unaware of what Hogon meant by his song, or whether this was a case of entrapment. Either way, implicitness served as protection for both parties: Hogon's words did not become unmistakably seditious until they were explained; but the Norfolk men could not be accused of troublemaking if they had not understood the meaning of the song without Hogon explaining it to them. They asked Hogon to clarify what he meant by 'the hunt is up'. He replied that he meant that the northern men were up. Bek asked Hogon what lay behind the line, 'The Duke of Suff[olk] myght a made Ingland mery'. Hogon answered, 'I meane this by that if the Duke off Suff[olk] hadde lete the lyncoulnshire mene & suffred them to a gone to the nurthen men then they to gether xuld or this tyme a brought Ingland to a better stay than it is now'. He went on to explain that 'the Duke of Suff[olk] promysed and was bounde vnto the lyncolnshire mene to gette ther p[ar]don for them all and that noen of them xuld suffer dethe and contrary to that the same Duke dyd vij men to be hangyed aft[er] that and dyu[er]se moe ar sent for'. Suffolk was indeed sent by the king in October 1536 to put down the Lincolnshire rebels, who had nevertheless disbanded before his arrival. The Lincolnshire rebels felt let down by Suffolk, whom they thought had promised to sue for their pardon. They disbanded because they believed that the herald had granted them the king's pardon. Instead, Henry demanded executions, which Suffolk carried out. Although Suffolk had probably not made any legally binding promise to the rebels for their pardon, it was public perception that mattered and the popular belief, as expressed by John Hogon, was that Suffolk was a double-dealer.[66]

It is clear, though, that whether or not the Norfolk men already understood the implications of his song, they believed that Hogon was spreading news. Their deposition describes how Hogon 'dyd goo from house to house and dyd syng that songe & made the report afore seyd'. Hogon entertained with his song and informed with his report of the news. Here, then, was a balladeer cashing in on a popular song that had its roots in court culture. *The Hunt is Up* had been transformed and politicised in order to comment on the Pilgrimage of Grace. Henry VIII considered the Pilgrimage of Grace to be so serious a threat that he sent the senior Duke, Norfolk, and the equally eminent Earl of Shrewsbury to suppress the rebels. There was no more topical subject in January and February 1537, given the attempt by Sir Francis Bigod and John Hallam to revive the rising in the north-east.[67] Hogon's audience questioned him about the meaning of his song; then, on the strength of those connotations, they reported him for sedition.

Ballads, News and Implicitness

During the mid-sixteenth century, there was no freely available genre that provided unmitigated access to knowledge of political affairs. Perhaps, then, reliance on a knowing audience worked in favour of the ballad as a news genre. Primarily an oral form, the ballad was often performed in public, which allowed the audience to ask questions if they did not understand every detail. Hogon's audience at the butcher's house claimed not to be in the know, but they were aware that there was more to the song than a simple hunting reveille. What is more, they were confident enough to engage with the singer to find out the implications of his ballad by asking him what he meant. The contrafactum on *The Hunt is Up* allowed a travelling minstrel to spread news as well as seditious opinion through the use of a catchy tune. It provoked discussion about the news of the day under the rule of a monarch who, in response to the continued troubles in the north, ordered the Duke of Norfolk to

> cause suche dredfull execuc[i]on to be doon vpon a good nomber of thinhabitau[n]ts of ev[er]y towne village and hamlet that have offended in this rebellion ashall by the hanging of them uppe on trees, as by the quartering of them, and the setting of ther hedd[es] and quarters in ev[er]y town... as they may be a ferefull spectacle to all...[68]

It was, perhaps, their very nature as entertainment that made sixteenth-century ballads potentially dangerous, especially in oral rather than printed form. They were difficult to control and yet they were influential, because their simple tunes made them attractive, adaptable and easy to remember. They were aimed at the very widest market and yet they could be composed by anyone, regardless of how much or how little knowledge that person had of the political, religious, social and economic problems of the sixteenth century. Before the news sheets of the seventeenth century, when the great existential battles between Protestant and Catholic confessions assumed military form on a Europe-wide scale, the social exchange of information had of necessity to rely on what channels were then available, and this ineluctably meant recourse to the less precise, less informative, and, inevitably, less rigorous forms of dissemination which were rhyming ballads set to catchy tunes. In the seventeenth and eighteenth centuries, more regular and explanatory methods became available, but nonetheless, in the mid-sixteenth century, the ballad operated as a medium of news.

Notes

1 Thomas Bette, *A newe ballade intituled, Agaynst rebellious and false rumours To the newe tune of the Blacke Almaine, vpon Scissillia* (London, 1570), STC (2nd ed.) / 1979. It is my belief that Thomas Bette's instruction that the song be sung 'To the newe tune of the Blacke Almaine, vpon Scissillia' meant that the duple-time melody of 'The Black Almain' (see Chapter 3) be adapted to the compound-time rhythm of the Siciliana, as shown here. From the late sixteenth century to the eighteenth, the term *La Siciliana* often referred to a dance form about which little is now known. According to the *Grove Dictionary*, it was a form of slow gigue (or jig) in compound time, but whether it is in some way related to the choreography for dances entitled 'Cycyllya Alemayne' and 'Cycyllia Pavan' in Oxford, Bodleian Library MS Rawlinson Poet. 108 is as yet unproven. 'Cecilia Pavan' was certainly used as the melody for a song in *A Handefull of Pleasant Delites.* The characteristic Siciliana rhythm of dotted quaver-semiquaver in 6/8 or 12/8 time (here extended to dotted crotchet-quaver in 6/4, in keeping with the other standard transcriptions of the period since it makes no difference to how it is heard) fits perfectly with the rhythm of Bette's lyrics. The final two phrases of music have been repeated in order to accommodate the words. For more on La Siciliana, see its entry in the *Grove Dictionary.* The chapter title is taken from BL MS Cotton Vespasian A-XXV, *Newes newes newes newes,* f. 126^v.

2 *TRCS,* i, p. 436.

3 Steven Peele, *A proper new balade expressyng the fames, concerning a warning to al London dames to the tune of the blacke Almaine* (London, 1571), STC (2nd ed.) / 19551.

4 For more on the development of the periodical press in the seventeenth and eighteenth centuries, see Richard Cust, 'News and Politics in Early Seventeenth-Century England', *Past & Present,* 112 (1986), pp. 60–90; Joseph Frank, *The Beginnings of the English Newspaper, 1620–1660* (Cambridge, MA: Harvard University Press, 1961); Joop W. Koopmans, *News and Politics in Early Modern Europe 1500–1800* (Leuven: Peeters, 2005); Andrew Pettegree, *The Invention of News: How the World Came to Know About Itself* (London: Yale University Press, 2014); Joad Raymond, *The Invention of the Newspaper: English Newsbooks, 1641–1649* (Oxford: Clarendon, 1996); Joad Raymond, *News, Newspapers, and Society in Early Modern Britain* (London: F. Cass, 1999); Joad Raymond, *Pamphlets and Pamphleteering in Early Modern Britain* (Cambridge: Cambridge University Press, 2002); Joad Raymond, *News Networks in Seventeenth-Century Britain and Europe* (London: Routledge, 2006); Joad Raymond (ed.), *The Oxford History of Popular Print Culture, Vol. 1, Cheap Print in Britain and Ireland to 1660* (Oxford: Oxford University Press, 2011); C. John Sommerville, *The News Revolution in England: Cultural Dynamics of Daily Information* (Oxford: Oxford University Press, 1996).

5 Sommerville, *News Revolution in England,* pp. 4–5.

6 Joad Raymond, 'Introduction: The Origins of Popular Print Culture', in Joad Raymond (ed.), *The Oxford History of Popular Print Culture, Vol. I, Cheap Print in Britain and Ireland to 1660* (Oxford: Oxford University Press, 2011), p. 9.

7 Joad Raymond, 'News', in Joad Raymond (ed.), *The Oxford History of Popular Print Culture, Vol. I, Cheap Print in Britain and Ireland to 1660* (Oxford: Oxford University Press, 2011), p. 377.

8 Pettegree, *Invention of News,* pp. 117, 4 and 24.

9 In a digital age, it is sometimes difficult to remember that modern understandings of 'recent', 'present', and 'topical' may be rather different to those of the

sixteenth century, when the transmission of information took much longer than it does now. For more on the idea of 'the present', see Daniel Woolf, 'News, History and the Construction of the Present in Early Modern England', in Brendan Dooley and Sabrina Baron (eds.), *The Politics of Information in Early Modern Europe* (London: Routledge, 2001), pp. 80–118.

10 Rollins, 'Black-Letter Broadside Ballad', p. 265.

11 M. A. Shaaber, *Some Forerunners of the Newspaper in England, 1476–1622* (Philadelphia: University of Pennsylvania Press, 1929), p. 193.

12 Würzbach, *Rise of the English Street Ballad*, pp. 147 and 235.

13 See for example Ian Atherton, 'The Itch Grown a Disease: Manuscript Transmission of News in the Seventeenth Century', in Joad Raymond (ed.), *News, Newspapers, and Society in Early Modern Britain* (London: F. Cass, 1999), p. 39; Pettegree, *Invention of News*, p. 10; Raymond, 'News', p. 378.

14 Rospocher and Salzburg, 'Evanescent Public Sphere', p. 105; Massimo Rospocher and Rosa Salzburg, 'Street Singers in Italian Renaissance Urban Culture and Communication', *Cultural and Social History*, 9:1 (2012), p. 15.

15 Kate Van Orden, 'Cheap Print and Street Song Following the Saint Batholomew's Massacres of 1572', in Kate Van Orden (ed.), *Music and the Cultures of Print* (London: Garland, 2000), p. 273.

16 Henk de Vries, 'Ballads, Literature, and Historical Fact - ("Voces Corren", "Celestina, Don Quijote")', *Jahrbuch für Volksliedforschung*, 44 (1999), p. 13.

17 Angela McShane, 'The Gazet in Metre; or the Riming Newsmonger: The Broadside Ballad as Intelligencer. A New Narrative', in Joop W. Koopmans (ed.), *News and Politics in Early Modern Europe 1500–1800* (Leuven: Peeters, 2005), p. 140.

18 Angela McShane, 'Ballads and Broadsides', in Joad Raymond (ed.), *The Oxford History of Popular Print Culture, Vol. 1, Cheap Print in Britain and Ireland to 1660* (Oxford: Oxford University Press, 2011), pp. 361–2.

19 McShane, 'Gazet in Metre', p. 145.

20 R. B., *A new balade entituled as foloweth. To such as write in metres, I write of small matters an exhortation, by readyng of which, men may delite in such as be worthy commendation. My verse also it hath relation to such as print, that they doe it well, the better they shall their metres sell. And when we haue doen al that ever we can, let vs neuer seke prayse at the mouth of man* (London, 1570), STC (2nd ed.) / 1058.

21 Raymond, *Pamphlets and Pamphleteering*, p. 105.

22 William Gibson, *A discription of Nortons falcehod of Yorke shyre, and of his fatall farewel The fatal fine of traitours loe: by iustice due, deseruyng soe* (London, 1570), STC (2nd ed.) / 11843; John Heywood, *A Balade specifienge partly the maner, partly the matter, in the most excellent meetyng and lyke Mariage betwene our Soueraigne Lord and our Soueraigne Lady, the Kynges and Queenes Highnes* (London, 1554), STC (2nd ed.) / 13290.3.

23 William Elderton, *The true fourme and shape of a monsterous chyld, whiche was borne in Stony Stratforde, in North Hampton shire The yeare of our Lord, M.CCCCC.LXV* (London, 1565), STC (2nd ed.) / 7565.

24 Alexandra Walsham, *Providence in Early Modern England* (Oxford: Oxford University Press, 1999), p. 33.

25 *L&P* xiii, SP 1/130 ff. 150^r–150^v, p. 225, no. 615, 'The Royal Supremacy, 28 March 1538'.

26 Shakespeare, *The Winter's Tale*, V.ii.20–5.

27 Shakespeare, *Winter's Tale*, IV.iv.273–9.

28 Shakespeare, *Winter's Tale*, IV.iv.281–2. On the characters' attitudes to the truth of Autolycus's ballads: Frances E. Dolan, 'Mopsa's Method: Truth Claims, Ballads, and Print', *Huntington Library Quarterly*, 79:2 (2016), pp. 173–85.

29 Shakespeare, *Winter's Tale*, IV.iv.260–5.

30 C. J. Ferdinand, 'Newspapers and the Sale of Books in the Provinces', in Michael F. Suarez and Michael L. Turner (eds.), *The Cambridge History of the Book in Britain* (6 vols. Cambridge: Cambridge University Press, 2009), iv, pp. 434–5.

31 See Fox, *Oral and Literate Culture*, Chapter 7.

32 Adam Fox, 'Rumour, News and Popular Political Opinion in Elizabethan and Early Stuart England', *Historical Journal*, 40:3 (1997), p. 598.

33 For a slightly later example of the detail which can be found in ballads, see Marotti and May, 'Two Lost Ballads of the Armada Thanksgiving'. This article also brings to the fore the links between ballads in manuscript, print, and the oral tradition.

34 Thomas Watertoune, *A Ninuectyue Agaynst Treason* (London, 1553), STC (2nd ed.) / 25105.

35 Henry Machyn, *The diary of Henry Machyn: Citizen and Merchant-Taylor of London*, ed. J.G. Nichols (London: Camden Society, 1848), old series, xlii, p. 37. On the nature of Machyn's diary, see Gary Gibbs, 'Marking the Days: Henry Machyn's Manuscript and the Mid-Tudor Era', in Eamon Duffy and David M. Loades (eds.), *The Church of Mary Tudor* (Aldershot: Ashgate, 2006), pp. 281–308; Ian Mortimer, 'Tudor Chronicler or Sixteenth-Century Diarist? Henry Machyn and the Nature of His Manuscript', *Sixteenth Century Journal*, 33:4 (2002), pp. 981–98.

36 Pettegree, *Invention of News*, p. 8.

37 Paul Griffiths, Adam Fox, and Steve Hindle, 'Introduction', in Paul Griffiths, Adam Fox, and Steve Hindle (eds.), *The Experience of Authority in Early Modern England* (Basingstoke: Macmillan, 1996), p. 1.

38 Martin Ingram, 'The Reformation of Manners in Early Modern England', in Paul Griffiths, Adam Fox, and Steve Hindle (eds.), *The Experience of Authority in Early Modern England* (Basingstoke: Macmillan, 1996), p. 48.

39 Raymond, 'News', pp. 378–9.

40 Raymond, *Pamphlets and Pamphleteering*. On the development of news and pamphleteering during the Civil War, see Jason McElligott, *Royalism, Print and Censorship in Revolutionary England* (Woodbridge: Boydell Press, 2007); Jason Peacey, *Politicians and Pamphleteers: Propaganda During the English Civil Wars and Interregnum* (Aldershot: Ashgate, 2004); Jason Peacey, *The Print Culture of Parliament, 1600–1800* (Edinburgh: Edinburgh University Press for the Parliamentary History Yearbook Trust, 2007).

41 Carolyn Nelson and Matthew Seccombe, 'The Creation of the Periodical Press 1620–1695', in Michael F. Suarez and Michael L. Turner (eds.), *The Cambridge History of the Book in Britain* (6 vols. Cambridge: Cambridge University Press, 2009), iv, pp. 533–5.

42 For an account of the Rising in the North, see K. J. Kesselring, *The Northern Rebellion of 1569: Faith, Politics and Protest in Elizabethan England* (Basingstoke: Palgrave Macmillan, 2007). On the polemical literature of the period, see James King Lowers, *Mirrors for Rebels: A Study of Polemical Literature Relating to the Northern Rebellion, 1569* (Berkeley: University of California Press, 1953).

43 Edward Wilson-Lee, 'The Bull and the Moon: Broadside Ballads and the Public Sphere at the Time of the Northern Rising (1569–70)', *Review of English Studies*, 63:259 (2012), pp. 230–2.

44 William Elderton, *Newes from Northumberland* (London, 1570), London, Society of Antiquaries, Book of Broadsides, STC (2nd ed.) / 7560; William Elderton, *A ballat Intituled Northomberland newes* (London, 1570) STC (2nd ed.) / 7554; William Kirkham, *Ioyfull newes for true subiectes, to God and the Crowne the rebelles are cooled, their bragges be put downe. Come humble ye downe, come humble ye downe, perforce now submyt ye: to the Queen and the Crowne* (London, 1570), STC (2nd ed.) / 15015. This use of 'news language' has also been highlighted by Wilson-Lee, 'Bull and the Moon', p. 232.

45 Peele, *letter to Rome*; Preston, *Lamentation from Rome*.

46 Wilson-Lee, 'Bull and the Moon', pp. 231 onwards.

47 Elderton, *ballat intituled Northomberland newes*.

48 Kesselring, *Northern Rebellion of 1569*, p. 8.

49 *CSPDom*, xv 24, SP 15/15, f. 43, p. 107, 'Earl of Sussex and four others of the Council of the North to the Queen, 15 November 1569'.

50 *A Ballad Reioysinge the Sodaine Fall, of Rebels That Thought to Deuower Vs All* (London, 1570), STC (2nd ed.) / 1326.

51 Kirkham, *Ioyfull newes for true subiectes*.

52 Elderton, *Newes from Northumberland*.

53 K. J. Kesselring, 'Mercy and Liberality: The Aftermath of the 1569 Northern Rebellion', *History*, 90:298 (2005), p. 230. See also Kesselring, *Northern Rebellion of 1569*, pp. 136–41.

54 Preston, *Lamentation from Rome*.

55 Elderton, *A newe well a daye*.

56 John N. King, *Tudor Royal Iconography: Literature and Art in an Age of Religious Crisis* (Guildford: Princeton University Press, 1989); Kevin Sharpe, *Selling the Tudor Monarchy: Authority and Image in Sixteenth-Century England* (London: Yale University Press, 2009).

57 William Cornwallis, *Essayes* (London, 1601), STC (2nd ed.) / 5775, sig. I7[r].

58 John Barnard, 'Introduction', in John Barnard and D. F. Mckenzie (ed.), *The Cambridge History of the Book in Britain* (6 vols. Cambridge: Cambridge University Press, 1998), iv, p. 3.

59 *L&P* xi, SP 1/113 f. 58, p. 556, no. 1403, 'Richard Oldfelden to his son Philip, 1536'; *L&P* xii, p. 181, no. 389, 'Carriage of Letters, 10 February 1537'.

60 William Griffith registered a ballad entitled *the hunte is vp &c* in 1569–70 (*TRCS*, i, p. 417). For more on the variant forms of the tune 'The Hunt is Up', see John M. Ward, 'The Hunt's Up', *Proceedings of the Royal Musical Association*, 106 (1979), pp. 1–25.

61 George Puttenham, *The arte of English poesie contriued into three bookes: the first of poets and poesie, the second of proportion, the third of ornament* (London, 1589), STC (2nd ed.) / 20519.5.

62 FSL V.a.159, f. 12[r].

63 London, British Library Add. MS 15233, John Thorne, *The Hunt ys Up*, ff. 33[r]–34[v]. The initial anacrusis is editorial in order to accommodate the words. The ear would hear a D as the first note of each of the first two bars: the upward leap to the D above is here purely editorial, but as well as being in keeping with later versions of the tune, it has a much greater impact than dropping to the lower D. The B at the beginning of bar 3 has been extended from a quaver to a crotchet (also in keeping with later sources) and is a natural progression of the tune. Likewise, the final note of the tune has been set to the home note, D, as the F sharp is likely to form part of the accompaniment.

64 Louise Rayment, 'A Note on the Date of London, British Library, Additional Manuscript 15233', *Notes and Queries*, 59:1 (2012), pp. 32–4. For more

on the social connections of the contributors to this manuscript, see
Louise Rayment, 'A Study in Sixteenth-Century Performance and Artistic
Networks: British Library, Additional Manuscript 15233', PhD Thesis, Uni-
versity of Southampton, 2011. A transcription of and commentary on 'The
Hunt ys Up' appears at p. 184.

65 *L&P* xii, SP 1/116 f. 30, p. 206, no. 424, 'Seditious Songs [15 Feb.] 1537'.
66 K. J. Kesselring, *Mercy and Authority in the Tudor State* (Cambridge: Cambridge University Press, 2003), pp. 168–9.
67 Richard W. Hoyle, *The Pilgrimage of Grace and the Politics of the 1530s*
(Oxford: Oxford University Press, 2001), pp. 274–88.
68 *L&P* xii, SP 1/116 f. 92, p. 226, no. 479, 'Henry VIII to the Duke of Norfolk,
22 Feb 1537'.

6 'Of popyshnes and heresye'
Political Ballads and the Fall of Thomas Cromwell

Trolle on away, trolle on awaye
Syng heaue and howe rombelowe trolle on awaye.

Bothe man and chylde is glad to here tell
Of that false traytoure Thomas Crumwel
Nowe that he is set to spell[1]

Synge trolle on awaye, trolle on awaye
Syng heaue and howe rombelowe trolle on awaye.[2]

In 1540, a series of 11 ballads and pamphlets examined the biggest news story of the year: the sudden fall from grace of Henry VIII's chief minister and vicegerent in spirituals, Thomas Cromwell, Earl of Essex. These ballads took the form of a flyting of verse libels in which the poets abused each other with rhyming invective. It is possible that it was the speed at which a ballad could be produced that attracted the authors to that particular medium. After all, the events of summer 1540 were fast-paced: Cromwell was taken to the Tower on 10 June 1540; Henry VIII's marriage to Anne of Cleves was annulled on 9 July; Henry married Catherine Howard on the day of Cromwell's execution, 28 July. Nevertheless, broadsides were not an expensive medium, so we might assume that these songs were available to the socially mixed, popular audience that ballads are known to have attracted.[3] Furthermore, if the authors did not anticipate a wide and diverse audience, they could have circulated the ballads in manuscript rather than going to the effort of having them printed. Manuscript would surely have been quicker than setting a press for printing, unless a wide circulation was a pre-requisite. It is possible that the ballads were mass-produced to give away, but it seems much more likely that they were sold, especially as the Cromwell flyting was not the only example of its kind in the mid-Tudor period. During the 1550s, a flyting between Thomas Churchyard and Thomas Camel was so popular that it eventually resulted in the publication of an anthology. Clearly, there was an audience for this sort of print contention, so it is reasonable to believe that the Cromwell ballads had a wide audience.

This chapter provides the first of my two case studies of the way in which the development of a major political event was presented in cheap print. It first explains why I consider these items of print to be ballads even though there is no indication of their tunes. It then tracks the progress of the flyting and examines some of the significant themes that it brought to light. Throughout the chapter, the focus is on how implicitness created a space for debate by protecting the authors from prosecution.

Broadsides to Be Sung

The high level of erudition displayed by the ballads might make us question whether they were actually intended for performance as songs.[4] Although none of the ballads names a tune, most have refrains and at least eight were printed as black-letter broadsides in the same style as other known songs so it is highly likely that they were intended to be sung. Eight of the ballads include the word 'troll', which refers to singing jovially, with gusto, in the manner of a child's nursery rhyme. While the biblical marginalia perhaps relate to reading rather than singing, we must remember that the broadside ballad was a multimedia source; in no way does such marginalia preclude singing and these ballads were not the only ones to include them.

Furthermore, it is possible that several of the ballads were con-trafacta. They have the same or very similar metrical patterns that could easily fit the same tune and, as we have seen, the recycling of the melody would immediately remind a knowing audience of previous lyrics. In Figures 6.1–6.3, the first verse of each of the first three entries in the flyting has been set to the contemporary tune 'Half Hannikin'.[5] These are, of course, only conjectural settings, as no tunes are indicated on the broadsides; however, 'Half Hannikin' seems a particularly suitable tune to use for these songs given that the name Hannikin or Hankin was used for several literary clowns and the term 'hankin booby' was one of abuse. A tune by that name certainly existed by 1537.[6] These musical examples clearly show how a single tune could be adapted to accommodate the words of the different songs. It is a simple, child-like, lilting melody in compound time, with lots of repetitive phrases. It is in a major key and covers a range of only six notes. The short phrases with dotted rhythms are perfect for hurling insults, with each line of the lyrics only taking two bars of music. The first phrase of music fits naturally to the refrain of *A newe Balade made of Thomas Crumwel*, while the line 'Synge trolle on away' is also a perfect fit for the final phrase when the words are repeated (bars 11–12). In Figure 6.2, the rhythms have been altered slightly to suit the scansion of the lyrics of the second song, *A balade agaynst malycyous Sclaunderers.* The final two bars of music have been repeated because the verse is five lines long but there is no suggested extra refrain. In Figure 6.3, bars 5–8 are repeated because the verse of the third ballad, *A lytell treatyse agaynst Sedicyous persons*, has seven lines. Further rhythmic alterations are also required, including an anacrusis at the start. Although these seem substantial alterations when described in this way, in fact, they come as second nature to someone who sings this type of music.[7]

Figure 6.1 Conjectural setting of *A newe Balade made of Thomas Crumwel* from *Reliques of Ancient English Poetry: Consisting of Old Heroic Ballads, Songs, and Other Pieces of Our Earlier Poets (Chiefly of the Lyric Kind.) Together with Some Few of Later Date. The Second Edition*, Ed. Bishop Percy (3 vols. London: J. Dodsley, 1765; repr. London: J.M. Dent & Sons, 1906), p. 327, to 'Half Hannikin' from Playford's *English dancing master* (London, 1651).

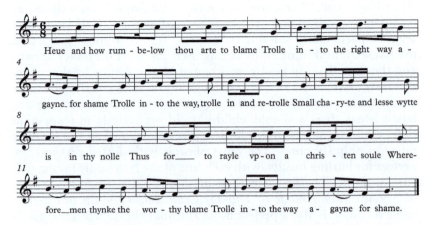

Figure 6.2 Conjectural setting of *A balade agaynst malycyous Sclaunderers* (London, 1540) to 'Half Hannikin'.

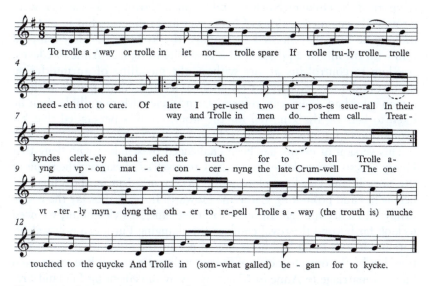

To trolle a - way or trolle in let not___ trolle spare If trolle tru-ly trolle_ trolle

4 need - eth not to care. Of late I per-used two pur - pos-es seue-rall In their way and Trolle in men do___ them call___ Treat -

7 kyndes clerk-ely hand - eled the truth for to tell Trolle a-
yng vp - on mat - er con - cer - nyng the late Crum-well The one

9 vt - ter -ly myn - dyng the oth - er to re-pell Trolle a - way (the trouth is) muche

12 touched to the quycke And Trolle in (som-what galled) be - gan for to kycke.

Figure 6.3 Conjectural setting of Thomas Smyth's *A lytell treatyse agaynst Sedicyous persons* (London, 1540) to 'Half Hannikin'.

Themes in the Flyting

The ballad flyting debated the nature of reforms to the church, with each side attacking the other as treacherous. Alongside the concerns about the unity of the Henrician church, the songs used Cromwell's fall from grace to attack new men at court, questioning the monarch's choice of political advisers. That this took place in the public arena of print suggests that there was a significant level of political debate both at court and in the streets, despite the regime's attempts to prevent the discussion of matters of state. Furthermore, none of this comment was aimed at Henry himself. It did not form part of the familiar trope of counselling a king and none of the known protagonists were members of the Privy Council, who might have been allowed to discuss matters of state and advise the king on policy. Instead, the discussion took place among courtiers and presumably, through the medium of cheap print, it even spread through London's streets. The main theme of the flyting was a debate over the nature of Henry's religious reforms and what constituted orthodox religious belief, but it also brought in aspects of citizenship: who had a right to advise the king, and whose responsibility it was to be a counsellor?

Although the ballads soon degenerated into mud-slinging and sectarianism, they responded both to one another and to the rapid changes occurring at court, discussing Cromwell's crimes in some detail. For many years, scholars were heavily influenced by Geoffrey Elton's account of these eventful months: Cromwell's sudden fall was a result of trickery on the part of the Duke of Norfolk and Stephen Gardiner. These men were Cromwell's enemies, jealous of his power and influence, but in order to undermine him they needed to manage the king's ego. They tempted him with the alluring prospect of a new wife to replace Anne of Cleves, freedom to control his affairs without the meddling of an interfering upstart and a new chance for religious unity among his people without a man who had dangerous reformist tendencies. More gullible than he liked to believe, the king fell for the story. He was persuaded that his promotion of Cromwell had in fact 'nurtured a Sacramentarian viper'.[8]

This version of events has been challenged by scholars who deny that Henry was so manipulable. For them, Cromwell's fall was not the result of the Norfolk and Gardiner plotting the vicegerent's demise, spreading malicious lies and promoting Catherine Howard. Instead, they lay the blame firmly on Henry himself. In order to understand this viewpoint, we need to look far beyond the royal court to the changing European political situation. Henry's mind had been altered not by the influence of court faction, but by the outside factor of foreign policy. Cromwell had engineered Henry's marriage to Anne of Cleves as a way of cementing England's relationship with the Lutheran states in Europe against an alliance between the Roman Catholic powers. Although the wedding had only taken place in January 1540, by June, the rapport between the Roman Catholic French and German monarchs which posed such a threat to English security had cooled. Henry was beginning to regret his marriage to Anne in its own terms, famously referring to her as 'the Flanders mare', while the Lutheran alliance which it represented had become 'a disposable commodity'.[9] The easiest way for the king to extract himself from the unwanted marriage was to remove Cromwell. Moreover, if Henry achieved this by allowing Cromwell to fall victim to the allegations made by his enemies rather than directly dismissing him from the earldom of Essex, he could avoid the embarrassing admission that he had made a mistake elevating this commoner in the first place. Whatever the true cause of his disgrace, Cromwell was charged with 'most detestable treasons'.[10] It was only later, in the final Act of Attainder, that the specific charge of sacramentarianism was laid upon him.[11] It is this charge of denying the Real Presence of Christ's body and blood in the bread and wine of the Eucharist that is central to the ballads.

Controlling Discussion

The ballads, then, debated matters at the heart of Henry's religious policy. What did it mean to be a Protestant or a papist? What were acceptable beliefs for an Englishman to hold? These were confused matters, because although the Pope no longer had authority over the English church, that church was not actually Protestant. It could be difficult to know what you were supposed to believe. This was precisely the sort of discussion that Henry's regime sought to curb, especially as it fell against a background of increased religious anxiety. At the time that these ballads were written, English fear of imminent invasion from the continent was at its height. The previous year, in Lent 1539, Bishop Tunstall of Durham had preached a sermon against papal authority that presented the religious issue in simple terms: if the English did not unite behind Henry's reformed Catholicism, foreigners would take advantage of the dissonance. Tunstall threatened that the Pope was plotting an invasion of England. Foreigners would steal English money, plate and goods, then distribute them amongst themselves. They would drive out English cattle to be sold. But, more frighteningly, their treatment of the English themselves would be even worse:

> And thou mayste be sure to be slayne, for they wylle not suffer the nor none of thy progeny to lyue to make any clayme afterward, or to be reuenged, for that were theyr vnsuertie. Thy wyfe shall be abused before thy face, thy doughter likewise defloured before the. thy chyldern slayne before thyne eyes.[12]

Tunstall alleged that Cardinal Pole, who had been a prominent opponent of Henry's divorce of Catherine of Aragon and was currently in self-imposed exile, was being used by the Pope as an emissary to incite continental rulers to declare war on England. This inflammatory language was intended to frighten people into support for the king and his religious settlement, the Act of Six Articles. Originally referred to as an act to end diversity in religion, it was an attempt to restore unity to a church in flux, a church in which the twin issues of religious controversy and foreign policy had combined to cause confusion and dissension. It laid out the central doctrines of Henry's church, which were actually essentially Catholic in nature. A royal proclamation of 1539 demanded an end to the scorn with which Protestants treated others, and the excessive superstition which was associated with popery. Henry's subjects were ordered to keep the rites and ceremonies of the English church and

> neyther by dede worde ne behauyour despice these ceremonyes afore mencioned, nor supersticiously abuse them, nor any of them, as they woll auoyde his maiesties moste greuouse indignation and displeasure.[13]

Despite the Six Articles and the regime's repeated efforts to make its position clear, there was still discord in the realm. It was a cause of disquiet, and the 'stryfe' between Smyth and Gray was representative of the religious dissonance not only in England but in Europe as a whole.[14] It is hardly surprising that discussion of these matters was something that Henry VIII sought to avoid.

Censoring Debate

Although various models of early modern press censorship have been posited by scholars in recent years, one thing is clear: efforts to control the outputs of the London presses were haphazard and irregular. Visions of censorship as equally reliant on the author and the law have been criticised for making too many assumptions. One was that censorship operated in the same across the whole early modern period. Another assumption was that the term censorship was self-explanatory and did not require any further definition.[15] With regard to the Cromwell flyting, it is perhaps more helpful to focus on the broader question of transgressive language: words which sought to challenge official attempts to control what people discussed. This model of censorship is closely related to the language of defamation.[16] The sort of slander exemplified by these ballads, based on religious beliefs and occupational stereotypes, had the 'perceived capacity to subvert existing social hierarchies'. Models of censorship nevertheless varied over time as a response not only to the perceived threat from both home and abroad, and shifting political circumstances, but also to changes in the regime's ability to enforce its own rules.[17] Nevertheless, Annabel Patterson's suggestion that 'functional ambiguity' allowed authors to encode their opinions in order to avoid a direct confrontation with authority might help us to understand how implicitness helped to protect the authors of the Cromwell ballads.[18]

The Cromwell flyting was published at a time when the regime felt vulnerable. Henry's marital and dynastic difficulties, coupled with his moves to change the country's religion, caused embarrassing public displays of criticism. This sensitivity was made manifest in the 1534 Treason Act, which allowed the regime to deal effectively with those who spoke out against the king and his family or who disavowed the Act of Supremacy.[19] The real significance of the 1534 legislation, drawn up by Cromwell, was that the spoken word, as well as printed words and physical acts, was now formally recognised as treasonable. In effect, the Treason Act had the power to silence anyone who dared to indulge in loose talk about the king or his reformation of the church. In suppressing any opposition, treason law promoted *de facto* unity within Henry's reformed church. It also forced the Cromwell balladeers to rely on implicitness in order to protect themselves from the consequences of discussing popishness and heresy in cheap print.

Ballads and the Public Sphere

The ballads contributed to a temporary or proto-public sphere which discussed religious identities and divisions, as well as court rivalries.[20] They formed an early example of disagreement and debate between opposing groups within the regime. The songs, however, did not have the authority of being commissioned by the regime, nor were they legitimised by the time-honoured trope of counselling the monarch. Instead, they bore witness to a sophisticated and apparently independent debate about issues at the heart of Henrician government, a debate that, presumably through music, played out among the people.

As the men who wrote them were close to the government, they might be expected to have intimate knowledge of what had been happening at court. Several of the pro-Cromwell ballads were written by one William Gray. Given his rather bald description in the Privy Council records as 'so[m]tyme s[er]v[a]nt to the late Lord Crumwell' it seems unlikely that this was the same William, Lord Gray de Wilton who was Lieutenant of Hammes in the Calais pale, despite his obvious leanings towards the reformed faith.[21] Instead, it seems that he was the same Gray who was popular at Henry's court for writing *The Hunt is Up*. He was a former monk who had given over his Catholic vocation in favour of Protestant teachings and would go on to become MP for Reading in 1547.[22] Gray later presented poems as New Year's gifts to the Protestant Protector Somerset.[23] Other balladeers who took part in the flyting, however, prove more elusive. Thomas Smyth is, of course, a very common name, making a positive identification extremely difficult. Styling himself 'clerke of the Queenes graces counsell', the queen in question was Catherine Howard.[24] It seems quite possible, then, that Smyth had only been in his post for a short time. The Queen's Council had existed as an administrative body since the medieval period. Its function was to administer the queen's landholdings, primarily those lands given as part of her dowry on her marriage to the king. The council also had a judicial function in dealing with disputes between the queen's tenants.[25]

It is possible that Smyth was in attendance at court prior to his association with Queen Catherine Howard's council. During investigations into the clandestine betrothal of the Duke of Norfolk's younger brother, Lord Thomas Howard, with the king's niece, Lady Margaret Douglas, in 1536, one Thomas Smyth gave evidence about the affair. His statement simply says that he saw Lord Thomas 'reasorte vnto [Lady Margaret]... div[er]se tymes in somuche that he wold watche tyl my lady bulleyn was goon and thenne stele in to her chamber'.[26] It is not possible to tell from the record how he knew about the affair, whether he was in fact in Anne Boleyn's household or Lord Thomas's.[27] It would be quite plausible to suggest that Smyth was Thomas Howard's servant, as Lady Margaret later had to dismiss two of his former servants from her own employ. She claimed that she had taken them in after her husband's death 'ffor the poverty that I saw them in'.[28] It is possible that the two servants that she had taken on were the two who were examined – Smyth and John Ashley. If Thomas Smyth had been in Howard's household rather than Anne Boleyn's, this would put him among religious conservatives at court. Norfolk was one of Cromwell's enemies. Even if Smyth were part of Queen Anne's household (could he have been clerk to that queen's council too?), by the time of her execution she was part of the group ranged against Cromwell at court.

Conversely, it is unlikely that the balladeer Smyth was the Sir Thomas Smyth who would become Secretary of State under Elizabeth I. During the period of May 1540 to January 1542, that man was travelling on the continent between Orléans, Paris and Padua. Meanwhile, the participants in the flyting were summoned to appear before the Privy Council in January 1541 and were subsequently imprisoned in the Fleet.[29] What is more, there is no evidence that the man who would become Elizabeth's secretary held a position as the clerk of the Queen's Council at this time. He is not known to have had such a close association with the court until 1547, under the Protectorate of the Duke of Somerset. A letter preserved in the State Papers was sent from a Thomas Harvard to a Thomas Smyth in March 1538, but there is no further evidence to the identity of either of these characters.[30] In 1542, a 'citizen and mercer of London' named Thomas Smith was owed £30 by a chapman named Nicholas Warde of Ocliff in Surrey.[31] Chapmen were petty merchants and pedlars, who were often associated with the selling of ballads and small books, but it seems unlikely that this Smith was the balladeer, because he is described as a merchant rather than a clerk.

What is clear, however, is that neither Smyth nor Gray was among the privileged few with access to a legitimate space to debate these issues. Instead, they audaciously attacked each other in a public sphere that used music to spread its message. In discussing the implications of religious reforms among themselves, the courtiers responsible for the ballads and pamphlet spread information around court and beyond. This flyting provided news and comment for the Tudor audience, but it also clearly shows evidence of a discussion of current affairs and matters of state taking place in the public domain. This might be considered a temporary public sphere, created to debate a matter so significant and exciting that it was of interest to a much wider community than that of the court or parliament. The songs might conveniently be seen as echoes of the debates which took place in official circles.[32]

Disrespecting Cromwell

The ballad that sparked the explosive exchange was called *A newe Balade made of Thomas Crumwel, called, Trolle on Away*. Although it was published anonymously, it was written by Thomas Smyth, who attempted to prove his loyalty to the 'redolent rose' Henry VIII by denouncing Thomas Cromwell. His song is missing from the collection in the Society of Antiquaries, London, but it was found in manuscript by Bishop Percy and published as part of his *Reliques of Ancient English Poetry*.[33] Each of its 16 verses has a rhyme scheme of AAA and a metrical pattern of 9.9.7, while the refrain has a rhyme scheme of BB with a metrical pattern of 9.11. Throughout the verse and chorus, there are four stressed beats in each line.

Thomas Smyth stated his position immediately: Cromwell was a false traitor. What is more, he expected his audience to share the opinion that 'bothe man and chylde is glad to here tell'. He accused Thomas Cromwell of being a 'false heretycke' 'of the newe trycke' who 'hast bene so longe a scysmatyke'. Schism divided one from the established church, undermining the religious harmony that Henry sought to promote. The song must have been written before Cromwell's execution on 28 July 1540. Even though the inclusion of the sacramentarianism charge in the ballad suggests that the song was not written until after the Bill of Attainder was introduced to the House of Lords on 17 June, several phrases hint that Cromwell was still alive. The singer invited Cromwell to 'lay downe thy heade vpon this blocke'.

Alluding to the charge of sacramentarianism in Cromwell's attainder, Smyth stated that 'Both sacramentes and sacramentalles / Thou woldest not suffre within thy walles'. The denial of the Real Presence in the Eucharist was a view so extreme that even most Protestant reformers found it unacceptable. Only the Zwinglians denied that the bread and wine became the body and blood of Christ when consecrated in the Eucharist. The first of the Six Articles reinforced the importance of the Real Presence as a tenet of Henrician Catholicism:

> that in the most blessed Sacrament of the Aulter, by the strengthe and efficacy of Christ[es] myghtie worde, it beinge spoken by the prest, is p[re]sent really, under the forme of bread and wyne, the naturall bodye and bloode of our Saviour Jesu Criste, conceyved of the Virgin Marie, and that after the consecrac[i]on there remayneth noe substance of bread or wyne, nor any other substance, but the substance of Criste, God and man.[34]

The implicit references to historical and newsworthy individuals in the ballads also relate to the second major theme in the songs: Henry's promotion of new men. The contrast between humble background and high office is apparent throughout the flyting. It obviously caused a great deal of resentment on one side and self-justification on the other. Cromwell's attainder foregrounded his enemies' objections to his base origins. It acknowledged that Henry had 'elected chosen and made divers as well of yo[ur] nobles as others to be of yo[ur] moste honorable Counsell, as to the hono[ur] of noble prince app[er]teynethe'.[35] Even so, the act was at pains to re-emphasise Cromwell's low birth at every opportunity. It described

> Thomas Crumwell now Erle of Essex, whome yo[ur] ma[jes]tie tooke and receaved into yo[ur] trustie service, The same Thomas then beinge a man of very base and lowe degree, and for singuler favor trust and confydence, w[hi]ch yo[ur] ma[jes]tie beere, and had in him did not only advaunce the same Thomas vnto the Estate of an

Erle and enriched him w[i]th manifolde giftes as well of goodes as of
Landes and offices, but also him the said Thomas Crumwell Erle of
Essex did elect and make one of yo[ur] moste trustie Counsellors, as
well concerninge yo[ur] Graces supreme iurisdic[i]ons Eccle[siastic]
all, as yo[ur] moste high secret affaires temporall.[36]

Cromwell had been raised to Earl of Essex in April 1540, just weeks
before his death. Yet throughout the Cromwell flyting, he was referred
to only as 'Lord Cromwell' by both sides, suggesting that the promotion
was considered to have been a mistake. What is impossible, given that
two of the participants in the flyting are known to have had court connections, is that they were unaware of his change of designation.

Indeed, the flyting drew heavily on the recent Act of Attainder, which
had described Cromwell as 'a p[er]son of as lowe degree as fewe be
w[i]thin this yo[ur] Realme'.[37] *Trolle on Away* included a similar personal attack on the vicegerent, suggesting that he owed his position to
fortune rather than birthright. Cromwell's low parentage was not only
well known, it was used as a source of ridicule. Cromwell's father was a
brewer and fuller. An allusion to Cromwell's parentage appeared in verse
14 when Smyth suggested that 'Thou myghtest haue learned thy cloth
to flocke / Upon thy gresy fullers stocke'. 'Greasy' was a conveniently
double-edged offensive epithet. Fulling was a process that felted woollen
cloth through the action of repeated beatings either by the fuller's feet or
a stock powered by a water mill. Urine was used to remove the grease,
lanolin and other impurities from the cloth. Smyth claimed that the king
was moved by 'petye and made the hys seuyture'. The idea that Henry
VIII's promotion of Cromwell had been motivated by pity is laughable.
Instead, the suggestion served to insult Cromwell, insinuating that he had
only achieved his position at court through the king's magnanimity.

Opposition to Cromwell, of course, had been longstanding. During the
Pilgrimage of Grace in 1536, grievances around religion, politics and the
economy had fused together in an attack on Cromwell's power and influence
over the king. *Trolle on Away* reflected similar suspicions that Cromwell
had abused his position by purloining revenue from the dissolution of the
monasteries in order to line his own pockets: 'Thy cofers with golde thou
fyllydst a pace', and 'Both plate and chalys came to thy fyst / Thou lockyst
them vp where no man wyst / Tyll in the Kynges treasure suche thinges
were myst'. Likewise, the Act of Attainder described how Cromwell

acquired and obteyned into his possession by oppression brybery
extort power and false promises made by him to yo[ur] subiect[es]
of yo[ur] Realme Innumerable somes of money and Treasure and
benige [sic] so inriched hath had yo[ur] Nobles of your Realme in
great disdayne derision and detestac[i]on and by expresse wordes by
him moste approbrously spoken hath appeared.[38]

Defending Cromwell

Trolle on Away provoked William Gray to write anonymously in support of Cromwell. His song was entitled *A balade agaynst malycyous Sclaunderers* (although it is also known as *Trolle In*). Despite echoing the first ballad, it has verses of five lines rather than three, with an AAABB rhyme pattern, and a further rhyming couplet for a refrain. Like *Trolle on Away*, *A balade agaynst malycyous Sclaunderers* has four stressed syllables in each line, so although the scansion is different, *A balade agaynst malycyous Sclaunderers* could have fitted the same tune as *Trolle on Away* if two phrases of music (perhaps the first two of the verse) were repeated. *A balade agaynst malycyous Sclaunderers* was written after 28 July 1540, because Gray's comment that 'this mortal life, full godly he ended' shows that Cromwell had already been executed.[39]

Reprising *Trolle on Away*'s insistence that the king was merciful, *A balade agaynst malycyous Sclaunderers* nevertheless contradicted Smyth, claiming instead that Cromwell's rise to vicegerent was a just reward for his abilities. According to Gray, rather than being motivated by pity, Henry had recognised Cromwell's aptitude: despite the fact that 'of byrth [he] were but bace / yet he was set up of the kynges noble grace'.

Even though he was writing in Cromwell's defence, his former client Gray was forced to acknowledge that Cromwell was a traitor. He suggested that 'the kynge of his grace / Hath forgyven him that gret trespas'. If this were true, it begs the question of how the author knew. If, on the other hand, it were merely conjecture, it would surely risk serious consequences for the author if his identity were revealed. Furthermore, if Cromwell had been forgiven for his offence by the king, why had he been executed? There is some evidence to suggest that Henry quickly regretted the loss of his trusted minister. For example, as Cromwell's son Gregory was made a baron, he must have been restored in the blood.[40] Still, Gray's belief that Cromwell would be exonerated is intriguing because the rest of the ballad seems to have been written after Cromwell's execution. Perhaps it was an expression of hope that in time Cromwell's memory would be rehabilitated, a process that Gray hoped to begin.

Like Cromwell at his execution, Gray was forced to concede that because 'the law he hath offended / By the lawe he is iustly condempned', but he also claimed that 'This mortall lyfe / full godly he ended'. Furthermore, the evangelicals needed to maintain the fiction that Henry was being held back by the religious conservatives around him. Gray described how Cromwell asked forgiveness not only of God and the king, but also the world at large: 'no man', even if his name were Thomas Smyth, was able to deny the forgiveness that God was pleased to give.

Protestants held strong views on obedience, so they needed to maintain and promote the belief that the king, in the long run, was on their side. The ballad represents not only an attempt to begin the process of rehabilitating Cromwell's memory, but also, by stressing evangelical loyalty to the king, it helped to keep open the lines of communication between the king and his more reformist subjects.[41]

Moreover, Cromwell's followers were keen to absolve their patron from the charge of sacramentarianism, not least because it reflected badly on them. Cromwell's close links with a group of English scholars who visited Zwingli's successor, Heinrich Bullinger, indicated that his personal theology was probably that of a Zurich-style sacramentarian.[42] But if Cromwell were a sacramentarian, then Gray, as his client, was at risk of a similar fate to that of his benefactor. Instead, it was safer to argue, as Cromwell himself had done, that

> The sacrament of the aulter, that is most hyest
> Crumwell beleued it to be the very body of Chriest
> Wherfore in thy writing, on him thou lyest
> For the kynge & his counsell wyll wytnesse the same.[43]

The third ballad in the series, *A lytell treatyse agaynst Sedicyous persons*, continued this theme of Cromwell's sacramentarianism. The author, Thomas Smyth, commented that 'Trolle away tolde trouth... / Declaryng the offence, wherin Crumwell offended'.[44] This ballad used a more complicated ABABBCC rhyme scheme with a two-line, rhyming chorus, but again, it had four stressed syllables in each line. The inclusion of a prayer for Queen Catherine dates *A lytell treatyse agaynst Sedicyous persons* after 15 August 1540, when news of Henry's fifth marriage was made public. The song accused Gray of being a closet Protestant. The 'olde heresy' was Lollardy, a religious movement set up by John Wycliffe in the mid-fourteenth century which demanded reform of the Catholic church. Wycliffe was branded a heretic in 1415 and his writings were banned, while his followers, the Lollards, were considered to be a threat not only to religious stability but also to social order.

Fear of Heresy

Building on fear that this old heresy posed a new threat, Smyth made mention of a much more recent heretic, Robert Barnes. One of the architects of the reformed Henrician church, Barnes had links with Martin Luther and other continental Protestants. Indeed, he had been used by Henry VIII as an ambassador to the Lutheran states during the 1530s. *A lytell treatyse agaynst Sedicyous persons* intimated that Cromwell's clients were adherents of that same Protestant faith:

The confessyon of an heretyke, that lately dyd offende
And amonges others, suffred for his deseruyng
Secretly they embrace, as a most precyous thyng
And yet playnly wyll I proue, by good lawe and reason
Contayned therin, both heresy and treason.

Furthermore, even though Cromwell acknowledged the authority of
the law by which he was condemned, he denied that he was a heretic,
calling for those attending his execution 'to beare me recorde, I die in
the Catholike faythe, not doubtyng in any artycle of my faythe, no nor
doubtyng in any Sacrament of the churche'. By contrast, John Foxe asserted that Barnes 'declared his faith and his Articles'.[45]

Although Smyth did not explicitly name Barnes, the suggestion that
he suffered among others would seem to indicate the five other men who
were executed the same day. Through Barnes's execution on 30 July 1540,
alongside the reformers William Jerome and Thomas Garrard, Henry was
publicly disassociating himself from the Protestant reformation. By purg-
ing his regime of three heretics, Henry could be seen to set his execution
of Cromwell in a wider context of dangerous evangelicalism.[46] Likewise,
Henry showed that he, not the Pope, was in charge of the English church:
three papists were hanged, drawn and quartered at the same time as
the three prominent reformers went to the flames. The execution of
Thomas Abell, Edward Powell and Richard Fetherstone, for refusing to
acknowledge the Act of Supremacy, illustrated that there would be no
return to papal authority in England.

Attacking Papistry

The anonymous author of the next entry in the flyting, *A brefe apologye or Answere to a certen craftye cloynar, or popyshe parasyte, called
Thomas smyth,* aimed to capitalise on this anti-papal feeling. The cloynar of the title was a cheat or a deceiver, with the author claiming that
A lytell treatyse had dressed up papistry in loyalty to the king's religious
conservativism. He attacked the popish character and religious beliefs of
Thomas Smyth:

Soche one as ye areywys
As popyshe prestes may blys
For wher all treason ys
Ye fynde nothynge amys

Your hate ye can not hyde
Nor yet you popyshe pryde
God wyll for hys prouyde
Whan ye shall stande asyde[47]

The author commented that 'All them that abhorre, ther olde pylde popery / For the worde of God, they accuse of heresye', and

> All ys sedycyon, that please not popyshe hartes
> All insurreccyon, whan menne from you declyne
> Of your sort manye, hath trolled trayterous partes
> And yet agaynst them, no trollynges ye dyffyne
> One relygyous zele, doth you and them combyne
> All heretyckes freyle, ye may touche in your spyght.

A *brefe apologye*, however, used an altogether different format to the other entries in the flyting. It is a true libel, a little book, rather than a broadside. This suggests, perhaps, a new author entering the debate, using a different method to attack Smyth for his alleged papism. It is quite possible that this author was the Protestant evangelical John Bale, who later claimed also to have taken part in the flyting.[48]

As a book, A *brefe apologye* was probably not a song. But because early modern print was aimed at oral transmission as well as literate readers, even the pamphlet A *brefe apologye* could have been performed. It opened with a set of 12 four-line verses with a simple AAAA rhyme scheme, but, following these introductory verses the book turned to a dialogic form, alternating a verse from Smyth's *A lytell treatyse* with two answering verses that sought to undermine Smyth's claims. It is possible (albeit with a fair degree of speculation) that a performer could characterise the three sections, perhaps adopting differing styles for the introductory and concluding verses, Thomas Smyth's verses and the text that was intended as a rebuttal of papism. At the very least, it is likely that the book was read aloud, although it is true that of the entries in the flyting, it was the least likely to have been sung.

It nevertheless shows how seriously cheap print had to be taken. To Bale, it was worth the effort of producing a short book in order to undermine what he saw as the papist propaganda of Thomas Smyth. Each verse was annotated with marginal references to the Bible that told the reader precisely where to look up exegetical information as well as highlighting the author's erudition. The book, therefore, appears to be aimed at an educated audience, an impression reinforced by the presence of Latin text within the verses, which was uncommon in ballads of this period.

Moreover, this biblical marginalia implies that God and Henry's church are on the side of the author, further denying papal authority over the scriptures. Taken in conjunction with its use of the word 'troll' to derogatory effect ('Trolle nomore with the scripturs, except ye haue better grace'), A *brefe apologye* claimed to know its Bible better than the author of A *lytell treatyse*. For example, the verse

your spyryt is verye drye
The scripturs to applye
ye rather them denye
Then ther trewthe fortyfye

has the marginal notation 'Ezec.13.'. This chapter of Ezekiel begins

The worde of the Lorde came vnto me, sayinge: Thou sonne of ma[n]. Speake, prophecye agaynst those p[ro]phetes, that preach in Israel: & saye thou vnto them that prophecye out of theyr awne hertes: heare the worde of the Lord, thus sayeth the Lord God: Wo be vnto those folysh prophetes, [tha]t folowe theyr awne sprete and speake where they se nothyng.[49]

In *A brefe apologye*, John Bale argued that there was more treason and heresy in hypocritically quoting scripture to further one's own ends than there was in the confession of a heretic. The wrangling over the true meaning of scripture in the ballads was symptomatic of confessional disputes over true and false churches. Catholics had the weight of centuries on their side to give them authority in this dispute. Protestants, by contrast, claimed that popes had corrupted the church over many generations through their reinterpretation of scripture. By asserting the right of men to access God's word for themselves, Protestants were able to claim that their beliefs were those of the 'true' church and therefore had the greater longevity.[50] Henry VIII, meanwhile, was trying to steer his church down a middle way. He saw himself as the Biblical David, the unifier of the church. He was represented in this fashion in the woodcut cover illustrations of the Coverdale Bible and the Great Bible. Both were vernacular translations to which he gave his support.[51] Echoing this official imagery, John Bale's ballad commented that 'Dauid commended a vnitie in the Lorde / Which with your peltrye, wyll vs not to accorde'. Although the balladeers all stressed the importance of unity, in the form of loyalty to the king and his church, they nevertheless competed over who was more loyal: the reformer or the conservative.

Honesty and Reputation

Thomas Smyth's response to the book that tore apart his *lytell treatyse* was to pen another broadside ballad by the name of *A treatyse declarynge the despyte of a secrete sedycyous person that dareth not shewe hym selfe*.[52] The verses of *A treatyse declarynge the despyte* have the same rhyme scheme as *A lytell treatyse* (ABABBCC) and a metrically similar chorus, suggesting that the same tune might have been used for both. Here Smyth claimed that his honesty, in revealing his name rather than publishing anonymously, made him superior to his opponent. The contrast between Gray's anonymity and Smyth's use of his name served to accentuate Gray's subterfuge and conspiracy in the face of Smyth's honour: 'His doyngs amo[n]ge trewe men, shuld not be had in place / That feareth to tell his name, & shameth to shewe his face'. Although Smyth threatened to reveal the identity of his poetic adversary, saying 'Though as a lurky[n]g lorrel, your name you woll not write / Bothe you shalbe knowen, and your deuelysshe despyte', instead, he relied on the belief that

> As the tree by her fruytes, is always chyefely knowen
> So I doubte not, by your workes, before this mater ende
> you shalbe well perceaued, & what blastes you haue blowe[n]
> And what kyndes of sede, euery other man hath sowen
> Wherfore I do aduyse you, be sure you stande vpryght
> I doubte not to ouerthrowe you, in your owne despyte.

Despite the fact that Gray claimed his anonymity was for modesty's sake, Smyth's threats to reveal Gray's identity implied his belief that it was really 'neministic' or fugitive anonymity to avoid prosecution. The use of initials might also restrict authorial identity only to the knowing.[53]

Flaunting Knowledge

Where *A brefe apologye* provided marginal citations from the Bible, Smyth played a game of educational one-upmanship by providing a gloss that included Biblical quotations in Latin. Smyth directly related his ballad to David and the psalms. This allusion to the psalmist raises the possibility that it may have been sung to a religious rather than a secular tune. It is possible that the ballads were intended to be intoned in the manner of plainsong, but the pronounced and relatively regular rhythm of the words suggests that a metrical psalm tune was more likely, in the same way that broadside ballads were set to psalm tunes later in the Tudor period.[54]

A culture of domestic psalm-singing might indeed have been familiar in the circles in which Smyth and Gray moved. Although congregational psalm-singing was still a long way in the future in 1540, collections of vernacular metrical psalms for private use had been circulating in London since the 1530s. They were designed to appeal to members of the court who appreciated poetry, song and scripture. Miles Coverdale's *Goostly psalmes and spirituall songes* had been published in 1535. The evangelical Thomas Sternhold, who produced what would later become the most popular vernacular psalter of the early modern period, was a member of the Privy Chamber by the end of 1540, being Groom of the Robes.[55] The use of a metrical psalm tune (similar to those which Sternhold would later publish) might even have been an ironic, implicit gesture which helped to satirise the reformers.

Gray's allegation that Smyth was a papist implicitly suggested that Smyth denied the king's supremacy over the Pope and that, as such, Smyth was as much a traitor as Cromwell. *A treatyse declarynge the despyte* was, however, confident that Smyth's enemies would find no evidence of his alleged treachery:

> They name me a papyste, and saye, I do not loue
> None other but Papystes, and men of popysshe mynde
> The trewe tryall wherof, I referre to God aboue
> And consequently to others, what they can proue & fynde
> O man malycyous, that woldest so fayne blynde
> The good intentes of others, which truely do and wryte
> Labourynge theyr destruccion, through serpe[n]tyne despyte
>
> If iustely you can proue, as you declare in wrytynge
> That I loue none, but papistes, tha[n] may you wel may[n]tain
> Me to be a traytour, both to God, and our good Kynge
> To the iuste tryall of the whiche, I woll dryue you playne
> For you it is to late, to call in your wordes agayne.

Despite the allegations that he was a papist and therefore a traitor, Smyth reiterated that his intentions had always been noble. Furthermore, Smyth asserts that if his opponents knew he had committed treason, they themselves were remiss for not acting on the information:

> If you haue knowen, any such treason to be in me
> Then you in your dewtye, haue bene very neglygent
> The parte of euery true hert, towardes his Kynge shuld be
> what he knoweth agai[n]st his grace, furthw[ith] to make euyde[n]t
> Who conceleth others treason, as a traytour doth consent
> Wherfore this your doying, may appere, to each ma[n]s syght
> Nothynge for the truethes sake, but all for lewde despyte.

The underlying implication was that if Smyth's enemies had any real evidence that he was loyal to the pope rather than the king, they would have acted upon it. If anyone could prove that he was a papist, then he would accept that he was a traitor, but in fact, his enemies' accusations of treachery were just slander and would not stand up to scrutiny. Smyth claimed that his judge was God alone.

An Answere to maister Smyth returned to the theme of Cromwell's alleged heresy.[56] Metrically similar to *A lytell treatyse* and *A treatyse declarynge the despyte*, again it is possible that it used the same melody. The use and abuse of scripture was its central topic. Gray accused Smyth of 'scraping together scriptures, your madnesse to mayntayne'. He showed a particular concern about Smyth 'making stryfe' to upset the unity of the church by twisting the word of God to fit his own ends. Gray accused Smyth of taking

the holy scripture to be lyke a shypmans hose?
Nay nay, although a shypmans hose, wyll serue all sortes of legges
yet Christes holy scrypture, wyll serue no rotten dregges.

He went on to demand that Smyth

Counsell with some tayler, whan that ye wryte nexte
Take measure of diuinyte, before ye cut the facyon
So shall ye square your scryptures, and the better trym your texte
And than shall men of lernyng, commende your operacyon.[57]

It is highly likely that the tailor was a reference to Rowland Taylor, an evangelical clergyman. Taylor had links with William Turner, the Protestant naturalist who would attack Stephen Gardiner for restraining the reformation in his 1543 polemic, *The Huntyng and Fynding out of the Romish Fox*.[58] The passage therefore suggested that the religious conservative Smyth should take lessons in scripture from a radical cleric. The cobbler could refer to the cobbler of Aesop's fable, who, unable to make a living mending shoes and having no knowledge of medicine, nevertheless set himself up as a doctor. Without any skill to rely on, his reputation was built only on his own braggadocio. The smith who was unable to appreciate good wine therefore suggests a reference to Thomas Smyth, the author. According to Gray, Smyth did not pay close attention to his Bible and understanding the word of God. Instead, Gray accused Smyth of using biblical references to play to the crowds.

Social Status

As well as objecting to the way Thomas Smyth bragged about his scriptural knowledge, Gray took exception to Smyth's styling himself 'clerk to the queen's council' on a piece of cheap print. It echoed the issues at the heart of Cromwell's attainder which were symptomatic of wider concerns at court, where hostility to upstarts in positions of power was played out on a wider stage. It could be, especially since we know so little about his identity, that Thomas Smyth had been raised from humble origins to his position of clerk in much the same way Cromwell himself had risen to high office. Gray believed Smyth to be boasting about a position he owed, just like Cromwell, to royal favour. Indeed, it mirrored the Act of Attainder's accusation that 'Thomas Crumwell elated and full of pryde contrary to his moste bounde dutie of his owen authorytie and power not regardinge yo[ur] Ma[jes]ties Royall' had become conceited by his promotion.[59] Gray went to great lengths to imply that, like Cromwell, Smyth had lowly origins, for as well as casting aspersions on Smyth's taste and commenting that Smyth was 'scarsely a clerke', he opined

A wyse man wolde haue praysed god, and than prayed for the kyng
The which of their gret goodnesse, to your offyce dyd you call
And not to haue bragged therof, and than put it out in printyng
For ye stande not yet so sure, but it is possyble ye may fall
And though your offyce be great, I trust your power be but small
Or els parchau[n]ce ye wold quickly thurst a poore man amo[n]g
   the thornes
But god almyghty prouydeth well to sende a shrewde cow short
   hornes.

The use of the word 'scarcely' presented the opportunity for multiple
readings: perhaps Smyth became clerk to the council of the new queen,
Catherine Howard, which would make his a recent appointment; it
could be read as a derogatory remark about his abilities; it also suggested
that he had humble origins and was 'scarcely' part of the noble council.
Smyth's inflated sense of self-worth was also described ironically as the
primrose peerless, a phrase used to label an ideal specimen. As 'scarcely
a clerk', Smyth had no right to comment on scripture or the king's policy.

This bluster regarding Smyth's inflated ego contrasted with Gray's concern to maintain his own good reputation in the face of Smyth's slander.
Instead of swaggering about his own abilities and position, Gray employed
a self-effacing yet loyal tone, claiming that his ballad was written 'By me a
poore man whose herte if ye knewe / Wolde be the kynges seruant as fayne
as you'. This show of loyalty was important, coming from someone who
continued to support Cromwell, an executed traitor. Gray's image was
also in need of rehabilitation following the downfall of his master.

There followed two closely related ballads, *An Enuoye from Thomas
Smythe* by Thomas Smyth and *The ret[ur]ne of M. smythes enuoy* by
William Gray.[60] *The ret[ur]ne of M. smythes enuoy* used many of the
same lyrics as *An Enuoye from Thomas Smythe*, but changed critical
words in order to refute Smyth's argument. So when the first verse of *An
Enuoye from Thomas Smythe* complained that

Nowe with no lesse salutacyon, that to such doth pertayne
Unto you I do present, this lytell poore treatyse
Wyllynge you to vnderstande, and also to knowe playne
I haue receued, your lewde lybell, wherin you enterpryse
Both me and my doynges, full proudely to despyse
But bable what you lyst, it skylleth not a whyt
Remember well this worde, hereafter cometh not yet.

The ret[ur]ne of M. smythes enuoy then replied

EUen with the same commendacion that to you dothe pertayne
I sende you here myne answer, which is no great treatyse

Desyrynge you to marke, and to vnderstande playne
That I haue receyued your enuyous and proude enterpryse
The mater wherof, I trust, all honest men dothe despyse
But bragge and face what you can, I care not a whyt
I take tyme as tyme is, though hereafter commeth not yet.

Despite the fact that the metre and syllable count are different, there are four stresses in each line, so although there is no evidence of what the tunes for these ballads might have been, it is possible to speculate that *An Enuoye from Thomas Smythe* and *The ret[ur]ne of M. smythes en-uoy* was sung to the same tune as *A lytell treatyse, A treatyse declarynge the despyte* and *An Answere to maister Smyth*. If the same tune was indeed used for all these ballads, this in itself would constitute a form of implicitness. The knowing audience would instantly associate *The ret[ur]ne of M. smythes enuoy* with the ongoing musical debate in four previous ballads.

The inclusion of a prayer that there might be children born to the royal couple, 'lyke other braunches for to sprynge', indicates that *An Enuoye from Thomas Smythe* was probably written in late August. By 21 July 1540, a week before her wedding to Henry was solemnised, there were rumours that Catherine was pregnant. Writing to the Constable of France, Montmorency, about the annulment of Henry's marriage to Anne of Cleves, the French ambassador, Marillac, confided that he

> Must not omit that the cause of this sudden settlement of so import-ant an affair is said to be that this King has already consummated marriage with this last lady, relative of the Duke of Norfolk, and it is feared she is already *enceinte*. Cannot affirm this otherwise; for these are things which are kept secret.[61]

Nevertheless, Marillac claimed that, although rumour was rife, the king's marriage was not confirmed publicly until 15 August 1540, when Catherine was included in prayers said for the royal family in church.[62] The Howard marriage was not exclusively of concern to wagging tongues in London. Reinforcing the international context to Henry's domestic problems, it shows that the French contingent was interested in gossip about Henry's marital affairs. The breakdown of relations between Francis I and Charles V was followed by Henry's rapprochement with the Habsburg emperor so, as a result, Henry could marry one of his own subjects rather than entertain another diplomatic wedding to strengthen his relationship with a foreign power.

Smyth and Gray, however, were more concerned with matters closer to home. They were particularly troubled by their social status and how this affected their honour. Replying to the accusation that he was merely a clerk of lowly status, Smyth argued 'Yet better is a cobbler than an ydell vagabounde'.[63] He implied that unlike the hardworking cobbler or smith, Gray, as a masterless man, did little but sponge off court society following the death of his patron, Cromwell. He also refuted the accusation of bragging, presenting his self-promotion as an admirable desire to take responsibility for his words and actions. He stated his name only because it would be dishonourable to remain anonymous. He had revealed his position at court simply in order to differentiate himself from the many other men named Thomas Smyth.

Furthermore, Smyth picked up Gray's occupational analogy from *An Answere to maister Smyth* and took it even further. Not only did he use it to dismiss Gray's claims that he was a papist, but he employed it to suggest once more that Gray was a heretic. Gray's name presented Smyth with the opportunity to pun on his abandoned monastic vocation: 'Tyme shall try your colour, be it russet, black, or graye'. He further claimed that Gray could not 'hyde your secte, nor yet your brotherly sorte / (A Clergy for the deuyll) you shewe your selfe the same / As Taylours, Cobblers, and Tylers, doctous of worthy fame'. Tyler was a reference to Wat Tyler, leader of the 1381 Peasants' Revolt and, indeed, a tiler by trade. Tyler's demands included the division of church goods amongst the laity and the abolition of serfdom and villeinage, but he was also famous for the uncouth behaviour that ultimately led to his death. Froissart's *Chronicle*, printed in 1523, described how the Mayor of London

> sawe and harde howe Watte Tyler demeaned hym selfe, and sayde to hym. Ha thou knaue, howe arte thou so hardy in the kynges presence to speke suche wordes. It is to moche for the so to do. Than the kynge began to chafe, and sayd to the mayre. Sette handes on hym. And while the kynge sayde so, Tyler sayd to the mayre, A goddesname, what haue I sayde to displease the? yes truely quod the mayre, thou false stynkynge knaue, shalt thou speke thus in the presence of the kynge my naturall lorde?[64]

Associating Gray with Wat Tyler not only suggested that his religious beliefs were highly suspicious, but cast doubt upon his personal honour and called into question his loyalty to the king.

Whereas in *An Enuoye from Thomas Smythe*, Smyth accused Gray of hiding his Protestantism and awaiting the return to power of the reformists ('In rayling is your ruffe, in your spelunke whan ye syt'), in *a brefe apologye* Gray described Smyth as 'the bolsterar of sedicion' whose 'auctoryte maketh bolde'.[65] Smyth claimed that the allegation of papistry which he faced was merely a result of Gray's heresy, because the only way in which a Protestant could defend himself from an accusation of heresy was by making a counter-accusation of papistry: 'Who rebuketh your secte, or wolde refourme your heresye / Amonge you strayte he is a mayntaynour of popery'. In an implicit appeal to history, Smyth likened Gray to a Lollard, plotting to overthrow the king:

> We shulde beware your secte for surely you wolde fayne brynge
> Some other to rayne ouer vs, yf you wylte, by whata shyfte
> Example we haue, herof, Reade of kynge Henry the fyfte.[66]

This passage related to Oldcastle's Revolt, the attempted Lollard coup of 1414. Cromwell was compared to Sir John Oldcastle, who was indeed hanged as a traitor *and* burnt as a heretic. Smyth hoped that Gray would suffer the same fate as the Lollards for his support of Cromwell.

In *The ret[ur]ne of. M. smythes enuoy*, however, Gray inverted this section of the poem to complain about the papist factions and sects that caused discord in England:

> We shulde beware of your treason, for surely I feare ye wolde
>   brynge
> Your romyshe ruffeler to be our heed, by some maner of shyft
> To the whiche your papisticall flocke, not longe agoo gaue a lyft.[67]

This was an implicit reference to the rise of the conservative religious faction at court, blaming the fall of the reformer Cromwell on the prestidigitation of his 'papist' enemies. Smyth further alleged that Gray was in appropriate company when he cited the tailor, cobbler and tiler, 'doctous of worthy fame', because they were 'vagabou[n]ds, ruffyens' and, indeed, the type of unsavoury characters whose counsel should be ignored. Implicit in these remarks was a belief that Gray should no more have a place at court than they did. Resorting to even more salacious comment, Smyth claimed that it was among such characters of low repute that 'you rynge your bell'.[68] As well as having an ironic Catholic overtone (the bell was rung at the elevation of the host during the mass), the phrase also meant to participate in sexual activity and referred in particular to the male genitals.[69] Of course, many of these allusions were funny as well as knowing, so collusion with the knowing section of the audience made the songs more entertaining.

A Missing Link

The ninth entry in the flyting may be considered a 'known unknown'. Although neither copy nor title seems to survive, its existence can be inferred from the tenth ballad, *An artificiall Apologie*, where R. Smyth P. refers to a woman who has not been mentioned in any of the previous extant ballads:

> As for the woman, alas it was no wonder
> She was a whore, and he hath such a charme
> If she be arrant, to brynge her shortly vnder
> And yet I promyse you, he doth them lytle harme
> But bryngs them to his house, where they parte not asonder
> He couereth her, he colleth her & keps her good and Warme.[70]

The words 'As for the woman' indicate that she had been specifically mentioned in a previous ballad rather than suggesting a general comment. She was a known entity, not someone who was just being introduced. In order for this verse to make sense, then, either a ballad is missing, or the audience are expected to know about another exchange that took place in an entirely separate forum.

Promoting Unity

The tenth entry in the flyting is the ostentatiously-entitled *An artificiall Apologie, articulerlye answerynge to the obstreperous Obgannynges of one W. G. Euometyd to the vituperacion of the tryumphant trollynge Thomas smyth. Repercussed by the ryght redolent & rotounde rethorician R. Smyth P. with annotacio[n]s of the mellifluous and misticall Master Mynterne, marked in the mergent for the enucliacion of certen obscure obelisques, to thende that the imprudent lector shulde not tytubate or hallucinate in the labyrinthes of this lucubratiuncle.* It is a macaronic ballad. Even its title relies on a knowing audience, as presumably the identities of R. Smyth P and Master Mynterne are meant to be known to those who read the ballad.[71] They have, however, been lost to the mists of time. One candidate for the author, R. Smyth, is the Oxford theologian Richard Smyth. During the 1530s and early 1540s he remained a religious conservative. Even if Richard Smyth himself did not write *An artificiall Apologie*, we cannot discount the possibility that it was written by someone pretending to be him. Alternatively, an intriguing document in the State Papers relates how a servant to the king named Thomas Smyth reported a priest named Sir Roger (whose surname and misdemeanour were not recorded), but although it is interesting to speculate if this was in some way a precursor to the flyting, there is no way to tell.[72]

The song has a different structure to the contrafacta *An Enuoye from Thomas Smythe* and *The ret[ur]ne of M. smythes enuoy*, so therefore would have been sung to a different tune. It employs a simple ABABAB rhyme scheme and is glossed with Latin marginalia, as well as using Latin text within the ballad verse itself. This suggests again that the intended audience was educated, a suggestion strengthened by the sesquipedalian nature of the title, an ironic device that also ridiculed the overblown and loquacious nature of the public disagreement between Smyth and Gray. In the case of these ballads, the purpose of irony is to belittle the author's opponent. The Latin text and marginalia, as well as appealing to an educated audience, also mocked the inflated egos of the two main authors, both of whom claimed to be well educated and influential. *An artificiall Apologie* seems to have been designed to bring an end to the flyting, and it certainly castigated both Gray and Smyth, pointing out somewhat hypocritically that they were harming the unity of the church by their disorderly balladry. *An artificiall Apologie* insisted that Henry VIII's reformed church was the true church. The author attacked Gray for calling Smyth a papist and invoked the authority of the 'olde auncyent mother holy church'. This type of appeal to the continuity of church history was common to both Protestant and Catholic reformers, who vied with each other to claim that their version of Christianity was the closest to scripture and Jesus's teachings.

The final broadside ballad, *A Paumflet compyled by G, C* was addressed to both Smyth and Gray and attacked them both in equal measure for 'the vncharyte / Of two that nowe with hatefull spyte / Do blame eache other openly'. Perhaps the Six Articles themselves were the 'precyse wordes' that forbade the English Christian to withstand Christ and his chosen governor, King Henry,

> Whych teacheth vs to loue and dread
> Hym that hathe power vnder God.[73]

It urged Smyth, Gray and 'we, in euery parte' to 'fyrmly stande in one belefe'. The trouble was that, as the flyting itself had showed, it was no longer clear what that 'one belief' should be. What is more, the Cromwell ballads illustrate the way in which people were prepared to talk about their confusion over royal policy using a medium as public as the broadside ballad. Which was worse: heresy or papistry? Could you be either of these terrible things and still be loyal to the king? Cheap print allowed a debate about these matters of high politics to take place in a proto-public sphere.

These entertaining songs hid powerful messages and empowered those who were in the know. The flyting shows how people outside the group of Henry's close advisers took sides, actively discussing the news, and how that news spread beyond court through the medium of cheap print. They framed their public discussion of Cromwell's fall against their wider understanding of politics, religion and personality, a power struggle that had both domestic and European ramifications. Furthermore, through the use of the religious insults 'heretic' and 'papist', the balladeers revealed confusion about Henry's religious reforms. The debate, which took place in the public domain, presumably through the medium of music, touched on aspects of Henry's policy that should not have been challenged at court, let alone discussed in the streets. These ballads highlighted the fact that any religious non-conformity was divisive and potentially seditious but, in so doing, they debated the nature of the sacraments and what beliefs constituted heresy.

The ballad form, with its heavy reliance on irony and metaphor, was the perfect medium for casting aspersions not only on the author's opponents but also on state policy, through implicit references. Some parts of the ballads were only comprehensible to the knowing section of the audience who shared the lyrics' common points of reference.

Knowingness flattered the exclusive group who had the power to understand the balladeers' vague references, while encouraging those who did not fully comprehend the songs to seek answers. Even so, the fact that an anti-Cromwell ballad provoked a pro-Cromwell response shows that sharing the values implicit in the words was not a prerequisite to understanding them. The coded nature of many of the references in the Cromwell flyting broke up the audience into those who knew and those who knew not. Furthermore, the implicit meanings of the songs divided the audience into reformers and conservatives. Smyth, Gray and the other protagonists clearly understood the knowing references in each other's songs, but their responses were far from sympathetic. Gray understood the common reference points that Smyth had utilised, but he did not share a belief in them. Implicit in Gray's response was a rejection of Smyth's form of Catholicism. Although he was keen not to be branded a heretic like Cromwell, and, indeed, he sought to rehabilitate his former patron's memory, he implied that Smyth's Catholicism was papistry by any other name and, therefore, treason. Implicitness, therefore, created a space for public debate, in which members of the audience were able to choose a ballad supporting or condemning Cromwell. With that decision, they rejected or supported specific aspects of Henry VIII's religious policy.

Nevertheless, implicitness could not protect the balladeers forever and such a scurrilous and disobedient public debate on religious policy could not avoid censure indefinitely. The records of the Privy Council for 3 January 1541 show that

> Thomas Smyth[e] Clerk of the Quenes Counsaill and Will[ia]m Graye so[m]tyme s[er]v[a]nt to the late Lord[e] Crumwell wer examined[e] of the caus[e] of their writting invectives oon[e] against another, and after long examinac[i]on of them they wer co[m]maundede to attende uppon the Counsaill the next mornyng at vij. of the clock.[74]

The following day 'Thomas Smyth Willm Graye Richard Grafton Thomas Walpole and Thomas Cottisford prist were comitted to the Flytt there to remayn during the King pleas[ure]'.[75] Smyth and Gray were released in February, the others in May.[76]

Ultimately, for the Henrician regime, part of the danger of these songs lay in their very form: the images and complaints would stick in the memory through the use of rhyme and melody. Although they were at pains to emphasise their obedience to the king, the balladeers debated Henry's religious policy and his choice of advisers, matters that were crucial to the politics of the day. Unity and obedience were common themes through many ballads, not only those in this ballad flyting but also, as we shall see in the next chapter, during the reign of Mary I. Again and again in the Cromwell flyting, authors condemned extremism and implied that there was a middle way between 'popyshnes and heresye'.[77] That way lay loyalty to the king and his dynasty, but the final years of Henry VIII's reign were overshadowed by uncertainty about the succession. The king's only son, Prince Edward, was still a young boy, while Henry's health was failing. This presented the worrying prospect of a political vacuum and an ensuing power struggle if Henry died before Edward reached the age of majority. Throughout the remainder of the Tudor period, however, hereditary right was the trump card held by Henry's children, surpassing issues of gender and religious belief when it came to retaining the loyalty of the English people. The issue of loyalty and obedience can be examined in more detail through a case study of the ballads in the reign of Mary I, England's first queen regnant.

Notes

1 'Set to spell' was possibly an allusion to spilling his blood at his execution, but also, perhaps, to spelling forth his beliefs and/or confession in public at his execution. The chapter title is taken from *A Paumflet compyled by G, C. To master Smyth and Wyllyam G. Prayenge them both, for the loue of our Lorde, To growe at last to an honest accorde* (London, 1540), STC (2nd ed.) / 4268.5.

2 *Reliques of Ancient English Poetry: Consisting of Old Heroic Ballads, Songs, and Other Pieces of Our Earlier Poets (Chiefly of the Lyric Kind.) Together with Some Few of Later Date. The Second Edition,* Ed. Bishop Percy (3 vols. London: J. Dodsley, 1765; repr. London: J.M. Dent & Sons, 1906). All entries in the flyting except this and one other (*A Brefe Apologye or Answere to a Certen Craftye Cloynar, or Popyshe Parasyte, Called Thomas Smythe* (London, 1565), STC (2nd ed.) / 22880.7) are held in a book of broadsides in the library of the Society of Antiquaries, London.

3 Peter Lake, 'Ministers, Magistrates and the Production of "Order" in Measure for Measure', *Shakespeare Survey, Vol. 54: Shakespeare and Religions,* p. 165.

4 Cathy Shrank, 'Trollers and Dreamers: Defining the Citizen-Subject in Sixteenth-Century Cheap Print', *The Yearbook of English Studies,* 38:1/2 (2008), pp. 104 and 117. The flyting has often been seen as an exercise in how far the participants could stretch their insults without falling foul of the libel laws (see Christopher Boswell, 'The Culture and Rhetoric of the Answer-poem, 1485–1626', PhD thesis, University of Leeds, 2003, pp. 128 and 127); for other previous scholarship on the flyting, see, for example, Ernest Dormer, *Gray of Reading: A Sixteenth-Century Controversialist and Ballad-Writer* (Reading: Bradley & Son, Ltd, 1923); Livingston, *British Broadside Ballads,* pp. 821–28.

5 John Playford, *The English dancing master: or, Plaine and easie rules for the dancing of country dances, with the tune to each dance* (London, 1651), Wing (2nd ed.) / P2477, p. 43.

6 William Chappell, *Popular Music of the Olden Time: A Collection of Ancient Songs, Ballads, and Dance Tunes* (2 vols. London: Cramer, Beale & Chappell, 1855, repr. Elibron Classics 2005), i, p. 73.

7 *Reliques of Ancient English Poetry,* p. 327; *A balade agaynst malycyous Sclaunderers* (London, 1540), STC (2nd ed.) / 1323.5; Thomas Smyth, *A lytell treatyse agaynst Sedicyous persons* (London, 1540), STC (2nd ed.) / 22880.4.

8 G. R. Elton, *Reform and Reformation: England, 1509–1558* (London: Edward Arnold, 1977), p. 194.

9 J. A. Guy, *Tudor England* (Oxford: Oxford University Press, 1988), p. 186; Glyn Redworth, *In Defence of the Church Catholic: The Life of Stephen Gardiner* (Oxford: Basil Blackwell, 1990), p. 119.

10 *State Papers Published under the Authority of his Majesty's Commission: King Henry the Eighth, 1830–1852*, viii: part 5, SP 1/160 f. 140, p. 349, 'The Council to Wallop 10 June 1540'.

11 Redworth, *In Defence of the Church Catholic*, pp. 122–24.

12 Cuthbert Tunstall, *A sermon of Cuthbert Bysshop of Duresme made vpon Palme sondaye laste past, before the maiestie of our souerayne lorde kyng Henry The. VIII. kynge of England [and] of France, defensor of the fayth, lorde of Ireland, and in erth next vnder Christ supreme heed of the Churche of Englande* (London, 1539), STC (2nd ed.) / 24322a.

13 *A proclamation, concernynge rites and ceremonies to be vsed in due fourme in the Churche of Englande, and the kynges most gracious pardon for certeyne fautes conteyned in the same* (London, 1539), STC (2nd ed.) / 7791.

14 Glyn Redworth, 'A Study in the Formulation of Policy: The Genesis and Evolution of the Act of Six Articles', *Journal of Ecclesiastical History*, 37:01 (1986), p. 45.

15 M. Lindsay Kaplan, *The Culture of Slander in Early Modern England* (Cambridge: Cambridge University Press, 1997), p. 3; Annabel M. Patterson, *Censorship and Interpretation: The Conditions of Writing and Reading in Early Modern England* (London: University of Wisconsin Press, 1984), pp. 14–15.

16 Kaplan, *Culture of Slander*, p. 7.

17 Steven Veerapen, 'Slander and Sedition in Elizabethan Law, Speech and Writing', PhD Thesis, University of Strathclyde, 2014, pp. 30 and 13.

18 Patterson, *Censorship and Interpretation*, pp. 18 and 12.

19 G. R. Elton, *Policy and Police: The Enforcement of the Reformation in the Age of Thomas Cromwell* (London: Cambridge University Press, 1972), Chapter 6; I. D. Thornley, 'The Treason Legislation of Henry VIII (1531–1534): Alexander Prize Essay, 1916', *Transactions of the Royal Historical Society*, 11 (1917), pp. 87–123.

20 Peter Lake and Steve Pincus, 'Rethinking the Public Sphere in Early Modern England', *Journal of British Studies*, 45:2 (2006), pp. 274–75.

21 *L&P* xvi, PC 2/1 f. 99, p. 212, no. 422, 'The Privy Council, 3 January 1541'.

22 Dormer, *Gray of Reading*, pp. 17, 42 and 23.

23 Poems reprinted in Dormer, *Gray of Reading*, pp. 114–24; Jennifer Loach, *Edward VI* (London: Yale University Press, 1999), p. 44.

24 Smyth, *A lytell treatyse agaynst Sedicyous persons*.

25 Anne Crawford, 'The Queen's Council in the Middle Ages', *English Historical Review*, 116:469 (2001), pp. 1193–211; N. R. R. Fisher, 'The Queenes Courte in Her Councell Chamber at Westminster', *English Historical Review*, 108:427 (1993), pp. 314–37.

26 The National Archives of the U.K., E36/120, f. 53^v.

27 Bradley J. Irish, 'Gender and Politics in the Henrician Court: The Douglas-Howard Lyrics in the Devonshire Manuscript (BL Add 17492)', *Renaissance Quarterly*, 64:1 (2011), p. 83; Alison Weir, *The Lost Tudor Princess: A Life of Margaret Douglas, Countess of Lennox* (London: Vintage, 2015), pp. 56–57 and 429. I am grateful to Dr Irish for his assistance in tracking down this Thomas Smyth reference.

28 Henry Ellis (ed.), *Original Letters Illustrative of English History 3rd series* (4 vols. London: Richard Bentley, 1846), iii, p. 137.

29 *L&P* xvi, PC 2/1 f. 99, p. 212, no. 422, 'The Privy Council, 3 January 1541'; *L&P* xvi, p. 214, no. 424, 'The Privy Council, 4 January 1541'.

30 *L&P* xiii, SP 1/130 f.9.1, p.203, no. 550, 'Thos. Havard to Thos. Smyth, 19 March 1538'.

31 *State Papers Domestic: Supplementary*, SP 46/2 'Certificate of Statute Merchant, 20 January 1549, for the recovery of the debt of £30, of Nicholas Warde of Ocliff, co. Surrey, chapman, to Thomas Smith, citizen and mercer of London, entered in July 15'.

32 Rospocher and Salzburg, 'Evanescent Public Sphere', p. 97.

33 *Reliques of Ancient English Poetry*, pp. 327–29.

34 *Statutes of the Realm*, iii, 31 Henry VIII c. 14 (London 1810–28), p. 739.

35 London, British Library, Add. MS 48028 (Yelverton MS), 'Act of Attainder of Thomas Cromwell, Earl of Essex; 29 June 1540', f. 160^v.

36 BL Add. MS 48028, 'Act of Attainder of Thomas Cromwell, Earl of Essex; 29 June 1540', f. 160^v.

37 BL Add. MS 48028, 'Act of Attainder of Thomas Cromwell, Earl of Essex; 29 June 1540', f. 161^v.

38 BL Add. MS 48028, 'Act of Attainder of Thomas Cromwell, Earl of Essex; 29 June 1540', f. 164^r.

39 *A balade agaynst malycyous Sclaunderers*.

40 G. R. Elton, 'Thomas Cromwell's Decline and Fall', *Cambridge Historical Journal*, 10:2 (1951), pp. 182–83; D. M. Loades, *Thomas Cromwell: Servant to Henry VIII* (Stroud: Amberley Publishing, 2013), p. 238.

41 Michael Riordan and Alec Ryrie, 'Stephen Gardiner and the Making of a Protestant Villain', *Sixteenth Century Journal*, 34:4 (2003), p. 1046.

42 Diarmaid MacCulloch, 'Heinrich Bullinger and the English-Speaking World', in P. Opitz and E. Campi (eds.), *Heinrich Bullinger (1504?–1575): Leben, Denken, Wirkung* (Zürcher Beiträge Zur Reformationsgeschichte, 2006).

43 *A balade agaynst malycyous sclaunderers*.

44 Smyth, *A lytell treatyse agaynst Sedicyous persons*.

45 *TAMO*, 1563 edition, p. 654–59.

46 Susan Brigden, 'Popular Disturbance and the Fall of Thomas Cromwell and the Reformers, 1539–1540', *Historical Journal*, 24:2 (1981), p. 267.

47 *A Brefe Apologye*.

48 Cathy Shrank, 'A Work by John Bale Identified?', *Notes and Queries*, 53:4 (2006), pp. 421–22.

49 *The Byble in Englyshe that is to saye, the content of all the holye scrypture, bothe of the olde and newe Testament, truly translated after the veryte of the Hebrue and Greke textes, by the diligent studye of dyuers excellent lerned [men e]xperte in the fore[saide] tongues* (London, 1540), STC (2nd ed.) / 2069, f. xcix.

50 Riordan and Ryrie, 'Stephen Gardiner', p. 1045.

51 King, *Tudor Royal Iconography*, pp. 72–81.

52 Thomas Smyth, *A treatyse declarynge the despyte of a secrete sedycyous person that dareth not shewe Hym selfe* (London, 1540), STC (2nd ed.) / 22880.6.

53 Raymond, *Pamphlets and Pamphleteering*, pp. 64–65.

54 For example, John Pyttes, *A prayer or supplycation made vnto God by a yonge man that he woulde be mercifull to vs, and not kepe his worde away from vs, but that the truth maie springe / quod John Pyttes* (London, 1559), STC (2nd ed.) / 19969.4, indicated the tune of Psalm 119, while John Awdelay's 1569 ballad, *A godly ditty or prayer to be song vnto God* was intended to be sung to the tune of Psalm 137 from Sternhold and Hopkins' *whole boke of psalmes*.

55 Quitslund, *Reformation in Rhyme*, pp. 19 and 24.

56 William Gray, *An Answere to Maister Smyth, seruaunt to the kynges most royall maiestye. And clerke of the Quenes graces counsell though most unworthy* (London, 1540), STC (2nd ed.) / 12206a.3.

57 The reference to the shipman's hose introduced a section of verse that related to various occupations, including the tailor and doctor. It was a metaphor which described a statement which could be interpreted so widely it would fit any meaning. In personal correspondence, Professor Diarmaid MacCulloch provided much useful feedback for this chapter, particularly on Cromwell's religion and the wider issues of Henry's reformation of the church, but I have difficulty in accepting his suggestion that the association of shipman's hose with trousers is a common misunderstanding. Instead he advised that the shipman's hose was a flexible tube used for taking on or removing water from a ship. The *Oxford English Dictionary* defines 'shipman's hose' as 'wide trousers worn by sailors. (Contrasted with the tight-fitting hose then worn.)', or as an obsolete expression for 'a sailor's wide trousers; often *fig.* a statement of wide application that can be turned to fit any case' and indeed, in this latter definition it cites *An answere to maister Smyth* as the first example of such a usage. Ultimately, whether the hose was a tube to carry water or a stocking to cover a leg, the meaning is the same: the object was flexible and could be shaped to suit an individual's needs.

  During the mid-Tudor period, the phrase seems to have been used particularly in relation to quoting scripture to prove a point, but often these references failed to clarify which type of hose. For example, Miles Coverdale wrote 'Thus make ye of gods holy scripture, a shipmans hose, wresting and wringing it to what purpose ye will' (Miles Coverdale, *A confutacion of that treatise, which one Iohn Standish made agaynst the protestacion of D. Barnes in the yeare. M.D.XL. Wherin, the holy scriptures (peruerted and wrested in his sayd treatise) are restored to their owne true vnderstonding agayne by Myles Couerdale* (1541), STC (2nd ed.) / 33.03, sig. Dvii^v), while John Jewel agreed 'Hereunto they adde also a Similitude not very agreeable, how the *Scriptures* be like to a *Nose of Waxe, or a Shipmans Hose:* how thei may be fashioned, and plied al manner of waies, and serue al mennes turnes' (John Jewel, *A defence of the Apologie of the Churche of Englande conteininge an answeare to a certaine booke lately set foorthe by M. Hardinge, and entituled, A confutation of &c. By Iohn Iewel Bishop of Sarisburie* (London, 1567), STC (2nd ed.) / 14600.5, p. 464).

  Nevertheless, on reflection I maintain that in the case of *An answere to maister Smyth*, the hose refers to trousers. Gray's shipman's hose 'wyll serue all sortes of legges', a comment which does not ring true if the hose in question was for carrying water. Similarly, in 1533, Sir Thomas More used the phrase with reference to legs, again making the point that men twisted God's word to fit their own ends: 'tha[n] haue there ben some prechers such ere this, the techyng playne heresies to theyr familiars secretely, wold prech in such wyse abrode, that theyr word[es] shold haue two senses, & one bote serue for eyther legge like a shypmans hose' (Thomas More, *The debellacyon of Salem and Bizance* ([London], 1533), STC (2nd ed.) / 18081, p. xxxv^r).

58 William Turner, *The huntyng and fyndyng out of the Romyshe foxe which more then seuen yeares hath bene hyd among the bisshoppes of Englonde, after that the Kynges hyghnes had commanded hym to be dryuen owt of hys realme. Whosoeuer happeneth vpon thys boke, yf he loue God beter then man, and the Kynges hyghnes beter than the bysshoppes false hypocrisye, let hym gyue it to the Kyng, that he may rede it before the bysshopes condemne it* (London, 1543), STC (2nd ed.) / 24353.

59   BL Add. MS 48028, 'Act of Attainder of Thomas Cromwell, 29 June 1540', ff. 161^{r-v}.

60   Thomas Smyth, *An Enuoye from Thomas Smyth Vpon Thaunswer of One W.G. Lurkyng in Lorrells Denne, for Feare Men Shulde Hym See* (London, 1540), STC (2nd ed.) / 22880.2; *The ret[ur]ne of. M. smythes enuoy, servaunt to the Kynges Royall Maiestye and Clerke of the Quenes graces counsell (though most unworthy)* (London, 1540), STC (2nd ed.) / 12206a.7.

61   *L&P* xv, p. 447, no. 902, 'R.O. Marillac to Montmorency, 21 July 1540'.

62   *L&P* xv, p. 490, no. 976, 'R.O. Marillac to Montmorency, 15 August 1540'.

63   Smyth, *Enuoye from Thomas Smyth.*

64   Jean Froissart, *Here begynneth the first volum of sir Iohan Froyssart of the cronycles of Englande, Fraunce, Spayne, Portyngale, Scotlande, Bretayne, Flau[n]ders: and other places adioynynge. Tra[n]slated out of frenche into our maternall englysshe tonge, by Iohan Bourchier knight Lorde Berners: at the co[m]maundement of oure moost highe redouted souerayne lorde kyng Henry the. viii. kyng of Englande and of Fraunce, [and] highe defender of the christen faythe* (London, 1523), STC (2nd ed.) / 11396, f. CCxiii^v.

65   The spelunk was intended as a biblical reference to the Old Testament cave of Adullam, the bandits' cave in which David took refuge from Saul while awaiting his opportunity to return to power. I am grateful to Prof. Diarmaid MacCulloch for this reference.

66   Smyth, *Enuoye from Thomas Smyth.*

67   *The ret[ur]ne of. M. smythes enuoy.*

68   Smyth, *Enuoye from Thomas Smyth.*

69   *Dictionary of Sexual Language*, i, pp. 94–97.

70   R. Smyth P., *An artificiall Apologie, articulerlye answerynge to the obstreperous Obgannynges of one W. G. Euometyd to the vituperacion of the tryumphant trollynge Thomas smyth. Repercussed by the ryght redolent & rotounde rethorician R. Smyth P. with annotacio[n]s of the mellifluous and misticall Master Mynterne, marked in the mergent for the enucliacion of certen obscure obelisques, to thende that the imprudent lector shulde not tytubate or hallucinate in the labyrinthes of this lucubratiuncle*, STC (2nd ed.) / 22877.6.

71   Smyth P., *An artificiall Apologie.*

72   *L&P* viii, SP 1/92 f. 56, p. 225, no. 595, 'Head of the Church, 27 April 1535'.

73   G, C., *A Paumflet compyled by G, C.*

74   *L&P* xvi, PC 2/1 f. 99, p. 212, no. 422, 'The Privy Council, 3 January 1541'.

75   *L&P* xvi, PC 2/1 f. 101, p. 214, no. 424, 'The Privy Council, 4 January 1541'. Cottisford's imprisonment was for a different offence.

76   Livingston, *British Broadside Ballads*, p. 827.

77   G, C., *A Paumflet compyled by G, C.*

7 'Lyege lady and queene'

Discourses of Obedience in the Reign of Mary I

How manie good people, were long in dispaire,
That this letel england, shold lacke a right heire:
But nowe the swet marigold, springeth so fayre,
That England triumpheth, without anie care.[1]

This anonymous ballad summed up widespread doubts about the long-term stability of the Tudor dynasty that preoccupied the mid-sixteenth century. King Henry VIII died in 1547, leaving Edward Seymour, Duke of Somerset, to lead a regency council as Protector during the minority of Edward VI. Following Somerset's downfall in 1549, the council was led by the Duke of Northumberland. Although Northumberland insisted that Edward was old enough to rule in his own right, he remained in tight control of the government as Edward learned his trade.[2] Edward's death in 1553, aged only 15, led to a coup in favour of Lady Jane Grey, but this was quickly overthrown by forces loyal to Edward's Catholic half-sister, Mary. She would die childless only five years later. The throne passed to Elizabeth I, famous as the queen who refused to marry. Throughout this period, Henry VIII's offspring drew on their father's memory for their legitimacy and authority.[3]

Mary I is an interesting case study to examine attitudes to obedience, not least because she is acknowledged as the first queen regnant.[4] Nevertheless, ballads have been underused as a historical resource for investigating popular attitudes to Mary's reign. Kevin Sharpe identified a dichotomy between representations of Mary by others and authorised Marian iconography such as proclamations, speeches, portraits and coins. He noted that popular ballads resembled royal speeches and proclamations in their emphasis on lineage and virtue rather than religion. Because he set out to investigate Mary's official iconography, Sharpe analysed only those three ballads whose authors could be connected to court circles. He studied opposition views only briefly, stating that Mary 'allowed others to present her religion as un-English', before concluding that it was neither Mary nor Catholicism that was unpopular, but her husband Philip and the Pope.[5] Furthermore, Sharpe's concentration on Mary's Catholicism meant that he did not specifically investigate how the ballads addressed the issue of gynarchy.

But popular ballads were not afraid to tackle the unusual issues raised by the accession of a female monarch whose intent was to restore Catholicism to a country in schism.[6] This chapter demonstrates the ballads' continued emphasis on obedience and loyalty. Equally importantly, it highlights the way in which ballads were able to respond quickly to news of religion and of gendered monarchy, in a public sphere. The chapter first shows that a practical understanding of dynastic right shaped the ballads that greeted Mary's accession, before examining the attitudes to female rule that the songs displayed. Through a focus on the imagery employed in four ballads, the chapter then shows that religious belief was at the heart of the balladeers' responses to the Marian regime. Issues of gynarchy were also thrown into sharp relief by Mary's marriage to Philip of Spain, which brought with it fears that England would be subject to a foreign power. The chapter therefore examines the two extant ballads that presented views opposed to the queen and goes on to show that Protestants could nevertheless support a female, Catholic monarch. Finally, the chapter demonstrates that the regime took ballads seriously enough to take action against them. The ballads written during the period 1553 to 1558 provide evidence of an 'evanescent public sphere' that was created when there was important news to be discussed but faded when it was no longer required.[7] Of course, ballads functioned primarily as entertainment and allowed their authors and performers to make a profit; however, listeners might also learn from their content.

Mary's Lawful Inheritance

Ballads attempted to influence the opinion of their audience, albeit in a way that was neither co-ordinated nor officially sponsored. The ballads printed in the immediate wake of the queen's accession portrayed Mary's ascendance as widely popular. The most important feature of these ballads was their emphasis on Mary's dynastic right, which highlighted the return to the rightful succession after Northumberland's coup. Thomas Watertoune's ballad *A ninuectiue agaynst Treason*, for example, described Mary as the 'ryghtful queene' and the lawful inheritor of the crown of England. Moreover, Watertoune foregrounded the moral aspects of recent events, appropriating history in order to support Mary's accession.[8] He placed Northumberland at the end of a long list of traitors, describing the unpleasant ends met by individuals who attempted to usurp the crown's authority. In doing so, he not only asserted the authority of the new queen, he invoked religious authority and normative moral values. A just God would always ensure that there was retribution for those that did wrong and 'most rightfully, doth always punyshe treason'.

Simultaneously, Watertoune cast aspersions on the Plantagenet line. His ballad laid the blame for the murders of Henry VI and the Princes in the Tower at the door of Richard III. Richard got his comeuppance, however, when 'at the last for his desartes, at Boseworth was he slayne'. In oral cultures, singers tell traditional stories in a traditional manner, and, although they are creative, this creativity is fixed within boundaries, such as the syntax of the storyline.[9] The traditional syntax for the Tudor period was to denigrate Richard III, the last of the Plantagenet line, who was defeated in battle by Henry VII, the first Tudor king. As Henry VII's claim to the throne had scarcely been any more credible than those of other descendants of the houses of York and Lancaster, the Tudors were always keen to promote their legitimacy and disparage their immediate predecessor. Watertoune's ballad therefore echoed the way in which Richard III was represented in several contemporary chronicles. Polydore Vergil described how 'the miserable man had suddaynly suche end as wont ys to happen to them that have right and law both of god and man in lyke estimation, as will, impyetie, and wickedness'.[10] Even though Vergil's text was only available in either a Latin printed edition or English manuscript at the time, Edward Hall's popular *Chronicle* was based on Vergil's. Written in English, it was also more widely available, having been printed in 1542, 1548 and 1550. Hall described Richard's murder of the princes in a similar manner:

> two noble princes, these innocente tendre children, borne of the mooste royall bloude and brought vp in greate wealthe, likely longe to liue, to reigne and rule in the realme, by trayterous tirannye taken and depriued of their estate, shortely shut vp in prison and priuely slaine and murthered by the cruel ambicion of their vnnaturall vncle and his dispiteous tourmentours: whiche thynges on euery parte well pondered, God gaue this world neuer a more notable example, either in what vnsurety standeth this worldes weale, or what mischiefe workethe the proude enterprise of an highe harte, or finally, what wretched ende ensueth suche dispiteous crueltie.[11]

Richard's murder of the young princes was believed to have been motivated by the threat that they presented to his authority. Likewise, Watertoune described how Northumberland and his supporters were responsible for the deaths of Protector Somerset and his younger brother, Sudeley, before trying to usurp the succession through Jane:

> At last they dyd attempt agaynst, theyr liege Lady and Queene:
> Mary by the grace of god, of Englande and of Fraunce
> And also right heyre of Irelande, most comly to be sene,
> Whom the mighty lorde preserue, from all hurt and mischaunce
> For she to ioyful godlynes. ledeth the parfect daunce
> Whom god at her great need doth helpe, workynge nothing in vayne
> Subdueth to her, her enemies al, which wrought with dredful crayne.

Finally, when Mary gained the throne, her people were able to celebrate: 'Such myrth was made in euery place as the lyke was neuer seene / That god had shewed on vs his grace in geuyng a ryghtful queene'. Northumberland, on the other hand,

> ...came a traytourin full sad, with hart that might be colde
> The same whom al before dyd feare, and were in most subiection
> The people wolde in peeces teare, yf they might haue election.

This suggests not only relief that Northumberland's plot had been foiled, but also that the council wanted people to believe that they had acquiesced to his plans only because they had been afraid of him.[12] It emphasised their loyalty to the new queen. Not only did Watertoune reinforce the social norm that traitors were always brought low, but he reminded his listeners that legitimate succession was by far the most important consideration in the continuity of the monarchy. His use of the inclusive words 'we' and 'us' implicitly placed the audience on the side of Queen Mary. It divided the audience by excluding those who did not support her, affiliating them with those traitors who were, of course, always punished. These phrases formed the basis of the personal element in the relationship between the ballad-monger and his audience.[13] As a narrative device, they reinforced the collective nature of listening in a group, inviting individuals to become part of the dominant ideology.[14]

Coming to Terms with a Queen Regnant

It is, of course, likely that celebratory ballads would sell in significant numbers following the accession of a new monarch, both because of people's interest in the news and because of a genuine mood of celebration. But the balladeers were not afraid to acknowledge that a reigning queen was unfamiliar. Mary I was something new and different, of which 'the lyke was neuer earst seene here'. William Forrest greeted Mary's accession with *A New Ballade of the Marigolde*, which lauded Henry's elder daughter as 'Marie, our Queene, that Floure so sweete'.[15] Like Watertoune, he exhorted all men to obey her rule. He argued that her position as queen regnant was God-given, a direct result of her virtue, education and faith: she had come to the throne through God's favour and his 'Graces many folde'. Forrest was an ordained priest and a prolific poet whose flattering portrait of the queen is unsurprising, considering his family connections. He was related to Catherine of Aragon's chaplain, the Franciscan friar, John Forest, who continued to visit the embattled queen during the six years of Henry VIII's divorce proceedings. John Forest was eventually executed for heresy in 1538, after being tried for his religious conservatism and allegiance to the pope.[16] Indeed, he was the only Tudor or Stuart papist who was burned as a heretic rather than hanged as a traitor.

William Forrest, however, continued to publish and dedicate his works to members of the royal family throughout the mid-sixteenth century's religious changes, suggesting that he put fealty to his monarch and the material need for patronage above his spiritual convictions.

Forrest's first known poem was dedicated to Queen Catherine Parr's brother, William, in 1545. The Parrs were a prominent Protestant family. In 1548, Forrest dedicated the *Pleasaunt Poesye of Princelie Practise* first to 'the moste worthie and famouse Prince Edward... Vncle vnto oure most dreade soueraigne lord, kinge Edwarde the Sexthe'.[17] Interestingly, this reflects the roles of the Protector, Edward Seymour, and the minor, King Edward: Forrest first addressed the arbiter of power and, only several pages later, the titular monarch. He also used the courtesy title 'prince' for the Lord Protector. In addition, Forrest composed metrical translations of 50 psalms for the Edwardian regime. It seems likely that Forrest found that it was the boundaries of religious toleration which changed around him, rather than his own beliefs.[18]

The *New Ballade of the Marigolde* is one of a number of works that Forrest dedicated to Queen Mary, the longest of which was his *History of Grisild the Second*, a versified history of Mary's mother, Catherine of Aragon. He presented it to Mary I shortly before her death in 1558.[19] Of course, dedications such as those made by Forrest did not necessarily reflect actual patronage by the dedicatee.[20] They could be purely speculative, written in the hope that the author would gain some sort of favour. In Forrest's case, his dedication of works to the queen seems to have been successful, despite his contribution to the Protestant cause, as Mary made him one of her chaplains in 1555. The *New Ballade* began by comparing the virtues of various English flowers:

> In Yeare, first springeth the Violet:
> The Primerose then, also doth spred:
> The Couslip sweete, abroade doth get:
> The Daisye gaye, sheweth forth her hed:
> The Medowes greene, so garnished,
> Most goodly (truly) to beholde,
> For which, God is to be Praised:
> Yet I commende, the Marigolde.

Flowers were imbued with popular meanings and associations for those who were in the know. The primrose and violet were associated with sadness, because they flower so early in the year that they do not live to see the summer sun. The violet was also linked with death while the primrose alluded to perpetual spinsterhood.[21] Other flowers came and went, but only the marigold was a constant companion, flowering early in the year and dying off in the winter.

The marigold, though, was also an especially potent symbol for Mary I. It played on her name, her position as queen regnant with a golden crown and, of course, the flower's association with the Virgin Mary. Forrest described how

> Shee may be calde, Marigolde well,
> Of Marie (chiefe) Christes mother deere,
> That as in heauen, shee doth excell,
> And Golde in earth, to haue no peere:
> So (certainly) shee shineth cleere,
> In Grace and honour double folde,
> The like was neuer earst seene heere,
> Suche is this floure, the Marigolde,

Mary was obviously peerless in England, given that she was an unmarried queen. She held the most exalted position of any woman that England had ever seen. She was an anomaly, an aberration even, that Forrest needed to explain. Forrest could directly address this thorny matter of female monarchy, without relying on implicitness, because he was writing in praise of the reigning monarch's education and her meekness.

Queens regnant, who sat on the throne in their own right rather than by virtue of their husband or son, posed two significant challenges to the social norms. The first was that their power was believed to increase their masculinity. Women were expected to be meek, yet to be an effective ruler, Mary also needed to display masculine the traits of strength and dominance. This was precisely the problem that Matilda, the Lady of England, had faced when she attempted to assert her right to inherit the throne in 1141. Humility was a highly regarded feminine quality and it was one that Matilda was accused of losing through masculinity. The anonymous author of the medieval *Gesta Stephani* displayed typical concerns about 'manly women' when, writing in support of King Stephen, he complained that Matilda had become 'a woman of subtlety and a man's resolution', 'mightily puffed up and exalted in spirit'.[22] The second challenge faced by women with power was the subversive example that they were believed to set to other women. This was less to do with misogyny than it was about men's fears that women would become assertive and independent.[23]

By using the iconography of the Virgin Mary, however, Marian balladeers were able to counteract fears that as queen regnant Mary would become an unnaturally masculine virago. The Virgin Mary was, of course, the model of womanhood, 'chaste, merciful, pure and unthreatening'.[24] She was a reassuring image of a woman in power as much as she was an image of Catholicism. The Mother of God helped Mary I to achieve a double-gendered status: her masculine role as king was feminised by images of the Virgin Mary and the emphasis on her feminine virtues. Forrest's ballad suggested that Mary had been able to ascend the throne while maintaining her feminine qualities because of God's grace, in the same way that the Virgin Mary had taken on a role of authority and kept her femininity intact.

Mary's Catholicism

But it was only once Forrest had dealt with Mary's dynastic claim that the issue of the queen's Catholicism came to the fore. Forrest clearly believed that Mary would restore the Catholic faith to England. He hoped that this would plant peace among the people and expressed the wish that 'That Errour may go hide his face'.[25] Far from a suggestion that Mary should root out heresy, at this early stage in the queen's reign it was more of an appeal for religious unity. Like an echo of the Cromwell ballads, Forrest suggested that unity was required in order to heal the commonwealth. After all the religious and political upheavals, an outward show of conformity would bring much needed stability to the country.

Forrest claimed that Mary's reluctant acceptance of Henry VIII's headship of the Church of England was an error that God had forgiven.[26] His intriguing verse

> Yf she (in faith) had erred a-misse,
> which God, most sure, doth vnderstande,
> wolde hee haue doone, as provéd is,
> Her Enmies so to bring to hande?

was placed immediately after a description of Mary's education and virtue. It is possible that to many people, this simply suggested that Mary's accession to the throne was proof that she had never sinned. For those who were in the know, however, it could be heard as a reference to the articles that Mary had been forced to sign in June 1536, rejecting the Pope's authority in England. As a member of the court, it is entirely possible that Forrest was aware of that youthful submission to her father, made under duress and indeed in fear for her life. The imperial ambassador, Eustace Chapuys, had counselled Mary to sign the articles in 1536, advising that

> if the King persisted in his obstinacy, or she found evidence that her life was in danger, either by maltreatment or otherwise, to consent to her father's wish, assuring her that such was your advice, and that, to save her life, on which depended the peace of the realm and the redress of the great disorders which prevail here, she must do everything and dissemble for some time…

> After the Princess had signed the document she was much de-
> jected, but I immediately relieved her of every doubt, even of con-
> science, assuring her that the Pope would not only not impute to her
> any blame, but would hold it rightly done.[27]

Despite receiving this assurance from Chapuys that she would receive
absolution from the Pope for her actions, in fact she was given no such
preferential treatment. Although there is no evidence that Mary's submission to her father was widely publicised, it is clear that it was the subject of much comment in royal circles because Chapuys described how
'As soon as news arrived of her subscription, incredible joy was shown
in all the Court' and 'Innumerable persons sent to me to congratulate me
on the reconciliation of the King and the Princess'.[28]

Forrest's opinion seems to be that, although Pope Paul III had refused
to absolve her for her Nicodemite submission to the English schism, God
had understood the impossible situation in which she had found herself
and had finally proved this by vanquishing those who would have kept her
from the throne. Pope Julius III agreed that Mary's succession had come
about because of her unfaltering commitment to Roman Catholicism. Of
course, at the time of the Henrician schism there was no reason to think
that reformation of the Catholic church and the repudiation of papal
authority would inevitably lead England to the heresy and damnation of
Protestantism, but in a letter to Cardinal Pole at the beginning of August
1553, Pope Julius stated that 'God has given the crown to Mary, who has
never deviated from the Catholic faith'.[29] Mary's personal piety had, for
Forrest and Pope Julius, never been in question. Moreover, she had endured 'paciently / The stormes of such as list to scolde / At her dooynges,
with cause why, / Loth to see spring this Marigolde'. These words could
be read either as an indictment of the attempt to put Jane Grey on the
throne, or, for a more knowing section of the audience, as another veiled
reference to Mary's tribulations at the hands of her father.

Forrest wrote other verses in praise of Mary, based on the Lord's
Prayer and the Te Deum. Published in 1555, they aroused the ire of
John Foxe, who included them in his *Actes and Monuments* to show
how Catholics 'wrasted and depraued' God's word. Forrest's *Pater
Noster to gods glory, With prayer to him for Quene Mary* and *Te
Deum, lauding god specially with prayer therin, for our Quene Mary*
interspersed lines based on the English translation of the Lord's Prayer
and Te Deum with lines on a similar theme praying for God's protection of the queen, for example:

> Thy kyngdome be vs here among,
> As in our hartes to raigne,
> Quene Mary prosper thou here long,
> Her honour none to stayne.[30]

Nevertheless, despite Foxe's disapproval, many of the population were undoubtedly sympathetic to Mary's Catholic beliefs.[31] As well as using biblical imagery for Mary, *An Ave Maria in Commendation of Our Most Vertuous Queene* took the Hail Mary as a starting point for each verse in turn. It was a vibrant statement of support for the queen.[32] Its author, Leonard Stopes, was one of the original scholars of St John's College, Oxford, in 1555. St John's was founded by Sir Thomas White to train Catholic priests to counter the threat of Protestantism. By 1559, Stopes was described as a priest. Refusing to conform to Protestantism under Elizabeth I, he fled to the English College at Douai and later returned to England as a Roman Catholic missionary. Lemon's *Catalogue of Broadsides and Ballads* erroneously dates the *Ave Maria* to Mary's accession in 1553.[33] But Stopes's reference to plural 'Catholike Capitaynes, to gouerne the same' dates the song after the marriage of Philip and Mary in July 1554. If the *Ave Maria* were written during Stopes's time at Oxford, this would place publication not only after burnings of Protestants began in 1555, but furthermore, at around the time that the heresy trials of Cranmer, Latimer and Ridley were taking place in the same city. Their executions were carried out just outside the city walls, with Latimer and Ridley dying on 16 October 1555, and Cranmer in March the following year. The *Ave Maria* described Mary's efforts to stamp out Protestantism:

> Of sectes and of schysmes a riddaunce to make,
> Of horrible errours and heresies all;
> She carkes & cares & great trauell dooth take,
> That vertue may flourish and vice haue a fall.

If the ballad were published at the time of these executions, it would present a timely reminder of Mary as 'the mirrour of mercifulnesse', placing the virtues of conformity in contrast to the theatre of persecution. Furthermore, it would lend an extra degree of topicality and newsworthiness to the ballad.

Biblical Imagery

As well as eliding the queen with the Virgin Mary, the song invoked two other biblical women: Esther and Judith. The use of such iconography was not particularly unusual, but in Mary's case, it was especially relevant. These were strong women who stood up for their faith and their people. Esther was the wife of king Xerxes. When Haman plotted genocide against the Persian Jews, she put her own life in peril in order to save her people by admitting to her husband her own Jewish identity. Likewise, Judith's apparent weakness belied her ability to behead the Assyrian general Holofernes, allowing the people of Israel to expel their

foreign invaders. Images of Judith were included in a coronation pag-
eant and in the border art of an unpublished prayer book, as well as in
Stopes's ballad, which shows that there was a crossover between official
and popular representations of Mary.[34] Mary was a strong, Catholic
heroine, victorious over the Protestant usurpation of the true church,
just as Judith had been over the tyrant Holofernes.

   Biblical imagery was familiar to the sixteenth-century population,
but Stopes was rather more unusual in invoking Mary as a 'princely
Mynerue', the Roman goddess of wisdom, who was believed to have
sprung, clothed in armour, directly from the head of her father, Jupiter.
As well as stressing Mary's rightful inheritance from her father, the classical figure of Minerva highlighted the masculine aspects of a reigning
queen, reinforced by the images of combat in the sixth verse:

> Our life is a warfare, the worlde is the fielde:
> Her highnes her army hath alwayes at hande;
> For Hope is her helmet, Faith is her shielde,
> And loue is her brestplate, her foes to withsta[n]d.

These masculine images, however, were softened by the stress on Mary's
femininity and, in particular, the allusion to the Virgin Mary that gives
the whole piece its structure.

   The strongly Catholic nature of ballads such as the *Ave Maria* and
the *Te Deum* show that, once Mary's dynastic right had been established, her religious beliefs were central to her rule and helped to define her popular image. Although several of the ballads were in the
panegyric genre, one clearly refers to doctrinal differences between
Protestants and Catholics. *An exclamation[n] upo[n] the erroneous
and fantasticall sprite of heresy, troubling to the Unitie of the Church,
deceavi[n]g the simple Christia[n] with her unperfect, unprofitable
and vayn words*, was published in late 1553 or during 1554.[35] It contains references to the seven sacraments of the Catholic rite (five of
which had been reduced in significance by the reformed church) and
to the intercession of saints. The ballad decried married priests, claiming that they 'livest in aduoutry'. It stated that good Catholics would
excel in virtue while, conversely, heretics would surely 'burne in hell'.
What is more, it contains a possible implicitly derogatory reference to
Princess Elizabeth:

> Fro[m] her ne swerue, lest thou do sterue
> with childer reprobate
> whose parentes be iniquitie
> gotte by the sprite debate,
> Thu[n]lauful spouses, whose works, doutles,
> As hypocrites God doth hate.

Elizabeth's parents, Henry VIII and Anne Boleyn (whose affair had helped to end Henry's marriage to Catherine of Aragon, resulted in Mary's bastardy and provoked the break with Rome), were seen by some as iniquitous. This was calculated to appeal to the many Catholics thought their union to have been unjust and sinful. William Forrest's *History of Grisild the Seconde* described how 'sundrye and many ad-noted the case, / That well they wiste they wolde togeathers knytt, / What soeauer lawe dyd oyghtys prohybyt'. Forrest commented that the afflictions of the church were 'myschifes, with a hundredefolde moe' that 'began / At the incummynge of this new Queene *Anne*'.[36] If the verse in the ballad related to Henry VIII, Anne Boleyn and Princess Eliza-beth, then the ballad also justified the succession of Mary as the rightful, Catholic heir, and sidelined Elizabeth as the bastard daughter of parents who had never been married in God's eyes.

Marriage of a Queen

Mary's name and Catholic faith combined to create a gift to the Marian apologists, who could invoke potent imagery of a strong but gentle woman of unimpeachable faith. Nevertheless, the Virgin Mary had no power except through that of her son. Mary the Mother of Jesus was a mediator between earth and heaven, who cherished the future king, but she was never a ruler in her own right and her power was drawn from God.[37] Consequently, the balladeers' emphasis on Mary's unusual posi-tion as an unmarried queen was unsustainable in the long term. In stark contrast to the Virgin Mary, Mary I would need a husband in order to conceive a future king. Mary's intent to marry brought with it the fright-ening prospect of a foreign king.

On 25 July 1554, Mary married Philip of Spain at Winchester Cathedral. John Heywood celebrated the 'meete match' between the Habsburg 'ea-gle' and Tudor 'rose' in a *Balade specifienge partly the maner, partly the matter, in the most excellent meetyng and lyke Mariage betwene our Soueraigne Lord and our Soueraigne Lady, the Kynges and Queenes Highnes*.[38] Heywood was the closest the Marian regime came to a popu-lar propagandist. Although he had been indicted for treason under Henry VIII for his part in the Prebendaries Plot to discredit Thomas Cranmer, he had been pardoned and made to recant publicly at Paul's Cross. His unswerving loyalty to Mary was eventually rewarded by a pension and the grant of a manor in Yorkshire. He and his family remained Catholic throughout the religious changes of the mid-sixteenth century, eventually leaving England for Brabant in 1564 rather than convert. Nevertheless, even for a loyal supporter of Mary like Heywood, Mary as queen reg-nant and the lion of England, 'Namelie the beaste most furious... may seeme straunge'. Despite using masculine stereotypes, Heywood insisted, like William Forrest, on Mary's femininity. Mary was 'No rampant lion masculine' but a 'lamblike lion feminyne'. He emphasised the peculiarity of the queen regnant, which required the addition of the male monarch to normalise it. Men (and indeed women) believed that women's lives were defined by their marital status: they were maids, wives or widows. They were, in short, defined by their men.[39] There was, of course, a discrepancy between these feminine identities and the *de facto* business done by women, as many gentlewomen were able managers of homes and estates during their husbands' absences.[40] But despite this, the population received 'constant reiteration of the principles of husbandly authority over wives'.[41] As Heywood saw it, through marriage to Philip, the Habsburg eagle, 'this birde dothe bring / A queenlie queene, a kinglie king'. Queen Mary was completed by King Philip and the natural order was restored.

This view of normality can be seen in two socio-economic protest songs, *In a pleasante earber, very quaynte and quadrente* and *Who lovithe to lyve in peas*. Both these ballads close with loyal prayers for Philip and Mary, rather than Mary and Philip. For example, Henry Sponare finished his ballad with a verse in praise of the royal family:

> Let us pray for Philepe and Mary, the firste of the name,
> That God ther ryall majestice may longe prosspare and mayntayn;
> And with trewthe and veryté ther harttes to inflame,
> Graciously to rull all the tyme of ther rayne
> And for my lady Elsabethes grace pray we also a meane,
> With all the noble cownssell worthé to resyghte
> That God offe his enfluence may put into ther brayne
> For to exsalte vertu and put downe vice quyghte.[42]

It is significant that the king is mentioned before the queen in these ballads. Since Philip and Mary are both words of two syllables with the stress on the first, it makes no difference metrically. These ballads presumably reflect the way in which the couple were actually seen by outsiders, confirming the patriarchal assumptions made by people at the time. It is certainly the order in which their style named them and the order in which their names appear on official documents.[43] The *Ballad of Ioy* even presents the royal family in Trinitarian fashion, praising first Philip, then Mary as the mother of a king:

> Blysse thou swete Jesus, our comforters three
> Oure Kynge, our Quene, our Prince that shal be:
> That they three as one, or one as all three,
> Maye governe the people, to the plesure of the.[44]

On the other hand, while the balladeers welcomed a return to the natural order of things, marriage for a reigning queen also brought the concomitant problems of patriarchy into sharp relief. Although she held the most powerful position in England, in her own household Mary would surely be subordinate to her husband. Because in England a woman's property passed to her husband when she married, this would potentially hand the country over to Philip's control.[45] Parliament discussed the constitutional implications of the wedding. The articles of a royal marriage treaty were published for the first time, specifically in an attempt to quell fears about domination by a foreign power. The marriage settlement attempted to limit Philip's authority over English affairs in a way that he felt to be emasculating.[46] Heywood's ballad, likewise, subverted traditional gender roles. Even if this was not an example of implicitness, Heywood's ballad reinforced the image of a queen assuming a king's power and a king in the role of consort:

> A birde, a beast to make to choose
> Namelie the beast most furious
> It may seeme straunge, and so it doose
> And to this birde iniurious
> It semthe a case right curious
> To make construction in suche sens
> As may stande for this birds defens

The text might also contain an implicit reference to the dispute that had taken place in court circles over who would be the better husband for Mary: a foreign prince, with whom came the potential threat of England's subordination to an external power, or an Englishman, who would be Mary's social inferior. Philip and Mary were 'lyke to lyke' and a 'meete ... matche in parentage', whereas marriage to the English contender, Edward Courtenay, would have promoted him above his place in society. Heywood stressed that Philip and Mary matched 'Croune vnto croune'. Mary, the reigning queen, was the Tudor rose and a 'crounid lion', while Philip had been made king of Naples shortly before the ceremony in order to raise him to her rank. Their wedding was therefore one of equals.

Mother of a King

It was hoped that the return to order signified by Philip and Mary's wedding would be cemented by the birth of a son. On the surface, *The Ballad of Ioy* was a celebration of the queen's pregnancy and hope for an heir, but a closer reading of the text provides some interesting insights into attitudes to Mary, Philip and the continuity of the monarchy. Although the date and author of the ballad are not given, it is unlikely that it was written during Mary's second false pregnancy (after January 1558 when Mary felt certain that she was six months pregnant and informed Philip). A conjectural setting of the words to the sixteenth-century tune of 'Nancie' can be found in Figure 7.1.[47] The version of the ballad in the Pepys collection includes a note that there is 'pasted on the Backside of this Ballad, a printed copy of a Letter sent from the Council to the Bishop of London, to sing Te Deum for her Maj[es]tie's being w[i]th Child'. This corresponds to a reference in Henry Machyn's diary in November 1554 that

> The xxix day of November was commondyd by the byshope of London, thrughe ys dyosesse, that thay shuld say the masse of the Holy-gost (with) prossessyon, and to syng *Te Deum*, and ryngyng, [and to] pray to God to gyffe hym thankes of owr [gracious] quen of her qwyckenyng with chyld, and to pray.[48]

The singing of the Te Deum in 1554 is confirmed by *The Chronicle of the grey friars of London*, but there is no mention of the Te Deum being ordered in 1558.[49] In early 1555, several London women were censured for suggesting that the queen was not pregnant, but would take another woman's baby and pass it off as her own.[50] This corroborates doubts about Mary's fertility even during the first pregnancy and, alongside the evidence of the Te Deum, it increases the likelihood of the ballad being contemporary with the earlier pregnancy. The earliest possible date for the ballad, therefore, is late November 1554 when the Te Deum was sung across London to give thanks for the queen's quickening. Its latest possible date is August 1555, when the queen returned to her public life following the acceptance that her pregnancy was false.

Even though Mary had been on the throne for a year, the anonymous poet expressed relief at the restoration of the rightful succession after the seizure of power by Northumberland's faction, and commented on the 'thraldomes' under which England had lived prior to Mary's accession. The song, however, clearly shows that there had been doubts about the success of Mary's marriage to Philip and the possibility of the queen (who was already 38 by the time of her marriage) becoming pregnant. The central section of the song brought into the open the opposition that her marriage to Philip had engendered:

> And suche as envied matche and the make
> And in their proceedinges, stoode styffe as a stake:
> Are now reconciled, their malis doth slake,
> And all men are wilinge, theyr partes for to take.

> Our doutes be dissolved, our fancies contented,
> The mariage is joyfull that many lamented:
> And suche as envied, like foles have repented,
> The Errours and Terrours, that they have invented.[51]

Figure 7.1 Conjectural setting of *The Ballad of Ioy* to 'Nancie' from *The Fitzwilliam Virginal Book*, ed. J. A Fuller-Maitland & W. Barclay Squire, i, p. 57. © Dover Publications.

As well as being a common means to include the audience, the balladeer's use of the word 'our' suggests that the fears he acknowledged were widespread.[52]

Furthermore, the words 'Her subjects were dubtful, of her highnes increse' imply that there was significant uncertainty about Mary's fertility. Philip was 11 years Mary's junior and had already fathered a son by his first wife. Just like her mother, Catherine of Aragon, Mary would be the one to get the blame if the couple failed to provide an heir to the throne and secure the dynasty. Even Charles V's ambassador, Renard, cast doubt on Mary's fertility. Writing to the emperor in March 1555, he expressed fears that 'supposing the Queen is not with child and dies without issue there will certainly be strife'.[53] In June, the king's friend and advisor Ruy Goméz commented that he doubted 'whether she is with child at all, greatly as I desire to see the thing happily over'.[54] Although Renard attempted to reassure Charles V that Mary really was pregnant, by early July 1555 the queen was once more receiving her privy councillors and in August she made a full return to public life, tacitly admitting she was not, in fact, expectant.[55]

Anti-Catholic Propaganda

But by no means all of Mary's subjects were pleased by her Spanish marriage and the prospect of a Catholic succession. The wedding cemented Mary's Catholicism in a European context, with the might of the Spanish Habsburgs willing to support her wish to return the English church to papal authority. The return to Rome (and indeed the restoration of Catholicism itself) was divisive, and some oppositional ballads did find their way into print from a position of safety among the Protesant exiles on the continent. *A tragicall blast of the Papisticall trompette for the maintenaunce of the Popes kingdome in Englande* was an ironic ballad that was appended to the end of a 50-page letter from a servant, John Bradford, to the Earls of Arundel, Derby, Shrewsbury and Pembroke.[56] The book appears to have been printed by Protestant exiles in the German town of Wesel, on the Rhine, not far from the border with the Spanish Netherlands. Its publication took advantage of Philip's absence from England between August 1555 and March 1557, a period when he was leading his armies in Flanders. It is tempting to think that *A tragicall blast* made the ideas presented in Bradford's letter more accessible to those of limited literacy; however, although they are both xenophobic in outlook, the contents of the two items differ quite substantially. It is not clear why the aggressively anti-Catholic ballad was appended to the more tolerant, anti-Spanish letter, although it seems that the publisher felt that the two would appeal to the same market. This in itself shows that those who were opposed to the Spanish marriage were also assumed to be open to anti-Catholic propaganda.

In his letter, Bradford comes across as a moderate, reformed Catholic, while his emphasis on unity echoes that of the Cromwell ballads. Despite his objections to papal authority, Bradford's letter was intriguingly positive about the need for Christians of different creeds to live in peace, saying

> And speciallye leaue those most deuilishe names of Papystes, here-
> tikes, Lutherans, protestauntes and suche like, accordyng to the
> Quenes most gracious proclamacion. Ioyne youre selues to gether
> wyth loue & amite, reioysinge to take vpon you the moste blessed
> name of oure sauiore Iesus CHRISTE, the GOD of equitee, peace,
> loue and tranquillite, and to bee called Christians.[57]

Bradford's twin anxieties were what he saw as the lax moral standards of the Spaniards and his fear that they would steal England's wealth. He was concerned that the Spaniards dissimulated in order 'to disceaue oure nobilite' and instead 'loue her treasure faithfully, and her crowne hartely'. This belief was reiterated by the balladeer, who advised that 'Our golden hatte we must defende' and 'The Spaniards hath sworne vs to defe[n]d / So that we betraye Englande to them'.[58] Bradford cited evidence from his experience 'at this present among Spaniards' to suggest that they would violate English wives and daughters. Although the early part of the letter avoids directly condemning Philip, later Bradford spread gossip about the king's sexual improprieties and referred to 'the king and all our enemies'.[59]

For Bradford, the return to papal authority was not the issue: he was neither anti-papal nor anti-Catholic – he was simply anti-Spanish. The ballad attached to the letter, however, conflated the two positions by blaming England's return to Catholicism on Spanish influence. The Pope was equated to Antichrist, 'the devil to him wil neuer say nay'. The re-frain played on the words 'croune', meaning both the crown of a king and the shaven head of a friar, and 'rome', which could be read as both 'Rome' and 'room': 'Now al shauen crounes to the standerd, / Make rome, pul down for the Spaniard'. The ballad's consistent xenophobic and anti-papistical theme laid the blame for the persecution of Protes-tants on Philip, 'the Spaniard'; Mary, on the other hand, is merely re-ferred to as the balladeer's 'foe'. Even John Foxe's *Actes and Monuments* avoided placing the blame for the executions directly on Mary, instead maligning two of her bishops, Bonner and Gardiner, the latter of whom had already died.

Indeed, the *tragicall blast* seems to be the only contemporary printed ballad that contained a clear reference to a specific incident of persecu-tion by Philip and Mary: 'Doe you not see this Englishe in feare: / Their hart is driuen into their hose / Xiii we burned of late to gether'.[60] What is more, the reference to the execution of the Protestants helps to date the publication more precisely, as it must date from after the only known burning of 13 martyrs at the same time. This took place at Stratford le Bow on 27 July 1556. The martyrs included servants, blacksmiths, brewers and two women, all from the county of Essex. Three other men were examined with them, but, agreeing to the articles put before them, they received dispensation from Cardinal Pole and were set free. Foxe provided a detailed account of the martyrs' backgrounds and the examinations which took place before they were executed. It recorded how they

> prayed earnestly vnto God, and ioyfully went to the stake and kyssed it and embraced it most meryly. The eleuen men were tied to foure stakes, and the twoo women lose in the middest without any stake, and so were they all burnt in one fyre, with suche loue to eche others, and constancie in our sauior Christ, that it made all the lokers on to maruell.[61]

Stafford's Rebellion

The following year, opposition to Philip and Mary was made manifest in the seizure of Scarborough Castle by the Protestant rebel, Thomas Stafford. The raid, however, really only served to show how much loyalty there was to the king and queen. Stafford had been involved in the only rebellion to pose a serious threat to the Tudor monarchy, Wyatt's Rebellion of 1554, after which he fled to France. Wyatt's Rebellion had been intended to put an end to proposals for Philip and Mary's marriage and, interestingly, no ballads relating to it have been found. Unlike Wyatt's Rebellion, Stafford's never stood any chance of success. Even though Scarborough Castle was unprotected, the queen's forces were much stronger and were already on their way to meet him by the time he arrived in Yorkshire. Furthermore, the plot failed to gain popular support. Its significance, however, lay not in its immediate threat to the king and queen but in the involvement of the French: it precipitated the queen's decision to support her husband's war in France.[62]

Stafford's raid was the subject of a loyal ballad penned by the playwright and musician, John Heywood.[63] Heywood's refrain, 'Take we Scarborow warning euerichone', is based on an epigram he had already published in 1546.[64] Although this refrain suggests that the rebellion was a surprise (a misconception repeated by Strype in his *Ecclesiastical Memorials*), in fact there had been plenty of intelligence about Stafford's plans.[65] Stafford had been watched carefully since at least April 1554. His activities were being monitored by the treasurer of Calais, Edward Wotton, with the assistance of at least one spy. By November 1556 it was clear that there were plans afoot. Stafford had been heard to claim 'that if her Majesty were dead he were next heir to the crown of England'.[66] This assertion was based on the claim to the throne held by his grandparents, Henry Stafford, Duke of Buckingham, and Margaret Pole, Countess of Salisbury. It was not merely unfounded, but inexplicable, given that his parents and elder brother were still alive. On 27 April 1557, the queen received a letter from Wotton reporting that Stafford had been buying arms and had amassed more than 400 supporters, made up of exiles and Frenchmen. Stafford's two well-armed ships had left Dieppe, reportedly heading for Scotland. On the same date, Mary sent orders to the magistrates of Newcastle and Hull to arm against the incoming rebels.[67] Stafford and his men entered Scarborough on 28 April 1557, with Stafford proclaiming himself Protector of the Realm, but local troops led by the Earl of Westmorland quickly dealt with the rebels. The town did not rise in support of Stafford, despite his claim that King Philip was to be granted 12 English castles that would be garrisoned with Spanish soldiers. Stafford was arrested three days later and executed in London at the end of May.

Heywood's ballad set news of Stafford's rebellion securely in the context of a national sense of the past by referring to the wider significance of the event.[68] *A breefe balet touching the traytorous takynge of Scarborow Castell* celebrated that 'A fewe false traytours can not wynne a reame' and that good subjects knew that their place was to obey their king and queen. Like Watertoune, who appropriated history in support of Mary for his *A ninvective against treason*, Heywood's ballad presented the occurrences in Yorkshire as part of a national history. Heywood warned that his cautionary tale related not only to Scarborough, but served as a remonstrance to protect all the havens belonging to the 'good Kyng and Queene'. He described the rebels as a 'most traitorous sect', with the word 'sect' implying a religious line. He advised his audience to 'serue franke and free' 'One God, one Kynge, one Queene', while the ballad closed with a loyal prayer for Philip and Mary's longevity and prosperity.

Stafford's raid was just the sort of action promoted by William Kethe at the end of Christopher Goodman's 1558 book, *How Superior Powers oght to be obeyd of their subjects*. Goodman's book argued that obedience to an unjust monarch was 'all to gether damnable'. It examined the possibility that in order to obey God's word it might be necessary to disobey the monarch. He hoped to encourage Protestants to resist Mary's rule because she was 'a bastarde, and vnlawfully begotton'. She had 'ioyned her self to adulterous Philip, the Spanishe kinge... and doth continually labor to betray the whole kingdome'.[69] Unlike the *tragicall blast* which had been printed with John Bradford's letter but was very different in tone, the close relationship of Goodman's prose text and Kethe's verses suggests that Kethe was well acquainted with the contents of Goodman's book. The book's 100 pages were distilled into 19 succinct, four-line verses, easier to digest and remember than the prose and especially useful for those who could not read. Moreover, the message could still be spread from person to person through the use of rhyming song if the printed copies were destroyed. Using these two related media meant that the message could be spread to diverse audiences as widely and as effectively as possible.

According to Kethe, the king and queen used their authority unjustly to execute Protestants. Similarly, Goodman's treatise made frequent reference to the murder of Protestants by a queen that he likened to Jezebel:

> Counterfayte Christians this day, which euerie where (but especial-lie in iyr miserable countrie) imprison, famishe, murther, hange, and burne their owne countrymen, and deare children of God, at the commandement of furious Iesabel, and her false Priestes and Proph-etes, the blouddie Bisshops and shauelynges.[70]

Kethe was an aggressive Protestant who had published anti-papal ballads during the reign of Edward VI. An associate of John Knox and John Foxe, he exiled himself to Frankfurt on Mary's accession and continued his attacks on Catholicism from the continent. He was a hugely influential composer of metrical psalms, one of which, *Old Hundredth* (*All people that on earth do dwell*), is still popular to this day. His vitriolic ballad, however, rejects female rule as well as Catholicism, suggesting that those who have reason

> Shal learne how ill Rulers we oght to obeye.
> Whiche kill, how they ca[...]e not in their cruell rage.
> Respecti[n]g their will more, the[n] lawe, othe, or charge.
>
> Whose fury longe fostered by suffrance and awe,
> Haue right rule subuerted, and made will their lawe.[71]

The significance of Kethe's ballad, however, does not lie solely in the way it remodelled a much longer text for a different audience. It also used the same imagery as John Heywood's wedding ballad, subverting its imagery to undermine rather than celebrate the union. Drawing on Heywood's image of Mary as a 'beaste most furious' that 'may seeme straunge', Kethe instead described 'A brut beast vntamed a misbegot-then; / More meete to be ruled, then raigne ouer men'. This theme was developed in Goodman's treatise, which, among its arguments against a queen regnant, complained that the highest authority in England was now 'not a man accordinge to his [God's] appoyntment, but a woman, which his Lawe forbiddeth, and nature abhorreth'.[72] Goodman protested that, because women were forbidden local office and wives were subject to their husbands, the anointing of a queen regnant in like manner to a king was unnatural.

Like Heywood's wedding ballad, Kethe used the image of the Habsburg eagle to represent Philip. In contrast to Heywood's description of the eagle as 'All other birds far surmounting', however, Kethe's bird gorged itself on the wealth of a country before destroying it. Less equivocally than Bradford, Kethe portrayed the Spaniards as vile robbers and rapists who would subjugate England just as they had done Naples. Furthermore, they had involved England in their quarrel with France:

> For France spiteth Spayne, which Englend doth threat,
> And England proud Spanyards, with salte woulde fayne eate:
> Yet Englande proud Spayne aydeth with men, ships, and botes.
> That Spayne, (France subdued once) may cut all their throtes.[73]

Protestant Loyalty

Nevertheless, we should not assume that to be a Protestant was in itself indicative of a lack of loyalty to Philip and Mary's regime. Despite the rampant anti-Catholicism of ballads like William Kethe's and the emphasis on Catholicism in the pro-Marian ballads, many of the queen's Protestant subjects were also loyal to their monarch. One of these, Edward Underhill, was a member of the Gentlemen Pensioners under Edward VI and continued to serve during Mary's Catholic rule, despite his own Protestant beliefs. In 1561, Underhill wrote an account of Mary's accession and the first year of her reign, in which he refers to a ballad that he penned. As it apparently came into the possession of the Secretary of State, Sir John Bourne, in early August 1553, shortly after the queen's accession, it is quite possible that it had been written during Edward's reign. The Privy Council believed it to be seditious and, as a result, Underhill spent a month in Newgate prison, where he requested that an acquaintance send him his nightshirt, his Bible and, tellingly, his lute.[74]

Unfortunately, Underhill did not preserve any details of the ballad in his account of his examination, nor do any of the printed copies seem to have survived, but, by his own admission, the song was anti-papist.[75] What appears to have been at issue in his examination was whether denying papal authority was, in itself, seditious. Underhill's examiners clearly felt that his ballad was treasonable. They asked him to clarify who he thought were papists. Underhill protested that he had 'offended no laws' and that he had been loyal to Mary even when he had been commanded to rise against her in defence of Queen Jane. He commented that 'in this controversy thatt hathe byn sume be called papistes and sume protestaynes', but he protested that he was not the one who should make the distinction between the two.[76] As the Cromwell flyting showed, those who were seen to hold extreme views of either a Protestant or Catholic nature alienated their neighbours. Underhill's account of his examination, however, suggests that concern with defining the exact specifications of Protestantism and Catholicism was felt more by those in authority than the ordinary worshipper.

Of course, it is also reasonable to assume that, in front of the Privy Council, Underhill was trying to avoid implicating himself as a heretic. Having reported his local vicar in Stepney, Henry More, to Archbishop Cranmer under Edward VI, Underhill appears to have been afraid that he would be reported for heresy himself now that his 'ferce enemys' were back in control.[77] Nevertheless, despite his openly Protestant views and position as a Gentleman-at-Arms and Gentleman Pensioner, he managed to escape trial for heresy under Mary, partly by fleeing Stepney and partly through the protection of his friends at court. His move away from Stepney suggests not so much that he was not prepared to stand up for his beliefs, but that self-preservation through loyalty to the monarch was more important.

It is possible, however, that beyond court circles, Mary's unfaltering Catholicism was not well-known, at least in the early days of her reign, and that Protestants might have hoped that Mary would not upset the religious *status quo*. Mary's first proclamation on religion, issued on 18 August 1553, indicated that there would be a degree of religious toleration until the matter could be decided by 'common assent'.[78] Around this time, the Protestant Richard Beeard penned *A Godly Psalme, of Marye Queene*, published in 1553 (Figure 7.2).[79] His *Godly Psalme* displayed either a complete lack of understanding of Mary's religious persuasions or a hope that Mary might at least tolerate Protestantism. As a 'godly psalm', it is definitely more art music than popular song. It was printed with music in four parts that is not properly contrapuntal, but neither is it homophonic. Beeard's composition is, in fact, similar to the four-part harmonisations of the metrical psalms that were in domestic use during the Elizabethan and Jacobean period and, indeed, it prefaced a highly decorated edition of Latin paraphrases from three thanksgiving psalms.[80] It is written in the modes that were associated with prayer in Archbishop Parker's *whole Psalter*.

Whether Beeard's Protestantism was merely characterised by his psalm singing or he did indeed go on to become a Puritan, there was no doubting Beeard's loyalty in the early days of Mary's reign. The *Godly Psalme* condemned the usurpation of the throne by Lady Jane and Northumberland and praised God for his regard for 'equitie, / Treuth, iustice, law, and right'. Its text begins to appear unusual when it evokes Protestant belief in *sola scriptura*, declaring that Edward VI's 'Whole strength was gods trew word'. Beeard's Protestantism is also evident in his claim that 'the Lord hathe placed thus / His chosen and elect'. With the benefit of hindsight, we can see that his belief that Mary would 'strongly buyld vpon / Her brothers good fondacion' would not be borne out.

Figure 7.2 Transcription of Richard Beeard's *A Godly Psalme, of Marye Queene* (London, 1553).

Singing Sedition

Mary's 1553 proclamation also shows that the regime viewed the seductive language and attractive tunes employed by ballads as a potential menace. It ordered that ballads were not to be printed without a license in order to prevent the spread of 'diuersitie of opinions'. As well as Protestant preachers, 'the playing of Interludes and pryntynge of false fonde books, ballettes, rymes, and other lewd treatises in the englyshe tonge' had nourished sedition and rumour, dating back to 'tyme past' but also 'muche renewed' since Mary's accession. A similar catalogue of heretical and seditious material was probed in Bishop Bonner's visitation of 1554. He asked commissioners to investigate 'whether there be any, that hath prynted or solde slaunderous Bookes, Ballades, or playes, contrary to christen religion' and 'whether anye teacher or scholemayster doo teache or reade to any hys scholers any euyl or noughty corrupte boke, ballade, or wrytyng'.[81] Two years later, King Philip's Select Council wrote to inform him of a ban on the movement of minstrels and players, 'for such idle persons have commonly, in their songs and plays, spread heresy and sedition'.[82]

In a society where many were illiterate, the regime's apprehension about ballads is perhaps unsurprising, nor was it by any means a new concern during the 1550s.[83] There had been attempts to control the spread of ballads under both Henry VIII and Edward VI, and they would continue into the next century. Censorship could not be concerned solely with printed or even written texts, because much of society still relied upon the spoken word. Ballads entangled print, music and oral culture, and it was more difficult for the regime to pinpoint the authors of seditious songs than it was to close a print shop.[84] With their attractive melodies, bouncing metre and rhyming lyrics, ballads were a 'potent political tool' with the potential for 'a detrimental effect upon the spiritual and moral standards of the population', precisely because they were easy to pick up and remember.[85] By legislating against seditious songs, the Tudor regime was responding to what it saw as a credible threat.

English balladeers were certainly not above the use of 'rayling ryme' for seditious purposes. On 20 November 1553, the Privy Council ordered the arrest of a preacher named John Huntingdon, for making 'a rayling ryme against Doctour Stokes and the Blissed Sacrament'.[86] Huntingdon appeared before the Council in December, when 'uppon humble submission and promising to amende aswell in doctryne as lyving, [he] was suffered to departe'.[87] The following January, the Council asked Sir Henry Tirell

> to set one Wymberd, who sange a sedytious songe, upon the Pyllerie the next market daye, with a paper on his hed having this written therein, For leude and sedytious rayling, and after a good admonytion to set him at lybertye.[88]

Likewise, John Strype reported that a minstrel's boy named Cornet was taken in front of the Earl of Oxford for singing a ballad called *News Out of London* against the Mass and the activities of the queen.[89] Although efforts to control the activities of balladeers were sporadic, they can be seen as evidence that a proto-public sphere existed at least when there was something newsworthy to discuss.

The ballads in circulation during Philip and Mary's reign provided news and entertainment, telling stories of celebrities, coups and rebellions. These were, in fact, matters of state and therefore ballads were a threat to be taken seriously, not least because they had the potential to spread widely and be remembered due to their appealing tunes. Even though many of the balladeers were positive about female rule, the fact that they addressed it rather than ignoring it meant that they were discussing their duty of obedience. The presence of a woman on the throne subverted the natural and divine law, threatening the assumptions of a society that was based on patriarchy.[90] Nevertheless, the Marian balladeers did not shy away from addressing this problem. The majority of the ballads that acknowledged the issues surrounding gynarchy concluded that hereditary right was more important than the monarch's sex. These ballads represented the views of a section of society that was pleased to see the natural succession restored, even if it were through an unmarried female monarch who would marry a stranger in order to ensure the future of her line. They were happy to see the reformed Catholic faith re-established, or at the very least, happy enough to put fealty to their liege lady before loyalty to their faith. For the most part, they promoted obedience to the legitimate inheritrix of the crown and a tacit acceptance of the religious change that went with it. William Kethe's anti-gynarchical ballad is notable for its vitriolic hostility to Queen Mary and, although it is impossible to rule out the existence of other ballads that expressed opposition to female rule, Kethe's is the only specifically anti-Marian ballad surviving in print or manuscript that can be reliably dated to the period of her rule. Either Mary's reign was portrayed in popular song as more positive than we sometimes give credit, or the evidence of dissenting voices has almost entirely disappeared. Only a few distant echoes remain. Perhaps they avoided written means of transmission in an attempt to avoid prosecution. Radical ballads, which challenged the established norms, were safer to pass on by word of mouth. If they had to be written down, then manuscript was the place to do it.

Notes

1 Cambridge, Cambridge University Library, Registry guard book CUR 8, *The Ballad of Ioy, upon the publication of Q. Mary, Wife of King Philip, her being with child*, f. 7ʳ⁻ᵛ. The chapter title is taken from Thomas Watertoune, *A ninuectyue agaynst Treason*.

2 Loach, *Edward VI*, p. 101.
3 Alec Ryrie, 'The Slow Death of a Tyrant: Learning to Live without Henry VIII, 1547–63', in Mark Rankin, Christopher Highley, and John N. King (eds.), *Henry VIII and His Afterlives: Literature, Politics, and Art* (Cambridge: Cambridge University Press, 2009), p. 80.
4 One other candidate has a claim to this honour. Henry I named his daughter Matilda as his heir. Upon Henry's death in 1135, the throne was claimed by her cousin Stephen. Though her forces managed to defeat Stephen's at the Battle of Lincoln in 1141, she failed in her attempt to be crowned queen and was eventually driven back to her husband's lands in Normandy in 1148. Matilda's biographer acknowledged that we 'cannot be sure that Matilda ever called herself queen of England, though some chroniclers gave her the title' (Marjorie Chibnall, *The Empress Matilda: Queen Consort, Queen Mother and Lady of the English* (Oxford: Blackwell, 1991), p. 104). For more on women who held positions of power prior to Mary's accession, see Helen Castor, *She-Wolves: The Women Who Ruled England before Elizabeth* (London: Faber, 2011).
5 Sharpe, *Selling the Tudor Monarchy*, pp. 260 and 316.
6 Queen Mary's first parliament, in October 1553, overturned her half-brother's religious laws and returned the English church to its position following the 1539 Act of Six Articles. The restoration of papal authority, however, had to wait until the divisive issue of ownership of former church lands had been resolved in June 1554.
7 Rospocher and Salzburg, 'Evanescent Public Sphere', pp. 95–6.
8 Watertoune, *A Ninuectyue Agaynst Treason*.
9 Rubin, *Memory in Oral Traditions*, p. 36.
10 Polydore Vergil, *Three books of Polydore Vergil's English History, comprising the reigns of Henry VI, Edward IV, and Richard III, from an early translation preserved among the MSS. of the Old Royal Library in the British Museum*, ed. Henry Ellis (London: Camden Society, 1846), old series, xxix, p. 226.
11 Edward Hall, *The Vnion of the Two Noble and Illustre Famelies of Lancastre [and] Yorke* (London, 1548), STC (2nd ed.) / 12722, f. xxviij.
12 Susan Brigden, *London and the Reformation* (Oxford: Clarendon Press, 1989), p. 524.
13 Würzbach, *Rise of the English Street Ballad*, p. 17.
14 Marsh, *Music and Society*, p. 57.
15 William Forrest, *A New Ballade of the Marigolde* (London), STC (2nd ed.) / 11186.
16 Giles Tremlett, *Catherine of Aragon: Henry's Spanish Queen: A Biography* (London: Faber, 2010).
17 William Forrest, 'Pleasaunt Poesye of Princelie Practise', in Sydney J. Herrtage (ed.), *England in the Reign of Henry the Eighth Part 1: Starkey's Life and Letters* (London: Early English Text Society, 1878), p. lxxxii.
18 Christopher Haigh, *English Reformations: Religion, Politics, and Society under the Tudors* (Oxford: Clarendon Press, 1993), pp. 285–95.
19 William Forrest, *A History of Grisild the Second: A Narrative in Verse of the Divorce of Queen Katherine of Arragon Written by William Forrest, Sometime Chaplain to Queen Mary I* (London: Chiswick Press, 1875).
20 Heidi Brayman Hackel, *Reading Material in Early Modern England: Print, Gender, and Literacy* (Cambridge: Cambridge University Press, 2009), pp. 105–9.
21 Jessica Kerr and Anne Ophelia Dowden, *Shakespeare's Flowers* (London: Longmans Young Books, 1969), pp. 47 and 42–3, Bridget Gellert Lyons, 'The Iconography of Ophelia', *English Literary History*, 44:1 (1977), p. 66.

22 *The Deeds of Stephen (Gesta Stephani)*, trans. K. R. Potter (London: Thomas Nelson & Sons, 1955), pp. 81 and 79.
23 Fletcher, *Gender, Sex, and Subordination*, p. 401; Judith M. Richards, '"To Promote a Woman to Beare Rule": Talking of Queens in Mid-Tudor England', *Sixteenth Century Journal*, 28:1 (1997), p. 121.
24 Sarah Duncan, *Mary I: Gender, Power, and Ceremony in the Reign of England's First Queen* (New York: Palgrave Macmillan, 2012), p. 129.
25 Forrest, *New Ballade of the Marigolde*.
26 London, British Library, MS Cotton Otho C/X, 'Princess Mary to Henry VIII. [15 June?] 1536', f. 282. David Loades corrected this date to 22 June 1536 (D. M. Loades, *The Reign of Mary Tudor: Politics, Government and Religion in England, 1553–1558* (London: Benn, 1979), pp. 19–20).
27 *L&P* xi, p. 3, no. 7, 'Chapuys to Charles V, 1 July 1536'.
28 *L&P* xi, p. 3, no. 7, 'Chapuys to Charles V, 1 July 1536'.
29 Reginald Pole, *The Correspondence of Reginald Pole*, ed. Thomas Mayer (Aldershot: Ashgate, 2004), p. 129.
30 *TAMO*, 1563 edition, pp. 1203–5.
31 Eamon Duffy, *Fires of Faith: Catholic England under Mary Tudor* (London: Yale University Press, 2009), p. 10; Christopher Haigh, *Reformation and Resistance in Tudor Lancashire* (London: Cambridge University Press, 1975), p. 178; Judith M. Richards, *Mary Tudor* (London: Routledge, 2008), p. 125.
32 Leonard Stopes, *An Ave Maria in commendation of our Most vertuous Queene* (London), STC (2nd ed.) / 23292.
33 Robert Lemon, *Catalogue of a Collection of Printed Broadsides in the Possession of the Society of Antiquaries of London* (London: Society of Antiquaries of London, 1866), p. 12.
34 Sharpe, *Selling the Tudor Monarchy*, pp. 289 and 273.
35 Hyder E. Rollins (ed.), *Old English Ballads 1553–1625: Chiefly from Manuscripts* ([S.l.]: Cambridge University Press, 1920), pp. 27–32. *An exclamation[n] upo[n] the erroneous and fantasticall sprite of heresy* is anonymous and the ballad undated, but its printer, Richard Lant, gives an indication of its date. Two other ballads printed by Lant survive: Forrest's *New Ballade of the Marigold* and Stopes's *Ave Maria*. The former was printed in 1553 at Aldersgate Street, and the latter after July 1554 at Pater Noster Row. This suggests that Lant moved his workshop from Aldersgate Street to Pater Noster Row in 1553 or early 1554. As the *exclamation[n] upo[n] the erroneous and fantasticall sprite of heresy* was printed at Pater Noster Row, it cannot be contemporary with the Forrest ballad. Furthermore, the reverse of the surviving copy is printed with a papal bull in Latin, upon which is written, apparently by hand, 'viz 23 Decembris 1554'.
36 Forrest, *History of Grisild the Second*, p. 54.
37 Janet L. Nelson, 'Women at the Court of Charlemagne: A Case of Monstrous Regiment?', in John Carmi Parsons (ed.), *Medieval Queenship* (Stroud: Alan Sutton, 1994), p. 50.
38 Heywood, *Balade Specifienge Partly the Maner, Partly the Matter*.
39 Fletcher, *Gender, Sex, and Subordination*, p. 376.
40 Fletcher, *Gender, Sex, and Subordination*, p. 226. Evidence of this can be found, for example, in Arthur Plantagenet *et al*, *The Lisle Letters* (6 vols. London: University of Chicago Press, 1981), in which Lady Lisle displays a capable hand in running the household and an active interest in politics.
41 Fletcher, *Gender, Sex, and Subordination*, p. 205.
42 Bod. MS Ashmole 48, Henry Sponare, *In a pleasante earber, very quaynte and quadrente*, f. 57^v–60^r; Bod. MS Ashmole 48, *Who lovithe to lyve in peas*, ff. 37^v–39^r.

43 See Glyn Redworth, *A Family at War? King Philip I of England and Habsburg Dynastic Politics* (Coburg: Prinz-Albert-Ges., 2008).

44 *Ballad of Ioy.*

45 Judith M. Richards, 'Mary Tudor as "Sole Quene"?: Gendering Tudor Monarchy', *Historical Journal*, 40:4 (1997), p. 907.

46 Glyn Redworth, '"Matters Impertinent to Women": Male and Female Monarchy under Philip and Mary', *English Historical Review*, 112:447 (1997), pp. 598–9.

47 *Fitzwilliam Virginal Book*, i, p. 57. The tune is later known as 'All You That Love Good Fellows', but this early arrangement is by Thomas Morley. All anacruses are editorial, using the pitch which seemed musically appropriate based on the style of the accompaniment. Some further rhythmic alterations have been made in bars 2 and 19 in order to accommodate the words.

48 Machyn, *Diary*, pp. 76–7.

49 J. G. Nichols (ed.), *The Chronicle of the grey friars of London* (London, Camden Society, 1852), old series, liii, pp. 80–98.

50 Brigden, *London and the Reformation*, pp. 595–6.

51 *Ballad of Ioy.*

52 Richards, 'Mary Tudor as "Sole Quene"?', p. 907.

53 *CSPSpan* xiii, p. 150, no. 164, 'Simon Renard to the Emperor, London, March or April 1555'.

54 *CSPSpan* xiii, p. 222, no. 212, 'Ruy Gómez de Silva to Francisco de Eraso, Hampton Court, 8 June 1555'.

55 *CSPSpan* xiii, p. 227, no. 220, 'Simon Renard to the Emperor, Twickenham, 10 July 1555'; John Edwards, *Mary I: England's Catholic Queen* (London: Yale University Press, 2011), p. 268.

56 John Bradford, *The copye of a letter, sent by Iohn Bradforth to ... the Erles of Arundel, Darbie, Shrewsburye, and Penbroke, declaring the nature of the Spaniardes, and discovering the most detestable treasons, which thei haue pretended ... agaynste ... Englande. Wherunto is added a tragical blast of the papisticall tro[m]pet. by T.E.* ([Wesel?], 1556), STC (2nd ed.) / 3504.5. The number of pages in the book suggests that the ballad may have been included in order to fill up the final signature's remaining sheets.

57 Bradford, *copye of a letter*, sigs. Gv^v–Gvi^r.

58 Bradford, *copye of a letter*, sigs. Bvi^r, Bii^v and Gviii^v.

59 Bradford, *copye of a letter*, sigs. Aiiii^v, Fvi^v–Fvii^r and Dii^v.

60 Bradford, *copye of a Letter*, sig. Gviii^r.

61 *TAMO*, 1563 edition, p. 1594.

62 Edwards, *Mary I*, p. 294.

63 John Heywood, *A breefe balet touching the traytorous takynge of Scarborow Castell* (London, 1557), STC (2nd ed.) / 13290.7.

64 John Heywood, *A dialogue conteinyng the nomber in effect of all the prouerbes in the englishe tongue compacte in a matter concernyng two maner of mariages, made and set foorth by Iohn Heywood* (London, 1546), STC (2nd ed.) / 13291, sig. Eiii^r.

65 John Strype, *Ecclesiastical Memorials Relating Chiefly to Religion* (Oxford: Clarendon Press, 1822), p. 67.

66 *CSPFor*, SP 69/9 f. 146, p. 276, no. 559, 'Dr. Wotton to Queen Mary, 30 Nov. 1556'.

67 *CSPFor*, SP 69/10 f. 77, p. 298, no. 593, 'Dr. Wotton to Queen Mary, 27 Apr. 1557'; London, British Library, MS Cotton Vespasian C/XIV/2, 'An order of Q. Mary, to the magistrates of Newcastle, 27 Apr. 1557', f. 303.

68 Woolf, *Social Circulation of the Past*, p. 273.

69 Christopher Goodman, *How superior powers oght to be obeyd of their subiects and wherin they may lawfully by Gods Worde be disobeyed and resisted* (Geneua, 1558), STC (2nd ed.) / 12020, pp. 8, 98 and 100.
70 Goodman, *How superior powers oght to be obeyd*, pp. 61–2.
71 Goodman, *How superior powers oght to be obeyd*, pp. 235–6.
72 Goodman, *How superior powers oght to be obeyd*, p. 96.
73 Goodman, *How superior powers oght to be obeyd*, pp. 136–7.
74 Edward Underhill, 'Autobiographical Anecdotes of Edward Underhill, Esquire, One of the Band of Gentlemen Pensioners', in J. G. Nichols (ed.), *Narratives of the Days of the Reformation: Chiefly from the Manuscripts of John Foxe the Martyrologist* (London: Camden Society, 1859), old series, lxxvii, p. 146.
75 A set of four verses reprinted by Nichols at the end of Underhill's 'Autobiographical Anecdotes' (p. 176) are not anti-papal in character, so there is nothing to indicate that these were the contentious verses investigated by the Privy Council.
76 Underhill, 'Autobiographical Anecdotes', pp. 140–1.
77 Underhill, 'Autobiographical Anecdotes', p. 157.
78 *By the Quene the Quenes Highnes Well Remembrynge...* (London, 1553), STC (2nd ed.) / 7849. On Mary's use of this proclamation to consolidate her position and explain her actions directly to her people, as well as more generally on the monarchy's use of proclamations to spread the news, see Chris R. Kyle, 'Monarch and Marketplace: Proclamations as News in Early Modern England', *Huntington Library Quarterly*, 78:4 (2015), p. 783.
79 Richard Beeard, *A Godly Psalme, of Marye Queene* (London, 1553), STC (2nd ed.) / 1655.
80 Temperley, *Music of the English Parish Church*, i, p. 71.
81 Edmund Bonner, *Articles to Be Enquired of in the Generall Visitation of Edmonde Bisshoppe of London* (London, 1554), STC (2nd ed.) / 10248.
82 *CSPDom Mary* viii, SP 11/8 f. 83, p. 204, no. 421, 'The council to the king, 7 May 1556'.
83 For a discussion of literacy rates in early modern England, see Watt, *Cheap Print*, pp. 6–7.
84 Pettegree, *Invention of News*, p. 10.
85 Marsh, *Music and Society*, p. 225; Jonathan Willis, '"By These Means the Sacred Discourses Sink More Deeply into the Minds of Men": Music and Education in Elizabethan England', *History*, 94:3 (2009), pp. 294–309.
86 *APC* iv, PC 2/7, p. 368, '[Meeting] At Westminster, the xxth of Novembre, 1553', f. 43.
87 *APC* iv, PC 2/7, p. 375, '[Meeting] At Westminster, the thirde of December, 1553', f. 51.
88 *APC* iv, PC 2/7, p. 88, '[Meeting] At Westminster, the xiiijth of January, 1554', f. 195.
89 Strype, *Ecclesiastical Memorials*, p. 124.
90 Susan Dunn-Hensley, 'Whore Queens: The Sexualised Female Body and the State', in Carole Levin, Jo Eldridge Carney, and Debra Barrett-Graves (eds.), *'High and Mighty Queens' of Early Modern England: Realities and Representations* (Basingstoke: Palgrave Macmillan, 2003), p. 102.

8 'Some Good Man, for the Commons Speake'
Radical Ballads and the Commonwealth

> Suche foly is fallen
> And wise out blawen
> That grace is gone
> And all goodness.
> Then no marvell
> Thoght it thus befell,
> Commons to mell
> To make redresse.[1]

Popular rebellion was a feature of the years 1530–70. Religious change and political upheavals combined with a broad range of economic and social concerns to create a contemporary perception that society was in a state of flux.[2] In 1536, the Pilgrimage of Grace saw the commons take up arms in opposition to the dissolution of minor religious houses and the imposition of new taxes. Large-scale rebellions broke out across England. Speaking in the voice of the common people, a contemporary radical ballad linked Thomas Cromwell's financial policies to Henrician attacks on the papal supremacy. The balladeer was not content merely to make generalisations about how the church was

> Robbyd, spoled and shorne
> From catell and corne,
> And clene furth borne
> Of housez and landes.

In addition, he attacked specific aspects of Henrician policy. He asserted that the rebels' actions were 'no marvell', because they were justified in attempting to undo the regime's folly. Notably, the final verse held 'Crim, crame and riche' and the 'thre ell' responsible for the economic and religious policies that were the subject of the pilgrims' protests. This relied on a knowing audience to recognise the identities of the protagonists. 'Crim' was Henry VIII's chief minister, Thomas Cromwell; 'Cram', the evangelical archbishop of Canterbury, Thomas Cranmer; while 'Rich' was Richard Rich, whose testimony as Solicitor-General during the trial of Sir Thomas

More secured the martyr's conviction for denying the royal supremacy. The slightly more obscure reference to the 'thre ell' probably relates to the evangelicals Sir Thomas Legh, Richard Layton and Hugh Latimer.[3] Legh and Layton's rough treatment of members of the monastic orders during their 1535–36 visitation of the north of England engendered much personal hatred, whereas Latimer provoked animosity for his radical evangelicalism during his tenure as Bishop of Worcester. Although many would have recognised the allusions to these men, disguising their identities in this way helped the authors to express their personal opinions on news and current affairs in a way that might 'break through political restraints and cultural assumptions'.[4] It helped to protect the balladeers from the allegation that they were intentionally criticising Henry VIII through his key ministers, because the act of identifying Crim is 'inherently provisional and partial'.[5]

It is inconceivable that this ballad could have appeared in print without risking the wrath of the Henrician regime, identifying and criticising as it did six individuals who were significant in creating and enforcing Henry VIII's policy of suppressing the monasteries. Instead, someone chose to write down the lyrics in manuscript. This chapter investigates the transmission of seditious ballads, looking first at the culture of collecting ballads in manuscript. It then investigates four manuscript collections in detail to illuminate the types of material that people chose to bring together. Next, the chapter investigates the nature of this moralistic and devotional material, before turning finally to the more radical songs which displayed something of a social conscience.

Collecting Ballads

Manuscript miscellanies therefore provide a different kind of resource for the study of ballads: rather than being random survivals, these songs were accumulated as part of a conscious process of collection and their circulation was rather more controlled than that of the printed broadsides. The first section of this chapter will examine the four contemporary manuscript collections of mid-Tudor ballads, establishing similarities in their thematic content. In acknowledging these four manuscript miscellanies to be significant in their own right, the chapter demonstrates that it was possible to combine a broad interest in ballads with a particular interest in works that had a more radical edge. These then form the chapter's basic source material, supplemented by printed material when appropriate. The chapter provides an analysis of ballads that include moralistic and socially critical themes in order to demonstrate that people of the middling sort were interested in news and politics as it affected them. The songs help to explain how people in the mid-sixteenth century negotiated the economic, legal and political changes of the period. These changes represented the lived experience of many people. Economic trends affected the lives and livelihoods of the common man and woman.[6] Socially critical ballads show people trying to understand what was going on in their lives. These miscellanies show that their compilers had an awareness of economic problems and a sophisticated understanding of social changes in the world around them. It was a world in which they wanted to play an active role.

The ballad collectors who put together these miscellanies decided to include songs that had a radical agenda. Presumably, this was because they shared that agenda or because they wanted to understand the political issues that affected them during the upheavals of the mid-sixteenth century. Although it was possible to buy a broadside ballad for a penny, the writing out by hand of a ballad text represented a considerably higher degree of engagement on the part of the scribe. These collectors were not passive consumers; instead, they were active in choosing ballads that suited their wants and needs. Collecting allowed a person or group to forge an identity based on the way in which they related to the material they collected. It was a personal activity, but it might rely on social interaction with other parties.[7] These ballad manuscripts represented collections of songs that people heard and enjoyed, but in order to create them the collector presumably heard people singing and joined in. They might have borrowed a broadside, or asked someone to sing. The collections therefore illuminate unseen and unheard social interactions as well as the material remains of the collections.

There was, of course, a culture of commonplacing in the period, in which people drew together short texts that they considered to be valuable and relevant to their lives. Unlike the ballad collections examined here, commonplace books were often made up of a wide variety of texts, including, recipes, herbal remedies, accounts, copies of correspondence and quotations from literary texts, gathered under headings which had been previously entered into the manuscript.[8] Indeed, several sixteenth- and seventeenth-century documents held in the British Library, such as the Aston manuscript, the Shann family manuscript and the Stanhope manuscript, contain a wide variety of material, including a number of ballads.[9] What is special about the four volumes studied in detail here, however, is that they are almost exclusively made up of ballads. This shows that these were compilations made by collectors who had a special interest in balladry. The songs that they contain cast light on the subjects that appealed to the tastes of these individual ballad collectors. As such, manuscript compilations are likely to contain ballads to which the scribes were particularly attached.

Ballad Communities

Individual objects in a collection 'are... socially meaningful, but their meaning is produced by arranging them in sets, both mentally and physically'.[10] To put it more simply, manuscript miscellanies represent collections of ballads that individuals or groups heard, knew and chose to keep.[11] It has been argued that this type of collecting culture emerged in the second half of the sixteenth century as an attempt to make sense of the mass of new information that was available as a result of 'a radical transformation in the intellectual climate and in the arts'.[12] Collections such as these demonstrate personal predilections and indicate the individual's preferences.[13] Their interest, therefore, lies as much in the fact that someone chose to gather these items together as it does in their individual value. Even where a manuscript contains more than one hand, meaning that it is not the collection of a single person but of a group, that miscellany epitomises the cultural identity of the group as a whole.[14]

Although the dominant theme of the manuscripts is religious and moralistic material, several ballads in each manuscript contain unmistakeable social criticism. The existence of these manuscript miscellanies shows that certain individuals had an active interest in ballads that attempted to make sense of the changes taking place in mid-Tudor England. Circulation of manuscript miscellanies such as these four took place mainly within what Harold Love termed 'scribal communities', for example, the Inns of Court, universities or family groups.[15] These social circles were groups of like-minded individuals who had an important defining characteristic in common, such as recusancy or nobility. Indeed, several of the manuscript miscellanies and poetry anthologies that survive are thought to relate to recusant families. Love argued that Catholic poetry and prose circulated in manuscript rather than print because it was 'more congenial' during times of persecution.[16] Although manuscripts were not unregulated, that regulation was particularly weak and inefficient. This meant that their authors were less likely to be caught.[17]

It seems possible that, in the same way, these politically aware, socially critical songs represent another area in which manuscript circulation, and certainly oral transmission, could be used to promote contentious ideas. Love pointed out that the scribal communication of texts was not just inclusive for the chosen recipients; it actively excluded those to whom access was denied.[18] The closed manuscript community was a safer means of circulating radical social criticism because it was easier to prevent copies falling into the wrong hands. If the oral tradition of Catholicism was an act of subversion under a Protestant regime, so too were socially critical ballads. Although they complained more than they called to action, the act of giving voice to these thoughts was 'one of defiance, and of what we would now call consciousness-raising'.[19]

Bodleian Library Ashmole 48

The four manuscript miscellanies were chosen because they represent a decision on the part of the collector or collectors to accumulate a set of ballads in one place. They are the only extant manuscripts of the period that display this trait rather than a more wide-ranging habit of collecting a wide variety of material. The one to have received most scholarly attention is also the most varied: Oxford Bodleian Library MS Ashmole 48.[20] A small book, measuring about 192 × 159 mm, it contains 86 items in total on 141 folios. Eight are pieces of prose, so the number of metrical items is 78. Two of these duplicate other pieces, reducing the total of individual items to 76. Of these, two items by Henry, Lord Morley and five short pieces do not fit the ballad genre; the former because their language is less demotic than that usually found in ballads and the latter because they are only a few lines long. This leaves 69 items that may be considered ballads. Careful analysis of the handwriting has identified the interplay of 11 different hands (identified as hands A-K) within the manuscript, sometimes with more than one hand copying a single ballad.[21]

Using internal evidence from several of the ballads, Thomas Wright dated the large majority of the items in the volume between 1554 and 1558. Several of the ballads are signed 'Richard Sheale'. Sheale was a minstrel in the pay of the Earl of Derby, who also, apparently, wandered the country with his pedlar wife.[22] Sheale's occupation prompted Wright to suggest that the book was a minstrel manuscript: a small and easily portable volume in which Sheale wrote down his repertoire.[23] Hyder E. Rollins suggested a slightly later date for the manuscript by identifying, with varying degrees of confidence, printed versions of 33 of the ballads contained within it. Based on the assumption that the manuscript had been copied from printed ballads, he concluded that the volume was written during the period 1557–65. He also challenged Wright's suggestion that the collection was that of Sheale's minstrel repertoire, commenting that it was unlikely that Sheale hoped to make money from singing these ballads when they were being sung for free by the ballad sellers who made their money from the sale of broadsides.[24] Since Sheale's wife was a hawker, it is possible that she sold copies of the ballads too.

Andrew Taylor explained these links to the broadside ballad trade in quite the opposite way. He made the radical suggestion that, rather than being copied from broadsides, the manuscript was used to collect material for the London printers to publish. If Taylor's supposition is correct, then despite the fact that Bod. MS Ashmole 48 is in many hands, it nevertheless represents collection on behalf of an individual. By providing internal evidence from the texts that much of the manuscript was written between 1557 and 1558, Taylor argued that several of the ballads were notated in the manuscript before they were registered with the Stationers' Company.[25] In fact, if the *Descripcion of an ungodly worlde* in Tottel's *Miscellany* was printed from Bod. MS Ashmole 48's *Who lovithe to lyve in peas*, the date of the central section of the manuscript cannot be later than June 1557, when the *Miscellany* was first registered. Nevertheless, given the sparsity of records before the late 1550s, it is difficult to know whether the ballads were new when they were registered with the company. Although Taylor's work adds much to our understanding of Richard Sheale and his world, his conclusions regarding the date and purpose Bod. MS Ashmole 48 are necessarily speculative and must, therefore, be treated with caution. Although it seems likely that the material in the central section of the manuscript dates from the reign of Philip and Mary, it is impossible to know whether the ballads were written down before or after their publication as broadsides. All that can be said with certainty is that the majority of these ballads were in circulation by 1565 at the latest.

Despite claims that many of the pieces in Bod. MS Ashmole 48 are more suited to recitation than singing and that they do not fit comfortably within literary definitions of the ballad, several of the songs include a tune instruction.[26] Many more can be linked to ballads registered with the Stationers' Company. There is every reason to think that this was, in the main, a collection of songs. As previous chapters have shown, the ballad was a malleable genre and there is no musical reason why this material could not have been sung.

British Library Manuscripts

Substantial excerpts from another manuscript miscellany, BL Sloane MS 1896, can be found in Hyder E. Rollins's *Old English Ballads, 1553–1625, Chiefly from Manuscripts*. The handwriting and subject matter of the ballads contained within it suggest that BL Sloane MS 1896 dates from the early Elizabethan period. The volume contains several ballads that relate to historical events, such as the executions of the Protestant preacher John Bradford in 1555 and the murderess Anne Saunders in 1572. The death of the Earl of Essex in 1576 provides the subject for the final ballad in the manuscript and Rollins suggested that 'there is no reason to believe that any part of the MS. is of a later date'. Measuring about 114 × 203 mm, the vast majority of its 59 folios are written in the same hand. This is the only one of the four manuscripts to contain a table of contents, which is also written in the same hand. The origins and ownership of the manuscript are unknown, although Rollins points out that the names of Thomas Hatcheman and John Blount both appear on a leaf at the back of the volume. BL Sloane MS 1896 comprises exclusively metrical compositions. Personal repentance dominates the mainly religious material, alongside complaints about the evils of vice and the declining moral standards of the world. There is a distinctly Protestant feel to many of the ballads, which are unleavened by humorous material.[27] Three of the 35 ballads fall outside the scope of this study because they deal with events that took place in the 1570s. Rollins suggested printed equivalents for ten of the items.

BL MS Cotton Vespasian A-XXV is by far the least studied of the four miscellanies. Despite the Victorians' interest in publishing collections of early modern ballads, a reliable printed edition was published only as recently as 1978.[28] The volume is about 153 × 16 mm and made up of

205 folios of paper and vellum. It includes 50 ballads as well as several other fragments of verse. Six of the ballads fall outside the date range of this study. Of the remainder, 14 have been identified with items in the Stationers' Registers, although some of these links are based rather tenuously on subject matter rather than title.[29] Earlier scholarly inattention notwithstanding, Peter Seng described this collection as 'second in importance only to the [later] Percy Folio MS'. The first five poems in the manuscript may date from the reign of Mary I, Edward VI or even as far back as that of their father, Henry VIII, and the collection was completed by 1576. The names of Johi[n] Anstis and Henry Sauill appear near the front of the book. Henry Savile inherited some of his collection of manuscripts from his father and grandfather, but acquired others from a fellow Yorkshireman, a Catholic schoolteacher named John Nettleton.[30] During the 1580s, Nettleton was known to the authorities for collecting books that had belonged to monasteries prior to the dissolution.[31] Indeed, this third miscellany contains mainly religious ballads and where they are of a discernibly denominational nature, the songs display a distinctly Catholic bias. Most of the social criticism also has a religious undertone, although two of the moralistic ballads contain no reference to God or faith. Nevertheless, BL MS Cotton Vespasian A-XXV also contains several drinking songs and a nonsense song; in terms of themes, therefore, it is the widest ranging of the manuscripts studied.[32]

More overtly Catholic in its nature is BL Additional Manuscript 15225. Indeed, it was described by Alison Shell as 'one of the most important surviving manuscripts of Catholic verse'.[33] It has 60 leaves and measures about 153 × 203 mm. Although the folio numbers run from 1 to 124, folios 95–98 are missing. The presence of a title but no lyrics at the bottom of folio 124[v] suggests that further leaves have also been lost from the end of the book. The latest date in the manuscript is 1616, but, according to Rollins, many of the ballads collected in the miscellany were registered with the Stationers' Company much earlier. The collection contains 36 items, of which one is in prose and one is a known poem. Of the 34 ballads, one item is duplicated, making a total of 33 individual ballads. Seven items fall outside the date range of this study, leaving 26 to be included, of which 16 can be identified with printed versions, albeit rather weakly in some cases.[34] BL Add. MS 15225 contains mainly moralistic and religious songs, many of which Rollins included in his *Old English Ballads* as a contrast to the Protestant material from BL Sloane MS 1896.

Themes in the Miscellanies

Table 8.1 shows the number of ballads on different themes which appear in these four manuscripts and the extant printed ballads. Political ballads made mention of activities relating to matters of authority and government, including monarchy or the form and organisation of the state.

Table 8.1 Thematic classification of ballads in manuscript miscellanies, surviving printed ballads and all ballads included in the study

	Ashmole 48	Sloane 1896	Cotton Vespasian A-XXV	Add. MS 15225	Surviving Printed Ballads	Total Ballads in Study
Total	69	32	44	26	206	433
Political	10 *(14%)*	8 *(25%)*	1 *(2%)*	6 *(23%)*	42 *(20%)*	77 *(18%)*
Socially critical	13 *(19%)*	5 *(16%)*	3 *(7%)*	4 *(15%)*	35 *(17%)*	66 *(15%)*
Moralistic	37 *(54%)*	13 *(41%)*	18 *(14%)*	15 *(58%)*	58 *(28%)*	168 *(39%)*
Religious of which:	31 *(45%)*	23 *(72%)*	27 *(61%)*	18 *(69%)*	102 *(50%)*	231 *(53%)*
Denominational	6 *(9%)*	8 *(25%)*	1 *(2%)*	9 *(35%)*	44 *(21%)*	75 *(17%)*
Non-denominational	25 *(36%)*	15 *(47%)*	26 *(59%)*	9 *(35%)*	58 *(28%)*	156 *(36%)*
Love	16 *(23%)*	0 *(0%)*	8 *(18%)*	2 *(8%)*	39 *(19%)*	72 *(17%)*
Other	12 *(25%)*	11 *(34%)*	12 *(27%)*	2 *(8%)*	86 *(42%)*	142 *(33%)*
Printed	33 *(49%)*	12 *(38%)*	14 *(32%)*	16 *(62%)*	N/A	276 *(63%)*

Percentages have been rounded to the nearest whole number.

Ballads were deemed to be socially critical if they specifically reflected on social structure, power and/or agency, but were classified as moralistic if they related more generally to human character or behaviour which was considered good or bad. Religious ballads dealt with aspects of religious belief, of which many are so general that they cannot be identified as coming from either side of the confessional divide. The subset of denominational ballads expressed explicitly Protestant or Catholic beliefs, perhaps related to the sacraments, the afterlife, the crucifixion or the hierarchy of the church. Love songs expressed amorous sentiments.

The raw number of ballads in each class has also been converted to a percentage of the total number of ballads. Since it is common for a ballad to contain more than one theme, a single ballad can appear under multiple headings and so the classifications are not mutually exclusive. This is also why the percentages do not add up to 100: they merely represent the number of ballads given each classification, as a proportion of the total number in the manuscript. Furthermore, some ballads do not fit any of the main themes. The difficulty of precisely dating the manuscripts renders it impossible to make a distinction between topical ballads (dealing with a current event) and ballads that deal with past events as history, so these ballads appear under the umbrella category 'Other'. This classification also contains ballad themes that appeared only rarely in the collections, such as the nonsense ballad and drinking song. Consequently, the results can only give an indication of the overriding themes within each of the manuscript miscellanies. Nevertheless, on the basis of this analysis, the contents of the four manuscript miscellanies are remarkably similar in many ways.

At first glance, the four miscellanies appear to have striking links to printed material, but these figures should be treated with caution for two reasons. First, some of the links to printed material are, to say the least, tentative. Many of these identifications were made by Hyder E. Rollins. A few of the links are indisputable because a printed version of the ballad also survives. For example, *Who lovithe to lyve in peas*, found in three of the manuscripts, is included in Tottel's *Miscellany*. Other identifications were made on the basis of the close similarity of titles or first lines with those entered in the Stationers' Registers. These include *Wysdom woold I wyshe to have* (entered in 1563) and *The prymerose in the greene forest* (entered in 1563–64) from Bod. MS Ashmole 48. Some manuscript ballads, however, were associated with registered titles on the strength of subject matter alone, without any further evidence. Rollins himself was circumspect about suggesting that *Thoughe weddynge go be destenye* from Bod. MS Ashmole 48 might have been registered in 1558–59 as *The proverbe ys tru that weddynge ys destyne* or in 1561–62 as *in prayse of a serten Ladye*.[35] Second, the higher correlation between ballads in BL Add. MS 15225 (the latest dated manuscript) and printed ballads might be explained by the increased survival rate of ballads later in the sixteenth century and the fact that more ballads were registered as the printing industry grew. Conversely, it also reminds us just how many early Tudor ballads might have been lost. It must be stressed, therefore, that the proportion of each manuscript that may have been taken from print is an estimate based on very limited information. If Rollins were overenthusiastic in linking ballads to the Stationers' Registers, the figures could be too high; alternatively, considering the number of printed ballads that we can be certain existed but that have not survived, the true figures might be much higher.

The collectors had a strong interest in material of a moralistic and religious nature. The largest single theme in Bod. MS Ashmole 48 is moralistic ballads, whereas the other three manuscripts are dominated by religious material. Nevertheless, the overlap of these themes in the manuscripts tended to be relatively high, as many of the moralistic songs have a religious bias. Furthermore, BL Sloane MS 1896, BL MS Cotton Vespasian A-XXV and BL Add. MS 15225 contain a higher proportion of religious material than the surviving printed ballads, while Bod. MS Ashmole 48, BL Sloane MS 1896 and BL Add. MS 15225 include a higher proportion of moralistic material than the printed ballads. BL Sloane MS 1896 contains the highest proportion of religious songs, but no love songs, while it and BL Add. MS 15225 had higher proportions of denominational material (Protestant and Catholic respectively) than printed survivals. The amount of socially critical material in Bod. MS Ashmole 48, BL Sloane MS 1896 and BL Add. MS 15225 is roughly equivalent to the proportion surviving in print. BL MS Cotton Vespasian A-XXV, on the other hand, is the most varied of the miscellanies, having only a minority of political, socially critical and denominational material, much less than the other three collections or the printed material. Although these figures can only be impressionistic, they show that the collectors were discerning in what they added to their collections. Far from being a random group of ballads on disparate subjects, each manuscript contains a assemblage of songs that show that the collectors were interested in their interior world as well as exterior issues of morality.

Table 8.2 compares the average numbers of ballads in the four miscellanies with the printed survivals and the total number of ballads in the study. The higher number of political and denominational ballads in print than manuscript perhaps reflects three related issues. First, during this period of religious upheaval it was often difficult to divorce matters of state and matters of confessional identity. Second, this was reflected in the agenda of the balladeers, because many of the ballads that were selected to go into print were written with a specific didactic purpose. Finally, the discerning consumers who created the four miscellanies chose ballads with timeless themes, rather than topical and explicitly denominational material that might quickly become dated. Indeed, there was a significant overlap between these categories. There was a great deal of interest in topical ballads, but it seems that, although this genre accounts for a substantial proportion of printed ballads, sixteenth-century collectors had little interest in keeping for posterity songs that directly related to current affairs. Their value was as news.

These collections show that, among their devotional ballads, collectors made an active decision to accumulate politically sensitive material, perhaps even that they found it interesting, stimulating and enjoyable. The rest of this chapter focuses first on moralistic ballads, which formed part

Table 8.2 Comparison of the average numbers of ballads in manuscript miscellanies with the printed survivals and the total number of ballads in the study, by classification

	Manuscript Miscellanies	Surviving Printed Ballads	Total Ballads in Study
Total	171	206	433
Political	25 *(15%)*	42 *(20%)*	77 *(18%)*
Socially critical	25 *(15%)*	35 *(17%)*	66 *(15%)*
Moralistic	83 *(49%)*	58 *(28%)*	168 *(39%)*
Religious of which:	99 *(58%)*	102 *(50%)*	231 *(53%)*
Denominational	44 *(21%)*	75 *(17%)*	79 *(18%)*
Non-denominational	58 *(28%)*	156 *(36%)*	160 *(37%)*
Love	26 *(15%)*	39 *(19%)*	72 *(17%)*
Other	37 *(22%)*	86 *(42%)*	142 *(33%)*
Printed	75 *(44%)*	N/A	276 *(63%)*

Percentages have been rounded to the nearest whole number.

of the personal devotional literature of the collectors, and then on socially critical songs, which formed one part of a culture of passive resistance in the mid-Tudor period. These form significant subsets of the mid-Tudor ballads that have, in the past, received less comprehensive attention from scholars, but nevertheless tell us about the way in which the collectors engaged with the world around them. They speak of a culture in which people could challenge the social order through the medium of song.

Ballads and the Commonwealth

During the sixteenth century, beliefs about morality and social order were bound up in the idea of the commonwealth. This was the belief, understood by everyone, that the different social orders (or estates) should work together, playing their own part, in order that everyone might thrive.[36] The concept pervaded politics in theory and practise at all levels. The commonwealth required due obedience to and worship of God, as well as the upholding of law and order. It looked to the wellbeing of the whole community and hoped for a degree of universal social improvement. Writers who used the term did so to suggest social reform that would benefit everyone.[37]

The mid-sixteenth century, however, was a time of dearth and inflation when some observers believed that the commonwealth was being undermined by local officials who put greed and personal ambition before the wellbeing of the community. The most celebrated work on the commonwealth was Thomas More's *A fruteful, and pleasaunt worke of the beste state of a publyque weale, and of the newe yle called Vtopia.*[38] *Utopia* was first printed in Latin in Leuven in 1516, but was not published in English until 1551. More identified several vested interests that stood in the way of prosperity and caused poverty, while his description of Utopian society created the image of an ideal community in which the arbiters of power applied their authority in the best interests of all. So powerful was his vision that it still resonates today.

Moralistic Ballads

Ballads likewise provided exemplary patterns of behaviour, albeit at a less erudite level. Their guidance implied that the failure of people to live in harmony would cause the breakdown of the commonwealth. For those who failed to live up to society's expectations of honesty, sobriety, chastity and thrift, for example, ballads presented patterns of repentance for inappropriate behaviours. Nevertheless, ballads such as *Who lovithe to lyve in peas, Thys miserable world in dede* and *Take hede in time* show that there was a pre-existing, informal code of moral conduct, which was only later reinforced by the Elizabethan and Stuart regimes' attempts to regulate behaviour by statute. *Thys miserable world in dede* described the many and varied problems with society, sometimes using personification to make the images more powerful: 'Meknes of pryde ys so agaste, he dare not shewe his heade. / Covettusnes, that cursyde cryme, dothe nowe rayne over all; / And whordome but for good pastime, ys hold with great and small'. The ballad's author, Henry Sponare, went on to claim that 'Pore charitie ys chacide owte, mercy hathe lyttle myghte; / Extorsion was never so stowte, with envy and disspyghte'. Nevertheless, Sponare invoked no criticism of the regime. Instead of assigning blame for society's ills to the monarch or even to the local gentry, Sponare attributed the malaise to man's failure to 'lyve well intende'.[39] He expressed no expectation that the regime should take responsibility for collective social problems; instead, men should forsake their sins and appeal to God for forgiveness and help.

Such ballads are wholly in keeping with a tradition that blamed the problems facing the commonwealth on society's depravity. Nevertheless, what appears to be passivity and a highly conservative wish to maintain the *status quo* on the part of the poor and oppressed might actually be 'a realistic, pragmatic view of the situation as they experience it'. Compliance with the day-to-day equilibrium might be based on a reluctant acceptance that the situation was inevitable rather than equanimity. Unless there was a political situation which created the possibility of change or a rebellious uprising, pragmatism tended to win out over aspiration. Moments of revolutionary change were rare, so for the most part, little changed.[40] This dichotomy is reinforced by the sharp division between socially critical ballads, for example, that which opened this chapter, which justified the Pilgrimage of Grace as 'no marvell', and the majority of moralistic ballads that were stoic in the face of a constant struggle against sin.

Devotional Songs

All four manuscript miscellanies are dominated by religious and moralistic material, suggesting that their collectors enjoyed and found useful songs on which placed their emphasis on sin and repentance. This was the tradition on which the English 'godly ballads' of the first half of the Elizabethan period drew. According to the ballads, sin was ubiquitous and immorality permeated everyday life. One could hope for salvation by turning away from sin, but the promise of heaven was far from certain. The fear of burning in hell for eternity, however, was constant.[41] Divine providence loomed large in these devotional songs, just as it did in other forms of cheap print and in messages from the pulpit.[42] This is reflected by the high number of moralistic ballads that, throughout the sixteenth century, catalogued the failings of society and linked the wellbeing of the commonwealth to personal repentance and/or greater faith in God:

> Ther is noe man so lewde of lyfe,
> so fond in fylthy talke,
> That doth not still perswade him selfe

in perfect path to walke.
The covetous carle whose hart and hand
doth lust and reache for coyne,
He thinckes it is a glory great
his bages and heapes to Joyne.[43]

These songs were intensely personal, providing the sort of self-scrutiny
and mortification that would become linked to the Puritan movement in
the late sixteenth and early seventeenth centuries.[44]

After the Reformation, such devotional songs provided people with a
way to practise their faith outside formal public worship. These pieces
allowed people to confess their sins, ask God's forgiveness and even request the punishment that was the consequence of their sinful actions.
This devotional material was used as a substitute for the Catholic pen-
itential cycle.[45] Nevertheless, the evidence from these four manuscripts
and printed material shows that interest in this devotional literature
existed both before and after the Reformation and, therefore, it was
not the exclusive preserve of the Protestant. Although BL Sloane MS
1896 and BL Add. MS 15225 contrast in their denomination, they
are in fact strikingly similar in their moral stance. Like their printed
counterparts, the songs in all four miscellanies concentrate on issues
of lechery, lust, drunkenness, charity and lying as well as more general
comments about vice and sin. These matters are frequently connected
to the idea of divine judgement, with balladeers pointing out that God
will always punish those who sin. *How every vice crepeth in vn[der]
the name and shew of a vertue* in the Protestant BL Sloane MS 1896
describes how

Licentious dealing beares the sway,
and all delightes the same;
Noe feare of hell nor Judgement great
can aught their wildnesse tame.[46]

Similarly, *To Passe the Place Where Pleasure Is* in the Catholic BL Add.
MS 15225 points out that

The liues that we long liued haue
in wantonnesse and iolitie,
Although the[y] seeme and show full braue,
yet is their end plaine miserie.
Let vs therefore, therefore,
now sinne noe more,
but learne this lore:
all remedie gone
except in Christ alone.[47]

Even though these songs were, at heart, popular entertainment, they nevertheless 'sketch the basis of a coherent layman's theology'.[48] That they became a staple of both printed broadside ballads and manuscript collections only serves to demonstrate that people absorbed their messages and enjoyed the songs.

Personal Morality

In a period when people could be uncertain about what constituted orthodox religion, these ballads provide a picture of personal morality based on penitence. Even though a solifidian belief in justification by faith alone was supposed to be reassuring to the faithful Protestant, there was still 'uncertainty, confusion, and indifference' to the officially sanctioned forms of religion by 1570.[49] Printed religious material such as *To Passe the Place Where Pleasure Is* could be multivalent in order to appeal to both sides of the confessional divide. In the voice of a Protestant, the refrain 'all remedie gone / except in Christ alone' sounds an affirmation of solifidianism. It reinforced the belief that only a steadfast faith could lead to redemption and that good works in this life had no direct effect on the next. To a Catholic, by contrast, those same words could become a complaint about the removal of a traditional framework of intercession and good works.

Whether the singer was Catholic or Protestant, the songs served the same function. They allowed people to contemplate their sinful conduct and explore their relationship with God as part of their personal devotional life. Furthermore, many of the ballads collected in the four manuscript miscellanies played a part in normative social influence, providing a code of conduct for people to emulate. They encouraged their audience to make the best of their lives in the interests of their own spiritual welfare, personal wellbeing and the wider community. For example, *Take hede in time* promoted financial responsibility to ensure a secure future:

> The servynge man that takythe wage,
> Lett hyme not spende, but kepe for age;
> For servys ys none erytage;
> Therfor take hede.[50]

Meanwhile, an untitled ballad in BL Add. MS 15225 reminded its listeners to

> Wast thou noe more then thou has got;
> if thou dost want, yet borrowe not;
> Thoughe coyne be sweete when thou dost borrow,
> yet wilt thou pay it home with sorrowe.[51]

The collectors' accumulation of moralistic songs reinforces the argument that there was already a significant interest in codes of behaviour and declining moral standards prior to any Puritan Reformation of Manners. Moral issues such as idleness, illegitimate births and inebriation were at the heart of the Tudor regime's social programme. In fact, the collectors' accumulation of moralistic songs show that these themes were prominent in both Protestant and Catholic ballads throughout the century. By the end of the Tudor era it seemed that personal morality had become a matter in which the regime (and indeed, other authorities) could intervene. To a certain extent, the middling sort fashioned their own sense of identity through their behavioural choices. If they detested 'noisy, repulsive and contaminating' behaviours, then this chapter shows that the process had been foreshadowed for many years in songs that identified a wide range of sinful and morally weak behaviours.[52] Manuscript miscellanies, by their very nature, showcase the interests not of the poorest members of society but those of the same middling sort who rejected immorality; after all, the collectors were literate and had sufficient disposable wealth to purchase their writing materials.

Social Conscience

The presence of a social conscience in popular music is a timeless theme which continues to this day. Although it must be stressed that the majority of ballads concentrated on issues of morality, a tantalising few were far more specific in their allocation of blame for society's ills, linking social injustice to those groups who were perceived to be responsible. These more radical ballads can be seen as social criticism, offering accounts of social structure and the relative agency of groups within it. They allowed the population to navigate their world, which was changing rapidly around them. English society was attempting to come to terms with what its members saw as major socio-economic upheavals. Even if the economic problems that those people perceived were not the same ones that actually existed, the songs offered a popular way of expressing the difficulties that people at the time believed they faced.[53] Whether or not these changes were more imagined than real in England is beside the point: these were the issues that many balladeers thought would appeal to their audience.

Ballads were, on occasion, able to display a precise engagement with particular ills such as enclosure, vagrancy and inflation. Rather than simply complaining that the community was in a process of decay, these ballads directly addressed the social and economic policy of the Tudor regime and the way in which this policy was perceived to affect society at large. This reflected the experience of the middling sort during the mid-sixteenth century. For example, protests against Somerset's radical religious policy broke out in Cornwall in 1548. Discontent escalated in the summer of 1549, with an outbreak of rioting in Norfolk resulting from the local gentry's continued enclosure of common land. This developed into a widespread insurrection that saw members of the gentry imprisoned while a series of rebel camps were established across East Anglia. The rebels were led by wealthier commoners and it was their grievances that dominated the various complaints that were sent to Somerset. During this 'commotion time', these grievances centred around a popular belief that local officials abused their power to the detriment of the middling sort.[54] Rather than presenting a coherent set of demands, however, the grievances reflected the concerns of individual camps.[55] In contrast to the Pilgrimage of Grace and the Prayer Book Rebellion, the eastern risings of summer 1549 pitched the commons against their local lords – the very men who should have been responsible for protecting their interests. Rather than complain about how Westminster had mismanaged its affairs, these men wanted to mobilise royal government in support of its complaints about local abuses of power; something upon which Somerset's government had promised to act.[56] A verse pamphlet printed in 1550 by Thomas Raynald painted these abuses in stark colours. *A Ruful complaynt of the publyke weale to Englande* stated that 'Ryche men lyue by vserye / Craftes men by dysceate / And vyttelers, by subtil[t]ye'. It described how

> Such offices, as heretofore
> Apparteyned, to the yomans ryght
> Be taken awaye they get nomore
> and geuen to Lorde or knight.

Finally, it expressed a desire that 'Some good ma[n], for the commons speake / That ryche men marre not all'.[57] A ballad in BL Add. MS 15233 likewise reminded those who had power and authority to exercise it with caution and care

> Yf thow be set to do Iustice,
> Regard virtu and poonysh vyce;
> O pres no man, I thee advyce;
> Abuse not thyne auctorytee
> To vexe poore men for vanité.[58]

A ballad in BL Sloane MS 1896 even claimed that abuse of power would lead directly to the downfall of the commonwealth:

> If England will take heede,
> as cause ther is indeede,
> Then let them lo[o]k about,
> and wede abuses out.
> For if they range, the state will change
> from weale to wo, no doubt.[59]

Similarly, Thomas Camel recommended that unity was essential for society to prosper, 'synce we be members of one common wealthe. / Let vs ioyne aptly, as fyttes for our health'.[60] William King agreed:

> Euery Kyngdome,
> Both all and some.
> That is deuided within it selfe:
> Desolate shalbe,
> Without feare truly
> Of God, be in that Commen welth.[61]

The *Ruful Complaynt* emphasised, however, that not only did England have the 'godlyest kynge' who was the 'worthiest governour in euery thynge', it also had 'the most mercyfullyst counsayle'. It closed with a loyal prayer:

> God save Edward our kyng
> And his counsellers worthye
> and send theym grace, to help thys thinge
> For the weale of the communaltye.[62]

This is highly significant considering the background of political intrigue at court. The years 1549 and 1550 saw the ousting of Somerset as Lord Protector in favour of Northumberland's leadership of the Privy Council. The *Ruful complaynt* made no hint of 'the world turned upside down'. Instead, he recommended the king and his council should rule in the best interests of society as a whole so that order would be maintained. This reflected the vision of a reformed commonwealth that was central to government propaganda during Somerset's rule.[63] Nevertheless, in accusing the lords and knights of abusing their power, the ballad called into question the very counsellors that he professed to support: they had failed in their responsibility to prevent this sort of exploitation. Throughout the summer of 1549, the rebels used economic and religious rhetoric in their exchanges both with the regime and the wider community. The agitators were fully aware of Protector Somerset's political strategies and they were able to appropriate and utilise the regime's rhetoric, confident that it would be understood by everyone from the elite to the poor. The rebels tailored their negotiations around policy areas that they knew interested the government. By engaging with Somerset's regime on its own terms, the rebels were able to win significant concessions.[64]

   If there was an active engagement in politics at all levels of society, then the mid-Tudor ballads which had a militant edge were implicitly aimed at just those sorts of people: knowing individuals who were interested in and able to understand how change affected them. Each of the manuscripts in the case study contains a small yet significant number of these socially critical songs, thereby indicating that each collector had a specific interest in songs of a radical nature. While these more radical ballads did not advance as far as to advocate a call to arms, they can be seen as part of a culture of passive resistance or even subversion. Juliet Ingram pointed out that contemporaries such as Thomas Elyot recognised that there were 'potentially subversive elements' in common-wealth discourse, such as its 'focus on the welfare of the multitude' and the idea that wealth should be held in common. She posited a 'framing of texts using the binary division between rich and poor', yet the situation revealed by the ballads was in fact much more complex.[65] Rather than a dichotomy, the ballads display a degree of affinity between rich and poor by invoking the time-honoured traditions of the commonwealth. The songs argue that the elite should use their wealth and power in the best interests of society as a whole, supported by those who worked the land. The division was between these common interests and the self-aggrandisement of the knights and lords. Nevertheless, although the focus of the protests is the gentry, a clearly stated desire for the mainte-nance of the *status quo* cloaked an implicit and subversive insinuation that the aristocracy had neglected their obligation to look after the needs of the community as a whole.

Who Lovithe to Lyve in Peas

One socially critical ballad, however, stands out for being present in three of the four miscellanies described above, as well as being published in 1557 in Tottel's *Miscellany* and as a single broadside (now lost) in September 1564.[66] Indeed, it is the only ballad to appear in more than one of the four miscellanies. The four versions of *Who lovithe to lyve in peas* are each slightly different. It is impossible to know if Tottel's text predated the version in Bod. MS Ashmole 48. If Bod. MS Ashmole 48 was a printer's collection, then it seems likely that this was an exemplar text from which the other versions stemmed. As Bod. MS Ashmole 48 dates from the 1550s, this suggests that, if BL Add. MS 15225 were in-deed compiled about 1616, as Hyder E. Rollins put forward, *Who lovithe to lyve in peas* sustained a degree of longevity that few sixteenth-century ballads attained.[67]

In BL Add. MS 15225, *Who lovithe to lyve in peas* is entitled *A dittie most excelent for euerie man to reade*. It is marked to be sung to the tune 'John Come Kiss Me Now' or 'A Rich Merchant Man'.[68] The earliest version of 'John Come Kiss Me Now' is found in FSL V.a.159 (Figure 8.1).[69] Over the years, it became associated with divine intervention to punish greed and the need to be charitable.[70] It is in simple time in the Ionian mode and contains lots of repetition, making it very easy to pick up and remember. The alternative tune, 'The Rich Merchant Man', appears to have taken its name from a ballad registered in 1594. Although no tune called 'The Rich

Whoe lou - eth to liue in peace: & mark - eth___ eu[e] - rie change, shall

see such newes from time to time: as seem-eth won - drous strang.

Figure 8.1 Setting of *A dittie most excelent for euerie man to reade* from London, British Library, Add. MS 15225, ff. 87ʳ–88ʳ, to 'John Come Kiss Me Now' transcribed from FSL V.a.159, ff. 7ʳ–7ᵛ.

Merchant Man' survives, *Pills to purge melancholy* contains a song called *The Merchant and the Fidler's WIFE* which begins with the line 'IT was a Rich Merchant Man'. Although the tune identification has so far been given only tentatively, Figure 8.2 shows that the much earlier words of *Who lo-vithe to lyve in peas* fit perfectly to this melody.[71] The tune is in compound time with a predominant dotted crotchet, quaver rhythm. It is unusual in that it ends on the third of the scale and the halfway point is reached on the leading note of the relative minor, which is an accidental (F sharp). Whereas some ballad tunes carried their own associations, the two alternatives given for *Who lovithe to lyve in peas* suggest that on this occasion, the tune carried no implicit meaning of its own. Nevertheless, either of these rousing melodies would have made this ballad, which catalogued a long list of specific problems afflicting England, more appealing, with the effect of making the song sound more like a rallying call than a cry of despair.

Who lovithe to lyve in peas criticised many sections of society for their behaviour. Censuring the wealthy for no longer choosing to be charitable to the poor, the balladeer complained that greed led to 'Suche brybyng for the purs, such gapynge after more / Such hording upe of worldly welthe, such kepyng mucke in store'. Likewise, the song exhorted men to accept their position in society because it 'Wear better be a pleane poor man / then leade a princis lyffe'. Man's fortunes were the result of 'Godes forsyght and provydence' and therefore had to be accepted with good grace.[72]

Whoe lou - eth to liue   in   peace:___   &   mar - keth eu[e] - rie___   change,___   shall

see___such   newes_from   time_to to time: as   seem - eth_____   won - drous strang.

Figure 8.2 Setting of *A dittie most excelent for euerie man to reade* from BL
Add. MS 15225, ff. 87ʳ–88ʳ, to 'The Rich Merchant Man' from
Henry Playford, *Wit and Mirth, or Pills to purge melancholy* (Lon-
don, 1719), v, p. 77.

Despite the relative paucity of extant radical ballads, the differences in the lyrics of *Who lovithe to lyve in peas* suggest that ballads which circulated in manuscript or oral tradition could be more
uncompromising than those that were printed. There are subtle differences between the manuscript lyrics and the printed text. If Bod.
MS Ashmole 48 were the exemplar text, then the *Miscellany* shows
that certain verses were edited out. If, on the other hand, Bod. MS
Ashmole 48 was taken from printed material, then it shows that extra
verses were added to the song, perhaps to make it more relevant to
the singer. Possibly these lines were passed on from person to person,
making the manuscript closer to the songs in oral transmission than
the printed ballads were.

The first verse that was missing from Tottel's *Miscellany* related to the
contrast between charity and extravagance:

> Such poverty abrowde
> and fewe men takyth them in;
> Suche juels warne and poore men want,
> which ys both shame and syne;

Perhaps these lines were seen as too sensitive to include in an unpro-
voking volume of poetry and song. Furthermore, they risked alienating
the very audience who might be expected to buy a work that demanded
more of a financial investment than a broadside ballad or an orally
transmitted song. Another of the missing verses was confessionally
controversial:

> Suche pryntynge off good bookys,
> such praychyng synn to fle;
> Suche ronnynge hedlong into hell,
> it pittiethe me to se.

This could easily be read as an endorsement of the Protestant emphasis on the importance of *sola scriptura*, which would have been provocative if published in 1557, during Philip and Mary's persecution of Protestants. A further two verses referred to God raising or reducing the status of man at his will:

> Yf that the boughe do breake
> be whiche the yous to clym;
> For God doth exsalte and overthrowe
> as he syeth caus and tym.
> The tymes apoyntyde be,
> and alteryde in ther kynde,
> Be Godes forsyght and provydence,
> whos knowlege fewe can fynde.

Two other sensitive verses dealt with the specific economic problems of engrossing and rising rents, linking them to greed and the decline of charity:

> Suche prolynge for fate farmes,
> such dublyng of small rente;
> Suche heppis of golde in sum mens handes,
> yete no man ys contente.
> Suche byldyng of fear bowars,
> suche honger kepte in hallys;
> Wher nydy men have fownde relyffe,
> nowe may the se bar wallys.

'Prolynge for fate farmes' was a reference to engrossing, the consolidation of two or more farms under the management of one landlord. *Who lovithe to lyve in peas*, therefore (in the manuscript edition at least) showcased the tensions between the different and competing sections of society. A knowing audience would be aware that it was landlords who were to blame for engrossing and rent increases. The Puritan pamphleteer Philip Stubbes remarked on the way that some men managed to produce ample amounts of grain from their land while others, with fat, fertile farms failed to make their land work: 'For some haue such fatte farmes, and tenements, as either will bring forth no corne at all (in a manner) or if it doe verie little, and that not without great cost bestowed vpon it'.[73] He complained that 'landlords, and gentlemen take all the lands, and lyuelode wherevpon there poore tenants shoulde liue into their owne hands', with the result that landlords 'suffer not the poore husbandmen to haue so much ground as will finde them corne for the maintenance of their poore families, nor which is more, scarcely to keepe one cow, horse or sheepe vpon, for their continuall reléefe'.[74] This was echoed by the ballad *Cleane witheowt feare*, which complained that

'Sum that be lordes off vyllages and townnes / Hathe covetyd to have away othar mens grondes'.[75] For those in the know, these ballads laid the blame for social problems unambiguously at the door of the local gentry.

But if there was one complaint that was perceived to bring together all the ills of society, it was the enclosure of common land. Enclosure increased the productivity and profitability of land by raising a boundary around a field in order to keep sheep rather than grow crops. It was a measure undertaken as a result of rising population and increased food prices.[76] In the early sixteenth century, woollen manufacturing was England's main industry, with the result that the use of land to support textile production provided far greater returns on investment than the cultivation of arable crops. Enclosure was associated with greed and avarice. Whilst it was good for the landowners, it was disruptive for tenants, undermined their traditional way of life and potentially reduced their income. They could even be evicted. Contemporaries believed that enclosure exacerbated 'unemployment and depopulation, reduced the corn harvest and aggravated local problems of grain scarcity'.[77]

As such, it was on this change of land use that the Tudor regime focused the attention of its agricultural policy. Tenants thought Protector Somerset's interest in the agrarian problem would improve their conditions. In fact, his interest in enclosure did not stem from a wish to protect the rights of the commons, but resulted directly from the resumption of war with Scotland. For Somerset, turning land over to pasture meant a reduction in the number of men working on the land and consequently, fewer strong, fit men to join his army.[78] Commissions were set up in 1517, 1548 and 1565 to investigate levels of enclosure and engrossing, but their results were patchy and incomplete. Although it was, perhaps, more a matter of perception than reality, enclosure was a highly visible problem that had changed the face of swathes of the English countryside. As one anonymous balladeer put it, 'Sum takys in commens, thus all men may se'.[79] Enclosure was an issue to which many people could relate, even if it did not directly affect them during the mid-sixteenth century.[80] This is one reason why words such as engrosser and encloser 'acted as powerful vehicles for a moralised explanation of change'.[81] They were considered to be insults and were levelled against those who put their own wealth before the common good.

Looking Back to a Golden Age

The sixteenth century was a time without a sophisticated understanding of economics. Issues such as enclosure and engrossing were instead closely associated with issues of vice and virtue on the basis of past experience and social norms. This in turn led to the belief that the past had been a better time – a golden age when men had been honest, treated one another fairly and had been, in modern parlance, socially responsible. By contrast, the present was a time of rampant iniquity. This nostalgia for an idealised past implied that the economic problems of the present had been brought about by decadence.[82] The ballads, however, show that although widespread moral decay upset the commons, there was also a specific concern about the iniquity of individuals who accumulated large amounts of land. According to the author of *Thys myserable world in dede*, greed was at the root of all evils against the commonwealth:

> Pryvate commoditie lykewyes,
> By treacherrye and stelthe,
> Dothe still consperacyes syrmyes,
> To sley pore commen welthe.[83]

Thomas More's *Utopia* similarly described how

> noble men, and gentlemen: yea and certeyn Abbottes, holy men god wote, not contenting them selfes with the yearely reuennues and profyttes that were wont to grow to theyr forefathers and predecessours of their landes, [n]or beynge content that they liue in rest and pleasure nothyng profytyng ye muche noyinge the weale publique: leaue no grounde for tyllage: they enclose all in pastures: they throw downe houses: they plucke downe townes, and leaue nothing stondynge but only the churche to make of it a shepehowse.

The enclosure of land by 'good holy men' turned 'all dwellinges places and all glebelande into desolation and wildernes'.[84] In the *Ruful Complaynt*, the authorial voice personified England, protesting that 'the ryche mans nead / To make pasture, away wyth ploughe / That they may cattle fead' led to dearth and poverty:

> My groundes they be imparked
> Corne feldes for beastes foode
> Poore by the ryche, are so pynched
> that of my ground, they take no good.[85]

Likewise, the ballad *Cleane witheowt feare* described how 'Hosbande men be brought so nakyde and poor, / That sum are not able to put a shepe owt ath dore, / To grayce uppone the commins, the lordes cloye them so sore'.[86] Demand for land rose in the sixteenth century as more land was enclosed and individual land holdings decreased in size. This had a knock-on effect on rents such as entry fines, which were charged to take up the lease on a piece of land. The theory was that the imposition of entry fines would help to keep rents at a nominal level, but in the mid-Tudor years, both seemed to be rising beyond the means of ordinary folk.[87]

Ballads found in Bod. MS Ashmole 48 and BL Add. MS 15225 stress the way landholders tightened their financial grip on their tenants. *Cleane witheowt feare* criticised 'Howe the heighten ther rent; / Besydes all othar things, wherin sum pas ther boundes' and *Winter could into summer hot* commented that 'Raysinge of rentes pi[c]kes poore men's purse'.[88] *Who lovithe to lyve in peas* complained of the 'doubling of smale rent', while on the other hand, *Remember man thy frayle estate* counselled that the wise man, living in fear of God, would 'repulse the vayne desyre of treasour, land, or rente'.[89] John Barker's 1561 *A Balade declaryng how neybourhed, loue, and trew dealyng is gone* censured landlords for their greed:

> To pourchace and bye, for lucre and gaine,
> Both leace and house, both wood and grounde,
> Thei double the rent, to poore mens payne;
> Of landlordes nowe fewe good are founde.[90]

A ballad in Bod. MS Ashmole 48, *That this great ware may stay*, suggested that by the time tenants had paid their entry fines, they could no longer afford to pay their rent:

> For no man cold get a farm
> Withowt a greyt fyne,
> Which makys them nowe to whyn,
> And ther bargins to repent,
> For the can skantly pay ther rent.[91]

Increased fines and high rents were seen to be a direct cause of theft, begging and vagrancy because they drove people off the land:

> Be incommys and fynes many tenantes decaye;
> Sum begge, sum steale, and sum ron away;
> And this caus sum landlordes sum teanantes saye,
> When the lacke ther rent
> All thing shal be strānyde, yf the poor man break day.[92]

The appearance of fines, rent increases, engrossing and enclosure in ballads points to a conscious attempt on the part of balladeers to appeal to their audience with songs about topical issues. That these issues were indeed relevant to the ballad-consuming public is demonstrated by the fact that each of the collections contained at least some of these socially critical songs.

Socially critical ballads drew on contemporary issues to which rural communities could relate. During the summer of 1549, the commons and the regime united to blame the ills of society on the landlords and gentlemen. The regime could claim that their greed and avarice caused economic decay; the commons protested about the effects of sheep-farming and enclosure on inflation.[93] *Who lovithe to lyve in peas* acknowledged that the middling sort was 'cryeng for redres' of local grievances.[94] Whether or not there was, for example, a high rate of enclosure between 1530 and 1570 is, in one sense immaterial, because it is clear that it was a matter of enormous concern to many individuals. These ballads dealt head-on with the perceived social ills of the day, relating the problems to an identifiable cause: the greed and avarice of local gentry. In so doing, they helped to spread a feeling of dissatisfaction with the local administration. These socially critical ballads played a part in a culture of passive resistance and subversion. That there are manuscript collections that place this more radical material centre stage suggests that there were individuals who used their song collections not just as devotional aids but also to understand the changes they experienced in the world around them.

Although there is some overlap between each of the miscellanies and printed material and the collectors certainly drew from the broadside market, songs circulating in manuscript were not necessarily the same ones being performed by balladmongers on the streets and sold for a penny to the poorest elements of society. Instead, they were collected by the very people who might be expected to have more in common with the rapacious landlords who were the subject of the balladeers' complaints. It is often assumed that manuscript miscellanies were copied from broadsides, but they might equally well have been written down from memory to aid the immortalisation of a favoured version of the lyrics. A clever and entrepreneurial ballad singer could take a popular song and alter the words in performance to make it relevant to contemporary politics. Ballads were able to address issues that had an impact on every member of society and, as such, they reflect people coming to terms with changes that had already taken place and which they perceived to be occurring around them. Assembling a collection of ballads that included socially critical items demonstrated an attempt to understand and perhaps to influence those changes. In addressing the themes of the commonwealth, ballads played a part in creating agency among those who were not the arbiters of power.

Notes

1 *L&P* xi, SP 1/108 ff. 186–87, p. 305, no. 786, 'Salley Papers, 1536'; see also Mary Bateson, 'The Pilgrimage of Grace', *English Historical Review*, 5:18 (1890), pp. 344–45. The chapter title is taken from *A Ruful Complaynt of the Publyke Weale to Englande* (London, 1550), STC (2nd ed.) / 5611.4.
2 E. H. Phelps Brown and Sheila V. Hopkins, 'Seven Centuries of Wages and Prices: Some Earlier Estimates', *Economica*, 28:109 (1956), pp. 296–314; Y. S. Brenner, 'The Inflation of Prices in England, 1551–1650', *Economic History Review*, 15:2 (1962), pp. 266–84.
3 *L&P* xi, SP 1/108, 'Salley Papers, 1536'.

4 Patterson, *Censorship and Interpretation*, p. 51.
5 Thomas Betteridge, *Literature and Politics in the English Reformation* (Manchester: Manchester University Press, 2004), p. 59.
6 Jane Whittle, 'Conclusion', in Jane Whittle (ed.), *Landlords and Tenants in Britain, 1440–1660: Tawney's Agrarian Problem Revisited* (Woodbridge: Boydell Press, 2013), pp. 220–21.
7 Susan M. Pearce, *On Collecting: An Investigation into Collecting in the European Tradition* (London: Routledge, 1995), p. 4.
8 Arthur F. Marotti, *Manuscript, Print, and the English Renaissance Lyric* (London: Cornell University Press, 1995), p. 19.
9 London, British Library, Add. MS 56279 (Aston Commonplace Book); BL Add. MS 38599 (Commonplace Book of the Shann Family of Methley, co. York); BL Add. MS 82370 (Stanhope Manuscript).
10 Pearce, *On Collecting*, p. 14.
11 Gregory, *Victorian Songhunters*, p. 22; Michael Mendle, 'Preserving the Ephemeral: Reading, Collecting, and the Pamphlet Culture of Seventeenth-Century England', in Jennifer Andersen & Elizabeth Sauer (eds.), *Books and Readers in Early Modern England: Material Studies* (Philadelphia: University of Pennsylvania Press, 2002), p. 202.
12 Koji Kuwakino, 'The Great Theatre of Creative Thought: The *Inscriptiones vel tituli theatri amplissimi* ... (1565) by Samuel von Quiccheberg', *Journal of the History of Collections*, 25:3 (2013), p. 303.
13 Adam Smyth, *Autobiography in Early Modern England* (Cambridge: Cambridge University Press, 2010), p. 152.
14 Marjorie Swann, *Curiosities and Texts: The Culture of Collecting in Early Modern England* (Philadelphia: University of Pennsylvania Press, 2001), pp. 155–56.
15 Harold Love, *The Culture and Commerce of Texts: Scribal Publication in Seventeenth-Century England* (Amherst: University of Massachusetts Press, 1998), pp. 180–82.
16 Marotti, *Manuscript, Print, and the English Renaissance Lyric*, p. 44.
17 Veerapen, 'Slander and Sedition', pp. 19–20.
18 Love, *Culture and Commerce of Texts*, p. 183.
19 Alison Shell, *Oral Culture and Catholicism in Early Modern England* (Cambridge: Cambridge University Press, 2008), pp. 82–83.
20 Wright (ed.), *Songs and Ballads*; Michael Chesnutt, 'Minstrel Poetry in an English Manuscript of the Sixteenth Century: Richard Sheale and Ms. Ashmole 48', in Flemming G. Andersen, Thomas Pettitt, and Reinhold Schroder (eds.), *The Entertainer in Medieval and Traditional Culture: A Symposium* (Odense: Odense University Press, 1997), pp. 73–100; Hyder E. Rollins, 'Concerning Bodleian Ms. Ashmole 48', *Modern Language Notes*, 34:6 (1919), pp. 340–51; Andrew Taylor, *The Songs and Travels of a Tudor Minstrel: Richard Sheale of Tamworth* (York: York Medieval Press, 2012).
21 Chesnutt, 'Minstrel Poetry'.
22 See Sheale's autobiographical song, *O God, what a world ys this now to se*, in Bod. MS Ashmole 48, ff. 95^r-98^r.
23 *Songs and Ballads*, pp. iv, vii and x.
24 Rollins, 'Concerning Bodleian Ms. Ashmole 48', pp. 349–50.
25 Taylor, *Songs and Travels*, pp. 91–98.
26 Taylor, *Songs and Travels*, p. 83.
27 Rollins (ed.), *Old English Ballads*, pp. xxx and xxxi.

28 Peter Seng (ed.), *Tudor Songs and Ballads from Ms Cotton Vespasian a-25* (Cambridge, MA: Harvard University Press, 1978). A previous transcription published in 1875–76 was marred by transcription errors and typographical mistakes.

29 See Seng's notes to each ballad in *Tudor Songs and Ballads*.

30 Seng, *Tudor Songs and Ballads*, pp. xx, xxi and xiii.

31 Hugh Aveling, *Post Reformation Catholicism in East Yorkshire, 1558–1790* (York: East Yorkshire Local History Society, 1960), pp. 31–60.

32 On drinking communities and their cultures, see *A Pleasing Sinne: Drink and Conviviality in Seventeenth-Century England*, ed. Adam Smyth (Cambridge: Brewer, 2004).

33 Shell, *Oral Culture and Catholicism*, p. 116.

34 See Rollins's introduction to each ballad in *Old English Ballads*.

35 Rollins, 'Concerning Bodleian Ms. Ashmole 48', pp. 347–48 and 243.

36 Ethan H. Shagan, *Popular Politics and the English Reformation* (Cambridge: Cambridge University Press, 2003), p. 91.

37 G. R. Elton, *Reform and Renewal: Thomas Cromwell and the Common Weal* (Cambridge: Cambridge University Press, 1973), pp. 1 and 5–7.

38 Thomas More, *A fruteful, and pleasaunt worke of the beste state of a publyque weale, and of the newe yle called Vtopia: written in Latine by Syr Thomas More knyght, and translated into Englyshe by Raphe Robynson citizein and goldsmythe of London, at the procurement, and earnest request of George Tadlowe citezein [and] haberdassher of the same citie* (London, 1551), STC (2nd ed.) / 18094 (hereafter: More, *Utopia*).

39 Bod. MS Ashmole 48, Henry Sponare, *Thys myserable world indede*, f. 52^r.

40 James C. Scott, *Weapons of the Weak: Everyday Forms of Peasant Resistance* (London: Yale University Press, 1985), pp 324–35.

41 Andrew Pettegree, *Reformation and the Culture of Persuasion* (Cambridge: Cambridge University Press, 2005), p. 73.

42 Walsham, *Providence in Early Modern England*, p. 33. For more on the popularity and decline of the 'godly ballad' in England, see Watt, *Cheap Print*, Chapter 2.

43 London, British Library, Sloane MS 1896, *How every vice crepeth in vn[der] the name and shew of a vertue*, f. 26^r.

44 Durston and Eales, 'Introduction: The Puritan Ethos, 1560–1700', p. 13.

45 Willis, *Church Music and Protestantism*, p. 203.

46 BL Sloane MS 1896, *A Warning vnto Repentaunce and of Christes Coming vnto Iudgement*, f. 46^r.

47 London, British Library Add. MS 15225, *To Passe the Place Where Pleasure Is*, f. 17^v.

48 Pettegree, *Reformation and the Culture of Persuasion*, p. 75.

49 Nancy Lee Beaty, *The Craft of Dying: A Study in the Literary Tradition of the Ars Moriendi in England* (London: Yale University Press, 1970), p. 155; Robert Whiting, '"For the Health of My Soul": Prayers for the Dead in the Tudor South-West', in *The Impact of the English Reformation, 1500–1640*, ed. Peter Marshall (London: Arnold, 1997), p. 139.

50 Bod. MS Ashmole 48, *Take hede in tyme*, f. 19^v. Heritage referred to inheritance or to the legal possession of something.

51 BL Add. MS 15225, *Seeke wisdome chiefly to obteine*, f. 38^v.

52 Hindle, *State and Social Change*, pp. 177 and 203.

53 Jennifer Loach, *A Mid-Tudor Crisis?* (London: Historical Association, 1992), p. 6.

54 Ethan H. Shagan, 'Protector Somerset and the 1549 Rebellions: New Sources and New Perspectives', *English Historical Review*, 114:455 (1999), pp. 34–63;

Ethan H. Shagan, '"Popularity" and the 1549 Rebellions Revisited', *English Historical Review*, 115:460 (2000), pp. 121–33; Shagan, *Popular Politics and the English Reformation*.

55 Wood, *Riot, Rebellion and Popular Politics*, pp. 55 and 64.

56 Shagan, '"Popularity" and the 1549 Rebellions Revisited', p. 131.

57 *A Ruful Complaynt of the Publyke Weale to Englande*.

58 BL Add. MS 15233 (transcribed in James O. Halliwell (ed.), *The Moral Play of wit and Science, and Early Poetical Miscellanies from an Unpublished Manuscript* (London: Shakespeare Society, 1848), p. 110).

59 BL Sloane MS 1896, *God doth blesse this realme for the receiving of straungers being persecuted for the gospel, although some do repine therat*, f. 56^v.

60 Thomas Camel, *To Dauid Dicars When* (London, 1552), STC (2nd ed.) / 4527.6.

61 William King, *Alteracio[n]s of Kindoms, for Despisi[n]g of God [and] How God Defendeth His* (London, 1550), STC (2nd ed.) / 14999.5.

62 *A Ruful Complaynt of the Publyke Weale to Englande*.

63 Juliet Ingram, 'The Conscience of the Community: The Character and Development of Clerical Complaint in Early Modern England', PhD Thesis, University of Warwick, 2004, pp. 57–58.

64 Shagan, *Popular Politics and the English Reformation*, p. 286.

65 Ingram, 'Conscience of the Community', pp. 59 and 119.

66 Tottel's *Miscellany*, ff. 87^r–88^r; *TRCS*, i, p. 116.

67 Rollins, *Old English Ballads*, p. xxviii.

68 BL Add. MS 15225, *A dittie most excelent for euerie man to reade*, ff. 56^r–58^r.

69 Simpson, *The British Broadside Ballad and Its Music*, p. 396; FSL V.a.159, ff. 7^r–7^v.

70 Una McIlvenna, 'The Rich Merchant Man, or, What the Punishment of Greed Sounded Like in Early Modern English Ballads', *Huntington Library Quarterly*, 79:2 (2016), pp. 279–99.

71 Edinburgh, National Library of Scotland, Henry Playford, *Wit and Mirth, or Pills to Purge Melancholy* (London, 1719), v, p. 77. An editorial anacrusis has been added at the beginning of the final phrase in order to make the timings match the other three phrases. Both Chappell and Simpson suggest editorial E flats in bars 5–7 (Chappell, *Popular Music of the Olden Time*, i, p. 381; Simpson, *British Broadside Ballad and its Music*, p. 602).

72 Bod. MS Ashmole 48, *Who lovithe to lyve in peas*, ff. 37^v–39^r.

73 Phillip Stubbes, *The second part of the anatomie of abuses conteining the display of corruptions, with a perfect description of such imperfections, blemishes and abuses, as now reigning in euerie degree, require reformation for feare of Gods vengeance to be powred vpon the people and countrie, without speedie repentance, and conuersion vnto God: made dialogwise by Phillip Stubbes* (London, 1583), STC (2nd ed.) / 23376, sig. O2^v.

74 Stubbes, *The second part of the anatomie of abuses*, sig. O3^r.

75 Bod. MS Ashmole 48, *Cleane witheowt feare truthe dothe me constrene*, f. 7^v.

76 Joan Thirsk, *Tudor Enclosures* (London: Routledge & Kegan Paul, 1959), p. 4.

77 Thirsk, *Tudor Enclosures*, p. 9.

78 M. L. Bush, *The Government Policy of Protector Somerset* (London: Edward Arnold, 1975), p. 57.

79 Bod. MS Ashmole 48, *Cleane witheowt feare truthe dothe me constrene*, f. 8^r.

80 See Loach, *A Mid-Tudor Crisis?*

81 Ingram, 'Conscience of the Community', p. 5.

82 Hindle, *State and Social Change*, pp. 54–55.

83 Bod. MS Ashmole 48, Sponare, *Thys myserable world indede*, f. 52^r.

84 More, *Utopia*, sig. Cvii^r.

85 *A Ruful complaynt of the publyke weale.*
86 Bod. MS Ashmole 48, *Cleane witheowt feare*, f. 8^r.
87 Brenner, 'Inflation of Prices in England', p. 234.
88 Bod. MS Ashmole 48, *Cleane witheowt feare*, f. 7^v; BL Add. MS 15225, *Winter could into summer hot*, f. 34^r.
89 Bod. MS Ashmole 48, *Who lovithe to lyve in peas*, f. 37^v; Bod. MS Ashmole 48, Richard Sheale, *Remember man thy frayle estate*, f. 36^v.
90 John Barker, *A balade declaryng how neybourhed loue, and trew dealyng is gone* (London, 1561), STC (2nd ed.) / 1419.
91 Bod. MS Ashmole 48, *That this great ware may stay*, f. 100^v.
92 Bod. MS Ashmole 48, *Cleane witheowt feare*, f. 7^v.
93 Shagan, *Popular Politics and the English Reformation*, p. 280.
94 Bod. MS Ashmole 48, *Who lovithe to lyve in peas*, f. 37^v.

Conclusion
'one hundred of ballits'

I must apologise, if it's written in these troubled skies.
We've been peddling lies, somehow forgotten what is true.
Though it's buried deep the poison never sleeps.
Through the ages seeps, to leave the reckoning for you.[1]

Mid-Tudor society relied on orality. If you wanted to buy something, you did so in person. If you wanted to pass on a message, you were most likely to do so face to face. If you wanted to learn a song, you asked someone else to sing it for you. Ballads were part of a social system and were sung in public places, often by people who travelled around the country to sell their goods at markets and fairs. In doing so, they carried news to the provinces. Ballads represent the ultimate in sixteenth-century multimedia sources: they united text, image and sound in one entertaining package.

Ballads were central to sixteenth-century culture because of their accessibility and broad appeal. They emphasised oral exchange and social interaction, urging consumers to become performers by joining in with their catchy tunes and simple language. Their lyrics created a dialogue between the performer and their audience, inviting them to share the opinions expressed in the songs. Though the broadside trade was centred on London, ballads themselves spread across the whole of the country. They were written in the voice of the people, and even though sometimes that voice was well educated, the songs reflected the needs and concerns of the middling and lower orders.

But if ballads were central to mid-Tudor entertainment, then melody was central to the ballad. Because they needed to be instantly memorable, ballad melodies were part of a musical impulse that was moving away from modal harmonies towards the eighteenth-century triumph of major/minor tonality. And we should never underestimate the power of a good tune. Put simply, it was the tune that made these words into a song and gave them their broad appeal. Sometimes, a tune grew by association with noteworthy lyrics, changing its name as it was attached to a particular hit, or even gathering implicit associations with a certain type of song. Such musical implicitness could amplify or destabilize the meaning of the words. Balladeers were also able to adapt their material to fit the circumstances. They could alter the rhythm of the words in order to accommodate different sets of lyrics, or even to adapt their words to suit to the political situation when necessary. Sometimes, the very material that an individual chose to sing could help them fashion their image in the eyes of others, perhaps by choosing a moralised ballad rather than a licentious one, or by choosing a ballad which condemned Thomas Cromwell rather than celebrating him.

Ballads certainly had a part to play in news culture. Many songs addressed themselves to the issues that concerned the populace and set that news in the context of editorial which helped people to understand how it might affect them. Even without a high level of detail, it is still easy to place many of these ballads at a certain time through their descriptions of major events. Others used the sort of language that we associate with news, and stressed their newness, novelty and topicality. Still more were related to what we might term 'current affairs' – the ongoing problems and issues which people worried about, such as land reform, fines and the continuing debate over the Reformation. Granted, this ballad news was unreliable in every sense: it was not a regular, periodical press, nor was it always completely true. Likewise, it often lacked detail and it was certainly not unbiased. But these were cheap texts, produced relatively quickly and easily, so it seems likely that many balladeers cashed in on major events that would soon become old news rather than relying on steady sales of timeless themes. This also suggests a ready market with an appetite for entertaining, topical songs and keen to hear the latest news.

Dressing the news in a cloak of moralising or religious material gave it a life beyond its immediate topicality and perhaps hoped to raise it from ephemerality, but the fact that fewer of these songs were treasured by manuscript collectors suggests that they were not valued in the same way that devotional material was. Instead, manuscript miscellanies bear testament to the enduring popularity of ballads with a significant moralistic or religious dimension, especially those related to personal devotion. What the manuscript collections show most clearly, though, is that people who collected ballads simply did not keep the ones that related to current affairs. Judging by the Stationers' Registers, plenty of topical ballads were printed; they were just not saved for posterity because they were news and quickly became stale.

The problem with discussing the news in the sixteenth century, though, was that it was nobody's business but the monarch's. People were clearly interested in the goings-on at court and in the church, just as they were interested in enclosure or rebellion, but they were not supposed to discuss it. It is just as clear, however, that people did exactly that. Sometimes, as in the songs which promoted Mary I's dynastic right and legitimate claim to the throne despite her gender, balladeers were able to tackle serious issues head on. When that topicality verged on sedition, or at times of political crisis, then the safer options were to circulate the song in manuscript, or not to write it down at all. At other times, when that news was particularly controversial, implicitness really came in to its own: rather than openly risking prosecution, implicitness created a temporary public sphere in which people could discuss the news. A balladeer could choose whether or not to highlight the implicit aspects of a song through his performance depending on the circumstances. If he were unsure of his audience, singing among people who might be total strangers or merely passing acquaintances, then implicitness could be the key to discussing the issues of the day. Among friends, and when passed on between people who knew each other well, implicitness created a space for discussion. These songs created some control over who understood. But always, the social context created opportunities for people to ask questions of their family, friends or the balladeer himself.

Those same tunes which made ballads appealing to the masses also presented a particularly potent threat when they were mobilised to carry the news. It made the lyrics, sometimes seditious but often on the very boundaries of legality, especially memorable. Despite the fact that many ballads stressed the importance of loyalty to God and obedience to the monarch, the Tudor regime made repeated attempts to control the dissemination of ballads. Entertainment they might have been, but they were influential too.

Implicitness Through the Centuries

As I came to the end of writing this book, two things made me think about the relationship between implicitness, music and information. First, my daughter was set a piece of English homework: she had to examine a set of song lyrics of her choice. She chose the verse from 'The Reckoning' by Steve Tilston with which I opened this chapter. The song is about the legacy of nuclear waste that we are leaving for generations to come.[2] She was fully aware that the extended metaphor meant something; she was just unsure exactly what that something was. So what did she do? She asked me.

By a second coincidence, the day's news was dominated by the British Prime Minister's decision to call a snap general election two years ahead of schedule. Watching the 6 p.m. news bulletin on BBC1, the story was so big that it had knocked all other topics from the programme.[3] It is clear that in itself, news of a general election would not take more than a few moments to deliver, but instead the whole half hour was taken up with context and analysis. As well as reports on the response of the different political parties, there was plenty of background information. There were *vox pops* from voters in marginal constituencies, in addition to reports on how news of the election had been received in the provinces of Scotland, Northern Ireland and Wales. Although there were no reports that the election was a result of divine providence, an expert on British elections was consulted and the voting patterns of marginal constituencies in the last general election were compared to those of the 2016 referendum on Britain's membership of the European Union. Indeed, Brexit was the main way in which the story was contextualised, even more so than the Conservative lead in the opinion polls. What is more, on Twitter, people discussed the news as it related to them. A few hours later, a quick glance at the social network revealed speculation about Teresa May's motivations and the possible outcomes. Others were posting memes that summed up their feelings in an entertaining fashion.[4]

Early modern balladeers did much the same thing. They set the news in context so that their audience could understand. The song did not need to be full of hard information, but not because the composer assumed that everybody already knew what had happened. Many probably did, but by no means everyone. Certainly, in the provinces we can see that balladeers were asked 'What news?' The one thing the balladeer did know was that his song was likely to be sung in a social situation, where the context could be explained. Far from undermining the ballad's role in news culture, the entertainment value of the ballad in fact tells us about the way in which news and information were experienced during a period when people did not have unfettered access to matters of politics. Ballads related the news in its widest sense to the other issues that people cared about – loyalty to the monarch, for example, or divine providence. In doing so, they set the news in context for their consumers. If the ballad's popularity and entertainment value made people pass the message from one person to another, then so much the better. The ballad, after all, was not synonymous with the broadside, and not all those messages toed the royal line.

One of the things that is different in Britain today is the amount of information that is freely available. Another is that we have a belief in free speech. There is no need to cloak the news or political opinion in secrecy unless your views are extreme. Over the years, implicitness has underwritten political song in many different cultures. It provided a means of communicating with like-minded people when you were not supposed to do so. Implicitness in the mid-Tudor period allowed balladeers to broach contentious subjects in a way that might circumvent censorship. We still use imagery, anecdote and even irony to deal with big issues, but we do it, in the main, because it is entertaining. The fact that it is enjoyable perhaps underlines its importance when it makes us think. It is effective, and it was no less so in the sixteenth century.

And so we come full circle, back to the Herricks in Leicester and London, sending and receiving ballads, singing and selling these deceptively simple songs. *A dolfull daunce & song of death* told the familiar, moralising story of the great leveller who would call on everyone eventually, regardless of their social standing.[5] Death, as the narrator, reminded his listeners that

Both high and low, both great & small
I nought doe feare your highe degree
the ladie fair the beldam ould
the champion stout, the souldier bould
must all with me to earthlie mould.

He even pointed out, in a nod to topicality, that

...on the solempe Syses last
how sodenlie in Oxfordshire
I came and made the Judges agast
and Iustises that did appeare
and took both bell and Baram away
and manie a worthie man that day
and all their bodies brought to clay.

Gossip like this was passed from person to person. News was framed in a similar context. While much of this news was local and probably personal, we can see that on occasion, matters of national import would be passed on in the same way. The social context of the news allowed people to discuss matters that were important to them. It was this same social context that made ballads a useful tool for those who wished to spread the news. Because ballads encouraged audience participation, they were able to play on the interest of their audience to spread messages across the country. If that message were in some way subversive, then it could be hidden in an implicit subtext. It was ultimately deniable, but it could be explained by those in the know.

Nevertheless, while scholars are keen to analyse and provide criticism, while we look for hidden meanings beneath the texts and in the tunes, the sorts of trivial pursuits and idle pastimes that were provided by ballads and jests invoke, at their heart, an elusive quality of pleasure and enjoyment.[6] This was one reason why they featured prominently in the Herricks' letters. Ballads were undoubtedly intended as a form of entertainment, generating income for those who produced, performed and sold copies. They were integral to the leisure activities of almost all sections of society. They were accessible to everyone. These popular songs provided the backdrop to so much of early modern life, from the alehouse to the marketplace, the countryside to the court. At turns moralising, topical or amatory, many combined several themes to ensure an appeal to the widest cross section of society, while encouraging people to join in, sing along, heckle and debate. Ballads, in particular, lose much of their fun when divorced from their music. Their entertainment value has sometimes been underestimated simply because they have been studied as texts alone. Moreover, it is often the music, as much as the words, which moves mankind's soul to elation or despair. As the balladeer Nicholas Whight put it, 'Musicke doeth appease, the dolours of the mynd'.[7]

While, at times, the music could provide an extra layer of meaning to the lyrics, catchy and memorable tunes such as 'Row Well Ye Mariners', 'The Lusty Gallant' and 'The Downright Squire' provided a means by which songs about sex, social ills, queens, heretics and rebellion could travel the country. They were able to spark debate and start conversations, which allowed people to play their part in a public sphere, even if it were at a modest level and relatively short lived. Censorship in Tudor England was generally reactive rather than proactive, so when successive regimes sought to curb the spread of ballads, they did so because they perceived these apparently simple songs as a significant threat. When people were enthused by the message and the music, they would pass on the songs. Even when we are unable to reconstruct the tunes to which these words were sung, we should never underestimate the power of the ballad to sing the news in mid-Tudor society.

Notes

1 Steve Tilston, 'The Reckoning', *The Reckoning* (HUB006: Hubris Records, 2011). Used by permission of the author. The chapter title is taken from Bod. MS Eng. hist. c. 474, f. 159^r.
2 *Steve Tilston*, 'Discography – The Reckoning', www.stevetilston.com/discography/the-reckoning/ [accessed 20 April 2017].
3 *BBC News at Six*, 18 April 2017, British Broadcasting Corporation.
4 Mathew Lyons (@MathewJLyons), 'Was May's decision triggered by upcoming election fraud charges? www2.politicalbetting.com/index.php/arch…', 19 April 2017, 12:01 a.m., Tweet; Rebecca Rideal (@RebeccaRideal), 'Did Paul Mason say Labour will win GE and then confess that he would 'vote tactically' (ie not Labour) in his constituency? #Newsnight', 19 April 2017, 12.03 a.m., Tweet; Kirsty Rolfe (@avoidingbears), 'I keep trying to be politically engaged but politics keeps being all [garbage fight GIF]', 18 April 2017, 4.51 p.m., Tweet. All used by permission of the authors.
5 *dolefull dance and song of death*.
6 Brown, *Better a Shrew Than a Sheep*, pp. 218–19.
7 Nicholas Whight, *A Commendation of Musicke and a Confutation of Them Which Disprayse It* (London, 1563), STC (2nd ed.) / 25350.

Appendix
A Note on Musical Analysis

The music that we hear can affect our mood. Our Renaissance ancestors were no different. Burgeoning interest in the history of the senses has highlighted the ways in which sound was heard and understood in the early modern period. The capacity for melody to make meaning and to provoke an emotional response was believed to have had its origins in the ancient scale patterns known as modes. Most obviously, the mode defined which notes could be used in a melody, but it also controlled the melodic and harmonic progressions (or cadences) at the end of a musical phrase. It even indicated the notes on which each part should begin, in polyphonic music that had several parts. Modes had been classified by music theorists over many hundreds of years. Eight Gregorian church modes were used for monophonic plainchant that had a single vocal line. In the mid-sixteenth century, the Swiss music theorist Heinrich Glarean advocated an extended system of twelve modes that became highly influential in Europe.

The relationship of ballad music to English musical theory, however, is not altogether straightforward. There were, in fact, two divergent but coexistent schools of English music theory. One was typified by the Renaissance composer, Thomas Morley, while the other was a more philosophically based theory that represented an apparently unusual intrusion of continental musical theory. Morley published the first popular English music textbook, *A plaine and easie introduction to practicall musicke*, in 1597.[1] The book explained a technique known as solmization, used to teach singing. Solmization was based, not on the modes, but on scales of six notes called hexachords that were used in sixteenth-century English composition. Solmization identified each of the six notes of the scale by a syllable (*ut, re, mi, fa, sol* and *la*). The process of moving from one hexachord to another in order to broaden the range of a melody beyond six notes was known as mutation. Where music mutated from one hexachord to another, singers were taught to sing the syllables belonging to both hexachords for the note where the change took place, then to continue solmizing in the new hexachord.[2]

Morley is, however, indicative of the 'muddled state' of English modal theory in the sixteenth century. Despite comprehensively covering the rudiments of music, he barely mentioned the modes, and even then only as they applied to the Gregorian psalm tones. If Morley is to be taken at face value, it would appear that sixteenth-century English composers did not use modes to construct their music.[3]

Nevertheless, although music teachers and composers in sixteenth-century England rarely described music in terms of modes, philosophers most certainly did. There was something of a divergence between formally trained musicians, whose interest was in practical methods of teaching and composing music, and philosophers, who showed a deep concern with the way that music affected the soul. Elizabethan humanists, for example, drew on a well of cultural discourse which contributed to the ways in which they understood and wrote about music and its practice.[4] Taking inspiration from Plato and Aristotle, university-educated men recognised that music affected the soul in different ways, depending on both its musical scale and the personality of the listener.

One of the most eminent of these men was the Elizabethan Archbishop of Canterbury, Matthew Parker. His *whole Psalter*, published in 1567, offered plenty of advice on how to choose suitable tunes for his metrical psalm translations. Parker appears to have been out of step with his English contemporaries, who, as Thomas Morley's textbook shows, had little knowledge or understanding of modal theory. It was Parker's continental counterparts in Germany and Italy, rather than other Englishmen, who were concerned with theorising about modes and how words would be affected by the music that carried them.[5] Parker, however, drew on ancient theories, such as Saint Athanasius's table of modal affect, to establish that the choice of a tune could have a huge impact on the meaning and character of the song:

> FIrst ye ought to conioyne a sad tune or song, with a sad Psalme, And a ioyfull tune and songe wyth a ioyfull Psalme, And an indifferent tune and song, with a Psalm which goeth indifferently.

He advised his readers that

> Psalmes of ioy be such as be constitute in the third and fift place of Athanasius table, which be Psalmes consolatory, and of thankesgeuyng with theyr Coniugates. Sad Psalmes be such as be set in the fourth common place, as Deprecatory, and Interpellatory, Indifferent be suche as be in the first and second place, as Propheticall, or such as do teach and exhort, and such also as be mixte containyng diuers of the sayd fiue places…

Parker nevertheless acknowledged that the music's effects varied from one person to another, for as there be diuersities of tastes in mens palaces: So bee there in mens spirites, and so also in theyr eares. For what Psalme or songe, one mans spirite shall iudge graue and sad, some other shall thinke it pleasaunt. And what one mans eare shall thinke pleasaunt, another shall iudge it sower and seuere.

Furthermore, Parker recognised that each mode provided a different context for the words, so he included a description of the 'Octo tonorum distinctiones & proprietates [Of eight distinct and special character tones]'.[6] He commissioned Thomas Tallis to write eight psalm tunes and a setting of the Veni Creator for his psalter.[7] Each of the eight psalm tunes was written in a different church mode, enabling Parker to suggest a tune in a suitable mode to match the content of each of his psalm translations.

Since Parker went to such an effort to show how important it was to use the right type of tune for each psalm, it raises questions about the source of Parker's modal theory. Even if Parker was out of step with English music theorists, he marched alongside the philosophy of transnational humanism and English balladeers. Though there is no evidence of an interest in music theory (such as Glarean's influential music treatise, *Dodecachordon*) in the holdings of the Parker Library at Corpus Christi College, Cambridge, it contains both Plato's *Republic* and Aristotle's *Politics*. Both these works discussed modal affect in the Gregorian modes. It appears likely, then, that Parker based his modal theory on classical scholarship rather than sixteenth-century music teaching. Nevertheless, the fact that Parker felt the need to give instructions on how to match the mood of the music with the mood of the words means that he saw the choice of music for his psalms as central to how they would be received.

Parker made a conscious decision not to use the same theory that musicians used to teach music. Instead, he was writing for an audience that looked to the continent for inspiration, perhaps as much musical as religious. He recognised that music touched the human spirit and that the practical application of this knowledge would affect the way his translations of the psalms were interpreted by their users: 'Us song shoule moue: as sprite therby / might tunes in concorde sing: / God graunt these Psalmes: might edifie, / that is the chiefest thing'.[8] As well as commenting on the effect of the music, Parker included patristic arguments for the ways in which the psalms should be used. He provided a 'textual avalanche of authority' that 'paradoxically frames the volume as an erudite undertaking even while it explicitly makes the case that psalm-singing should be both public and popular'.[9]

Although Parker's wish to frame his psalter against a background of patristic authority is clear, his determination to assign each of the versifications to what he saw as an apposite tune seems to reflect a personal desire to ensure that the music resonated with the text. Though some modes were thought to inspire devotion, by the mid-seventeenth century others were certainly thought to encourage levity.[10] Parker took care to ensure that the tunes he suggested for each psalm would neither detract from the words, nor generate inappropriate emotional responses.

Parker's *whole Psalter* highlights another problem in understanding and describing English Renaissance music, especially in the more demotic genre of the ballad. His table of modes did not include two of the most common modes used in ballad music: the Ionian and the Aeolian. This is because he invoked the authority of classical authors, who described only the effect of the eight Gregorian modes (Dorian, Hypodorian, Phrygian, Hypophrygian, Lydian, Hypolydian, Mixolydian and Hypomixolydian). The Ionian and Aeolian scales (which were part of the Glarean system but not the Gregorian) are nevertheless relatively familiar to modern audiences due not only to the fact that they form the modern major scale and the natural minor scale, respectively, but also through their constant use in early modern popular music.[11] In fact, most mid-sixteenth century ballad tunes can be classified as being in either the Ionian or the Dorian mode, or what today we might refer to as major and minor tonalities.[12]

The varying terms used to describe music both during and between the sixteenth and twenty-first centuries create difficulties for the modern author. Compositional practice certainly deviated from the systems prescribed by polyphonic modal theory. It thereby created discrepancies in the way the rules were applied. An alternative approach to understanding Renaissance polyphony was therefore popularised by Harold Powers, who recognised that, although the concept of mode might be used by modern scholars to classify early modern music, mode was rarely the underlying compositional principal on which the music was based. Instead, he used the term 'tonal type' to describe the *a priori* assumptions on which Renaissance composition was based. He argued that, for the most part, Renaissance composers chose to write pieces in one of twenty-four 'tonal types' rather than in one of eight, or even twelve, modes. Musicologists could identify tonal type by the tonal system, clef and final note of a piece of music, in order to give them a better indication of the way in which any given piece had been conceived. In contrast to tonal types, Powers argued that modes 'were originally thought of more as *a posteriori* categories for grouping items in a repertory'.[13]

To describe sixteenth-century ballad tunes in terms of the technical terminology of tonal type would be, for a general audience, obscure and unnecessarily complex. The same would be true of hexachords. The priority of this study has been to ensure that the musical analysis is accessible to the general reader, so it uses more familiar modal terminology. This approach, however, is not intended to suggest that mode was the conceptual framework for the composition of ballad tunes. Furthermore, I accept that the music can be analysed and described modally, but at the risk of being *avant la lettre*, I have sometimes chosen to refer to tonality as major and minor. In keeping with other historical texts on early modern music, it uses major/minor terminology whenever the music uses cadential patterns familiar to modern harmony.[14] It is vital to employ both sets of terminology because central to the argument of this study is the suggestion that the growth of a popular musical culture in this period helped power the move towards the eighteenth-century triumph of major/minor tonality. Ballads were not the exclusive province of academically trained ecclesiastical choirs or seasoned singers of madrigals, so they had to be based on melodic structures which were easier to recall and to sing. Their emphasis on melodies which were easy to remember and reproduce made them the forerunners of musical change. In their own small way, ballads were part of the vulgarisation of music, which went hand in hand with the opening up of the public sphere.

Notes

1 Thomas Morley, *A plaine and easie introduction to practicall musicke set downe in forme of a dialogue: deuided into three partes, the first teacheth to sing with all things necessary for the knowledge of pricktsong. The second treateth of descante and to sing two parts in one vpon a plainsong or ground, with other things necessary for a descanter. The third and last part entreateth of composition of three, foure, fiue or more parts with many profitable rules to that effect. With new songs of 2. 3. 4. and .5 [sic] parts. By Thomas Morley, Batcheler of musick, & of the gent. of hir Maiesties Royall Chapel* (London, 1597), STC (2nd ed.) / 18134.

2 See Gaston Allaire, *The Theory of Hexachords, Solmization and the Modal System: A Practical Application* (Rome: American Institute of Musicology, 1972).

3 Rebecca Herissone, *Music Theory in Seventeenth-Century England* (Oxford: Oxford University Press, 2000), pp. 174–75 and 77–78.

4 Willis, *Church Music and Protestantism*, p. 36.

5 I am grateful to John Milsom for correspondence in which he gave advice on this topic.

6 Parker, *whole Psalter*, sig. VVii[v] and Ei[v]. I am grateful to Marci Freedman for translating Parker's Latin table.

7 A modern transcription was edited by David Skinner: Thomas Tallis, *The Tallis Psalter, Psalms and Anthems, Canticles, Preces and Responses* (London: Novello Publishing Ltd, 2013).

8 Parker, *whole Psalter*, sig. Biii[v].

9 Quitslund, *Reformation in Rhyme*, pp. 252–23.

10 Charles Butler, *The principles of musik, in singing and setting with the twofold use thereof, ecclesiasticall and civil. By Charles Butler Magd. Master of Arts* (London, 1636) STC (2nd ed.) / 4196, p. 2.

11 The natural minor scale is the white-note scale from A to A, that is, the Aeolian mode.
12 Leonard Bernstein, 'Young People's Concert Series: What Is a Mode?', *Leonard Bernstein*, www.leonardbernstein.com/ypc_script_what_is_a_mode.htm [accessed 11 August 2014].
13 Harold S. Powers, 'Tonal Types and Modal Categories in Renaissance Polyphony', *Journal of the American Musicological Society*, 34:3 (1981), pp. 435 and 439.
14 See, for example, Marsh, *Music and Society*, p. 238, and John Milsom, 'William Mundy's "Vox Patris Caelestis" and the Accession of Mary Tudor', *Music and Letters*, 91:1 (2010), p. 26.

Bibliography

Audio-Visual Recordings

BBC News at Six, 18 April 2017, British Broadcasting Corporation.

Music Recordings

Show of Hands. 'Roots', *Witness* (HMCD23: Hands On Music, 2006).
Tilston, Steve. 'The Reckoning', *The Reckoning* (HUB006: Hubris Records, 2011).

Manuscripts

Cambridge, Cambridge University Library:
   Registry guard book CUR 8.

London, British Library:
   Add. MS 15225.
   Add. MS 15233.
   Add. MS 38599 (Commonplace Book of the Shann family of Methley, co. York).
   Add. MS 56279 (Aston Commonplace Book).
   Add. MS 82370 (Stanhope Manuscript).
   MS Cotton Vespasian A-XXV.
   Sloane MS 1896.
   Stowe MS 958.

Oxford, Bodleian Library:
   MS Ashmole 48.
   MS. Eng. hist. c. 474.

Paris, Bibliothèque nationale de France:
   MS Rés. 1186.

Facsimiles

Dublin, Trinity College:
   MS 408 (William Ballet Lute Book), http://digitalcollections.tcd.ie/home/index.php?DRIS_ID=MS408_001 [accessed 9 July 2014].

   MS 410 (Dallis Lute Book), http://digitalcollections.tcd.ie/home/index.php?DRIS_ID=MS410_003 [accessed 8 August 2017].

Edinburgh, National Library of Scotland:
Henry Playford, *Wit and Mirth, or Pills to Purge Melancholy* (London, 1719), v, p. 77, Glen Collection of Printed Music, Glen.145–145e, http:// digital.nls.uk/87908915 [accessed 26 June 2017].

Folger Shakespeare Library Digital Image Collection:
V.a.159, http://luna.folger.edu/luna/servlet/view/search?showAll=what&q=v.a. 159&sort=Call_Number, Author, CD_Title, Imprint [accessed 9 July 2014].

Kew, The National Archives:
State Papers Domestic: Supplementary, SP 46, The National Archives Online Catalogue, http://go.galegroup.com/mss/i.do?id=GALE|MC4320180111&v= 2.1&u=jrycal5&it=r&p=SPOL&sw=w&viewtype=Manuscript [accessed 31 July 2014].

London, British Library:
Add. MS 30513 (Mulliner Book), www.bl.uk/manuscripts/FullDisplay.aspx? ref=Add_MS_30513 [accessed 5 July 2017].

Add. MS. 48028 (Yelverton MS. 32), http://go.galegroup.com/mss/i.do?id= GALE|MC43186 80796&v=2.1&u=jrycal5&it=r&p=SPOL&sw=w&view type=Manuscript [accessed 31 July 2014].

Cotton Otho C/X f. 282, http://go.galegroup.com/mss/i.do?id=GALE|MC 4301881177&v=2.1&u=jrycal5&it=r&p=SPOL&sw=w&viewtype=Manu script [accessed 31 July 2014].

Cotton Vespasian C/XIV/2 f. 303, http://go.galegroup.com/mss/i.do?id=GALE| MC4318899470&v=2.1&u=jrycal5&it=r&p=SPOL&sw=w&viewtype=Ma nuscript [accessed 31 July 2014].

Printed Primary Sources

Acts of the Privy Council, ed. J.R. Dasent et al. (32 vols. London: HMSO, 1890–1907).
Awdelay, John. *The cruel assault of Gods fort* (London, 1560), STC (2nd ed.) / 989.
———. *A godly ditty or prayer to be song vnto God for the preseruation of his Church, our Queene and realme, against all traytours, rebels, and papisticall enemies* (London, 1569), STC (2nd ed.) / 995.
———. *An Epitaph, of Maister Fraunces Benison, Citizene and Marchant of London, and of the Haberdashers Company* (London, 1570).
A balade agaynst malycyous sclaunderers (London, 1540), Society of Antiquaries, London, Book of Broadsides, STC (2nd ed.) / 1323.5.
The Ballad of constant Susanna (London, 1624).
A Ballad Reioysinge the Sodaine Fall, of Rebels That Thought to Deuower Vs All (London, 1570), STC (2nd ed.) / 1326.
Barker, John. *A balade declaryng how neybourhed loue, and trew dealyng is gone* (London, 1561), STC (2nd ed.) / 1419.
———. *Of the horyble and woful destruccion of Ierusalem and of the sygnes and tokens that were seene before it was destroied: which distruction was after Christes assension. xlii. yeares. To the tune of the Queenes Almayne* (London, [1569?]), STC (2nd ed.) / 1420.

————. *The plagues of Northomberland. To the tune of Appelles* (London, 1570), STC (2nd ed.) / 1421.

Beeard, Richard. *A Godly Psalme of Marye Queene* (London, 1553), STC (2nd ed.) / 1655.

Bette, Thomas. *A newe ballade intituled, Agaynst rebellious and false rumours To the newe tune of the Blacke Almaine, vpon Scissillia* (London, 1570), STC (2nd ed.) / 1979.

Bonner, Edmund. *Articles to Be Enquired of in the Generall Visitation of Edmonde Bisshoppe of London* (London, 1554), STC (2nd ed.) / 10248.

Bradford, John. *The copye of a letter, sent by Iohn Bradforth to... the Erles of Arundel, Darbie, Shrewsburye, and Penbroke, declaring the nature of the Spaniardes, and discovering the most detestable treasons, which thei haue pretended... agaynste... Englande. Wherunto is added a tragical blast of the papisticall tro[m]pet. by T.E.* ([Wesel?], 1556), STC (2nd ed.) / 3504.5.

A Brefe Apologye or Answere to a Certen Craftye Cloynar, or Popyshe Parasyte, Called Thomas Smythe. ([Antwerp], 1540), STC (2nd ed.) / 22880.7.

Brooke, Thomas. *Certayne versis writtene by Thomas Brooke Ge[n]tleman in the tyme of his impriso[n]ment the daye before his deathe who sufferyd at Norwich the 30 of August 1570* (Norwich, 1570), STC (2nd ed.) / 3835.

Burdet, Robert. *The refuge of a sinner wherein are briefely declared the chiefest poinctes of true saluation* (London, 1565), STC (2nd ed.) / 4104.

Butler, Charles. *The principles of musik, in singing and setting with the two-fold use thereof, ecclesiasticall and civil. By Charles Butler Magd. Master of Arts* (London, 1636), STC (2nd ed.) / 4196.

The Byble in Englyshe that is to saye, the content of all the holye scrypture, bothe of the olde and newe Testament, truly translated after the veryte of the Hebrue and Greke textes, by the diligent studye of dyuers excellent lerned [men e] xperte in the fore[saide] tongues (London, 1540), STC (2nd ed.) / 2069.

By the Quene the Quenes Highnes Well Remembrynge... (London, 1553), STC (2nd ed.) / 7849.

Calendar of State Papers, Domestic Series, of the Reign of Mary I, 1553–1558, ed. C.S. Knighton (London: Public Record Office, 1998).

Calendar of State Papers, Domestic Series, of the Reigns of Edward VI, Mary, Elizabeth, 1547–1580, ed. R. Lemon and M. A. E. Green (12 vols. London: Longman, Brown, Green, Longmans, & Roberts, 1856–72).

Calendar of State Papers, Foreign, Mary, 1553–1558, ed. W. B. Turnbull (London: Longman & Co., 1861).

Calendar of State Papers, Spanish, xiii, ed. Royall Tyler (London: HMSO, 1914–54).

Camel, Thomas. *To Dauid Dicars When* (London, 1552[?]), STC (2nd ed.) / 4527.6.

Chronicle of the grey friars of London, ed. J. G. Nichols (London: Camden Society, 1852) old series, liii.

Churchyard, Thomas. *Churchyardes lamentacion of freyndshyp* (London, 1566), STC (2nd ed.) / 5223.

Cornwallis, Sir William. *Essayes* (London: 1601), STC (2nd ed.) / 5775.

Coverdale, Miles. *Goostly psalmes and spirituall songes drawen out of the holy Scripture, for the co[m]forte and consolacyon of soch as loue to reioyse in God and his Worde* ([London], 1535), STC (2nd ed.) / 879:22.

————. *A confutacion of that treatise, which one Iohn Standish made agaynst the protestacion of D. Barnes in the yeare. M.D.XL. Wherin, the holy scriptures (peruerted and wrested in his sayd treatise) are restored to their owne true vnderstonding agayne by Myles Couerdale* (1541), STC / 33:03.

Cranmer, Thomas. *Articles to be enquired of, in visitacions to bee had, within the Diocesse of Cantorbury: in the seconde yere of the reigne of our moste drad souereigne Lorde Edward the.VI. by the grace of God, Kyng of Englande, Fraunce, and Irelande, defender of the faithe and in yearth of the Churche of Englande and also of Irelande, the Supreme Hedde* (London, [1548]), STC (2nd ed.) / 10148.

The daunce and song of death (London, 1569), STC (2nd ed.) / 6222.

The Deeds of Stephen (Gesta Stephani.), trans. & ed. Kenneth Reginald Potter (London: Thomas Nelson & Sons, 1955).

The dolefull dance and song of death; intituled; Dance after my pipe To a pleasant new tune ([London], 1664), Wing (2nd ed.) / H2013B.

Dorne, John. 'The Daily Ledger of John Dorne, 1520', in *Collectanea*, First Series, ed. F. Madan (Oxford: Oxford Historical Society at the Clarendon Press, 1885), pp. 71–178.

Elderton, William. *The panges of Loue and louers ftts* (London, 1559), STC (2nd ed.) / 7561.

——. *The true fourme and shape of a monsterous chyld, whiche was borne in Stony Stratforde, in North Hampton shire The yeare of our Lord, M.CCCCC. LXV* (London, 1565), STC (2nd ed.) / 7565.

——. *A proper new balad in praise of my Ladie Marques, whose death is bewailed, to the tune of New lusty gallant* (London, 1569), STC (2nd ed.) / 7562.

——. *A proper newe ballad sheweing that philosophers learnynges, are full of good warnynges. And songe to the tune of My Lorde Marques Galyarde: or The firste traces of que passa* (London, 1569), STC (2nd ed.) / 7563.

——. *A ballad intituled, A newe well a daye / as playne maister papist, as Donstable waye. Well a daye well a daye, well a daye woe is mee Syr Thomas Plomtrie is hanged on a tree* (London, 1570), STC (2nd ed.) / 7553.

——. *A ballat intituled Northomberland newes Wherin you maye see what Rebelles do vse* (London, 1570), STC (2nd ed.) / 7554.

——. *Newes from Northumberland* (London, 1570), London, Society of Antiquaries, Book of Broadsides, STC (2nd ed.) / 7560.

The English and Scottish Popular Ballads, ed. Francis James Child (5 vols. London: H. Stevens, Son & Stiles, 1882).

Erasmus, Desiderius. *A booke called in latyn Enchiridion militis christiani, and in englysshe the manuell of the christen knyght replenysshed with moste holsome preceptes, made by the famous clerke Erasmus of Roterdame, to the whiche is added a newe and meruaylous profytable preface* [trans. William Tyndale?] (London, 1533), STC (2nd ed.) / 10479.

The Fitzwilliam Virginal Book, Edited from the Original Manuscript with an Introduction and Notes by J. A. Fuller Maitland and W. Barclay Squire; Corrected and Edited by Blanche Winogron; (translated into German by John Bernhoff, ed. J. A Fuller-Maitland & W. Barclay Squire (2 vols. New York: Dover Publications, 1963).

Forrest, William. *A History of Grisild the Second: A Narrative in Verse of the Divorce of Queen Katherine of Arragon Written by William Forrest, Sometime Chaplain to Queen Mary I*, ed. W. D. Macray (London: Chiswick Press, 1875).

———. *A New Ballade of the Marigolde* (London), STC (2nd ed.) / 11186.

———. 'Pleasaunt Poesye of Princelie Practise', in *England in the Reign of Henry the Eighth Part 1: Starkey's Life and Letters*, ed. Sydney J. Herrtage (London: Early English Text Society, 1878).

Froissart, Jean. *Here begynneth the first volum of sir Iohan Froyssart of the cronycles of Englande, Fraunce, Spayne, Portyngale, Scotlande, Bretayne, Flau[n]ders: and other places adioynynge. Tra[n]slated out of frenche into our maternall englysshe tonge, by Iohan Bourchier knight lorde Berners: at the co[m]maundement of oure moost highe redouted souerayne lorde kyng Henry the. viii. kyng of Englande and of Fraunce, [and] highe defender of the christen faythe. [et]c* (London, 1523), STC (2nd ed.) / 11396.

Fullwood, Francis. *The church-history of Britain from the birth of Jesus Christ until the year M.DC.XLVIII endeavoured by Thomas Fuller* (London, 1655), Wing / F2416 (Church-history).

G, C. *A Paumflet compyled by G, C. To master Smyth and Wyllyam G. Prayenge them both, for the loue of our Lorde, To growe at last to an honest accorde* (London, 1540), London, Society of Antiquaries, Book of Broadsides, STC (2nd ed.) / 4268.5.

G. W. *The faithful analist, or, The epitome of the English history: giving a true accompt of the affairs of this nation, from the building of the tower in London, in the days of William the Conquerour, to the throwing down the gates of the said city, by the command of the Parliament, which state before the secluded members were admitted, in the yeer 1660. In which all things remarkable both by sea and land from the yeer 1069. To this present yeer of 1660 are truly and exactly represented* (London, 1660), Wing (2nd ed.) / G69.

Gardiner, Stephen. *The Letters of Stephen Gardiner*, ed. James Muller (Cambridge: Cambridge University Press, 1933).

Gibson, Leonard. *A very proper dittie: to the tune of lightie loue Leaue lightie loue ladies, for feare of yll name: and true loue embrace ye, to purchace your fame* (London, 1571), STC (2nd ed.) / 11836.

Gibson, William. *A discription of Nortons falcehod of Yorke shyre, and of his fatall farewel The fatal fine of traitours loe: by iustice due, deseruyng soe* (London, 1570) STC (2nd ed.) / 11843.

Goodman, Christopher. *How superior powers oght to be obeyd of their subiects and wherin they may lawfully by Gods Worde be disobeyed and resisted* (Geneua, 1558), STC (2nd ed.) / 12020.

Gray, William. *An Answere to Maister Smyth, seruaunt to the kynges most royall maiestye. And clerke of the Quenes graces counsell though most unworthy* (London, 1540), Society of Antiquaries, London, STC (2nd ed.) / 12206a.3.

Hall, Edward. *The Vnion of the Two Noble and Illustre Famelies of Lancastre [and] Yorke* (London, 1548), STC (2nd ed.) / 12722.

Hall, John. *Certayn chapters take[n] out of the Prouerbes of Salomo[n], wyth other chapters of the holy scripture, [and] certayne Psalmes of Dauid, translated into English meter, by Iohn Hall. Whych prouerbes of late were set forth, imprinted and vntruely entituled, to be thee doynges of Mayster Thomas Sternhold, late grome of the kynges Maiesties robes, as by thys copye it maye be perceaued* (London, 1550), STC (2nd ed.) / 2760.

Heywood, John. *A dialogue conteinyng the nomber in effect of all the prouer-bes in the englishe tongue compacte in a matter concernyng two maner of mariages, made and set foorth by Iohn Heywood* (London, 1546), STC (2nd ed.) / 13291.

———. *A Balade specifienge partly the maner, partly the matter, in the most excellent meetyng and lyke Mariage betwene our Soueraigne Lord and our Soueraigne Lady, the Kynges and Queenes Highnes* (London, 1554), STC (2nd ed.) / 13290.3.

———. *A breefe balet touching the traytorous takynge of Scarborow Castell* (London, 1557), STC (2nd ed.) / 13290.7.

Howard, Henry, Earl of Surrey. *Songes and Sonettes, Written by the Right Hon-orable Lorde Henry Haward Late Earle of Surrey, and Others* ([London], 1557), STC (2nd ed.) / 13861.

Jewel, John. *A defence of the Apologie of the Churche of Englande conteininge an answeare to a certaine booke lately set foorthe by M. Hardinge, and entituled, A confutation of &c. By Iohn Iewel Bishop of Sarisburie* (London, 1567), STC (2nd ed.) / 14600.5.

King, William. *Alteracio[n]s of Kindoms, for Despisi[n]g of God [and] How God Defendeth His* (London, 1550), STC (2nd ed.) / 14999.5.

Kirkham, William. *Ioyfull newes for true subiectes, to God and the Crowne the rebelles are cooled, their bragges be put downe. Come humble ye downe, come humble ye downe, perforce now submyt ye: to the Queen and the Crowne* (London, 1570), STC (2nd ed.) / 15015.

Larke, John. *The boke of wisdome otherwise called the flower of vertue. Folowing the auctorities of auncient doctours [and] philosophers, deuiding and speak-ing of vices [and] vertues, wyth many goodly examples wherby a man may be praysed or dyspraysed, wyth the maner to speake well and wyselie to al folkes, of what estate so euer they bee. Translated first out of Italion into French, [and] out of french into English, by Iohn Larke* (London, 1565), STC (2nd ed.) / 3358.

Letters and Papers, Foreign and Domestic, of the Reign of Henry VIII, ed. J. S. Brewer et al. (21 vols. London: HMSO 1867–1910).

Machyn, Henry. *The diary of Henry Machyn: Citizen and Merchant-Taylor of London (1550–1563)*, ed. J.G. Nichols (London: Camden Society, 1848), old series, xlii.

Mell, George. *A proper new balad of the Bryber Gehesie Taken out of the fourth booke of Kinges the.v. chapter. To the tune of Kynge Salomon* (London, [1566]), STC (2nd ed.) / 17802.

A merry new song how a bruer meant to make a cooper cuckold and how deere the bruer paid for the bargaine. To the tune of, In somertime (London, 1590), STC (2nd ed.) / 22919.

The Moral Play of wit and Science, and Early Poetical Miscellanies from an Unpublished Manuscript, ed. J. O. Halliwell-Phillipps (London: Shakespeare Society, 1848; repr. 2014, Kessinger Publishing).

More, Thomas. *The debellacyon of Salem and Bizance* ([London], 1533), STC (2nd ed.) / 18081.

———. *A fruteful, and pleasaunt worke of the beste state of a publyque weale, and of the newe yle called Vtopia: written in Latine by Syr Thomas More knyght, and translated into Englyshe by Raphe Robynson citizein and goldsmythe of London, at the procurement, and earnest request of George*

Tadlowe citezein [and] haberdassher of the same citie, trans. Raphe Robynson (London, 1551), STC (2nd ed.) / 18094.

Morley, Thomas. *A plaine and easie introduction to practicall musicke set downe in forme of a dialogue: deuided into three partes, the first teacheth to sing with all things necessary for the knowledge of pricktsong. The second treateth of descante and to sing two parts in one vpon a plainsong or ground, with other things necessary for a descanter. The third and last part entreateth of composition of three, foure, fiue or more parts with many profitable rules to that effect. With new songs of 2. 3. 4. and.5 [sic] parts. By Thomas Morley, Batcheler of musick, & of the gent. of hir Maiesties Royall Chapel* (London, 1597), STC (2nd ed.) / 18134.

The Mulliner Book, ed. John Caldwell (London: Stainer and Bell, 2011).

A newe ballade intytuled, Good fellowes must go learne to daunce (London, 1569), STC (2nd ed.) / 12019.

The noble tryumphaunt coronacyon of quene Anne wyfe vnto the moost noble kynge Henry the.viij. (London, 1533), STC (2nd ed.) / 656.

Old English Ballads 1553–1625: Chiefly from Manuscripts, ed. Hyder E. Rollins ([S.l.]: Cambridge University Press, 1920; repr. Forgotten Books, 2012).

Original Letters Illustrative of English History 3rd series, ed. Henry Ellis (4 vols. London: Richard Bentley, 1846), iii.

Osborne, M. *A Newe Ballade of a Louer / Extollinge his Ladye. To the tune of Damon and Pithias* (London, 1568), Early English Tract Supplement / A3:4[26].

Parker, Matthew. *The whole Psalter translated into English Metre, which contayneth an hundreth and fifty Psalmes. The first Quinquagene* (London, 1567), STC (2nd ed.) / 2729.

Pater, Erra. *The pronostycacion for euer of Erra Pater: a Iewe borne in Iewery, a doctour in astronomy, [and] physycke Profytable to kepe the body in helth. And also Ptholomeus sayth the same* (London, 1562), STC (2nd ed.) / 439.15.

Peele, Steven. *A letter to Rome, to declare to the Pope, Iohn Felton his freend is hangd in a rope and farther, a right his grace to enforme, he dyed a papist, and seemd not to turne. To the tune of Row well ye mariners* (London, 1571), STC (2nd ed.) / 19549.

———. *A proper new balade expressyng the fames, concerning a warning to al London dames to the tune of the blacke Almaine* (London, 1571), STC (2nd ed.) / 19551.

Plantagenet, Arthur, et al. *The Lisle Letters*, ed. Muriel St Clair Byrne (6 vols. London: University of Chicago Press, 1981).

Playford, John. *The English dancing master: or, Plaine and easie rules for the dancing of country dances, with the tune to each dance* (London, 1651), Wing (2nd ed.) / P2477.

Pole, Reginald. *The Correspondence of Reginald Pole: Volume 2. A Calendar, 1547–1554: A Power in Rome*, ed. Thomas Frederick Mayer (Aldershot: Ashgate, 2004).

Preston, Thomas. *A Lamentation from Rome, how the Pope doth bewayle, / That the Rebelles in England can not preuayle to the tune of Rowe well ye mariners* (London, 1570), STC (2nd ed.) / 20289.

A proclamation, concernynge rites and ceremonies to be vsed in due fourme in the Churche of Englande, and the kynges most gracious pardon for certeyne fautes conteyned in the same ([London], 1539), STC (2nd ed.) / 7791.

Puttenham, George. *The arte of English poesie Contriued into three bookes: the first of poets and poesie, the second of proportion, the third of ornament* (London, 1589), STC (2nd ed.) / 20519.5.

Pyttes, John. *A prayer or supplycation made vnto God by a yonge man that he woulde be mercifull to vs, and not kepe his worde away from vs, but that the truth maie springe / quod John Pyttes* (London, 1559), STC (2nd ed.) / 19969.4.

R.B. *A new balade entituled as foloweth. To such as write in metres, I write of small matters an exhortation, by readyng of which, men may delite in such as be worthy commendation. My verse also it hath relation to such as print, that they doe it well, the better they shall their metres sell. And when we haue doen al that ever we can, let vs neuer seke prayse at the mouth of man* (London, 1570), STC (2nd ed.) / 1058.

R.M. *An epytaphe vpon the death of M. Rycharde Goodricke Esquier* (London, 1562), STC (2nd ed.) / 17145.3.

———. *A Newe Ballade* (London, 1560), STC (2nd ed.) / 17147.

Ravenscroft, Thomas. *Pammelia Musicks miscellanie. Or, Mixed varietie of pleasant roundelayes, and delightfull catches, of 3. 4. 5. 6. 7. 8. 9. 10. parts in one. None so ordinarie as musicall, none so musical, as not to all, very pleasing and acceptable* (London, 1609), STC (2nd ed.) / 20759.

Records of Early English Drama: Bristol, ed. Mark C. Pilkinton (Toronto, ON: University of Toronto Press, 1997).

Records of Early English Drama: Cambridge, ed. Alan H. Nelson (2 vols. Toronto, ON: University of Toronto Press, 1989).

Records of Early English Drama: Cheshire (including Chester), ed. Elizabeth Baldwin, Lawrence M. Clopper and David Mills (2 vols. Toronto, ON: University of Toronto Press, 2007).

Records of Early English Drama: Chester, ed. Lawrence M. Clopper (Toronto, ON: University of Toronto Press, 1979).

Records of Early English Drama: Coventry, ed. R. W. Ingram (Toronto, ON: University of Toronto Press, 1981).

Records of Early English Drama: Cumberland, Westmorland, Gloucestershire, ed. Audrey Douglas and Peter Greenfield (Toronto, ON: University of Toronto Press, 1986).

Records of Early English Drama: Devon, ed. John M. Wasson (Toronto, ON: University of Toronto Press, 1986).

Records of Early English Drama: Dorset, ed. Rosalind Conklin Hays et al. (Toronto, ON: University of Toronto Press, 1999).

Records of Early English Drama: Herefordshire, Worcestershire, ed. David N. Klausner (Toronto, ON: University of Toronto Press, 1990).

Records of Early English Drama: Kent: Diocese of Canterbury, ed. James M. Gibson (3 vols. Toronto, ON: University of Toronto Press, 2002).

Records of Early English Drama: Lancashire, ed. David George (Toronto, ON: University of Toronto Press, 1991).

Records of Early English Drama: Lincolnshire, ed. James Stokes (2 vols. Toronto, ON: University of Toronto Press, 2009).

Records of Early English Drama: Newcastle upon Tyne, ed. J. J. Anderson (Toronto, ON: University of Toronto Press, 1982).

Records of Early English Drama: Norwich, ed. David Galloway (Toronto, ON: University of Toronto Press, 1984).

Records of Early English Drama: Oxford, ed. John R. Elliott, Jr, and Alan H. Nelson (University); Alexandra F. Johnston and Diana Wyatt (City) (2 vols. Toronto, ON: University of Toronto Press, 2004).

Records of Early English Drama: Shropshire, ed. J. Alan B. Somerset (2 vols. Toronto, ON: University of Toronto Press, 1986).

Records of Early English Drama: Somerset, ed. James Stokes and Robert J. Alexander (2 vols. Toronto, ON: University of Toronto Press, 1996).

Records of Early English Drama: Sussex, ed. Cameron Louis (Toronto, ON: University of Toronto Press and Brepols Publishers, 2000).

Records of Early English Drama: York, ed. Alexandra F. Johnston and Margaret Rogerson (Toronto, ON: University of Toronto Press, 1979).

Reliques of Ancient English Poetry: consisting of Old Heroic Ballads, Songs, and other Pieces of our earlier Poets (Chiefly of the Lyric kind.) Together with some few of later Date. The Second Edition, ed. Bishop Percy (3 vols. London: J. Dodsley, 1765; repr. London: J.M. Dent & Sons, 1906).

The ret[ur]ne of. M. smythes enuoy, servaunt to the Kynges Royall Maiestye and Clerke of the Quenes graces counsell (though most unworthy) (London, 1540), London, Society of Antiquaries, Book of Broadsides, STC (2nd ed.) / 12206a.7.

Rider, Thomas. *A merie newe ballad intituled The pinnyng of the basket: and is to bee songe to the tune of The doune right squire* (London, 1590), STC (2nd ed.) 21037.

Robinson, Clement. *A Handefull of Pleasant Delites Containing Sudrie New Sonets and Delectable Histories, in Diuers Kindes of Meeter. Newly Deuised to the Newest Tunes That Are Now in Vse, to Be Sung: Euerie Sonet Orderly Pointed to His Proper Tune. With New Additions of Certain Songs, to Verie Late Deuised Notes, Not Commonly Knowen, nor Vsed Heretofore, by Clement Robinson, and Diuers Others* (London, 1584), ed. Hyder E. Rollins (New York: Dover Publications, 1965).

Robinson, Thomas. *The schoole of musicke wherein is taught, the perfect method, of true fingering of the lute, pandora, orpharion, and viol de gamba; with most infallible generall rules, both easie and delightfull. Also, a method, how you may be your owne instructer for prick-song, by the help of your lute, without any other teacher: with lessons of all sorts, for your further and better instruction. Newly composed by Thomas Robinson, lutenist* (London: 1603), STC (2nd ed.) / 21128.

A Ruful Complaynt of the Publyke Weale to Englande (London, 1550), STC (2nd ed.) / 5611.4.

Saparton, John. *Sapartons alarum, to all such as do beare the name of true souldiers, in england, or els wheare* (London, 1569), STC (2nd ed.) / 21745.

Shakespeare, William. *The Oxford Shakespeare: The Complete Works*, ed. Stanley Wells and Gary Taylor (Oxford: Oxford University Press, 1989).

The Shirburn Ballads, 1585–1616, ed. Andrew Clark (Oxford: Clarendon Press, 1907).

Simard, Marie Ange. *An Introduction to the Looue of God. Accompted among the Workes of S. Augustine, and Translated into English, by the Right Reuerend Father in God, Edmund, Bishop of Norwitch, That Nowe Is, and by Him An introduction to the looue of God. Accompted among the workes of S. Augustine, and translated into English, by the right reuerend father in God, Edmund, Bishop of Norwitch, that nowe is, and by him dedicated to the Queenes most excellent*

Maiestie, to the glorie of God, and comfort of his chosen. And newlie turned into Englishe meter by Robert Fletcher (London, 1581), STC (2nd ed.) / 936.

Smyth P., R. *An artificiall Apologie, articulerlye answerynge to the obstreperous Obgannynges of one W. G. Euometyd to the vituperacion of the tryumphant trollynge Thomas smyth. Repercussed by the ryght redolent & rotounde rethorician R. Smyth P. with annotacio[n]s of the mellifluous and misticall Master Mynterne, marked in the mergent for the enucliacion of certen obscure obelisques, to thende that the imprudent lector shulde not tytubate or hallucinate in the labyrinthes of this lucubratiuncle* (London, 1540), Society of Antiquaries, London, STC (2nd ed.) / 22877.6.

Smyth, Thomas. *An Enuoye from Thomas Smyth Vpon Thaunswer of One W.G. Lurkyng in Lorrells Denne, for Feare Men Shulde Hym See* (London, 1540), Society of Antiquaries, London, STC (2nd ed.) / 22880.2.

———. *A lytell treatyse agaynst Sedicyous persons* (London, 1540), Society of Antiquaries, London, STC (2nd ed.) / 22880.4.

———. *A treatyse declarynge the despyte of a secrete sedycyous person that dareth not shew Hym selfe* ([London], [1540]), London, Society of Antiquaries, Book of Broadsides, STC (2nd ed.) / 22880.6.

Songs and Ballads, with Other Short Poems, Chiefly of the Reign of Philip and Mary, from a Manuscript in the Ashmolean Museum, ed. Thomas Wright (London: J.B. Nichols and Sons, 1860; repr. Forgotten Books, 2012).

State Papers Published under the Authority of His Majesty's Commission: King Henry the Eighth, 1830–1852. Vol. 8: Part V: Foreign Correspondence, 1537–1542 (London: Her Majesty's Stationery Office, 1849).

Statutes of the realm, from original records and authentic manuscripts (1101–1713), ed. A. Luders et al. (11 vols. London, 1810–28).

Sternhold, Thomas, et al. *The whole boke of psalmes, collected into English metre by Thomas Sternhold, Iohn Hopkins, and others: conferred with the Ebrue, with apt notes to syng them wyth all.; Newlye set foorth and allowed to bee soong of the people together, in churches, before and after moring and euening prayer: as also before and after the sermon, and moreouer in priuate houses, for their godlye solace and comfort, laying apart all vngodly songes and balades, which tend onely to the nourishing of vice, and corrupting of youth* (London, 1566), STC (2nd ed.) / 2437.

Stopes, Leonard. *An Ave Maria in commendation of our Most vertuous Queene* (London), STC (2nd ed.) / 23292.

Strype, John. *Ecclesiastical Memorials Relating Chiefly to Religion* (Oxford: Clarendon Press, 1822).

Stubbes, Phillip. *The second part of the anatomie of abuses conteining the display of corruptions, with a perfect description of such imperfections, blemishes and abuses, as now reigning in euerie degree, require reformation for feare of Gods vengeance to be powred vpon the people and countrie, without speedie repentance, and conuersion vnto God: made dialogwise by Phillip Stubbes* (London, 1583), STC (2nd ed.) / 23376.

———. *The theater of the Popes monarchie wherein is described as well the vncleane liues of that wicked generation, as also their Antichristian gouernment, and vsurped kingdome: togeather with their horrible superstition, and blasphemous religion, as it is now vsed at this present, where Antichrist the Pope & his members do beare rule, by Phillip Stubbes* (London, 1585), STC (2nd ed.) / 23399.2.

Tallis, Thomas. *The Tallis Psalter, Psalms and Anthems, Canticles, Preces and Responses*, ed. David Skinner (London: Novello Publishing Ltd, 2013).

Thacker, R. *A godlie Dittie to be song for the preseruation of the Queenes most exclent Maiesties raigne* (London, 1586), London, Society of Antiquaries, Book of Broadsides, STC (2nd ed.) / 23926.

A Transcript of the Registers of the Company of Stationers of London, 1554–1640 A.D, ed. Edward Arber (3 vols. London: Privately printed, 1875).

Tudor Songs and Ballads from Ms Cotton Vespasian a-25, ed. Peter J. Seng (Cambridge, MA: Harvard University Press, 1978).

Tunstall, Cuthbert. *A sermon of Cuthbert Bysshop of Duresme made vpon Palme sondaye laste past, before the maiestie of our souerayne lorde kyng Henry the. VIII. kynge of England [and] of France, defensor of the fayth, lorde of Ireland, and in erth next vnder Christ supreme heed of the Churche of Englande* ([London], 1539), STC (2nd ed.) / 24322a.

Turner, William. *The huntyng and fyndyng out of the Romyshe foxe which more then seuen yeares hath bene hyd among the bisshoppes of Englonde, after that the Kynges hyghnes had commanded hym to be dryuen owt of hys realme. Whosoeuer happeneth vpon thys boke, yf he loue God beter then man, and the Kynges hyghnes beter than the bysshoppes false hypocrisye, let hym gyue it to the Kyng, that he may rede it before the bysshopes condemne it* (London, 1543), STC (2nd ed.) / 24353.

Tyndale, William. *That fayth the mother of all good workes iustifieth us before we ca[n] bringe forth anye good worke...* ([Antwerp], 1528), STC (2nd ed.) / 24454.

Underhill, Edward. 'Autobiographical Anecdotes of Edward Underhill, Esquire, One of the Band of Gentlemen Pensioners', in *Narratives of the Days of the Reformation: Chiefly from the Manuscripts of John Foxe the Martyrologist*, ed. J.G. Nichols (London: Camden Society, 1859), old series, vol. lxxvii.

Vergil, Polydore. *Three books of Polydore Vergil's English History, comprising the reigns of Henry VI, Edward IV, and Richard III, from an early translation preserved among the MSS. of the Old Royal Library in the British Museum*, ed. Henry Ellis (London: Camden Society, 1846), old series, vol. xxix.

Watertoune, Thomas. *A Ninuectyue Agaynst Treason* (London, 1553), STC (2nd ed.) / 25105.

Whight, Nicholas. *A Commendation of Musicke and a Confutation of Them Which Disprayse It* (London, 1563), STC (2nd ed.) / 25350.

Secondary Sources

Allaire, Gaston. *The Theory of Hexachords, Solmization and the Modal System: A Practical Application* (Rome: American Institute of Musicology, 1972).

Amussen, Susan Dwyer. 'The Gendering of Popular Culture' in *Popular Culture in England c.1500–1850*, ed. Tim Harris (Basingstoke: Macmillan Press Ltd, 1995), pp. 48–68.

Atherton, Ian. 'The Itch Grown a Disease: Manuscript Transmission of News in the Seventeenth Century', in *News, Newspapers, and Society in Early Modern Britain*, ed. Joad Raymond (London: Cass, 1998), pp. 39–65.

Atkinson, David. *The Anglo-Scottish Ballad and Its Imaginary Contexts* (Cambridge: Open Book Publishers, 2014).

Attridge, Derek. *The Rhythms of English Poetry* (London: Longman, 1982).

Aveling, Hugh. *Post Reformation Catholicism in East Yorkshire, 1558–1790* (York: East Yorkshire Local History Society, 1960).

Bailey, Peter. 'Conspiracies of Meaning: Music-Hall and the Knowingness of Popular Culture', *Past & Present*, 144 (1994), pp. 138–170.

Barnard, John. 'Introduction', in *The Cambridge History of the Book in Britain, Vol. 3: 1557–1695*, ed. John. Barnard and D. F. Mckenzie (6 vols. Cambridge: Cambridge University Press, 1998), pp. 1–26.

Bateson, Mary. 'The Pilgrimage of Grace', *English Historical Review*, 5:18 (1890), pp. 330–345.

Beaty, Nancy Lee. *The Craft of Dying: A Study in the Literary Translation of the 'Ars Moriendi' in England* (London: Yale University Press, 1970).

Betteridge, Thomas. *Tudor Histories of the English Reformations, 1530–8* (Aldershot: Ashgate, 1999).

———. *Literature and Politics in the English Reformation* (Manchester: Manchester University Press, 2004).

Blume, Friedrich. 'The Period of the Reformation', trans. F. Ellsworth Peterson, in *Protestant Church Music: A History*, ed. Friedrich Blume (London: Gollancz, 1975), pp. 3–123.

Bourdieu, Pierre. 'The Social Space and the Genesis of Groups', *Theory and Society*, 14:6 (1985), pp. 723–744.

———. 'Social Space and Symbolic Power', *Sociological Theory*, 7:1 (1989), pp. 14–25.

Bouza Alvarez, Fernando J. *Communication, Knowledge, and Memory in Early Modern Spain*, transl. Sonia López and Michael Agnew (Philadelphia: University of Pennsylvania Press, 2004).

Brayman Hackel, Heidi. *Reading Material in Early Modern England: Print, Gender, and Literacy* (Cambridge: Cambridge University Press, 2009).

Brenner, Y. S. 'The Inflation of Prices in Early Sixteenth Century England', *Economic History Review*, 14:2 (1961), pp. 225–239.

Brigden, Susan. 'Popular Disturbance and the Fall of Thomas Cromwell and the Reformers, 1539–1540', *Historical Journal*, 24:2 (1981), pp. 257–278.

———. *London and the Reformation* (Oxford: Clarendon Press, 1989).

Bronson, Bertrand H. 'On the Union of Words and Music in the "Child" Ballads', *Western Folklore*, 11:4 (1952), pp. 233–249.

———. *The Singing Tradition of Child's 'Popular Ballads'* (Princeton, NJ: Princeton University Press, 1976).

Brown, Howard Mayer. 'Emulation, Competition, and Homage: Imitation and Theories of Imitation in the Renaissance', *Journal of the American Musicological Society*, 35:1 (1982), pp. 1–48.

Brown, Pamela Allen. *Better a Shrew than a Sheep: Women, Drama, and the Culture of Jest in Early Modern England* (London: Cornell University Press, 2002).

Bush, M. L. *The Government Policy of Protector Somerset* (London: Edward Arnold, 1975).

Capp, Bernard S. *Astrology and the Popular Press: English Almanacs, 1500–1800* (London: Faber, 1979).

Castor, Helen. *She-Wolves: The Women Who Ruled England before Elizabeth* (London: Faber, 2011).

Chappell, William. *Popular Music of the Olden Time: A Collection of Ancient Songs, Ballads, and Dance Tunes* (2 vols. London: Cramer, Beale & Chappell, 1855; repr. Elibron Classics 2005).

Chesnutt, Michael. 'Minstrel Poetry in an English Manuscript of the Sixteenth Century: Richard Sheale and Ms. Ashmole 48', in *The Entertainer in Medieval and Traditional Culture: A Symposium*, ed. Flemming G. Andersen, Thomas Pettitt and Reinhold Schröder (Odense: Odense University Press, 1997), pp. 73–100.

Chibnall, Margaret. *The Empress Matilda: Queen Consort, Queen Mother and Lady of the English* (London: Basil Blackwell, 1991).

Christianson, C. Paul. 'The Rise of London's Book-Trade', in *The Cambridge History of the Book in Britain*, ed. Lotte Hellinga and J. B. Trapp (6 vols. Cambridge: Cambridge University Press, 1999), iii, pp. 128–147.

Coffin, Tristram P. 'Remarks Preliminary to a Study of Ballad Meter and Ballad Singing', *Journal of American Folklore*, 78:308 (1965), pp. 149–153.

Cogswell, Thomas. 'Underground Verse and the Transformation of Early Stuart Political Culture', in *Political Culture and Cultural Politics in Early Modern England: Essays Presented to David Underdown*, ed. Susan Dwyer Amussen, Mark A. Kishlansky and David Underdown (Manchester: Manchester University Press, 1995), pp. 277–300.

Crawford, Anne. 'The Queen's Council in the Middle Ages', *English Historical Review*, 116:469 (2001), pp. 1193–211.

Cust, Richard. 'News and Politics in Early Seventeenth-Century England', *Past & Present*, 112 (1986), pp. 60–90.

Darnton, Robert. 'Literary Surveillance in the British Raj: The Contradictions of Liberal Imperialism', *Book History*, 4 (2001), pp. 133–176.

Davenport, Edwin. 'Elizabethan England's Other Reformation of Manners', *English Literary History*, 63:2 (1996), pp. 255–278.

Davidson, Audrey Ekdahl. 'Review: The Acoustic World of Early Modern England: Attending to the O-Factor by Bruce R. Smith', *Sixteenth Century Journal*, 30:4 (1999), pp. 1160–1161.

Davis, Bryan P. 'John Day', in *The British Literary Book Trade, 1700–1820*, ed. James K. Bracken and Joel Silver (London: Gale Research, 1995), pp. 78–93.

Dolan, Frances E. 'Mopsa's Method: Truth Claims, Ballads, and Print', *Huntington Library Quarterly*, 79:2 (2016), pp. 173–185.

Donaldson, William. *The Jacobite Song: Political Myth and National Identity* (Aberdeen: Aberdeen University Press, 1988).

Dormer, Ernest. *Gray of Reading: A Sixteenth-century Controversialist and Ballad-Writer* (Reading: Bradley & Son, 1923).

Duffin, Ross W. *Shakespeare's Songbook* (London: W. W. Norton, 2004).

Duffy, Eamon. *Fires of Faith: Catholic England under Mary Tudor* (London: Yale University Press, 2009).

Duncan, Sarah. *Mary I: Gender, Power, and Ceremony in the Reign of England's First Queen* (New York: Palgrave Macmillan, 2012).

Dunn-Hensley, Susan. 'Whore Queens: The Sexualised Female Body and the State', in *'High and Mighty Queens' of Early Modern England: Realities and Representations*, ed. Carole Levin, Jo Eldridge Carney and Debra Barrett-Graves (Basingstoke: Palgrave Macmillan, 2003), pp. 101–116.

Durston, Christopher and Jacqueline Eales. 'Introduction: The Puritan Ethos, 1560–1700', in *The Culture of English Puritanism, 1560–1700*, ed. Christopher Durston and Jacqueline Eales (Basingstoke: Palgrave/Macmillan, 1996), pp. 1–31.

Edwards, John. *Mary I: England's Catholic Queen* (London: Yale University Press, 2011).

Elton, G. R. 'Thomas Cromwell's Decline and Fall', *Cambridge Historical Journal*, 10:2 (1951), pp. 150–185.

———. *Policy and Police: The Enforcement of the Reformation in the Age of Thomas Cromwell* (London: Cambridge University Press, 1972).

———. *Reform and Renewal: Thomas Cromwell and the Common Weal* (Cambridge: Cambridge University Press, 1973).

———. *Reform and Reformation: England, 1509–1558* (London: Edward Arnold, 1977).

Ferdinand, C. J. 'Newspapers and the Sale of Books in the Provinces', in *The Cambridge History of the Book in Britain*, ed. Michael F. Suarez SJ and Michael L. Turner (6 vols. Cambridge: Cambridge University Press, 2009), iv, pp. 434–447.

Firth, C. H. 'The Ballad History of the Reigns of Henry VII and Henry VIII', *Transactions of the Royal Historical Society*, 2 (1908), pp. 21–50.

———. 'The Ballad History of the Reigns of the Later Tudors', *Transactions of the Royal Historical Society*, 3 (1909), pp. 51–124.

———. 'The Ballad History of the Reign of James I', *Transactions of the Royal Historical Society*, 5 (1911), pp. 21–61.

Fish, Stanley. 'Short People Got No Reason to Live: Reading Irony', *Daedalus*, 112:1 (1983), pp. 175–191.

Fisher, N. R. R. '"The Queenes Courte in Her Councell Chamber at Westminster"', *English Historical Review*, 108:427 (1993), pp. 314–337.

Fletcher, Anthony. *Gender, Sex and Subordination in England, 1500–1800* (London: Yale University Press, 1995).

Fox, Adam. 'Ballads, Libels and Popular Ridicule in Jacobean England', *Past & Present*, 145 (1994), pp. 47–83.

———. 'Rumour, News and Popular Political Opinion in Elizabethan and Early Stuart England', *Historical Journal*, 40:3 (1997), pp. 597–620.

———. 'Remembering the Past in Early Modern England: Oral and Written Tradition', *Transactions of the Royal Historical Society*, 6th Series, 9 (1999), pp. 233–256.

———. *Oral and Literate Culture in England, 1500–1700* (Oxford: Clarendon Press, 2000).

Frank, Joseph. *The Beginnings of the English Newspaper 1620–1660* (Cambridge, MA: Harvard University Press, 1961).

Fumerton, Patricia, and Anita Guerrini. 'Introduction: Straws in the Wind', in *Ballads and Broadsides in Britain, 1500–1800*, ed. Patricia Fumerton, Anita Guerrini and Kris McAbee (Farnham: Ashgate, 2010), pp. 1–9.

Gartman, David. 'Bourdieu's Theory of Cultural Change: Explication, Application, Critique', *Sociological Theory*, 20:2 (2002), pp. 255–277.

Gibbs, Gary. 'Marking the Days: Henry Machyn's Manuscript and the Mid-Tudor Era', in *The Church of Mary Tudor*, ed. Eamon Duffy and David Loades (Aldershot: Ashgate, 2006), pp. 281–308.

Gowing, Laura. *Gender Relations in Early Modern England* (Harlow: Pearson Education, 2012).

Greenblatt, Stephen. *Renaissance Self-Fashioning: From More to Shakespeare* (London: University of Chicago Press, 1980).

Gregory, E. David. *Victorian Songhunters: The Recovery and Editing of English Vernacular Ballads and Folk Lyrics, 1820–1883* (Oxford: Scarecrow, 2006).

Griffiths, Paul, Adam Fox and Steve Hindle. 'Introduction', in *The Experience of Authority in Early Modern England*, ed. Paul Griffiths, Adam Fox and Steve Hindle (Basingstoke: Macmillan, 1996), pp. 1–9.

Guy, J. A. *Tudor England* (Oxford: Oxford University Press, 1988).

Habermas, Jürgen. *The Structural Transformation of the Public Sphere: An Inquiry into a Category of Bourgeois Society*, trans. Thomas Burger with the assistance of Frederick Lawrence (Cambridge: Polity, 1989).

Haigh, Christopher. *Reformation and Religion in Tudor Lancashire* (Cambridge: Cambridge University Press, 1975).

———. *English Reformations: Religion, Politics, and Society under the Tudors* (Oxford: Clarendon Press, 1993).

Herissone, Rebecca. *Music Theory in Seventeenth Century England* (Oxford: Oxford University Press, 2000).

———. *Musical Creativity in Restoration England* (Cambridge: Cambridge University Press, 2013).

Hindle, Steve. *The State and Social Change in Early Modern England, c.1550–1640* (Basingstoke: Macmillan, 2000).

Holman, Peter. 'Review: The Acoustic World of Early Modern England: Attending to the O-Factor by Bruce R. Smith', *Journal of the Royal Musical Association*, 125:1 (2000), pp. 115–118.

Hoyle, Richard. 'Taxation and the Mid-Tudor Crisis', *Economic History Review*, 51:4 (1998), pp. 649–675.

———. *The Pilgrimage of Grace and the Politics of the 1530s* (Oxford: Oxford University Press, 2001).

Hyatt King, A. 'The Significance of John Rastell in Early Music Printing', *Library*, 5th Series, 26:3 (1971), pp. 197–214.

Hyde, Jenni. 'William Elderton's Ladie Marques Identified', *Notes and Queries*, 260:4 (2015), pp. 541–542;

Ingram, Martin. 'The Reformation of Manners in Early Modern England', in *The Experience of Authority in Early Modern England*, ed. Paul Griffiths, Adam Fox and Steve Hindle (Basingstoke: Macmillan, 1996), pp. 47–88.

Irish, Bradley J. 'Gender and Politics in the Henrician Court: The Douglas-Howard Lyrics in the Devonshire Manuscript (BL Add 17492)', *Renaissance Quarterly*, 64:1 (Spring 2011), pp. 79–114.

Jauss, Hans Robert. 'Tradition, Innovation, and Aesthetic Experience', *Journal of Aesthetics and Art Criticism*, 46:3 (1988), pp. 375–388.

Jauss, Hans Robert, and Elizabeth Benzinger. 'Literary History as a Challenge to Literary Theory', *New Literary History*, 2:1 (1970), pp. 7–37.

Kaplan, M. Lindsay. *The Culture of Slander in Early Modern England* (Cambridge: Cambridge University Press, 1997).

Kempe, Alfred John. *The Loseley Manuscripts: Manuscripts and Other Rare Documents... Preserved in the Muniment Room of James More Molyneux, Esq. At Loseley House, in Surrey* (London: Murray, 1836).

Kerr, Jessica, and Anne Ophelia Dowden. *Shakespeare's Flowers* (London: Longmans Young Books, 1969).

Kesselring, K. J. *Mercy and Authority in the Tudor State* (Cambridge: Cambridge University Press, 2003).

——. 'Mercy and Liberality: The Aftermath of the 1569 Northern Rebellion', *History*, 90:298 (2005), pp. 213–35.

——. *The Northern Rebellion of 1569: Faith, Politics and Protest in Elizabethan England* (Basingstoke: Palgrave Macmillan, 2007).

King, John N. *Tudor Royal Iconography: Literature and Art in an Age of Religious Crisis* (Guildford: Princeton University Press, 1989).

——. 'The Book-Trade under Edward VI and Mary I', in *The Cambridge History of the Book in Britain*, ed. Lotte Hellinga and J. B. Trapp (Cambridge: Cambridge University Press, 1999), iii, pp. 164–178.

Koopmans, Joop W. *News and Politics in Early Modern Europe 1500–1800* (Leuven: Peeters, 2005).

Krummel, D. W. *English Music Printing, 1553–1700* (London: The Bibliographical Society, 1975).

Kuwakino, Koji. 'The Great Theatre of Creative Thought: The *Inscriptiones vel Tituli Theatri Amplissimi* ... (1565) by Samuel von Quiccheberg', *Journal of the History of Collections*, 25:3 (2013), pp. 303–324.

Kyle, Chris R. 'Monarch and Marketplace: Proclamations as News in Early Modern England', *Huntington Library Quarterly*, 78:4 (2015), pp. 771–787.

Lake, Peter. 'Ministers, Magistrates and the Production of "Order" in Measure for Measure', in *Shakespeare Survey Vol. 54: Shakespeare and Religions*, ed. Peter Holland (Cambridge: Cambridge University Press, 2006), pp. 165–181.

Lake, Peter, and Steve Pincus. 'Rethinking the Public Sphere in Early Modern England', *Journal of British Studies*, 45:2 (2006), pp. 270–292.

Lake, Peter, and Michael Questier. 'Puritans, Papists, and the "Public Sphere" in Early Modern England: The Edmund Campion Affair in Context', *Journal of Modern History*, 72:3 (2000), pp. 587–627.

Le Huray, Peter. *Music and the Reformation in England, 1549–1660* (Cambridge: Cambridge University Press, 1978).

Leaver, Robin A. *'Goostly Psalmes and Spirituall Songes': English and Dutch Metrical Psalms from Coverdale to Utenhove (1535–1566)* (Oxford: Clarendon, 1991).

Lemon, Robert. *Catalogue of a Collection of Printed Broadsides in the Possession of the Society of Antiquaries of London* (London: Society of Antiquaries of London, 1866).

Levin, Carole. 'A Good Prince: King John and Early Tudor Propaganda', *Sixteenth Century Journal*, 11:4 (1980), pp. 23–32.

Livingston, Carole Rose. *British Broadside Ballads of the Sixteenth Century: A Catalogue of the Extant Sheets and an Essay* (New York: General Music Publishing Co., 1991).

Loach, Jennifer. *A Mid-Tudor Crisis?* (London: Historical Association, 1992).

——. *Edward VI* (London: Yale University Press, 1999).

Loades, D. M. *The Reign of Mary Tudor* (London: Ernest Benn Ltd, 1979).

——. *Thomas Cromwell: Servant to Henry VIII* (Stroud: Amberley Publishing, 2013).

Love, Harold. *The Culture and Commerce of Texts: Scribal Publication in Seventeenth-Century England*, 2nd ed. (Amherst: University of Massachusetts Press, 1998).

Lowers, James King. *Mirrors for Rebels: A Study of Polemical Literature Relating to the Northern Rebellion, 1569* (Berkeley: University of California Press, 1953).

Lyons, Bridget Gellert. 'The Iconography of Ophelia', *English Literary History*, 44:1 (1977), pp. 60–74.

MacCulloch, Diarmaid. 'Heinrich Bullinger and the English-speaking World', in *Heinrich Bullinger (1504?–1575): Leben, Denken, Wirkung*, ed. P. Opitz and E. Campi (*Zürcher Beiträge zur Reformationsgeschichte*, 24 (2006)).

McElligott, Jason. *Royalism, Print and Censorship in Revolutionary England* (Woodbridge: Boydell Press, 2007).

McIlvenna, Una. 'The Power of Music: the Significance of Contrafactum in Execution Ballads', *Past & Present*, 229:1 (2015), pp. 47–89.

———. 'The Rich Merchant Man, or, What the Punishment of Greed Sounded Like in Early Modern English Ballads', *Huntington Library Quarterly*, 79:2 (2016), pp. 279–299.

———. 'When the News was Sung', *Media History*, 22:3–4 (2016), pp. 317–333.

McShane, Angela. 'The Gazet in Metre; or the Riming Newsmonger: The Broadside Ballad as Intelligencer. A New Narrative', in *News and Politics in Early Modern Europe 1500–1800*, ed. Joop W. Koopmans (Leuven: Peeters, 2005), pp. 131–150.

———. 'Ballads and Broadsides', in *The Oxford History of Popular Print Culture, Vol. 1, Cheap Print in Britain and Ireland to 1660*, ed. Joad Raymond (Oxford: Oxford University Press, 2011), pp. 339–362.

Marotti, Arthur F. *Manuscript, Print and the English Renaissance Lyric* (Cornell University Press, 1995).

Marotti, Arthur F. and Steven W. May. 'Two Lost Ballads of the Armada Thanksgiving Celebration (with Texts and Illustration)', *English Literary Renaissance*, 41:1 (2011), pp. 31–63.

Marsh, Christopher. *Music and Society in Early Modern England* (Cambridge: Cambridge University Press, 2010).

———. 'The Sound of Print in Early Modern England: The Broadside Ballad as Song', in *The Uses of Script and Print, 1300–1700*, ed. Julia C. Crick and Alexandra Walsham (Cambridge: Cambridge University Press, 2010), pp. 171–190.

———. '"The Blazing Torch": New Light on English Balladry as a Multi-Media Matrix', *The Seventeenth Century*, 30:1 (2015), pp. 95–116.

———. '"Fortune My Foe": The Circulation of an English Super-Tune', in *Identity, Intertextuality, and Performance in Early Modern Song Culture*, ed. Dieuwke van der Poel, Louis Peter Grijp and Wim van Anrooij (Leiden: Brill, 2016), pp. 308–330.

———. 'A Woodcut and Its Wanderings in Seventeenth-Century England', *Huntington Library Quarterly*, 79:2 (2016), pp. 245–262.

May, Steven W. 'Matching Hands: The Search for the Scribe of the "Stanhope" Manuscript', *Huntington Library Quarterly*, 76:3 (2013), pp. 345–375.

Mendle, Michael. 'Preserving the Ephemeral: Reading, Collecting, and the Pamphlet Culture of Seventeenth-Century England', in *Books and Readers in Early Modern England: Material Studies*, ed. Jennifer Andersen and Elizabeth Sauer (Philadelphia: University of Pennsylvania Press, 2002), pp. 201–216.

Milner, Matthew. *The Senses and the English Reformation* (Farnham: Ashgate, 2011).

Milsom, John. 'Songs and Society in Early Tudor London', *Early Music History*, 16 (1997), pp. 235–293.

———. 'Music, Politics and Society', in *A Companion to Tudor Britain*, ed. Robert Tittler and Norman Jones (Blackwell Reference Online: Blackwell Publishing, 2004) www.blackwellreference.com/subscriber/tocnode.html?id=g9780631236184_chunk_g978063123618435 [accessed 20 July 2014].

———. 'William Mundy's "Vox Patris Caelestis" and the Accession of Mary Tudor', *Music & Letters*, 91:1 (2010), pp. 1–38.

Monson, Craig A. 'The Council of Trent Revisited', *Journal of the American Musicological Society*, 55:1 (2002), pp. 1–37.

Mortimer, Ian. 'Tudor Chronicler or Sixteenth-Century Diarist? Henry Machyn and the Nature of His Manuscript', *Sixteenth Century Journal*, 33:4 (2002), pp. 981–998.

Nelson, Carolyn, and Matthew Seccombe. 'The Creation of the Periodical Press 1620–1695', in *The Cambridge History of the Book in Britain*, ed. Michael F. Suarez SJ and Michael L. Turner (6 vols. Cambridge: Cambridge University Press, 2009), iv, pp. 533–550.

Nelson, Janet L. 'Women at the Court of Charlemagne: A Case of Monstrous Regiment?' in *Medieval Queenship*, ed. John Carmi Parsons (Stroud: Alan Sutton, 1994), pp. 43–61.

Ong, Walter J. *Orality and Literacy: The Technologizing of the Word* (London: Methuen & Co Ltd, 1982).

Osborn, James M. 'Benedick's Song in "Much Ado"', *The Times*, 17 November 1958, p. 11.

Patterson, Annabel. *Censorship and Interpretation: The Conditions of Writing and Reading in Early Modern England* (London: University of Wisconsin Press, 1990).

Peacey, Jason. *Politicians and Pamphleteers: Propaganda During the English Civil Wars and Interregnum* (Aldershot: Ashgate, 2004).

———. *The Print Culture of Parliament, 1600–1800* (Edinburgh: Edinburgh University Press for the Parliamentary History Yearbook Trust, 2007).

Pearce, Susan. *On Collecting: An Investigation into Collecting in the European Tradition* (London: Routledge, 1995).

Pettegree, Andrew. *Reformation and the Culture of Persuasion* (Cambridge: Cambridge University Press, 2005).

———. *The Invention of News: How the World Came to Know About Itself* (London: Yale University Press, 2014).

Phelps Brown, E. H. and Sheila V. Hopkins. 'Seven Centuries of the Prices of Consumables, Compared with Builders' Wage- Rates', *Economica*, 23:92 (1956), pp. 296–314.

Platonov, Rachel. *Singing the Self: Guitar Poetry, Community, and Identity in the Post-Stalin Period* (Evanston, IL: Northwestern University Press, 2012).

Powers, Harold S. 'Tonal Types and Modal Categories in Renaissance Polyphony', *Journal of the American Musicological Society*, 34:3 (1981), pp. 428–70.

Quitslund, Beth. *The Reformation in Rhyme: Sternhold, Hopkins and the English Metrical Psalter, 1547–1603* (Aldershot: Ashgate, 2008).

Rayment, Louise. 'A Note on the Date of London, British Library, Additional Manuscript 15233', *Notes and Queries*, 59:1 (2012), pp. 32–34.

Raymond, Joad. *The Invention of the Newspaper: English Newsbooks, 1641–1649* (Oxford: Clarendon, 1996).

———. *News, Newspapers, and Society in Early Modern Britain* (London: F. Cass, 1999).

———. *Pamphlets and Pamphleteering in Early Modern Britain* (Cambridge: Cambridge University Press, 2002).

———. *News Networks in Seventeenth Century Britain and Europe* (London: Routledge, 2006).

———. 'Introduction: The Origins of Popular Print Culture', in *The Oxford History of Popular Print Culture, Vol. 1, Cheap Print in Britain and Ireland to 1660*, ed. Joad Raymond (Oxford: Oxford University Press, 2011), pp. 1–14.

———. 'News', in *The Oxford History of Popular Print Culture, Vol. 1, Cheap Print in Britain and Ireland to 1660*, ed. Joad Raymond (Oxford: Oxford University Press, 2011), pp. 377–397.

Redworth, Glyn. 'A Study in the Formulation of Policy: The Genesis and Evolution of the Act of Six Articles', *Journal of Ecclesiastical History*, 37:01 (1986), pp. 42–67.

———. *In Defence of the Church Catholic: The Life of Stephen Gardiner* (Oxford: Basil Blackwell, 1990).

———. '"Matters Impertinent to Women": Male and Female Monarchy under Philip and Mary', *English Historical Review*, 112:447 (1997), pp. 597–613.

———. *A Family at War? King Philip I of England and Habsburg Dynastic Politics* (Coburg: Prinz-Albert-Ges., 2008).

Richards, Judith M. 'Mary Tudor as "Sole Quene"?: Gendering Tudor Monarchy', *Historical Journal*, 40:4 (1997), pp. 895–924.

———. '"To Promote a Woman to Beare Rule": Talking of Queens in Mid-Tudor England', *Sixteenth Century Journal*, 28:1 (1997), pp. 101–121.

———. *Mary Tudor* (Abingdon: Routledge, 2008).

Riordan, Michael, and Alec Ryrie. 'Stephen Gardiner and the Making of a Protestant Villain', *Sixteenth Century Journal*, 34:4 (2003), pp. 1039–63.

Rollins, Hyder E. 'The Black-Letter Broadside Ballad', *Publications of the Modern Language Association of America*, 34:2 (1919), pp. 258–339.

———. 'Concerning Bodleian Ms. Ashmole 48', *Modern Language Notes*, 34:6 (1919), pp. 340–51.

———. 'The Date, Authors, and Contents of "A Handfull of Pleasant Delights"', *Journal of English and Germanic Philology*, 18:1 (1919), pp. 43–59.

———. 'William Elderton: Elizabethan Actor and Ballad-Writer', *Studies in Philology*, 17:2 (1920), pp. 199–245.

———. 'Ballads from Additional Ms. 38, 599', *Publications of the Modern Language Association of America*, 38:1 (1923), pp. 133–152.

———. 'An Analytical Index to the Ballad-Entries (1557–1709) in the Registers of the Company of Stationers of London', *Studies in Philology*, 21:1 (1924), pp. 1–324.

Rospocher, Massimo, and Rosa Salzburg. 'An Evanescent Public Sphere: Voices, Spaces, and Publics in Venice During the Italian Wars', in *Beyond the Public Sphere: Opinions, Publics, Spaces in Early Modern Europe*, ed. Massimo Rospocher (Bologna: Il Mulino, 2012), pp. 93–114.

———. 'Street Singers in Italian Renaissance Urban Culture and Communication', *Cultural and Social History*, 9:1 (2012), pp. 9–26.

Rubin, David C. *Memory in Oral Traditions: The Cognitive Psychology of Epic, Ballads, and Counting-Out Rhymes* (Oxford: Oxford University Press, 1995).

Ryrie, Alec. 'The Slow Death of a Tyrant: Learning to Live without Henry VIII, 1547–63', in *Henry VIII and His Afterlives: Literature, Politics, and Art*, ed. Mark Rankin, Christopher Highley and John N. King (Cambridge: Cambridge University Press, 2009), pp. 75–93.

Salgado, Gamini. *The Elizabethan Underworld* (Stroud: Sutton, 2005).

Scott, James C. *Weapons of the Weak: Everyday Forms of Peasant Resistance* (London: Yale University Press, 1985).

Scribner, Robert W. *The German Reformation* (London: Macmillan, 1986).

———. *Popular Culture and Popular Movements in Reformation Germany* (London: Hambledon, 1987).

Shaaber, M. A. *Some Forerunners of the Newspaper in England, 1476–1622* (Philadelphia: University of Pennsylvania Press, 1929).

Shagan, Ethan H. 'Protector Somerset and the 1549 Rebellions: New Sources and New Perspectives', *English Historical Review*, 114:455 (1999), pp. 34–63.

———. '"Popularity" and the 1549 Rebellions Revisited', *English Historical Review*, 115:460 (2000), pp. 121–133.

———. *Popular Politics and the English Reformation* (Cambridge: Cambridge University Press, 2003).

Sharp, Cuthbert. *Memorials of the Rebellion of 1569* (London: John Bowyer and Son, and William Pickering, 1840).

Sharpe, Kevin. *Selling the Tudor Monarchy: Authority and Image in Sixteenth-Century England* (London: Yale University Press, 2009).

Shell, Alison. *Oral Culture and Catholicism in Early Modern England* (Cambridge: Cambridge University Press, 2008).

Shrank, Cathy. 'A Work by John Bale Identified?' *Notes and Queries*, 53:4 (2006), pp. 421–422.

———. 'Trollers and Dreamers: Defining the Citizen-Subject in Sixteenth-Century Cheap Print', *Yearbook of English Studies*, 38:1/2 (2008), pp. 102–118.

Shuger, Debora. *Censorship and Cultural Sensibility: The Regulation of Language in Tudor/Stuart England* (Philadelphia: University of Pennsylvania Press, 2006).

Simpson, Claude M. *The British Broadside Ballad and Its Music* (New Brunswick: Rutgers University Press, 1966).

Skinner, Quentin. 'Motives, Intentions and the Interpretation of Texts', *New Literary History*, 3:2 (1972), pp. 393–408.

Smith, Bruce R. *The Acoustic World of Early Modern England: Attending to the O-Factor* (Chicago, IL: University of Chicago Press, 1999).

Smyth, Adam (ed.). *A Pleasing Sinne: Drink and Conviviality in Seventeenth-Century England* (Cambridge: Brewer, 2004).

Smyth, Adam. *Autobiography in Early Modern England* (Cambridge: Cambridge University Press, 2010).

Sommerville, C. John. *The News Revolution in England: The Cultural Dynamics of Daily Information* (Oxford: Oxford University Press, 1996).

Spufford, Margaret. *Small Books and Pleasant Histories: Popular Fiction and Its Readership in Seventeenth-Century England* (London: Methuen, 1981).

Swann, Marjorie. *Curiosities and Texts: The Culture of Collecting in Early Modern England* (Philadelphia: University of Pennsylvania Press, 2001).

Taylor, Andrew. *The Songs and Travels of a Tudor Minstrel: Richard Sheale of Tamworth* (York: York Medieval Press, 2012).

Temperley, Nicholas. *The Music of the English Parish Church* (2 vols. Cambridge: Cambridge University Press, 1979).

Thirsk, Joan. *Tudor Enclosures*, 2nd ed. ([London]: Routledge & Kegan Paul, 1989).

Thornley, I. D. 'The Treason Legislation of Henry VIII (1531–1534): Alexander Prize Essay, 1916', *Transactions of the Royal Historical Society*, 11 (1917), pp. 87–123.

Tremlett, Giles. *Catherine of Aragon: Henry's Spanish Queen: A Biography* (London: Faber, 2010).

Tsur, Reuven. 'Rhyme and Cognitive Poetics', *Poetics Today*, 17:1 (1996), pp. 55–87.

Van Orden, Kate. 'Cheap Print and Street Song Following the Saint Batholomew's Massacres of 1572', in *Music and the Cultures of Print*, ed. Kate Van Orden (London: Garland, 2000), pp. 271–323.

de Vries, Henk. 'Ballads, Literature, and Historical Fact - ("Voces Corren", "Celestina, Don Quijote")', *Jahrbuch für Volksliedforschung*, 44 (1999), pp. 13–23.

Wallace, Wanda T. 'Memory for Music: Effect of Melody on Recall of Text', *Journal of Experimental Psychology: Learning, Memory & Cognition*, 20:6 (1994), pp. 1471–1485.

Walsham, Alexandra. *Providence in Early Modern England* (Oxford: Oxford University Press, 1999).

Walter, John. *Crowds and Popular Politics in Early Modern England* (Manchester, Manchester University Press, 2006).

Ward, John. 'Music for "a Handefull of Pleasant Delites"', *Journal of the American Musicological Society*, 10:3 (1957), pp. 151–80.

———. '"The Hunt's Up"', *Proceedings of the Royal Musical Association*, 106 (1979), pp. 1–25.

———. 'And Who but Ladie Greensleeues?' in *The Well Enchanting Skill: Music, Poetry, and Drama in the Culture of the Renaissance – Essays in Honour of F. W. Sternfeld*, ed. John Caldwell, Edward Olleson and Susan Wollenberg (Oxford: Clarendon Press, 1990), pp. 181–211.

Warner, Christopher. *The Making and Marketing of Tottel's Miscellany, 1557: Songs and Sonnets in the Summer of the Martyrs' Fires* (Farnham: Ashgate, 2013).

Watt, Tessa. *Cheap Print and Popular Piety, 1550–1640* (Cambridge: Cambridge University Press, 1991).

Wells, Evelyn K. 'Playford Tunes and Broadside Ballads', *Journal of the English Folk Dance and Song Society*, 3:2 (1937), pp. 81–92.

Whiting, Robert. '"For the Health of My Soul": Prayers for the Dead in the Tudor South-west', in *The Impact of the English Reformation, 1500–1640*, ed. Peter Marshall (London: Arnold, 1997), pp. 121–142.

Whittle, Jane. 'Conclusion', in *Landlords and Tenants in Britain, 1440–1660: Tawney's "Agrarian Problem" Revisited*, ed. Jane Whittle (Woodbridge: Boydell Press, 2013), pp. 216–221.

Weir, Alison. *The Lost Tudor Princess: A Life of Margaret Douglas, Countess of Lennox* (London: Vintage, 2015).

Williams, Gordon. *A Dictionary of Sexual Language in Shakespearean and Early Stuart Drama* (4 vols. London: Athlone Press, 1994).

Willis, Jonathan P. '"By These Means the Sacred Discourses Sink More Deeply into the Minds of Men": Music and Education in Elizabethan England', *History*, 94.3 (2009), pp. 294–309.

———. *Church Music and Protestantism in Post-Reformation England: Discourses, Sites and Identities* (Farnham: Ashgate, 2010).

Wilson-Lee, Edward. 'The Bull and the Moon: Broadside Ballads and the Public Sphere at the Time of the Northern Rising (1569–70)', *Review of English Studies*, 63:259 (2012), pp. 225–242.

Wood, Andy. *Riot, Rebellion and Popular Politics in Early Modern England* (Basingstoke: Palgrave, 2002).

Woody, Robert H. 'Playing by Ear: Foundation or Frill?', *Music Educators Journal*, 99:2 (2012), pp. 82–88.

Woolf, Daniel. 'News, History and the Construction of the Present in Early Modern England', in *The Politics of Information in Early Modern Europe*, ed. Brendan Dooley and Sabrina Baron (London: Routledge, 2001), pp. 80–118.

———. *The Social Circulation of the Past: English Historical Culture 1500–1730* (Oxford: Oxford University Press, 2003).

Würzbach, Natascha. *The Rise of the English Street Ballad, 1550–1650*, transl. Gayna Walls (Cambridge: Cambridge University Press, 1990).

Unpublished PhD Theses

Boswell, Christopher. 'The Culture and Rhetoric of the Answer-Poem, 1485–1626', University of Leeds, 2003.

Duguid, Timothy. 'Sing a New Song: English and Scottish Metrical Psalmody from 1549–1640', University of Edinburgh, 2011.

Ingram, Juliet. 'The Conscience of the Community: the Character and Development of Clerical Complaint in Early Modern England', University of Warwick, 2004.

Rayment, Louise. 'A Study in Sixteenth-Century Performance and Artistic Networks: British Library, Additional Manuscript 15233', University of Southampton, 2011.

Veerapen, Steven. 'Slander and Sedition in Elizabethan Law, Speech and Writing', University of Strathclyde, 2014.

Websites

Associated Board of the Royal Schools of Music. *Practical Musicianship Examination Syllabus*, http://us.abrsm.org/en/our-exams/other-assessments/practical-musicianship/# [accessed 1 September 2014].

Bernstein, Leonard. 'Young People's Concert Series: What Is a Mode?', *Leonard Bernstein*, www.leonardbernstein.com/ypc_script_what_is_a_mode.htm [accessed 11 August 2014].

Broadside Ballads Online from the Bodleian Library, http://ballads.bodleian.ox.ac.uk/ [accessed 20 July 2017].

'Discography – The Reckoning', *Steve Tilston*, www.stevetilston.com/discography/the-reckoning/ [accessed 20 April 2017].

Early English Books Online (EEBO), http://eebo.chadwyck.com/home [accessed between 1 January 2014 and 30 September 2017].

English Broadside Ballad Archive, http://ebba.english.ucsb.edu/ [accessed 20 July 2017].

The English Folk Dance and Song Society. *The Full English*, www.vwml.org/search/search-full-english [accessed 31 August 2014].

Foxe, John. *Actes and Monuments of These Latter and Perillous Days, Touching Matters of the Church* [*The Unabridged Acts and Monuments Online* variorum edition] (Sheffield: HRI Online Publications, 2011), www.johnfoxe.org [accessed 6 February 2012].

Gale Cengage Learning. *State Papers Online*, http://gale.cengage.co.uk/state-papers-online-15091714.aspx [accessed between 12 May 2015 and 20 July 2017].

Grove Music Online, www.oxfordmusiconline.com/subscriber/book/omo_gmo [accessed 9 September 2014].

Lyons, Mathew (@MathewJLyons). 'Was May's decision triggered by upcoming election fraud charges? www2.politicalbetting.com/index.php/arch...', 19 April 2017, 12:01 a.m., *Twitter*, https://twitter.com/MathewJLyons/status/854469847849324546 [accessed 19 April 2017].

The Making of a Broadside Ballad, http://press.emcimprint.english.ucsb.edu/the-making-of-a-broadside-ballad/index [accessed 20 July 2017].

Oxford Dictionary of National Biography, online edition, ed. Lawrence Goldman (Oxford: Oxford University Press), http://www.oxforddnb.com [accessed 9 September 2014].

Oxford English Dictionary, online edition (Oxford: Oxford University Press), www.oed.com [accessed 9 September 2014].

Rideal, Rebecca (@RebeccaRideal). 'Did Paul Mason say Labour will win GE and then confess that he would 'vote tactically' (ie not Labour) in his constituency? #Newsnight', 19 April 2017, 12.03 a.m., *Twitter*, https://twitter.com/RebeccaRideal/status/854470595295268866 [accessed 19 April 2017].

Rolfe, Kirsty (@avoidingbears), 'I keep trying to be politically engaged but politics keeps being all [garbage fight GIF]', 18 April 2017, 4.51 p.m., *Twitter*, https://twitter.com/avoiding_bears/status/854361832315912192 [accessed 18 April 2017].

Index of Ballad Titles and Tunes

Number spans in italics refer to text within figures.

General Index

Number spans in italics refer to text within figures, while those in bold refer to text in tables.